WALKING HOME

THE LIFE AND ART OF MONIKA STEINHOFF

WALKING HOME

THE LIFE AND ART OF MONIKA STEINHOFF

A Memoir By The Artist

Sunstone Press
Santa Fe

Sunstone books may be purchased for educational, business, or sales promotional use.
For information please write: Special Markets Department, Sunstone Press,
P.O. Box 2321, Santa Fe, New Mexico 87504-2321.
Printed on acid-free paper
♾

Library of Congress Cataloging-in-Publication Data

Names: Steinhoff, Monika, author.
Title: Walking home : the life and art of Monika Steinhoff / Monika Steinhoff.
Description: Santa Fe, NM : Sunstone Press, [2023] | Includes index. | Summary: "A memoir of artist Monika Steinhoff's life and art, focusing especially on her figurative egg tempera paintings"-- Provided by publisher.
Identifiers: LCCN 2023039931 | ISBN 9781632933836 (paperback) | ISBN 9781632933843 (hardcover)
Subjects: LCSH: Steinhoff, Monika. | Women painters--New Mexico--Biography. | LCGFT: Autobiographies.
Classification: LCC ND237.S68277 A2 2023 | DDC 759.13 [B]--dc23/eng/20230907

LC record available at https://lccn.loc.gov/2023039931

WWW.SUNSTONEPRESS.COM
SUNSTONE PRESS / POST OFFICE BOX 2321 / SANTA FE, NM 87504-2321 /USA
(505) 988-4418

DEDICATION

I dedicate my book to David Bell, Art Critic for the *Santa Fe New Mexican* in the 1980s and poet, whose words I still remember, and all critics who gave my art serious and honest evaluation over the almost fifty years of my career, including the lady sent by the *Santa Fe New Mexican* to my ten-year Retrospective at St. John's College, whose critique never got published, but who took me aside and personally gave me her insightful opinion, which moved (and disturbed) me deeply at the time and ended my period of creating Santa Fe–, etc. interiors and catapulted me into what became my "mature" period of "Magic Realism."

And to my husband, Daniel J. O'Friel, who has not read what I have written nor would come into my studio to see what I was painting, nor ever suggested subject matter, but whose faith in me is steadfast, and whose integrity and love have sustained me. And to our four children, Sean Eddy, Paolo, Melissa and Heather.

And to the younger generation who will inherit the Earth, our nine grandchildren: Jericho, Jaden and Scarlet Joy O'Friel; Mia, Paolo Jr. (June) and Julian O'Friel; C J Smith; and Benjamin and Hailey Morton; all of whom I love so deeply and am inspired by.

CONTENTS

PREFACE

Monika Steinhoff's Achievement

Over a long career as a visionary artist, Monika Steinhoff has accomplished a prodigious body of work, whose intellectual complexity and subtlety are of a very high order. She often renders her subject matter panoramically, and the manifold world represented in her more ambitious pictures becomes a mash-up of both life today and time immemorial. Steinhoff casts her satirical and spiritual eye over the contemporary scene and zooms in on social and political issues that are of special concern to her. But the present day is not her singular focus: what is timeless for humanity and its planet earth is also a clear preoccupation. In her art she is able to see the microcosm of the present within the macrocosm of human history, sometimes cosmic in its reach. Without regard for simple chronology, she ranges through the past to resonate in the present, and even views the possible future.

Art historical references permeate her work, usually applied to some current dilemma she finds abroad in the world. Autobiography plays a significant role as well, not explicitly but merely as partial inspiration for the random earthly creation she portrays. Physical gravity is defied throughout her oeuvre, and supernatural or religious beings float freely in and out of her vision. Surrealism would seem to be the chief precedent for Steinhoff's work, but symbolism is to be found everywhere in it. As often as not, the imagery in her art operates above the literal level. That is, it stands for ideas beyond the objects depicted: it is therefore symbolic. The pictures can be mysterious, sometimes seeming to defy interpretation, but I have scarcely seen comparable contemporary paintings that require more prolonged looking, more mental exercise to extract all one can of the meaning invested in their respective representations of reality. Her imagination's limitless invention makes this a constant challenge for the viewer, but effecting this fundamental activity yields a recurring delight of discovery. Although her work has dedicated high seriousness of purpose, I find it to be more comic in its essence than tragic. She has a wry detachment from the disorderly and sometimes catastrophic nature of the life on earth she regularly deals with. She looks at the world not as a pessimist, but as an optimist.

As a former museum curator, I would have been eager to organize a retrospective for Monika Steinhoff, had I known about her work in those inspirited days. But that must now be the duty of some future curator. What is certain is that the future of art will take more notice of her work than the present has done heretofore, not that she has lacked for either recognition or acquisitions by collectors. But an artistic achievement of this profound magnitude can only grow in reputation: with the passage of time, the hindsight of history, and the foresight of those who responsibly value monuments of unageing intellect.

—James Mann, PhD

STEADFAST PASSION

for Monika Steinhoff

This lapse means chasing phantoms and fumbling keys,
The artist grumbles when doubt confounds her gaze—
Like stumbling through a forest of slanted trees,
Forever changing course in a shifting maze:
Scant headway weaving work between the pines.
But their shadows scatter patterns on the ground
Like seeds that burgeon and branch in fresh designs:
Directions to new perceptions all around.

Now mapping more fruitful pathways with her art,
She might uncover the crypt of lost time,
Persistent as if prying the world apart.
Falling down, then turning on a dime,
She spurs the steadfast passion feeding her heart
To hunt creation's fugitive sublime.

—James Mann, PhD

INTRODUCTION

While I have written many volumes of journals over fifty years plus, I decided to write this without consulting them as it would take too much time and be too detailed for this first book on my art. If "Fate" allows me to, I do want to go over them at some point and maybe write again. At any rate there is much material if biographers want to use it.

Some German words/concepts will be used periodically. The words one heard often as a child in one's formative years leave a lasting effect on one's psyche, so they are helpful to understanding oneself first, and then in communicating this awareness. I also include some astrology in that it became an important tool to understand reality and my role in it, as part of the exploration of idea vs. experience.

Creativity in my birth family had to be practical, certainly not critical of the dominant culture, and was not considered a way to make a living. At the beginning of my senior year at UCLA the Woodrow Wilson Fellowship committee interviewed me, finally telling me that while I deserved the scholarship due to my academic standing, but since I was engaged to be married, I would not be offered it. Had I been more politically aware and more of an activist at the time, it would have occurred to me to challenge their position, especially after I broke my engagement. At the time, my acquiescence of their decision had more to do with my own ambivalence about my future as a scholar of German literature. While I was far from being ready to commit myself to the path of an artist, receiving the fellowship could have further delayed it.

What compels one to be an artist? Certainly several in my extended family had artistic talent and exercised it. One aunt was a poet and story teller, another was a composer, a third was a jeweler and my god aunt Traute had established her own crafts school which became famous throughout Germany. Apparently my father had dabbled in art in his family attic while in school, and my mother who had had ambitions of studying medicine but decided to get married instead, became an accomplished painter of the wild birds she studied around her, once all of her own "chicks were out of the nest." So while in school I doodled and always drew in the margins of whatever notes I took, my path to being a practicing artist was a long and sometimes circuitous one. Every experience I recount, every memory, has contributed to bringing out and developing the artist in me.

I was born into a country at war, severely bombed: broken buildings, trees, broken bodies; a society almost totally destroyed for its own serious mistakes. Having once experienced and survived this destruction, even with no conscious memory of it, "hyper vigilance" can be the result. Now, in the present, people and societies all around the world are undergoing apocalyptic changes: fleeing violence and war, climate crisis, pandemics, homelessness, and hunger. The Covid pandemic forced me to close my gallery, which started as a co-operative hybrid ten years earlier. Not only had collectors disappeared, but visitors as well.

To me there is a level of surrealism to our present society. I'm reminded of Shakespeare's words that life is a play and we are all actors. When I "wake up," I assume I will more fully understand this drama. For over a year (and then again due to the Delta variant) we were all incognito, admonished to be masked whenever in public. What is cause and what effect: technology's role in this pandemic and in the human affect on global climate change? I have felt most of my adult life that modern technological societies have lost their connection to their own bodies, other species, and the Earth (Nature). Are we also morally adrift? All religions have codes of morality. Growing up with Christianity, I am most familiar with the Ten Commandments: "thou shalt not kill, not bear false witness, not covet...anything that is thy neighbors, love your enemies. Instead we insist on countries being our enemies perpetually because we profit from warfare, as we profit from illness. Leonard Cohen said, "When they said repent, repent, I wonder what they meant." I feel that I know.

In my childhood there were many mysteries and unanswered questions: would my mother have had a nervous breakdown while we lived on the farm if she had not become a born again Christian, along with two of my siblings. Why did my college and long term friend, spiritual sister, Heidi, tell me she would be worried about me taking my life if I were not a Christian? I am sort of a low key mystic, but don't believe in any of the organized religions as having exclusive handle on Truth. Her younger daughter many years later did commit suicide. Did my father have a sense of guilt about working first for Hitler and then (seemingly seamlessly) for the American Military Industrial Complex? In his seventies while recovering from a collapsed lung and broken ribs (a serious automobile accident on his way to see Reagan), it took three strong able bodied orderlies to stop his attempts to climb out the hospital window. He was convinced he was in a concentration camp.

In writing about one's life, one of course relies on memory, one's own as much as possible and where no or too little memory exists, on others who were present, on photographs, or on research. It's interesting, curious and important to examine what one's mind picks up and retains, and where and why there are gaps. I have almost no memory of my life until on board ship to America at age five. In Berkeley in my twenty-ninth year my live-in psychiatrist boyfriend, recommended I travel to Columbus, Ohio, where my parents were living at that time, and ask them questions about the years during the war. The visit both opened doors to the past and sadly, shut one door between my mother and myself (more on this later).

Some so-called facts in my story may have been experienced differently by others. While we were growing up, our parents did not mention topics like the World War we came out of, or Nazism to us children. Certainly professional decisions were not discussed with or in front of us, either, so some is speculation on what occurred and what I observed. My paintings explore the mysteries and contradictions in my life, personality, psyche and that of society.

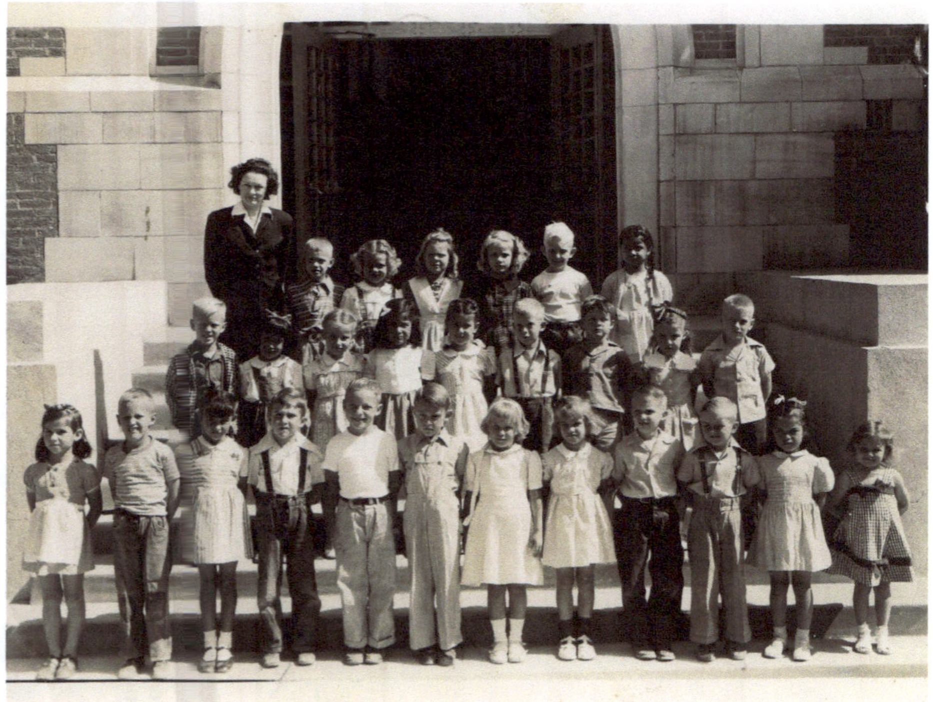

Kindergarten

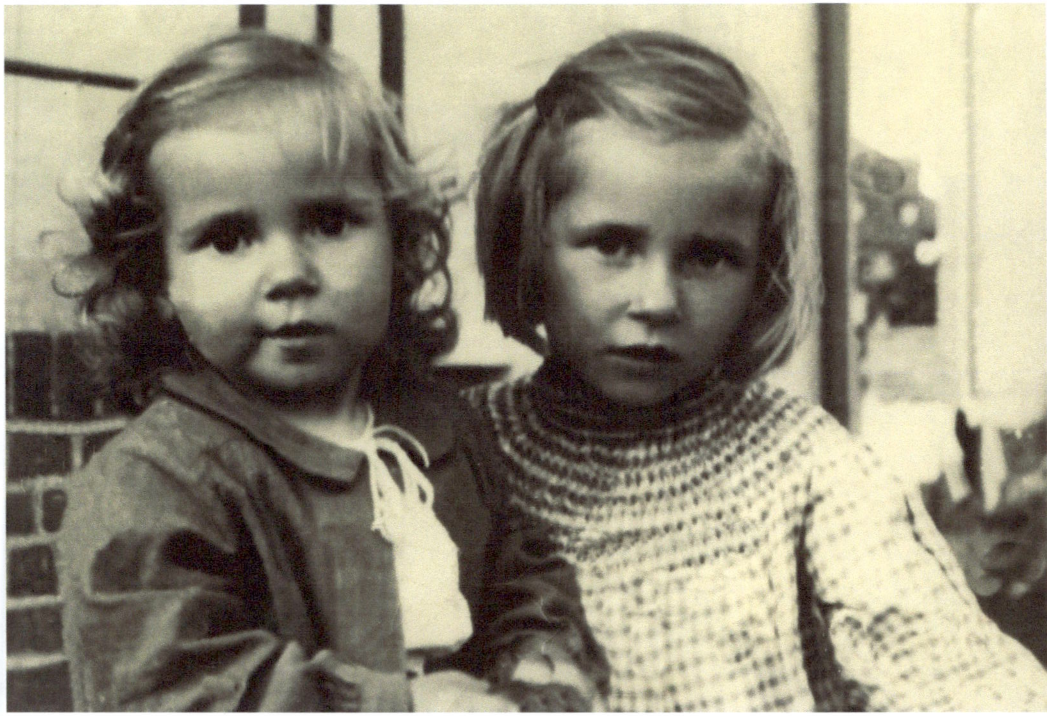

Hannelore (right) and me

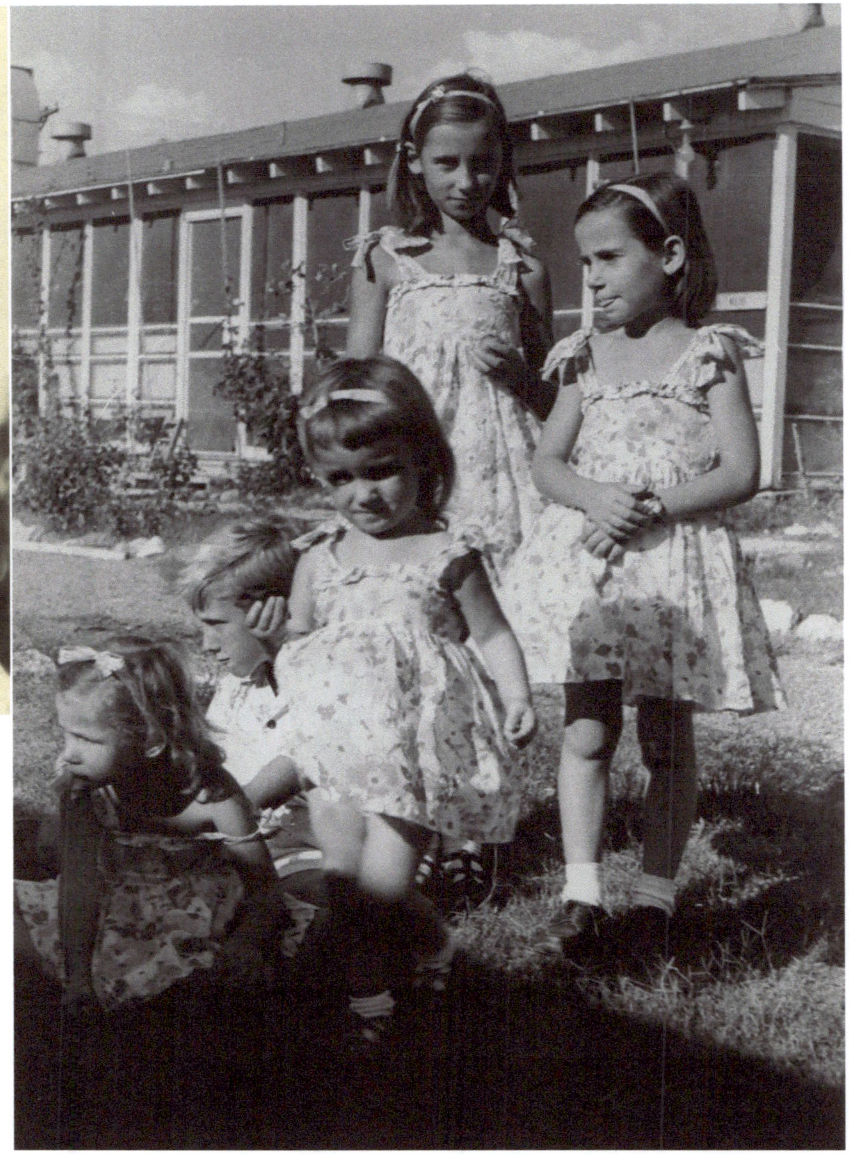

Four Sisters

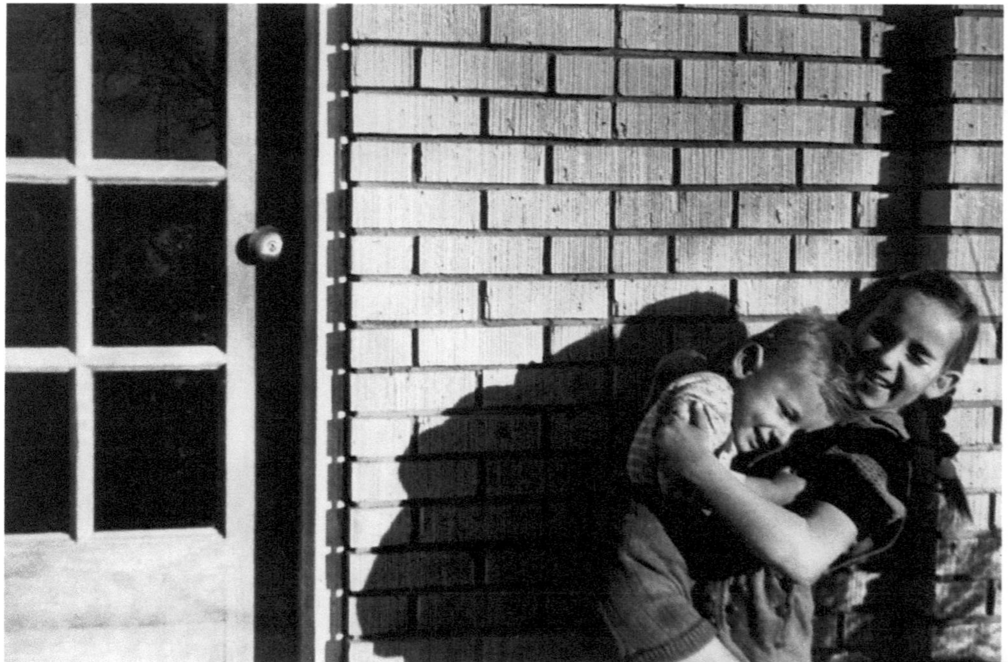

Playing with Ralph

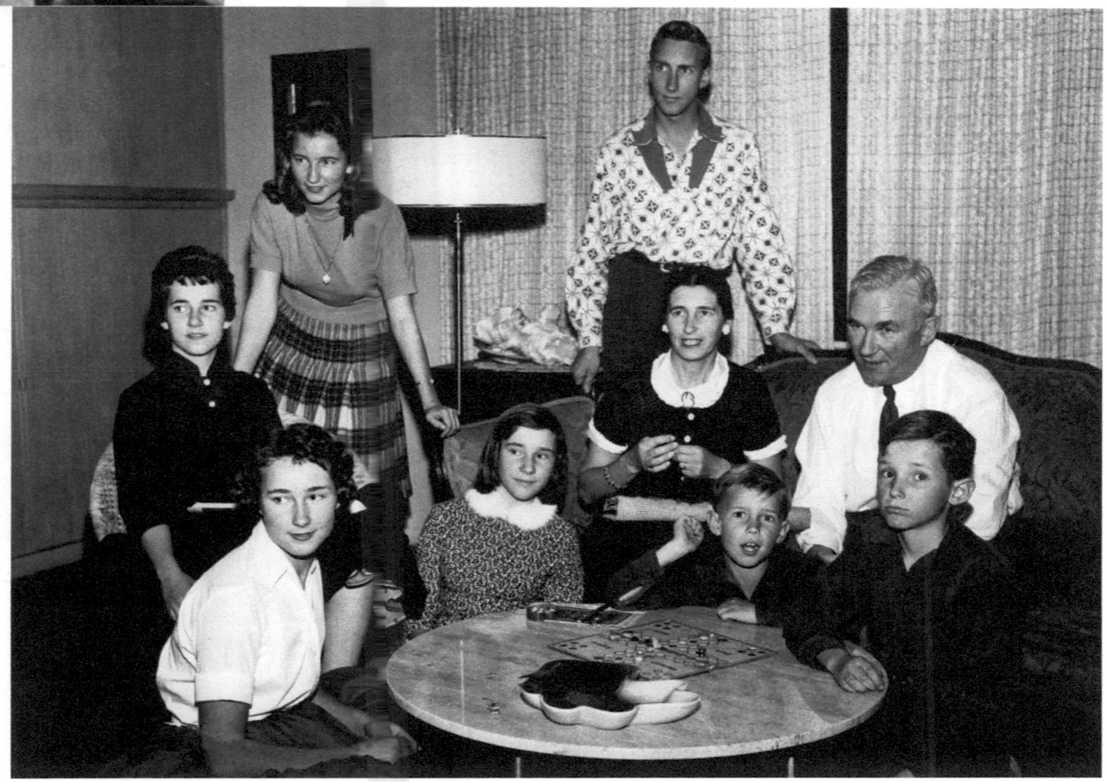

Family Game

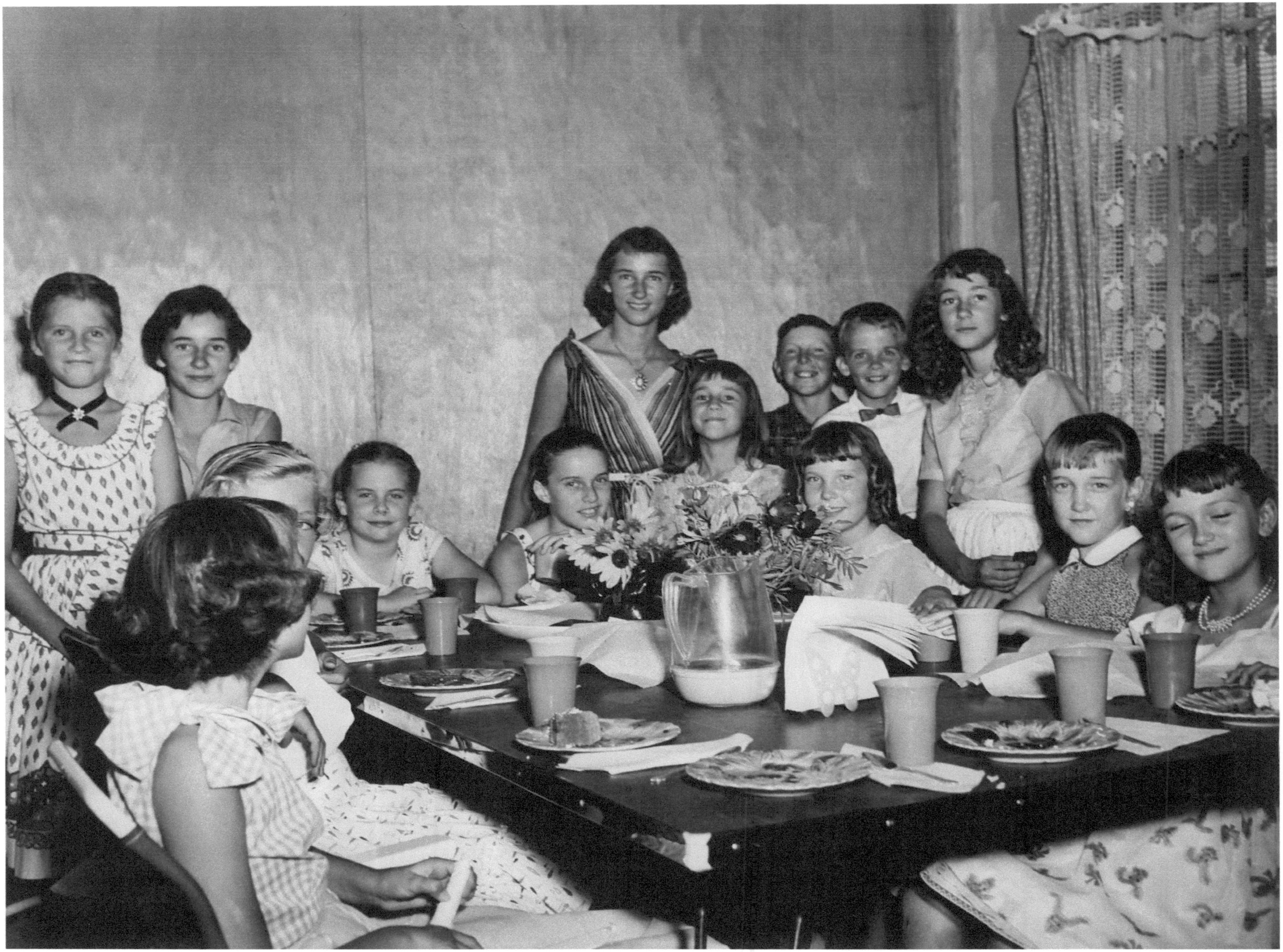

Celebration (me, 2nd from left, Hannelore, Gisela top right, Astrid just below Hannelore)

PART 1 / THE ARTIST

1 / BEGINNINGS

1947, El Paso, Texas

I am a five year old in Kindergarten learning English. My first report card states: "Monica disturbs the other children as they work." Over the years when I would come across it in our many family photo albums, I would be amused by it, though I'm sure my parents were not. They must have strongly impressed on me that I must behave better and focus on learning. Report cards were important in our family. Only A's were praised by my authoritarian father; B's were questioned and all marks below those meted some type of unwanted consequence. Striving for a level of excellence in all things was automatic in our family; both parents were good role models for that. On another level it was part of the immigrant fabric, not wanting to appear different, not wanting to stand out negatively. The spelling of my first name was automatically anglicized, a "c" replacing the "k." While at home our parents insisted we speak only German and my mother cooked the traditional German dishes (which included organ meats: kidneys, hearts, even brains, etc. a major and popular part of European cooking; but more importantly to my taste, she baked our hearty whole grain bread). My siblings swiftly and eagerly became Americanized. As soon as they were on their own, my three sisters switched completely to what they considered to be an American diet (especially spaghetti, pizza and hamburgers) while I became a lifelong vegetarian at twenty-six (with an occasional slip for necessary courtesy, ie. eating a little turkey on Thanksgiving). Our parents diet changed very little and while both worked hard to improve their English, were comfortable being German Americans. I was the only one of seven who later would seriously delve into our roots, returning regularly to Europe. My questions were not only personal, but about my whole family (both here and those left behind) and the community superimposed on the southern New Mexico town of Alamogordo.

Who were we? Where did we come from? Why did we leave and come here? One important clue is in the military history: the dropping of the first Atomic Bomb at what was then called the White Sands Proving Grounds, thirty miles northwest. This happened, of course, before my family arrived. I need to retrace more events in Germany first.

1939

My father, Dr. Ernst A. Steinhoff, professor of Mathematics at the Technical Institute in Darmstadt, Germany, had been recruited by Dr. Werner von Braun to take over the Telemetry Department of the rocket research at Peenemünde, on the Island of Usedom.

1941

In October by my birth in the hospital at Swienemünde, Germany, WWII was in full swing. My mother had filled in these details in answer to my questions. From August 1943 on we moved frequently due to being bombed out thirteen times. Once we were the only family in a whole block who survived without injury. Another time, in the general panic from an air raid, I was left outside in my portable crib (my reoccurring dream of Christmas trees falling from the sky, the spiraling flares preceding a bombing raid). Another time I could not be found in the bomb shelter though everyone agreed I was with the family as it entered. Another bomb shook the building, and suddenly they heard a muffled but frantic cry coming from an old unused stove I had crawled into. Ashes and soot from the chimney, loosened by the air raid had awakened, choking me, poured from the door.

In the spring of 1942 when I was about nine months old, I was quarantined in the same hospital in which I was born, at the other end of the long island of Usedom, with either Diphtheria or Scarlet Fever, and got the second from the hospital. My Mother recalled: "You were psychic. Even though you could not see me because you faced the other direction lying in your crib, as I peered through the big plate glass window, you always became agitated and started to cry." When I was finally released after six weeks, supposedly well, I had actually contracted Whooping Cough which my 12 year old baby sitter caught and became so ill she passed out. Having not seen or heard us for several days, the neighbors who were to look in on us, had to break the door down to rescue us. The successfully suppressed deep sense of abandonment must be part of the content of what I later objectified as my "black hole." In her telling of these events, my mother added that I was incredibly stubborn. I was not allowed to take my teddy bear to bed and cried all night for it. An astonishing story. We raised four children, one biological and three adopted; I can't imagine denying a small child the comfort of a stuffed animal, especially in such an acutely stressful time. Nazism had some really shocking rules governing child rearing: absolute obedience was one of them, and toilet training was even worse. But also, behavior in war time can seem strange to those who weren't there or have no memory.

The fact that my first actual memory is both primarily visual, and ironically humorous, is a clue to why I became a painter and of what kind. On the boat to America, I must have been on deck with one or more of our party, watching the sailors playing baseball with oranges, the bright fruit crashing against the deck's railing, part or whole falling into the dark water. On board we were given plenty to eat, especially ice cream, but the surrealism did not escape me, coming from a war torn country where food had been scarce.

There is a second visual image that has stayed with me through my entire life and helped with the scary decision to devote myself to art, times when I would walk the three miles home when my mother forgot me. I'm always reminded of the nursery rhyme line: "she had so many children she didn't know what to do." But after school, feeling abandoned, often in tears, the extraordinary New Mexico sunset through the giant cottonwood trees along the highway, comforted and inspired me.

Some of the German ladies let my mother know that they wondered why in the world they had seven children. My mother would repeat a rather salacious joke: every time I hung my undies on the bedpost I would get pregnant (that's worse than the stork story children were told). Seeing that in the "Dunigan Edition" (an impoverished settlement) there were kids with no rides, she would pile in as many as our station wagon could hold (no seat belts in those days) so it wasn't hard for a quiet child to be forgotten. A third clue or event, came much later, while I was in the PhD program at Berkeley. A friend introduced me to the tjanting tool (used in Batik to draw lines of different thickness from delicate to quite broad with hot bee's wax on cloth): The astonishing beauty this tool created gave me such a sense of ecstasy, that batik became my back door to becoming an artist. Later after I took a "Leave of Absence" from the PhD program and accepted a teaching job for the next fall, I hitch-hiked back to New Mexico and spent some time drawing at White Sands, creating black and white water colors of the dunes. In the house on Woolsey Street I shared the main floor with a married couple and their toddler. The closet off the living room became my tiny meditation room. One day I hung all my watercolors on its walls. I recognized: this is the work of an artist. I am an artist.

But first back to 1946. In late Spring one hundred scientists from the town of Peenemünde had been brought to White Sands. Without the authoritarian presence of our fathers, we children bonded with each other and our mothers, both in the year waiting in Germany and the long travel to join them. We had spent several weeks aboard ship (it sprang a leak and almost went under, and then took many more weeks to repair) then by train from New York. We had left all relatives, friends, our language and culture (or the chaos of what was left of it) to move to the desert of El Paso, Texas first, and then New Mexico. We were immigrants with the usual obstacles but also different ones.

The US Congress, in response to a wider uproar across the political spectrum, about these "Nazi" scientists down there close to the Mexican border, passed an Act declaring them (and us) illegal immigrants, so that the Pentagon arranged to have us all go to Mexico and be entered legally. While in El Paso, all the families were housed together behind barbed wire in converted barracks of the abandoned Army Hospital at Beaumont Annex. On week days the scientists were taken to White Sands Proving Grounds to work while their children were bused to local public schools. Nevertheless, Kindergarten lasted only a few weeks as I learned the language quickly and was promoted to first grade. I kept learning fast and eventually ended up in the University of California Berkeley PhD program for German literature, always wanting to learn more about my origins. Along with my academic pursuit I continued to explore and test the artistic waters. Growing up in New Mexico with its special environment and light that attracted so many artists, played a fundamental role in my becoming an artist.

After the deprivation and chaos in Germany, it must have seemed an almost idyllic existence. In this small ex-pat community traditional German celebrations were elaborately prepared and enthusiastically enjoyed. I still vividly recall the four identical beautiful flowery dresses tied at the shoulders with bows, and for winter the white corduroy skirts and matching orange and ivory sweaters our Mother sewed and knitted for her four daughters aged two to nine. For our first day of school in our new country we were all presented with enormous "Zuckertueten," (paper cones decorated and filled with goodies). Our Mutti's practice of baking an incredible variety of traditional German Christmas cookies lasted all our childhood. Once I could not wait and tried to climb up to the high shelf where they were stored and fell with my butt landing on the metal rim of the pail I had balanced on, an unforgettable lesson, or instant Karma as one would later call it. Mother, like all the ladies had periodic "Kaffeeklatsches" ("coffee and gossip") each with a handful of the wives/friends invited to our house. They were quite formal; she made beautiful German cakes, cookies or pies, beginning in El Paso and continued through the seven years in Alamogordo. We children looked forward to these celebrations. All dressed up, we were allowed to come in, curtsy (possibly), greet the guests. choose a modest selection from the desserts and then be dismissed to go out and play.

Unlike most immigrants, while the German scientists and their families were all outsiders in this small western desert town, they also created a kind of elite upper social class. Speaking only German together, which continued throughout my childhood, (though to a lesser degree in the case of my two U.S.A born siblings, Ralph and Reiner) made us all bilingual. For myself this would become an advantage but for a time made me seem less intelligent along with being somewhat dyslexic (Astrology: five planets retrograde). I would become tongue-tied while speaking English as vocabulary from the German language would flood my mind. I still know the names of many kitchen implements only in German. As more and more of our experiences were with English speaking persons, an atrophying of the original language occurred, so that studying German literature (to which the study of grammar was also the necessary foundation, a Saturnian discipline, both a challenge and a good grounding for a Neptunian dreamer such as myself) was important.

Compliance, hard work, and obedience were required of us seven children (some lingering influence of Nazism?) so much so that when I later entered college, and had some choices on what to study, I realized doing well in all subjects had been so uppermost, that I did not know what I liked or was particularly suited for. Liking or not liking did not enter the equation, just doing well, so in school I did well at everything. But I loved school; I could sit down and use my head. The idea of studying art, which mysteriously came into my head, met with clear, immediate resistance; in fact, my parents would not afford me any financial support, nor social acceptance, effectively disowning me. But being successful was such an important value in our upbringing, not studying art was okay with me. I didn't know if I'd be any good anyway, and German literature was an acceptable alternative, affording the real possibility of at some point returning to Germany to understand where we came from, meeting our relatives.

Could there be a greater contrast between the island in the Baltic Sea, Usedom, where I was born, and the southern New Mexico arroyos we roamed as children? While even in those early years, many of the families (as a whole or individually) returned to Germany for visits, we did not. Secretly our mother feared that we would become confused about where we belonged, and become critical of where we now were. She had witnessed this among some of the German ladies she was friends with and invited to her afternoon teas. My mother was resolutely committed to being happy in America and did not even visit Germany for many years, burying her feelings of how deeply painful it was to leave her estranged mother alone there. She never saw her alive, even though our Aunt Sophie, who immigrated through marriage to an American military man, and whom I would meet many years later, loved America enthusiastically and would happily offer me a piece of "God bless America Pie" (from the freezer)—freedom from the old enslavement of women). Uncles (Vati's cousins, the Bauses) visited us from Ohio and Kentucky several times and we also made one trip East to visit them. Our cousin, Susan Bause (who would later move with her husband to Albuquerque, New Mexico) invited us girls for a boat ride on the Ohio River, and almost panicked when two of my sisters and

I all jumped overboard to swim. We were all good swimmers; I had passed my life saving classes. And before I would finally get back to Germany, we had lived in Santa Barbara, Cincinnati, and Los Angeles. Through those two California residences (a combination of six years) I rediscovered my love for the ocean, swimming and what could have been culture shock was dampened by broadening experience.

After we had lived in El Paso for three years, the group of scientists were given a choice: the whole group could move with Von Braun as head, to Huntsville, Alabama (Redstone Arsenal) or one-half of the scientists could remain at White Sands under the leadership of my father. The latter was decided. Much as my father loved and admired von Braun, the pull of this wide, open landscape which he had come to love, and the independence to explore it's possibilities, won the day (not always with success, as we will see later). So work began in Alamogordo, on the yellow brick house on Florida Avenue that we occupied for three years, built by my father with lots of help from some of the other scientists and his oldest son, Hans, from his twelfth year on, a beautiful house but never finished until we moved out, inhabited by our family of nine as it progressed. As though that were not enough, soon a cow and a pig shared the back yard and my father's dream of farming this immense land (to the horror of my urban born Mother) was born.

We "homesteaded" 140 acres northwest of town, which would soon after result in building a second family home, this time a pre-fab metal house. My father was admired by the military men who visited us, and loved by the local ranchers and farmers. Not bothered or critical of his English, they embraced his enthusiasm for the land, his eagerness to learn and take up farming. He won prizes for the fruit, vegetables, pigs and cows he entered into the annual State Fair.

Compared to El Paso or the cities my parents knew, Frankfurt, Munich or Berlin, Alamogordo must have seemed like a cultural wasteland (though the natural surrounding landscape, especially the mountains were wonderful). The scientists' families, and the group as a whole was sophisticated, upper middle class professionals to even remnants of German nobility, so the quality of education in the public schools (there were no private ones) became high through their efforts, with often the best sports, chorus and orchestra in the state. Our mother insisted we all learn a musical instrument: the oldest, Hans, played cello; next, my older sister did well on the violin and I was talked into the viola, but not quite happily as it rarely had the melody in the pieces we played. At home we heard little music beyond our practicing, as we had no gramophone, only a radio (no TV: my father was convinced it would be America's ruination). While I played the viola for seven years, I was not conscious of how important music was to me until after I was on my own. From my Mutti I learned German folk songs, which she sang frequently as she did housework. The mystical bent present in my art can also be traced to my memories of growing up in Alamogordo. Alone, I sang familiar church hymns and read the Bible to myself, so my being attracted later to a Lutheran university is not surprising.

Living in a particular society, we all to some degree adopt the beliefs of the society in the areas of religion, science, politics and in general, how the world works. My family was officially Protestant, though I'd classify my father as a non-believer but not necessarily closed off to spiritual ideas. As a child I often thought if I were Catholic I would become a nun. Even more dramatic, my concern: would I have the courage of beliefs even to the point of dying as a martyr (where do these ideas come from?). We attended the Lutheran church in Alamogordo, where I was also confirmed at twelve years old. Peter, slightly older, joined me in the conformation class in wanting to ask questions about some texts we had to memorize. Pastor Zimbrick made clear that questions were not allowed. Here again I am an outsider of the group with my questioning of orthodoxy: the Lutheran beliefs I nevertheless submitted to. During high school I struggled to follow my mother's evolution toward "born again Baptist," but could not. Much later, in Berkeley, my awakening began and a new inner autonomy. Even in the paintings of what I call my mature period in which I draw attention to the USA bomb making industry and the "Military Industrial Complex," are balanced with this underlying mysticism, (two opposing sides of my reality: "Zwei Seelen").

Not only does it not surprise me that I disturbed the other children, it's like a leitmotif (aka. Thomas Mann), another clue of my outsider—not only status but a deeper internal state. At five years old I am suddenly in a whole different world, learning ABC's in a different language not only with the German kids I knew, but regular little Texan public school first graders. Isn't that strange to my childish mind? Is it any wonder I am disturbing those who act as if this is all normal, familiar, safe? Years later, after my marriage, whenever we were preparing to travel, especially to Europe, the deeply buried anxiety would start to surface and I could not sleep. One day

I revealed to my husband: "a part of me always expects that when we return I will find our house destroyed." In my psyche I'm sitting on a landmine. At any moment a drone might appear and destroy my home, my family, my relatives, my friends and me. So I make pictures of what disturbs me, but they also contain the humor that's always present (sometimes as my mother called it "Galgen Humor"), not with ugliness, with subtlety, archetypal because it seems to always be part of the human condition. Now it's 2021 when I'm writing these words; I am near the end of my career, still trying to disturb people: wake up! Isn't the reality around us strange? Are we all at a masked ball? Only it's not fun.

Growing up in a family of nine, there is naturally lots of comparing and competition, especially in a competitive culture like the U.S. Mutti, apologetically, often said we were growing up like weeds. I think she meant by this that we got little individual attention, guidance, or fostering of our abilities. I envied my only child friends who even got to take ballet lessons. At forty I treated myself to a ballet class. Natasha, my teacher, couldn't believe how easy it was for me. (My past life time as a Russian Ballerina?) Perhaps to make up for this a little, it seems our mother might have told each of us at some point that "you are my favorite." I was the only one with a nickname. In fact more than one: "Moni " was most frequent; "Moenchen" (an endearment "little moon"—though of course astrology did not play a role in this, but having the Moon conjunct Neptune on the Ascendant, remarkably accurate (or more in criticism when my attention was absent " Mondkind" (moon child) but still better than being considered one of the two black sheep which occurred later. Ralph, seven years younger, affectionately called me: "Cow Eyelashes" which I didn't mind either (noting cows shared my unusually long lashes), possibly compensating me for some of the teasing (or insults) due to my prominent nose. Later two spiritual names were added: first Pratibha (Lamp of Wisdom) by Hari Dass Baba, and decades later, Sherab Chodren (Intuitive Wisdom) when I took refuge in Buddhism.

The period in Alamogordo had two parts: town and farm. In the close knit German community, we all lived within walking distance of each other, walking to school, playing together in streets, yards and each others' houses. Ebers, Jaenke, Genglebach, Lau, Tanzen—we all knew each other. Our lives in town, centered around Florida Avenue; the Ebers' with three daughters lived further southeast as did the Zimbricks. Dr. Eber and his flirtatious wife, Hilde, entertained a lot. Whether from encouragement or pressure, our mother embraced the German Hausfrau image, giving up perms (and hair dressers) for her "Knotten" (her long hair in the knot at the nap of her neck) while I observed my father seemed to melt under Hilde Eber's charm. We recently saw the 1920s film, "Grand Hotel," which takes place in and around Berlin's Adlon Hotel. I told my husband that I really find the exaggerated dip and slid of the actresses in the film irritating. That's where I first saw it—in Mrs. Eber's style of attention to the males at their parties. My mother clearly was not threatened by the other Hilde, she liked her and probably even admired her style. To me in retrospect they were like two sides of the same coin; my mother also was not plain but an attractive, self-assured woman. Pastor Zimbrick with three handsome sons and one beautiful daughter, the stars of the church youth group, held parties that were as popular as any secular ones. "Spin the bottle" took first place, amidst much laughter, and embarrassment among the younger, less experienced like myself. Next door to the south lived a retired American couple who always had cookies for us and encouraged our visits enthusiastically. Our unfinished house progressed after work and evenings, sometimes late into the night.

Not everything went smoothly in this immigrant community due to language, laws, and human error. It was assumed safe in our neighborhood for my younger brother Ralph, an alert, smart four year old, to cross Florida Avenue on his way to visit his friends (both adult and pre-school). But one morning two adults made mistakes that almost got him killed. The Alamogordo street sweeper ran out of water, paying no attention, thus creating a visually impenetrable cloud of dust (against the law: his job description states he is to stop immediately when the water has run out). At that same moment, a speeding cleaners truck, ignoring the lack of visibility, ran over little Ralph. I can imagine the neighbors who all knew each child, running to the scene, aghast, shocked. Ralph would suffer from these injuries all his life. This event in my family has echoes for me of what Frieda Kahlo suffered but had the courage and creative instinct to make the basis of her life's work. Whenever I see a street sweeper I remember this event. While it was clearly neither his fault nor my parents, the city won the law suit: no compensation for the tremendous hospital bills nor suffering or rehabilitation. It's still shocking to me: he's been diseased (liver cancer) for more than two years now as I write this memoir. Perhaps only an artist's intuition would see a connection.

Was it being immigrants? Not wanting to complain, be critical, to stand out. Was the attorney incompetent? When Ralph was a teenager and I in college, on a visit home I begged my mother to send him to a dermatologist or other therapist. His acne was disfiguring in it's intensity. I had had my own experience with this confidence undermining problem, probably due at least in part to taking unnecessary thyroid medicine and was treated with radiation for it at Wittenberg, which didn't seem like a good remedy, but nothing like Ralph's problem. Mutti responded: "He is a Christian," (as though God willed it).

One day during the Alamogordo in town phase, Hans ran away from home. The milk pail had been turned over by the cow kicking it, spilling all that day's milk; he could not bear the anger he anticipated from Vati (both worked too hard). Between school work and all the help demanded on building the house and chores, he was overwhelmed. My parents argued heatedly. To my horror, I heard my father threaten to shoot himself (he did not have a gun as far as I know). I went outside into the backyard, put my arms around our German Shepherd's neck and cried, a not infrequent memory. She was called Veronica. Imagine the confusion that caused: are they calling me or our dog?

Of course we kids also had a lot of fun: playing with neighbor kids, walking to school together, socials at the Lutheran church; etc. Very special were the monthly trips to El Paso where we sometimes bought new clothes and always stopped at Kahn's German Bakery for bread and Broetchen. Picnics at "Dog Canyon" were frequent; the first when we still lived in El Paso. I was six or seven when Mutti had to extract the thorns from my butt when I sat on a cactus. We loved wading in the creek and hiking up the mountain (which I still do when visiting the area). Going to White Sands for the day with a big watermelon and other eatables, running, jumping or rolling down the big dunes, was probably our favorite. One day Hannelore and I played "Purzelbaum" on our bed in the unfinished bedroom. We were having so much fun and got so wild tumbling on the bed that Hannelore's head went through the plasterboard wall. (It must have hurt.) Rather than sympathy, our father, probably tense and irritable from overwork, made Hannelore sleep in the garage for a month, an overly harsh punishment I thought, especially since I still can't help wondering how it was known it was her head not mine and feeling a little guilty. After that event I limited my tumbling to the class in PE where mats, equipment and the teachers supervision made it safer; it was my favorite class.

New scientists and families continued to come from Germany to work at White Sands. I was a twelve year old child, probably unusually observant about underlying dynamics but whose awareness like everyone's, was colored by my own suppressed experiences. "Onkel Lau" not a relative of our family, but even closer in spirit, both father figure, favorite uncle, counselor; Heinrich Lau, "Lauli" to us children. He came alone but was followed a year or so later by his wife and their four children. He built their house next to our's to the north, between our house and the Gengelbach's. Unlike our own father who never spoke about his work because it was secret, nor about more personal subjects (I found out later in therapy, that my father's genius also probably had "Asperger" elements). Lauli was communicative; mother and he would talk for hours, filling an emotional and intellectual void for my mother. He could talk about and listen to all topics. In our experience, German men, especially scientists, never washed dishes, held children or (god forbid) changed diapers.

Lauli would drop by and immediately pitch in to help with whatever chores needed doing. Often I would see him in our kitchen with dish towel in hand, while he waited for his security clearance to work at White Sands. He was also a pilot, had bought his own plane to give flying lessons. Soon after his wife, Leutya, came with the children, we saw less of him, though my mother was aware of an underlying conflict: Lauli had a mistress and a daughter by her and wanted to bring them to America also. (Did a phrase I remember hearing more than once of "airing dirty laundry" in arguments between my parents relate to this?) This problem tragically resolved itself: there was an accident. Another pilot, neglecting to check the flight schedule, flew into Lauli's plane from below. Lauli was instantly killed. Soon after, compounding this terrible tragedy, while his stunned, bereaved widow was bathing, the electric razor fell into the water and electrocuted her.

I stand at Lauli's funeral. Something is wrong with me. I feel nothing. I know he meant so much to me, to all of us. Years later I am walking out of our bedroom, suddenly aware that my heart feels numb. I explored this theme in many paintings, especially in my "Door to my Heart" series.

The four children were sent to California to an aunt. Hartmuth, the oldest and Margaret, (Pushie) are the only ones I remember: her blond hair and dark eye brows over warm, brown eyes. Did her life ever become whole again? Astrid was closest to her. I don't remember a funeral for Luetja. Was it because it was uncertain whether it was an accident or suicide, and the church did not sanctify the latter?

What other "tragedies" did this seemingly close knit community experience? The Tarnovski's moved down the street from us and Hiltrud, a year my senior, became my closest friend. Her family life was different from ours. While not an only child (she had an older brother and younger sister), she arrived alone with her parents. Since she was in chorus and I in orchestra we saw a lot of each other. She had such beautiful, unusual clothes, ordered from a catalog, *Spiegel*, which she eagerly shared with me. I started saving my baby sitting earnings and modest clothing allowance to order from it. Pretty soon the catalog became the means to gain sophistication beyond the bounds of our small western town. Hiltrud instantly became popular, written up in the school paper, because of her physical beauty and angelic voice. My mother, surprisingly, was critical of my friendship, implying the family was not quite socially on our level? They were "hotel people." Germans both here and in the "old country" surprised me with their more rigid class structure. When we moved to the farm about a year later, 140 acres of desert of which forty were gradually cultivated, I was much less available due to added chores, more homework as I entered High School, and new extra extracurricular activities like "Pep Squad."

Tragically, her father died of a stroke before the family had really acclimated to living in the United States and especially to a small basically southern Baptist town. Without her father's stabilizing influence, her quick popularity attracted the fast crowd. A rumor spread throughout high school that she had spent the night in the room of one of the football heroes (the two groups were not to mix) during the Allstate Chorus and Orchestra trip. While the relationship apparently continued loosely for some years, her reputation was ruined. She had become pregnant, dropped out of school and was miserable. Later when she was employed at Holloman AFB, she remained living with her mother who had great compassion for her, overlooking her growing dependence on alcohol to numb her bitterness. Over the years whenever we returned to Alamogordo to visit, I would stop by Edel's, who always welcomed me and shared whatever news she had or introduced me to a grandchild. Even though Hiltrud was often at home, I never saw her again, nor forgot her. I always felt I would have moved to a big city like Albuquerque, gone to college and changed my life.

On a recent camping trip, I discovered the Alamogordo Community Art Cafe, a pleasant atmosphere, and sat working on my laptop at a small table. Nearby, two older women and a man where drinking coffee and chatting pleasantly. I wondered who they were: the woman facing my table looked so much like Hiltrud. I kept thinking I should have the courage to introduce myself and ask if she might have known Hiltrud, or even be Darlene, her daughter. She could be just the right age, While usually I am not shy about such actions, I could not do it. I still wonder; will there ever be another opportunity? Probably not. I actually went again this summer. No one I felt I might know.

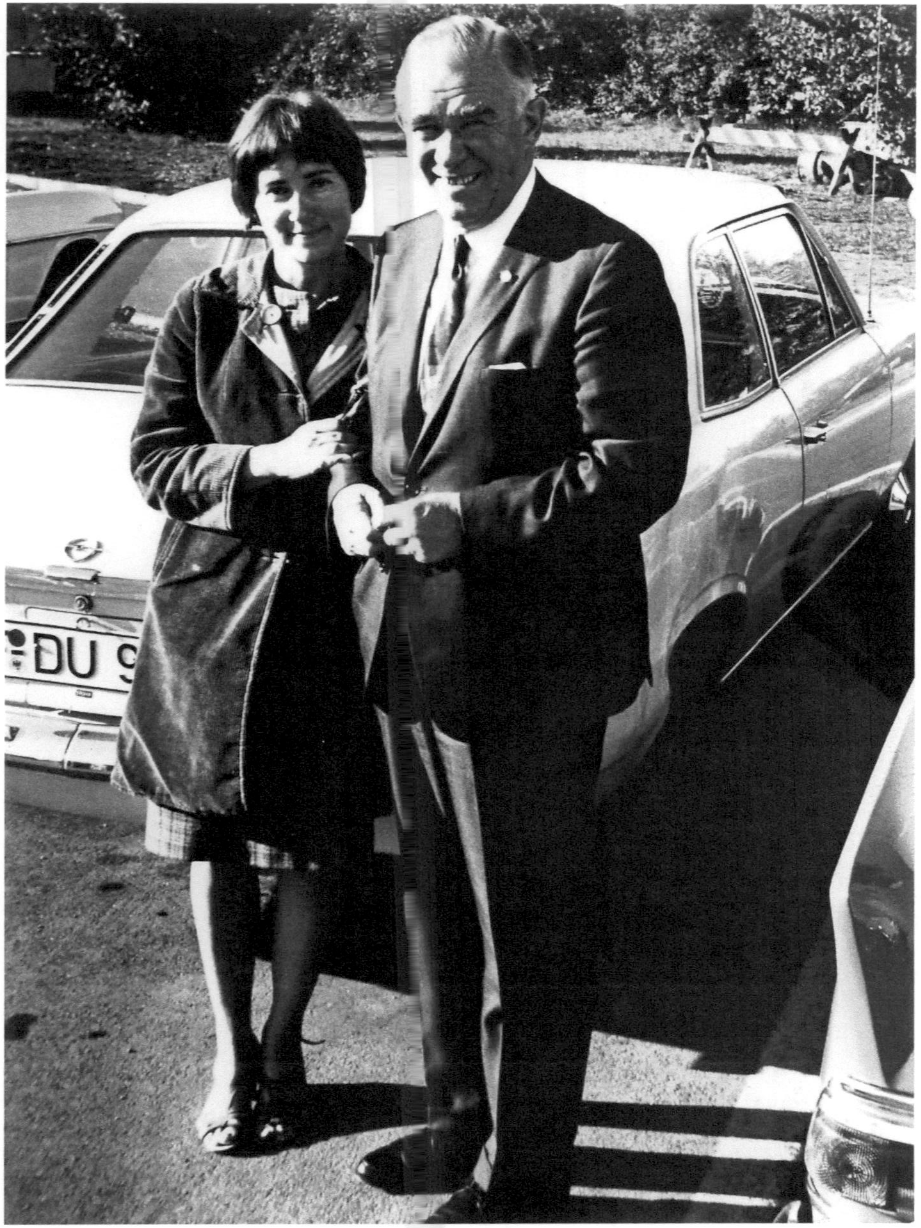

Dad and I in Germany

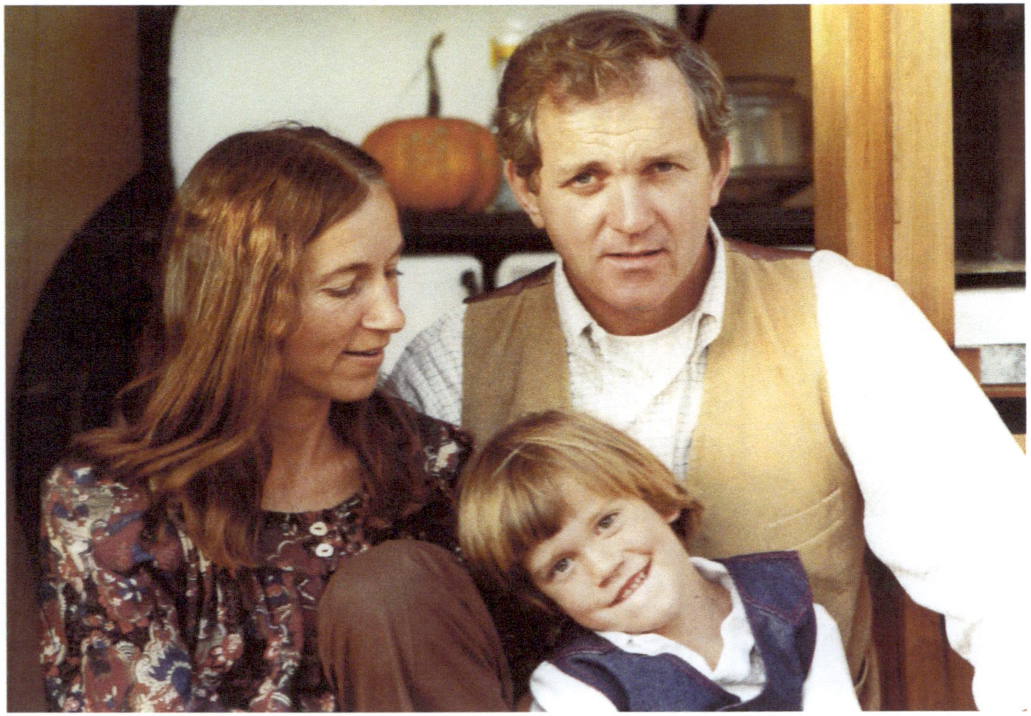

Dan, Sean and I

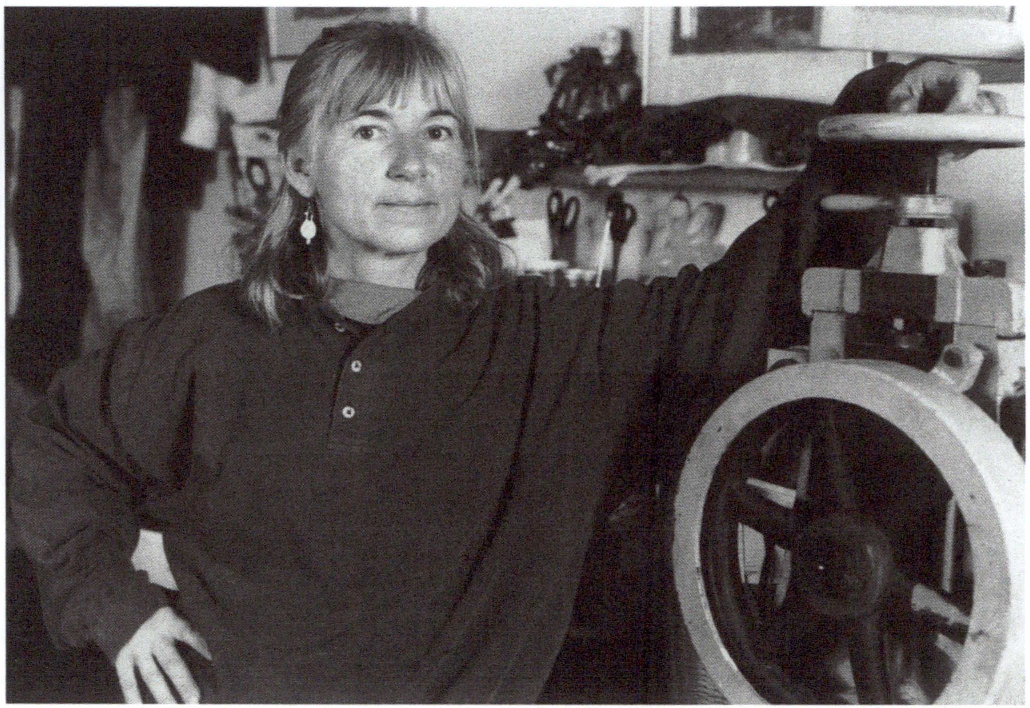

My etching press and I

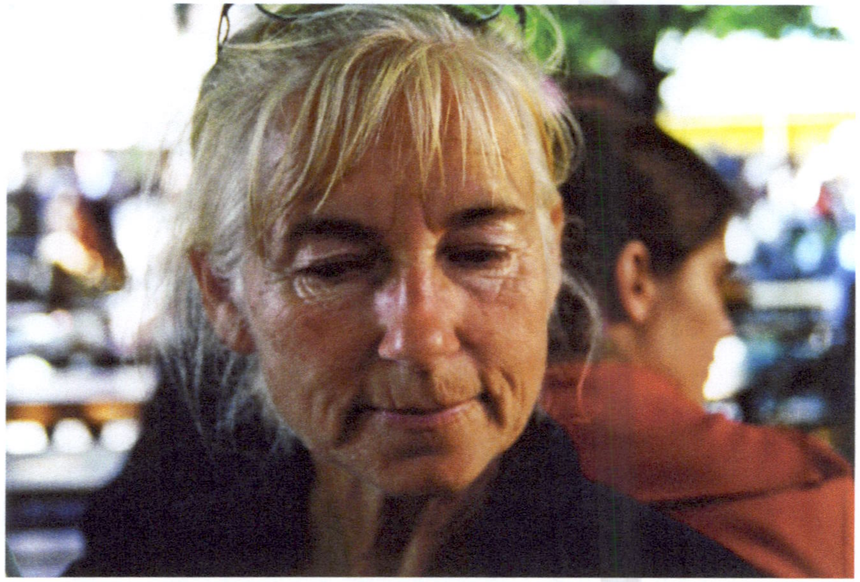

At the Austrian Biennale

Master class with Henriette

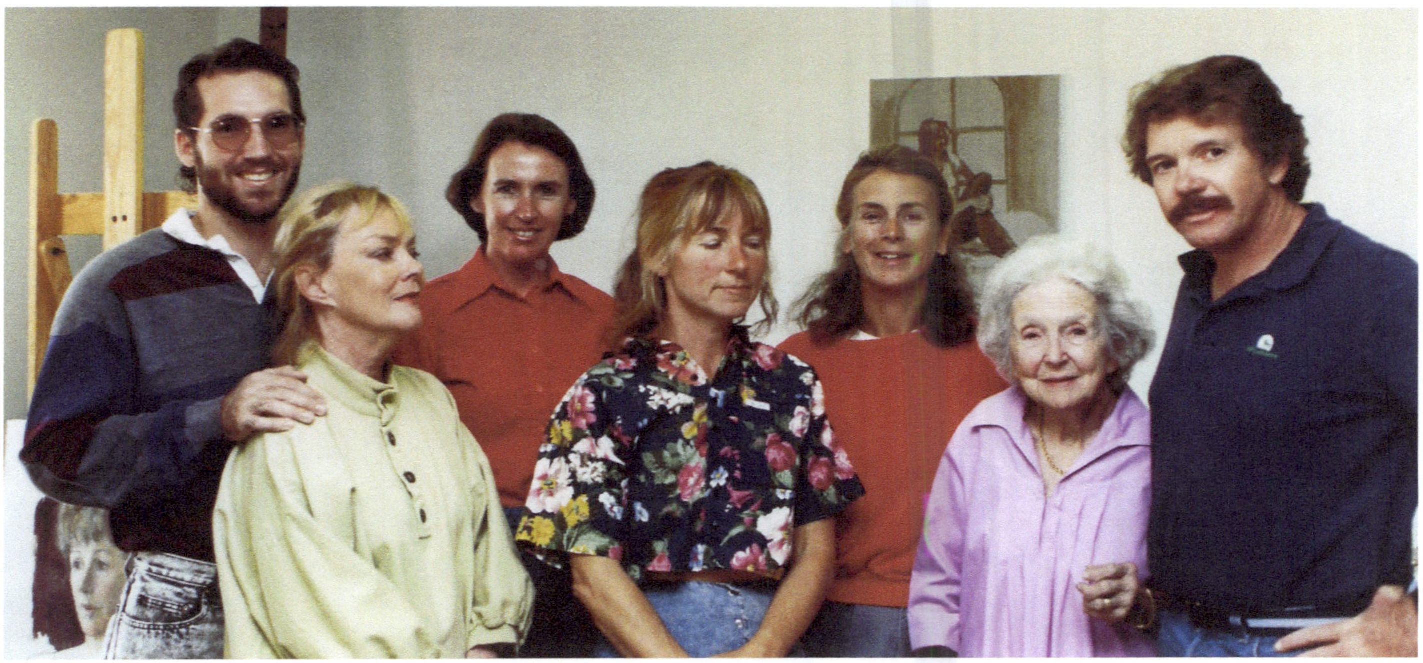

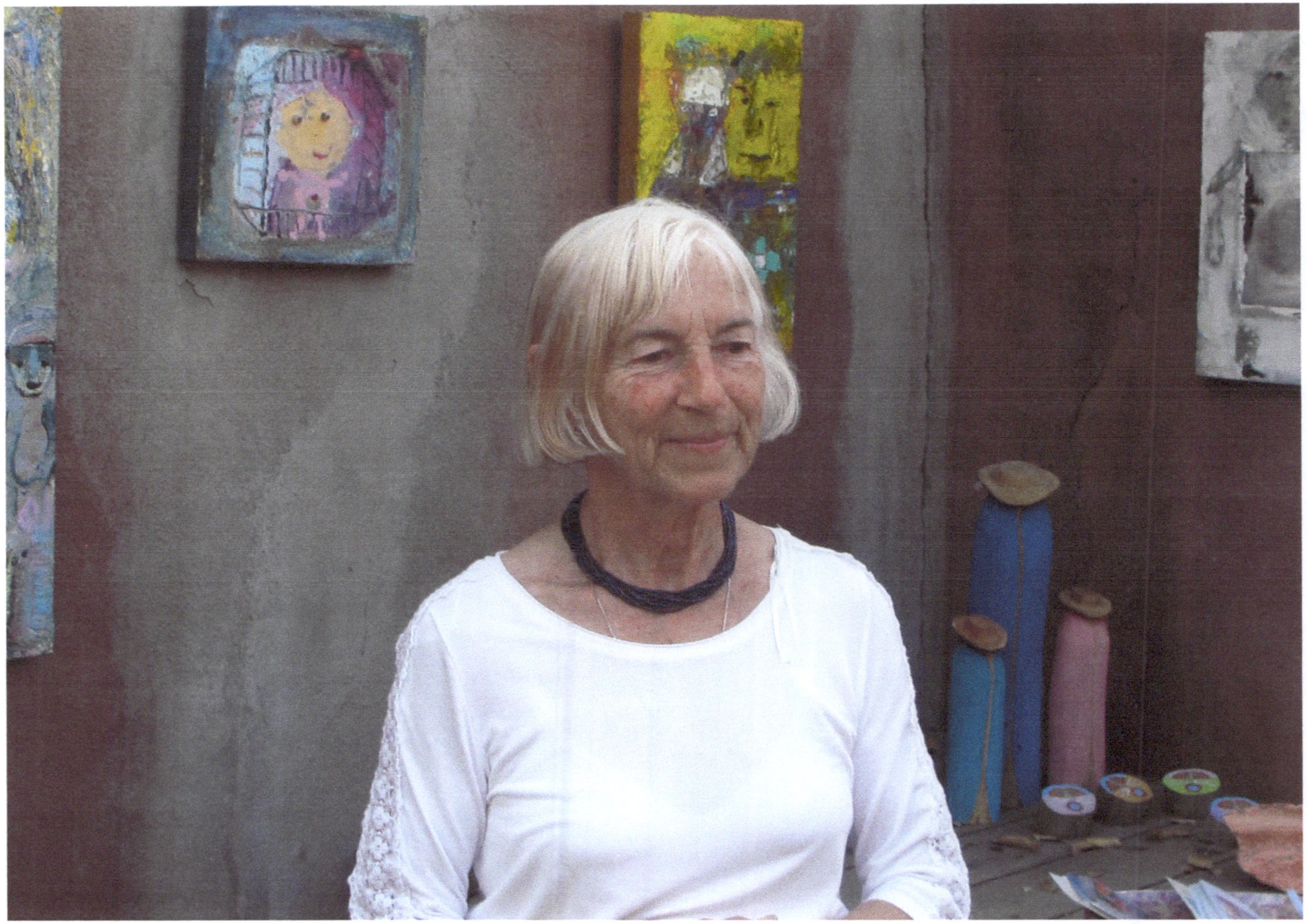

Almost 80

Mutti's "Kaffeeklatsches" continued: one happy, consistent reality from the three year "in town" phase that we children continued to be allowed to participate in. More cows were added; an electric milking machine, the "milk house" built and we began selling raw milk in town. Two dikes separated us from the desert, the metal prefab house sitting between them; there had been nothing but desert sand, mesquites and tumble weeds, an oasis began to take shape: fruit trees, a rainwater tank and a pond from well water. In the summer we swam in the second, in winter we shoe skated on the frozen rain water tank, often falling in when the ice broke, but it was shallow. No one could drown, just got a little wet and cold. We laughed.

We older three (I following Hans and Hannelore who often tried to lose me) roamed the nearby arroyo by the hour; it was endless, running all the way to the mountains. Flash floods could happen at any moment and they were dangerous. We learned to be wary, listening to all sounds for that distant rumble. There was one memorial flood, but not in the arroyo. We were on our way home, a flood blocked the road; we stopped, got out of the car, water was up to my thighs. A small crowd of people who could not get home had assembled. I felt a sense of excitement, not fear—confident that I could master any danger. Once, trying to follow my two older siblings, who had eluded me, I jumped barefoot from a shed roof I assumed they had been on, right into broken glass. I remember sitting with my feet in a basin of water as it turned red from the blood. The scars are still visible on my feet and often over the years I would feel a painful pull on one of them. In our family it seemed you had to be on death's door before a doctor was called or visited. Several times I had tonsillitis, but each time the doctor said we had to wait to take them out until the infection was gone. I was lucky. I still have them. At twelve because of a toothache, I had my first visit to a dentist. He asked me if I use Novocaine? I said no (not knowing what it was). After drilling out the large cavity, he said: "You are the bravest girl I've ever seen."

Farmer's children work hard; we helped plant the vegetable garden, watered and weeded. Mother's analogy with our upbringing as weeds, took on more graphic meaning in this period. Picking cotton became a fierce competition: whose sack weighed the most. Hannelore shot the rattler I had briefly mistaken for a giant bean in the vegetable patch. We played hide and seek among the sugar cane. One day, Burunda, the "wetback" (not a racial slur on my part, it was what they were called) hired as farm worker grabbed and kissed me (I was probably about thirteen, from his point of view, marriageable; his wife, I was told later by one parent, had died recently). That was the first of several instances that were confusing and where I later understood that my parents had little awareness of the appropriateness of their daughters' experiences or safety as we grew into puberty, and could have benefited from more protection and guidance. Other parents were protective in ways that seemed over done like not letting a girlfriend my age watch our German Shepherd, Veronica, give birth. We not only watched puppies being born but calves also. Gisela, three years younger than me, claimed a calf as her pet, heartbroken later when "Bullie" was taken to the slaughter house.

Puberty was something of a landmine, a landscape through which I passed at times scared, at other times confused. Uninitiated, when my breasts started to develop I wore really tight tee shirts under my clothes, to flatten and hide them. The beginning of my periods seemed so terrible to me, I told no one and calculated one fourth of my life was ruined. Having an older sister could have been helpful but we had an uneasy relationship. Church camp was not a safe place either. On a stormy, rainy night, Joan, a nineteen year old runaway from prison, her short black, greasy hair slicked back into a "duck tail," a knife at her waist, crawled into my bunk, held on to me, crying that the storm scared her. I felt sorry for her, patted her back and felt I could not ask her to leave. The next morning she told me: "you'll make a great love." I felt really embarrassed, uneasy. What had happened? Our mother invited Joan to stay at our house, misunderstanding our attempts to avoid her and our dislike of her, as prejudice. Had she "molested me"? Clearly, she was after Hannelore, who finally convinced our social worker mother to ask Joan to leave.

Another day my mother took me aside and said angrily: "Don't you try to take Red (his name) from your sister." I was shocked. I had no interest in my sister's boyfriend and had not been aware of any interest from him toward me. In fact, my friends thought my older sister "fast" because she was dating an airman. And then there was Tillman, another ranch hand but Anglo. He seemed really creepy to us girls. Living in his portable trailer on our property, within sight of our house, his attention to Hannelore and me was uncomfortable. Usually we worked right along with the hired help, but in this case, we did our best to avoid him.

At about the same time I had my first "crush" on one of my classmates. Being so visual, I couldn't help staring at the handsome football player whose desk faced mine in the first row of the semicircle in Biology class. (I wasn't really aware of staring, still to this day, I look at all things around me more intently if they are visually important to me.) Before this I wasn't conscious of staring at another classmate, a girl with beautiful skin and dramatically rosy cheeks. I think her friends thought I might be a lesbian. One of them actually made a comment to me. Soon after, a friend of Jim C. came up to me after class, saying he wanted to know if I would go out with him. I was so excited I couldn't sleep for several nights. We went on a double date to the ghost town, White Oaks. On the way home, Jim and I sat in the back seat; he tried to hold my hand. I was terrified he would think me fast and pulled my hand away. Since we each were so tongue-tied, our relationship fizzled out. That same summer we moved to Santa Barbara and an almost total drought that lasted years in the romantic part of my life began.

The Santa Barbara experience had sharp contrasts. Being near the ocean with hours of beach time and swimming was heaven for me. School with its accompanying social life was another thing. Alamogordo High School had about two hundred students; I knew a large number of them, both German and New Mexicans. It was a familiar, trusted place. I played my instrument in the orchestra, starting to enjoy the music. I joined the "Pep Squad" and got excited over games; felt at home (even with my broken heart). Santa Barbara was beautiful, sophisticated...a whole new horizon, but I was a stranger. It was not easy to fit in. It was ten times larger than the school I was used to, affluent in ways foreign to my parents: cashmere sweaters, the Tri High Y system (sororities and fraternities). If you weren't accepted into the best you felt you were banned. Academically the school was excellent, but so had Alamogordo High School been. The orchestra conductor was Dave Brubeck's brother who let you know how unfair fate was. Another violist was needed, that helped. But my period stopped, so I was tested and given thyroid medicine. The school counselor recommended I be given a room of my own to have more peace and quiet. My Mother's reaction: "who do you think you are?" I did not fully relax until Senior Prom (I'm leaving anyway, I don't care who likes me or not) so we danced the night away. Gary Rolle (the son of family friends) and I and had fun, a lot of it.

Besides school, I had been employed as a designer for a sporting goods company. The owner was so impressed with my skills that he wanted me to stay in Santa Barbara when the family moved. I had also won the California sewing contest with my sophisticated tailored suit, which would later help support me into my transition to becoming a free standing artist. I did make a few friends; and Wally, a grade below me and a year younger, whose closest Alamogordo friend, Heike now moved in higher circles, became my closest friend. We spent many hours enjoying playing tennis and our paths would cross again many times in the following years. Since I was unable to make plans for college (first it was unclear where we would be), and once my father had decided on Cincinnati, Ohio, I needed time to see what was available in terms of higher education there, and thus chose to put off college entry to the Spring semester.

While I knew this was a temporary break, I'm a person who lives very much in the moment, not being in school with my peers was hard for me. Hannelore remained at UC Santa Barbara, Hans had graduated but stayed in Golita also, beginning his career as an engineer and Gisela stayed with friends. For me one major phase had come to an end, but the next had not yet begun, so I was in limbo, a kind of "Purgatory." Without classmates or even my older two siblings I was lonely and a little lost.

I took a full-time retail job at Kenwood Shopping Center, about a mile and a half from our home. I walked to and from work, five days a week; this began my first criticism of technology: traveling in a car can be nice, but walking along a major thoroughfare, seemed pretty unpleasant. To alleviate the boredom of the job, I took a course (Logic and Semantics) in night school at the University of Cincinnati. My mother joined me by signing up for a course also and we drove together. I would make cards of what I needed to memorize and successfully hid them among the merchandise (socks) to be sold. This helped.

The summer after my high school graduation, for the second time since entering the USA, my father did not renew his contact due to moral? conflicts with the management of the company, all of which, whether military or private worked for the Pentagon. This would become a pattern, working with each company only two years (the initial probationary period?), moving from New Mexico, to Santa Barbara, then Cincinnati, Ohio then Los Angeles, then Columbus, Ohio, with a break as guest professor at MIT for a year, and finally, for his last employment, back again (Civil Service) with the federal government as head of White Sands Proving Ground. So when I returned to New Mexico to begin my art career there, my parents were again in Alamogordo along with my youngest brother, Riner (his name now anglicized) lived next to our parents on land deeded to him, with his wife, Karen and two children David and Gina. My youngest sister, Astrid had gone to the University of New Mexico and lived in Albuquerque with her husband Gary and soon two daughters, Melanie and Andrea. Ralph joined this part of the family in New Mexico, moving to Las Cruces after marrying Anne, and had three daughters. And finally when he retired, the eldest, Hans, also moved to southern New Mexico (Cloudcroft) with his wife; their two daughters, spouses and children remained on the West Coast. So Hannelore and Gisela were the only siblings who remained in California with their subsequent families, and finally becoming neighbors in Paradise, California until Gisela died of lung cancer and Paradise burned down. I used to joke, because Gisela's family were all "born again" Christians, that she was already in "paradise."

Did my parents avoid the soul searching, guilt and shame of other Germans when the truth came out about the fate of the Jews before and during WWII, by leaving Germany? I had grown up knowing nothing of "Nazi Germany," it's reality and it's causes. I did not remember ever even hearing that phrase before the moment I will now describe.

I had been reading the book, *Nineteen Eighty-Four*, for an English Literature class at UCLA, which generated a strong negative reaction in me: "Nothing like this could happen," I stated emphatically to my Jewish roommate and friend, Betty S., who responded: "What about "Nazi Germany?" I was dumbfounded; even the phrase had been non-existent to me. How could I have had such total ignorance of it? How could that be? I was born there, lived with a hundred families from there—highly educated people? I did ask my mother later, among the questions about my first five years the usual horrified question: "Why didn't you do more to stop it?" My mother's response: "We believed the English were telling lies about us to make us look bad in order to have a reason to attack us."

My father and the other scientists were criticized by some of the Germans for leaving, with their country in such desperate straits. His answer to this was that individual European countries (nationalism) did not count anymore; now it was only East vs West (Russia of course representing East). Due to his privileged status in Germany he was able to bring his young cousin, Walter Frahnert out of Stalingrad, thus saving his life, while millions died. His own youngest brother, Ludwig, lost one leg and then was blinded by a bomb as he tried to ride his motor cycle. The middle brother, however, Fritz, was a committed Nazi his widow, Ilse told me. Captain of a submarine fleet, he surrendered to the American military but died in captivity. My father was devoted to helping his extended family, sending money, packages of essentials and visiting as often as possible and later invited on lecture tours in Europe.

From that moment of Betty's question I began filling that void. I read (not everything) but volumes, and even visited the concentration camps. I had even read and was moved by, *The Diary of Anne Frank* as a thirteen year old, but had no idea of its context and relation to my life. My mother not only subscribed to and read the *Reader's Digest* to learn English more quickly, but also the *Reader's Digest* condensed books, which is where I found Anne Frank. Another book of that series that stood out, was Norman Vincent Peale's, *The Power of Positive Thinking*, popularizing an idea that later would resurface, and making it superficial enough for mass consumption. My mother's perfectionism in housekeeping was more difficult to maintain on the farm, with all the extra chores. I had told her once in the easier in town days: "My children may not have such a perfect house, but they will know they are loved." My mother was clearly taken aback. Her answer to my critique was surprising: "You are probably right." With Lauli gone, lonely and overwhelmed, her internal struggles around the demands on her energies, I think, made her receptive to the Apostles of Christ going door to door, who found someone who really needed to be listened to.

Did the ladies who came to Hilde's beautiful, afternoon coffees, discuss their past in Germany and how they felt about it? I will never know. I do know that Wally's parents had more understanding of their children's subsequent difficulties than my own parents revealed. Or in Germany, Tante Annemarie (my uncle Walter's wife,) when she told me her youngest son had therapy because she noted his nervousness/dis-ease. I believe the burden of the Nazi and war past ("Heimgesucht") was heavy on their psyches and played a role in their late years. First there was the terrible auto accident on the way to Washington DC to see Reagan, which left my mother with 7th Cranial nerve damage, causing one half of her face to be paralyzed, a disfigurement painful to see (and certainly even more to experience), also causing her eye to become painfully dried out. While she never sought a divorce, she decided she could not live with her husband. Keeping his affairs in order (I inherited his tendency to create chaos, lose or misplace things, but being female I was forced while growing up to combat that myself) was beyond her now. Riner who as an adult had dropped the "e" out of his name, built her a small house on his property. She took ever more refuge in church and Bible reading.

Character and Belief System

I was reminded of the German word "Ruecksichtslos" while my husband and I were reading a novel based on Rembrandt's life (and had a difference of opinion). From my perspective as an artist I defended Rembrandt's action of using the money he was supposed to use to make a payment on used furniture, to purchase a drawing at auction. I won't go into more of the circumstances and the excellent job the writer did in making deep, even irrational motives clear, that can cause anger and misunderstanding on the part of family or friends with a different outlook/belief system. In my own mind I can also easily defend Gauguin's leaving his family (wife with dependent children) and Van Gogh's internal struggles. I remember hearing the phrase: "Sei nicht (so) ruecksichtslos!" in different variations, probably from my mother directed both at myself and more frequently at my father. Ruecksicht means literally to look back, hindsight. Emotive: it's usually translated as irresponsibility. I felt I was seen as irresponsible, even in the decision to be an artist which led to other decisions that fit this reputation.

The first and most serious case was when I broke my engagement. To me it was deeply responsible and also deeply considered. I agonized and suffered over it. No one in my family talked with me about it, even though they must have known that I was unhappy and conflicted. Finally my roommate (one of three) Betty, whose mother was a therapist, suggested I go talk to Dr. Offman, a school counselor at UCLA. That was wonderful, helpful advice. Having someone outside of my frame of reference listen and share their perspective was healing. When Clyde and I became engaged and consummated our relationship for the first time, I was undone. My feelings of both attraction and literally, loathing—what I came to describe as my schizoid reaction to intimacy an inner voice said: if I marry this man I will end up in an institution.

Growing up I was sure my mother did not love my father and felt they were really incompatible, and I was determined I would not marry anyone I did not sufficiently love. That can become a dilemma. That notion of love and "sufficiency" is tricky; how does one know? It changes with time. But this degree of attraction and subsequent inner rejection which I could hardly admit to myself, much less discuss with my fiancée, took many years to understand/heal, though not necessarily completely. Offman advised me to end the engagement, quit graduate school and go into therapy with him for a year. While the first made sense, I could not commit to the latter. Continuing the university education which gave me the opportunity to explore my psyche while preparing for a career, gave me a sense of needed security.

Both my parents spent the last months of their lives in a nursing home; my father due to a stroke that paralyzed him. A mystery surrounds my father's death: a nurse with an assumed name who disappeared immediately afterwards caused his death through what seemed like a careless medical procedure. The young nurses aid who had been learning German from my father and had grown to love him, begged the head nurse to let her call an ambulance to take him to the hospital, as he was suffering incredibly. Riner heard about these events later from the young girl who was weeping broken heartedly at the funeral and as my brother approached her, asked to speak to him privately. Once in the hospital, all my father's organs poisoned, he was still so strong it took him forty-eight hours to die. For years I suspected the order of death might have come from the CIA, as Riner found in my dad's papers that he worked secretly for this organization on the question of UFO activity in New Mexico (Roswell and White Sands incidents) and came to believe, according to his notes, that there was actual extraterrestrial activity, a conclusion that was against the official U S position at that time. (Sounds more plausible in Russia?) Gi, supported my suspicion, telling me that once when my father visited the Voehringer's in their Pocano Mountain cabin, a CIA helicopter circled for some time over head, as if they were planning to land. Over the years it seems possible it was more closely related to our origins in Germany and Nazi-ism. I had heard several times that there were Jews who hunted down Germans they believed were Nazis. My dad was a scientist, not the best dad, but an ethical, conscientious human being, who like many Germans relied too much on the authority of the State. He once told me, when he realized I participated in demonstrations against Vietnam: "if you are critical of this country, go live in Russia." Just before her eightieth birthday, Mutti broke her hip; she never recovered from the surgery. Near the end, as she lay in the hospital bed, I felt that in spite of her "faith," she was frightened of dying. I held her hand for many hours, assuring her of God's love.

Hyper Vigilance

A part of me I now know is deeply affected by what I have experienced and what I see around me. How can one not be, when I have personally experienced the destruction of a world war, and continue to see the destructiveness, be it to man/woman, other species or Nature. People say: "I believe in science." But science is also pursued by corruptible humans; and science has often been wrong in the past. When the wireless transition occurred, I used a cell phone like everyone else. But I couldn't help noticing my body did not like it: my hand would become numb, bringing out the underlying "carpel tunnel syndrome." Like always, I read everything I could find on the new technology. These books soon disappeared from book shelves and even public libraries. I concluded it is not good for my body, nor for the Earth or any species. This realization was deeply distressing: nothing would ever be the same again. Generations yet unborn would not know how the Earth felt before this pervasive level of radiation.

But almost everyone embraced it, even those who initially distrusted it and possibly still do, but think they cannot engage productively with society without it. It is unquestionably believed to be the "new way"—without regard to consequences—a massive social and environmental experiment. Anyone not with it can feel isolated and alone. And then we had Covid-19 (and the Delta variation) and were again isolated, wearing masks indefinitely that caused us not to recognize faces and make it seem like we know no one. It's accepted that vaccination is absolutely necessary but will not end this. We are so divorced from Nature and ourselves, that we don't see how health, world-wide, has deteriorated to such an extent that viruses will continue to plague humanity. Like one scientist has said: the pandemic is wireless, the virus just the symptom and result. There are two parts to illness: the virus and the host just as a seed does not sprout without the right conditions, soil, water sun, nutrients, a virus thrives in an unhealthy body.

Health I

As I write this I am well into my eightieth year, the same age both my parents were when they died, though six years apart. Five of my six siblings have passed over, three from cancer, while my older sister Hannelore, two years my senior, partially paralyzed from stroke five years earlier, died March of 2021. The last remaining sibling, Hans, a brother four years older, looks physically quite frail, but his strong will and humor belie this. I've also had my share of pain and suffering. I broke both my wrists, three months apart; the left much more seriously and still painful over a year later. For over forty years I've had periodic intense "carpel tunnel syndrome" (over-working), so the resulting "Peripheral Neuropathy" of both breaks was intensely painful, causing many sleepless nights and despair. It is still mysterious why I broke my wrists; the right one isn't so surprising as I slipped on ice; the left, a much gentler fall, was a much worse break. My last bone density test had been good, and before I moved into the quadrant of the city of Santa Fe, Old Santa Fe Trail 500 block, that has high magnetic fields, I fell off my bike several times hitting the concrete hard so I had bad bruises, but never broke anything. The milligauss in the building was over 100 in spots and average was in the twenties. According to my research, the DOE states that inside spaces where humans live or work should not exceed 2.5 mg. High magnetic fields are a known health hazard causing leukemia in children. Can there be a connection?

My wrists are strong again. Once I decided to bike to Whole Foods here in Santa Fe and climb over the wall, avoiding the traffic on Cerrillos Road, which I hadn't done in years. It felt good. I also bought a 14 inch electric chain saw so that I could cut up all the dead branches surrounding my studio for firewood. It has only a wood stove for heat, cold water and a grandfathered in outhouse our son Sean renovated. I'm ready for a lower energy use future.

2 / COLLEGE AND CAREER

In Springfield, Ohio, only an hour from Cincinnati, surrounded by a rural setting of woods, my parents and I visited the small, idyllic, Lutheran Wittenberg University. After the anonymity of Santa Barbara High School, it's size and focus appealed to me and I was accepted with a partial scholarship for the first Spring semester. I was so highly motivated and scared of "flunking out" that I got straight A's. In my second semester, I was offered a quasi scholarship kind of job: every two years a female student with high academic standing was selected to live at the president's house with the other seasoned student who had also been trained for a year by an older one, to do light housekeeping, dinner and breakfast dishes in return for room and board. My being selected after only one semester was unusual, if not unheard of. The Universe works in unusual ways, and my mother's expert housekeeping and our weekly chores prepared me as well as possible.

My roommate and housekeeping coach, Heidi Voerhinger, though we each had our own room, separated by a corridor that stretched the length of the back part of the president of the university's house, was also born in Germany. We often spoke German together, though her "Schwaebisch" (southern German dialect), in contrast to the "high" German I learned from my parents was an astonishing contrast in it's much more lyrical but also seemingly crude, uneducated and naive cadence, to her sophisticated, intellectual English. The folk songs she had learned from her mother were also different from the ones I knew (central vs southern). I eagerly learned them from her. We had hilarious times cleaning the almost immaculate rooms (the weekly housekeeper did the serious stuff) while singing these folk songs as well as a few opera arias. This was the beginning of my conscious enthusiasm for music and also my introduction to Joan Biaz (whom Heidi had remarkable resemblance to) and Bob Dylan, and the guitar. With my years of playing the viola in Orchestras, learning to play the guitar was easy and fun; soon I could join Heidi, her brother Arnie and others in jam sessions. We would spend the evening playing music and singing folk, country western, and anti war songs. I rediscovered passion and joy.

I was somewhat in awe of Heidi, (and even to some degree her whole family), her intelligence, warmth and charisma. While we were only a year apart in age, I was a second semester freshman and she was already a senior. She had graduated from Girl's High School in Philadelphia in only three years and would have her B.A. also in three years. We became close over that year; I learned through her and shared her opinions on many things; the trajectory of my life became more focused through our relationship. Wittenberg University like Santa Barbara High School was a fraternity/sorority school. I went through "Rushing" as I did in Santa Barbara, with the same result. I did not fit the sorority model, though again I was invited to join the second tier sorority. I declined and proudly became an "independent," like Heidi and her friends. However the dating part of my social life became non-existent. Fraternity men (over 90 % of the campus) were not allowed to date "independents," but Heidi's circle filled the gap and around them I felt a spontaneous, innocent happiness. She and her older (only by one year) brother Arnie were almost like twins. He visited frequently from Fort Wayne, Indiana where he studied engineering. Next to music were the Bridge nights, which I enjoyed more for the company than excelling at it. I also loved and sympathized with Heidi's mother who like me had trouble keeping up with their sophisticated, witty repartee.

Heidi seemed like my soul-sister and I became part of the family, fitting much better and more easily than in my own, I was invited to spend the following summer and other vacations with her family in their cabin in the Pocono Mountains in Pennsylvania and their home in Philadelphia. While I had begun to work as a waitress in high school, I became more professional through the job Heidi procured for me. We drove to work together on the winding mountain roads in her old clunker, "Krushenka."

I was possibly responsible for the car's transmission failure. Still today I am not considered a cautious driver due to my speedy reaction time (mars in Aries) or dis-ease with machinery. I owe the family a lot for their patience and love for me. I continued to support myself through waitressing jobs all the way through my M.A. I was never bored as it was always challenging and I enjoyed the contact with the public as well as my fellow waitresses.

Though our families were different, there were significant similarities besides our origins. Both our fathers had PhDs, though at opposite ends of the ethical spectrum. Her father wanting to save "Heathens" in Africa, with Christianity and mine saving USA democracy with weapons of mass destruction, to put a complex story in simplistic, ironic terms. Both Heidi and I inherited through them, not just the value of higher education, but of ambition. Both fathers were charismatic, even visionary at times, traits which Heidi and I, though much later, exhibited. Like me Heidi was also the third child, each of us having an older male and female sibling. Notable height discrepancies, though not of essence to me, existed in both families. Both fathers were somewhat shorter than average, while both mothers were on the taller side. Heidi's older sister, Gisela (Gi), was petite, probably around 5' 2"; blond and fair skinned. She looked like an "exquisite china doll," as Heidi often described her. Gi made many of her clothes, even her wedding dress. I did the same; from about age twelve on, we were given a modest clothing allowance. So I learned to sew many of my own clothes, a skill that has always been valuable. Later while supporting myself through creating batiks, I also made high end silk dresses and quilted coats which were stitched, beautifully batiked and sold through Hills Gallery on the Santa Fe Plaza, at, it seemed to me, amazing high prices. Being one of the shorter members of my family, I was more attracted to taller men. Like my older sister and brother, Heidi was tall, with long dark hair, and tawny skin. Like both her parents, all four children had blue eyes; this last family trait was important to Heidi—it needed to be passed on. While my father's eyes were blue, almost turquoise and twinkled when he got enthusiastic, the gray of our mother's eyes became hazel in all but the oldest and youngest.

Eye color, of course, was not only emphasized in Nazism, just as skin color has lately again received prominence in the U.S. Both being/becoming a source of discrimination. The basic biological, and more complex emotional, social—even class for German born—process of who one is attracted to as a potential mate, was part of both the land mine and the black hole for me, though I understood nothing of this at the time. And while I was not conscious of height and eye color in our family or those around us (weeds are undiscriminating), it does play a role in the biological preferences (part of which are often unconscious) of choosing a mate. Heidi and I both had trouble in this department, but of a different nature. At Wittenberg University playing tennis one day, as I hit the ball, I had one of those sudden bolts of truth that grabs one in mid air: I had been reading Thomas Mann's *Buddenbrooks* for a class; the central theme about two parts of the German psyche seemed to describe my family perfectly. To put it simply for this context, my dad: blonder and blue eyed fit the image of the businessman, the go getter unencumbered by introspection or self-doubts; my mother, the darker, religious/mystical, creative. More than the physical, was the attitude toward life, of trust and confidence. Like Goethe's "Zwei Seelen leben, Ach! In meiner Brust." In me the two tendencies combine, battle each other or try to deny each other, but come to a synthesis in my art.

In my case, I more than any sibling, inherited my father's prominent nose, and felt ugly and was teased as a teenager because of it. A noticeable bout with acne during my first college months, for which the student health used radiation, did not help. In case of the former, my mother, trying to comfort me, said: "It shows that you will go far in life." Many years later after I had gone through my two engagements at UCLA, a wealthy aunt visiting us from Germany, offered to pay for a nose job. Synchronistically Andrea, one of my three roommates, encouraged me to also apply for a part-time job with the plastic surgeon who had hired her. When I did he said he would hire me if I had my nose "fixed" first. I refused both. I was now comfortable with my appearance. Later I learned that my older sister, Hannelore, actually did have a nose job. Hers followed a tendency on our father's side to be somewhat, even subtle, irregularly formed rather than classically perfect noses like my mother's and uncles. I had not noticed it, showing me how irrelevant small imperfections can be.

At this time I was invited to spend the summer with Andrea's (Fusako Tsukamoto) family whose father was a minister to the Japanese people in Central Los Angeles. While we had been apartment hunting earlier, I became conscious for the first time of racial prejudice even toward the Japanese in Los Angeles. Ironically, while she was attractive enough in appearance to work as a receptionist in a plastic surgeon's office, when Fusako went apartment hunting there never seemed to be any vacancies, while I and our other two friends had no such problems. She was indeed a rare, delicate beauty with a tall handsome father and lovely, petite dynamo of a mother whom I loved and admired. In her gracious oriental way, she ruled her roost. They never spoke of it, but I realized later that the family had shared the fate of many Japanese who had been interned in the war time internment camps through which they lost all their possessions. It makes their generosity to me even more surprising. In both these families, my early mystical inclination, still to Christianity, made me feel at home.

While I remember my senior year chemistry teacher at Santa Barbara

High School being complimentary to me saying: "Monika, you will excel at whatever you put your mind to," my art ability was recognized by Mr. Baker in whose drawing class I got the only A. The art department at Wittenberg was not inspiring to me. It always reminded me of a dusty forgotten attic. The best and most popular teacher taught design/advertising rather than fine art. For a time there was an evening "life drawing" class that I enjoyed and Heidi sometimes modeled for. It was her love of Gauguin's paintings that opened a permanent door to my art vision. Many times she would bring out her book of his Tahitian paintings and share with me her awe of the exquisite Madonna like faces. Critics, collectors and viewers have pointed out over the years that in my paintings the female figure often looks Madonna like. Though I was not conscious of this influence until later, Gauguin's retreat from modern commercial life, immersing himself in a more primitive and nature oriented society, the spiritual quest in his work, which became part of a larger movement, is also present in my own work and life style. Many years later when I had the opportunity to go to (then still) Leningrad, when the tour group visited the Hermitage a second time, I left the group and sought out the room of Gauguin's paintings.

Life is mysterious. I could have picked another school and not gotten the President's job. Our meeting and closeness was "Karmic," a term I did not know then. Heidi and I remained in touch for years, mostly through letters and a few visits. I adopted her family's practice of using real candles on the live Christmas tree and learned many German carols which I still love to sing on Christmas Eve. The Canyon Road in Santa Fe caroling always finds some German singers gravitating to the Quaker Meeting (fire). Christmas Eve as Canyon Road was closed to strollers and carolers during Covid, but car traffic was encouraged. I missed the caroling so much I went by myself and sang carols in front of the Meeting House as loud as I wanted, to the cheering of some enthusiastic occupants of the cars enjoying the Faralitos.

I was moved when Heidi shared a tragic secret with me: her desperate love of her older sister's husband whom she was convinced should have married her. Ted's tallness seemed to Heidi more suited to her than Gi. More importantly, she was convinced that Ted had the ability to become America's Dostoevsky and she, not her sister could help him realize this potential. Male writers throughout history have often cited a woman as Muse, a role Heidi felt she was destined for. The Voehringers and the Heinnegins had been neighbors and friends. Both fathers were professors at the Mount Airy Seminary in Philadelphia and the two brothers and two sisters, were friends since childhood. Heidi had even become engaged for a short time to Mickey, the younger brother who was blond, handsome and athletic: the role of biology. Ted became a successful publisher of others literary efforts and remained, surely happily, married to Gi. Heidi after finishing her M. A. through a Woodrow Wilson scholarship, met and married Rip, the only heir of a wealthy family; they joined the Peace Corps together and went to Africa, Heidi having developed a love and curiosity for that continent through her father's years there. She was convinced at the time, that her husband had the potential to become a great writer, over the years it became clear that this was a stress producing illusion; they eventually divorced. In spite of this Rip had agreed to support her financially to do a PhD at Harvard in theology and Arab history. But as she began to attend classes she found she could not keep up: Alzheimer's had already impaired her mental ability. Rip then paid for her care so that she could continue to live in their house at Saranac Lake.

Arnie's life was also touched by tragedy; I remember his quoting from Matthew Arnold's poem, *Dover Beach*: "Happiness is but a brief episode in a general drama of pain," a war scene, like that out of which our lives emerged. My response to this idea was opposition, evolving over time: first from Christianity, later from Buddhism. Already in my childhood, joy seemed more important than happiness. Arnie was born with a stomach ailment that had caused great physical suffering in his childhood and surgical loss of half his stomach. He married twice, both times to a nurse named Judy. Neither treated him well. He had two children, a son and a daughter; the former died in a fatal automobile accident on his first visit to Germany (where speed limits did not yet exist).

Some years after Heidi's death, Gi, who came semi-annually to Santa Fe with Ted on publishing business, would invite me to lunch; we always enjoyed a long talk over a beer. I looked forward to her visits; we had a lot more in common than I had with my own sister, Gisela. Visiting with her during a recent trip to Chicago where she still lived after Ted's death, I asked her on impulse (my husband always tells me I have no guile) if she was aware of Heidi' s obsession. While first she responded with shocked disbelief, answering that her sister was deluded, she did share this memory with me: the night before her wedding, Heidi came to her room and told her: "You have ruined my life!" I wonder what she felt about this? Did Ted and she discuss it? I had never looked at a chart of anyone in the Voeringer family because my interest in Astrology began much later, but as the new Moon is approaching and it happens to be on Heidi's birthday, August 8th, I looked it up. Wow! Saturn square her Sun (difficulty of achieving one's purpose) and Pluto conjunct her Venus (compulsivity in love); a Stellium in Leo (a sense of royalty) That can do it. World literature is full of tragic heroines like Heidi. My painting, *Passion,* though based on a different time and event, draws from, and harkens back to my store of memories. Now I see that I could have asked Heidi some questions, such as: before Gi returned from her year in Europe, did Ted give some indication he wanted to be with you? I would imagine he must have. I could have found out more but at that time it did not occur to me to ask. That is one reason I love literature: the author can tell you what occurs in the minds of all participants. In my "narrative realism" I create a view, often archetypal, that suggests several possibilities. In Thomas Mann's last novel, a trilogy, *Joseph und seine Brueder* (*Joseph and his Brothers*), Jakob had to marry Leah first, because she was the older sister, before he could marry Rachel, his true love...a more fluid society.

The Seductive Power of Ideas

I struggled with the story of Heidi: questioning whether it belongs in such length and detail in my memoir. I've finally understood why it grips me and that it goes right to the center of why I am an artist who addresses the ideas behind beliefs. Ideas put out by today's mass media or any other sources, such as parents, must be looked at with discrimination. Children of course are not capable of doing that, but adulthood is defined by this, and balanced by experience and moral conscience. My parents were, at the very least, influenced by Nazi-ism; certainly Hitler's attitude about art was part of their distrust of the artistic spirit, the need to follow one' s "Daemon" (Goethe and possibly CG Jung). While Heidi was convinced her role in life was to be the feminine facilitator of male genius, I decided my role was to explore my own.

After five semesters at Wittenberg, necessary due to my starting school in the Spring semester as well as my two year commitment to the Stoughtons, I was ready for a greater challenge than this more intimate and protective setting provided, and entered UCLA as an upper division student. Between the time of my crush on Jim C. in Alamogordo and that of my secret feelings for Arnie, there had been no one. In that summer before school started, Arnie and his parents visited us in L.A. To my surprise, Arnie attempted to seduce me toward the end of the visit. Part of the two years I knew him at Wittenberg he never expressed more than affection for me. I was part of the Family, everyone called me "Moni." I withdrew from his advances, probably to his surprise, since he certainly must have sensed my attraction to him. Later, he explained he probably could not support me at the level I was used to. (A misunderstanding or excuse?) In both Santa Barbara and L.A. we had, for the first time, a home that gave the appearance of affluence, which was superficial and not the basis of a relationship for me. Arnie seemed to have assumed I was experienced. Another misunderstanding, though I was twenty-one, it was something I was taught should happen after marriage or at least engagement; plus there weren't even opportunities. While my feelings for him did not immediately change, my social life expanded with the beginning of school and suddenly there were several men in my life.

The most determined suitor was a German Department graduate student, Clyde S., who worked hard at, and succeeded in awakening my dormant sexuality, while also introducing me to hiking, camping, improving my tennis skills, as well as taking me to numerous opera productions. A year later we became engaged. The immediate tremendous inner turmoil I experienced made clear that I was not ready for this step. While confused and ignorant of the cause, I eventually gave back his ring. When I entered UCLA I first moved into one of the co-ed dorms which seemed a good choice while being at a new school. Once Clyde and I became involved emotionally, the fact that he lived only a couple of floors below my own, became a problem: we would run into each other at meals and he could come to my room too easily. I did have a roommate, but it was hard to avoid one another without seeming rude. I had not yet learned how to maintain good boundaries. As soon as I could, I left the dorm, joining three girl friends in looking for an apartment. Too soon my emotional pendulum swung in the opposite direction and a handsome "post doc" from Cambridge, England with a beautiful speaking voice, convinced me to accept his marriage proposal. During my first engagement, my roommate, Betty. whose mother was a "shrink" and who had the wisdom to recognize my inner turmoil was deeper than a friendship could address, advised me to seek out Dr. Offman, the college counselor. I did. That was the first step to understanding my intimacy dilemma. I ended the second engagement, finished my M.A. and joined my father who was leaving for a lecture tour in Germany to spend a year getting to know my relatives from the northern most part, Cuxhaven and Hamburg, through central part around Frankfurt, down to Munich in the south.

Over the years as I returned to Germany, I would be greeted at the Frankfurt airport by my mother's best friend, Emma Pommeranz, whom I probably got to know more personally (the deepest feelings, deepest regrets) than any of my relatives. She lived in an apartment block in Frankfurt before the time of the displacement of small family or one owner grocery stores, replaced by chain and box stores. I usually spent several days with her because she was so eager to show me around. Among her favorite excursions would be one of the numerous beer gardens where we would sit together with a beer and enjoy "Handkaese und Musik," Frankfurt was famous for, a type of mild, soft aromatic cheese, topped with fried onion on the wonderful freshly baked rye bread, it was so delicious. She had two daughters close to my age, Siegfried, a year older and Mechthild, a year younger. The latter was studying medicine in Berlin at the time, visiting occasionally while I was there. Siegfried, was more available for friendship as she lived near Frankfurt; we enjoyed each other's company. I still have a photo of the incredible several days "Wanderung" from Munich over the Alps on cross country skis. Not only did we barely miss an avalanche but there was the exhilarating experience of crossing the Alps in her company. By the way, I picked up lice at the "Huette" we stayed at over-night to the horror of my landlady in Munich. Later I gave up downhill skiing and took up cross country permanently, more suitable to an artist's lifestyle as the other was so expensive. It seemed a capitalist's sport and my knee surgeon had warned me I could lose my leg.

Emma would proudly share her knowledge of the herbs she grew on her window sill, her organic diet and medical secrets, many of which I still use. The family had never recovered completely from the war; both daughters had a vulnerability I could sense. Emma's severely PTSD second husband (I think the first died in the war) had insisted that she (temporarily?) send her two and four year old's to an orphanage. Of course this turned out to be a terrible mistake which she deeply regretted. The children never regained their innocent trust. It was one of the instances that taught me that the damage of war goes far beyond the number of soldiers killed and cities destroyed. Siegfried died early of cancer, while Mechthild, a year after a serious auto accident, through which she became addicted to pain medicine, ended her own life. Left to Emma was Timmy, Mechthild's son, who on one visit told us about the incredible German "Unfall's Medicin." His arm had been severed in an auto accident and been miraculously re-attached and was healing well. The last time we saw Emma she was in a nursing home. She had Alzheimer's; the TV was on, to me an alienating practice. I don't know if she ever had watched TV.

For the winter semester of that first trip to Germany, I stayed with my Onkel Walter Madee's (my mother's brother) family. I was offered a job teaching a course in "American Studies" at the University of Saarbrueken and took a course in French conversation before attending the University in Munich for the summer semester. I quickly made friends with other students there. Rather than individual dating, students congregated in groups, going to parties, and movies. When you made one friend, you suddenly had several. The most fun and funniest was going to movies as a group. People brought alarm clocks, paper bags to make noise, while attending American westerns. It was loud, hilarious and innocent fun. When I had my wisdom teeth pulled there (much cheaper) the whole group around my friend Klaus came to visit me with homeopathic pain pills. Dr. Offman had suggested I leave graduate school and go into therapy for a year with him, but neither my family nor I were ready, or could consider, such a step. And looking back, finishing my M. A., going to Germany, seeing where I was born, getting to know my relatives, gave me an irreplaceable perspective on life in Germany, as well as America and of course, myself.

Along with all the beneficial experiences I also had a traumatic one that highlighted, but initially worsened, the source of my confused psyche—getting raped by a student in Munich whom I had trusted as a friend, but had no interest in as a potential partner. As I met each aunt or uncle, people who had known my father and/or mother all their lives, were so eager to meet me, embraced me so heartily, made me feel important and valued in a way I had never experienced before. To what degree we had lived in an emotional vacuum, is clearer and still moves me as I write this. In the Madee (my Mother's brother's) family, the afternoon hours we spent over coffee and the wonderful German Broetchen and cakes, talking about life, politics, philosophy, art, and personal experiences, similar as in Heidi's family, but not ours, was exiting and deeply healing. Also, of course, we project our desires, fears, and emotions on each other: I secretly envied Sybille, ten years younger than I. She, like me, had three brothers, but she was the youngest and only girl, not one of four, and seemed to be treated like a princess. In reality they all worked hard; two became medical doctors, and Sybille, who became a physical therapist with her own practice in which she earned more than her Italian medical doctor husband, also. Tragedy did come later; "In every life, some rain must fall."

Their father, my uncle Walter, an executive at Telefunken, always left for work before seven in the morning and returned after seven in the evening. It seemed to him they were spoiled: while he slaved, they partied) He had neither time nor interest to join his family's "Kaffee Klatsch'es." His own version was rejected by the rest of the family, secretly calling him the "old Nazi."

I was the only one who accepted his Sunday invitation to join his weekly long walk through the woods, stopping in the afternoon at one the restaurants for coffee and dessert. I had not recognized the cultural and emotional polarization in my uncle's family until I too became enmeshed in it just before I left for the University of Munich on a cold June 2nd. Rather than Frau Wager, a long-time family friend who had been embraced by my family during the war as a refugee, whom I would become close to over many decades until her death at over ninety, welcoming me, or my close friends from UCLA, or even the colleague of my father's and his family, who would repay my father's friendship and loyalty by hiring me to give me time to learn Latin while earning money, who had all promised to welcome me with open arms, all were absent. The warmth and trust I had experienced with my Uncle's family seemed to have suddenly cooled. From their point of view, I was siding with my uncle whom, of course I liked, enjoyed and respected. And was thus against them. Absurd! I am a person who can embrace two seemingly opposing points of view (double Libra). I've learned over the decades how opposites attract each other and can see that issues of Nazism and WWII had remained unresolved in the Madee family just as they were buried in my own family here in the U.S. and how at this time our whole society is polarized, and the lack of each side speaking truthfully, vulnerably with each other.

I still remember walking up the massive steps to the Munich University Library and feeling like I needed to throw up, an emotional vulnerability that my would-be rapist, might have sensed. He approached me with friendliness and curiosity. He was a student whom I was not attracted to physically, and never sensed that he was to me. We met often over a two week period to talk about life in America versus Germany. When he invited me to have dinner at his apartment, I had no warning clue. Before accompanying me to the bus, a surprising gesture for a rapist, it seemed to me, he told me he had read the *Kinsey Report* and got from it that American women always say no when they mean yes. Well, a dozen no's, begging and crying had no impact on his intent. Thankfully, a fellow student (not a friend, certainly) of his, who knew his history, visited me the next day, took me under his wing over several days, fed me homeopathic trauma medication, and listened while I cried.

Soon however I was able to connect with the people I had planned to meet in Munich. I visited Frau Irmtraut Wager, a free spirit, who immediately felt a renewed deep connection with me. She remembered me as a three to four year old, where she was convinced I was psychic because I always knew when she had managed to procure some small sweet—more difficult in wartime—and I would knock on her door with my little companions. "You haven't changed at all." A phrase I have heard many times over the years. Not only did we share a deep love of nature and hiking, as I later became a student and practitioner of Tibetan Buddhism, our interest evolved in parallel. It was hard to get to the mountains without a car; she could not afford to buy one so she played the State lottery with the intention/prayer of winning and thus getting a car. She won. Later she really wanted to visit Tibet, feeling concerned for the plight of the Tibetan people; winning the lottery again made the trip possible. Thus began the German "Tibet Hilfe" that she lead for several decades, raising millions for schools and other support. She told me that on one trip a Tibetan Lama noticed that she had a slight limp, a chronic pain she had for years. He was able to heal it permanently. Part of the healing of my rape trauma was through my friendship with Peter Steinhoff, no relative in the usual sense, an ex-priest who was retraining as a counselor in psychology at the university. At the end of the semester he wanted me to stay and marry him, but I knew my path did not lie in Germany. I could not be an artist there. It was a far more tightly structured society. I could only be an English teacher. I applied to Berkeley for the PhD program and was accepted. There I could explore my options further.

A "Free Education" was the gift of the time. I took out just one student loan after my first year at UC Berkeley to return to Europe in the summer. Of course I could justify it because it aided my PhD studies.

The teaching assistantship I received not only paid well, but helped me to overcome my stage fright and before long I loved teaching. The more in-depth German literature courses suited me even better than before. Both the teaching and doing well in the excellent courses substantially increased my self-confidence. To be an artist that's essential. I was the only student who passed the exploratory oral exam that year. Coming from another university, even within the University of California system, you had an oral exam in front of a committee of professors, as difficult as for the actual PhD oral, which let you into the program. This along with teaching and the normal class load took two years of study unless you came straight from an M.A. in "Germanistik" in Germany, which many did. This seemed kind of absurd in view of UCLA and UC Berkeley being part of the same University of California system, but each branch competed to be the best in a particular area. Berkeley's German department was considered the best in the USA at that time, even better than Harvard as their own students told us when they came to take a contemporary German literature course from my favorite and most challenging professor, Dr. Bluma Goldstein.

By my third year I had finished all requirements except the linguistics part. I have a natural interest in the formation of languages but I was not looking forward to being tested by Dr. Wilbur, reputed to be difficult both academically and personally. The Latin requirement was based on the German university's "Grosses Latinum" which constituted eight years of Latin, basically an almost impossible requirement. Most students did not try to master Latin, but instead memorized translations of important passages of Virgil and Homer and hoped they'd be lucky. I had started learning Latin at the University of Munich and continued on my own at Berkeley, not wanting to take the short-cut. Then came Reagan who, as governor, canceled the U of C language requirement. He probably never learned a foreign language; and who gives politicians such powers? This did not immediately go into effect and would not solve my dilemma with the requirement but which sent a wave of panic through the whole department—the loss of language teaching positions across the US, as the University of California was considered the leader in educational trends. Reagan was also against the low tuition. His famous position: why should the taxpayers pay for studies if students protest our military policies?

It was time to take the leap. I had proved I could succeed in the academic world; I wanted to try my hand at being the creator rather than studying the creative process. I decided on a "leave of absence," not because I did not do well, but because I had done so well. If I could do this so well on my second-best subject, I would take the risk to pursue what I am best at. I could always go back if I need to.

I signed a contract to teach German, English and Crafts at Holy Names High School. I had been working with clay on the potter's wheel in the Student Union basement pottery facilities as well teaching myself Batik. For some time I managed to stay several steps ahead of my students, teaching myself jewelry making and mosaics as well as other crafts. To wean myself from the intense intellectual activity of the PhD program I taught myself astrology, and shortly began casting charts and doing readings, finding my acutely active intuition helpful. Soon several of the nuns I worked with including the head nun, who was also Principal of the school, asked me to cast and read their charts. (More than fifty years later I'm still pursuing it, though not professionally; it's just part of the way I understand reality.) Having spent six months in the San Raphael Ashram with Yogi Bhajan, I also began teaching Kundalini Yoga, first at noon to my fellow teachers at the high school and several years later Astanga Yoga with Baba Hari Dass, as well as learning from Sufi Sam, Pir Valijat Kahn and Ram Dass whose lecture on eating meat and the adrenaline released by the animal's fear acts a poison for us humans, turned me into an instant vegetarian. And I was ready to test myself, not in one fell swoop, but in gradual steps.

Lovers as Muse(s): The Acid of Truth

Reading about Linda Durham's trips launched me into the central portion of this book on how I became an artist. A good introduction is my own acid trip, one of two, but the only significant one. While the first ended a longer, serious relationship, the second nipped a briefer one in the bud. Jon T. of Polish ancestry, who had a medical doctorate in psychiatry, moved into the small back bedroom off the main floor apartment of the building I shared. I have always had a deep and active interest in psychology; he was tall, attractive and charming. Over the months our friendship resulted in our decision to live together for at least a year. However, before the end of this commitment Jon was accepted by San Francisco General Hospital for his residency in psychiatry. Finding the commute too time consuming and exhausting, Jon wanted us to move to San Francisco.

We began house hunting together in the beautiful city; he decided on a modest, affordable two bedroom down the hill from a Eucalyptus grove.

One issue of conflict that had developed between us was my refusal or inability to get drunk. He saw it as an inhibition to emotion/erotic pleasure? While Jon was a private person, he was focused on emotional closeness and I felt pressured that I was not emotionally close enough. Having a partner so focused on one's psychology can be daunting. Since I was teaching in Oakland as well as establishing my art career, getting up early to do daily meditation and yoga, I was not eager to commute from San Francisco to Oakland five days a week. Perhaps to shed more light and solutions to our impasse, Jon suggested he could act as my guide for an acid "trip." While I was cautious, I had been interested in exploring LSD safely. I knew lots of people in Berkeley who dropped acid regularly, after all it was the sixties. My focus had always been on: what's below the surface beyond our normal or peripheral vision, what is Truth? I especially hoped for a mystical experience. So I agreed to his getting the LSD. What could be safer? For the event we naturally designated the living room of his San Francisco house.

After I took the dose he gave me, Jon stayed with me. He had bought a box of KFC and began eating a piece of chicken as I sat quietly waiting to see what would occur. It was not what I expected. The piece of chicken in his hand became a whole live bird, in full color, it's wings flapping madly, squeaking loudly, trying to get out of his grasp while Jon calmly proceeded to eat. I had been a vegetarian for about four years; it looked utterly disgusting, Jon like a cannibal. I decided to take a walk outside, turning left on his street, up the hill and sat down among the Eucalyptus trees. I started to cry due to an overwhelming sense of sadness, as if the trees were all suffering. Later I read in the newspaper that the trees had frozen due to a sharp drop in temperature. They were literally dying as I sat among them.

After some time, I returned to the house and sat back down in the same place. A young woman with long, flaming red hair walked in. Jon walked out of the room with her. She seemed agitated. I knew instantly that Jon was having an intimate relationship with her, even though Jon had said he was only renting the extra bedroom to her, and that they had no involvement. After she left, Jon came to the point of why he suggested the trip. He asked me whether I was willing to devote my life to him, put him first, above all other concerns. Wow! I knew he had lied to me about the "roommate." I still loved him, but could not say yes (she had said she could?). He said, "then it's over" and told me that he would not even drive me back. Driving while being "high" was dangerous if not impossible. Being in an altered state I prayed silently as I looked up at the dark sky; it was now night. "Show me the house where help is."

I walked down the hill until I came to a house that felt "right." I rang the doorbell. A little boy around two came to the door. He seemed lit up like a light bulb, laughing and dancing around. His father appeared and asked, "Are you on Acid?" Embarrassed, I said "Yes, I need help." The young man told me his son always gets a contact high. I explained my situation and he generously agreed to give me a ride back to Berkeley. I was grateful to both him and the Universe. That was the last time I saw Jon, but not the last time I saw my replacement.

I had signed up for a women's workshop with Anais Nin, which occurred soon after this event. Meeting her there brought out all my insecurity and sorrow about the end of this relationship. The intensity of my feelings totally surprised me. I felt jealous, insecure and sad to be suddenly alone again.

From today's perspective I understand what I did not understand then or for a long time: I needed a relationship wherein I am an equal, not subordinating myself to another. John's lying to me brought a sudden and easier end to that relationship. Equality between men and women is a major issue of our times; for centuries women were subordinated to men. I'm aware now how often I've just naturally subordinated myself to others, both male and female. Power issues are fundamental, but often not conscious and in my experience, rarely discussed. For me, being a woman artist and wanting to be in a serious, intimate relationship, has made it necessary to become aware of my power and learn to resist giving it away. That learning will continue to go on until I draw my last breath.

Clifford L. was doing a doctorate in Botany, but like me had a multitude of interests. He was head of the Sailing Club (Commodore) at Berkeley, and introduced me to Kundalini Yoga and Yogi Bajhan. While as lovers we were flawed, as friends we were steadfast. I met him early in my UC Berkeley sojourn, joined the yoga class, chanted Sat Nam and meditated. But something was missing. I was full of contradictions. I wanted to be equal, but also wanted someone I looked up to; was he too humble, too uncertain of himself? We both moved into the Ashram in San Raphael; We would rise at four o'clock in the morning for individual or group meditation and at seven o'clock I commuted weekdays to Oakland to my teaching job as well as doing my share of the community chores. Managing this schedule was challenging, leaving little time for the social life of the community. We had a commitment to be celebrate, to fast each Monday, meditate one or two hours daily and contribute to the smooth running of the community.

We women were urged to become part of the "Grace of God Movement" which I treasure to this day. I felt taken advantage of, owning a car and stereo, among other things, I was the only one with substantial possessions and a full-time job. While I hardly saw Cliff at the Ashram, still he was there for me in a crisis. When I left the Ashram after six months, in spring, lonely and unmoored, on a Friday the 13th, I had accepted a date with my new jeweler friend. The police broke into his apartment on a marijuana raid while we were making love (only once). Cliff was the one who held my hand and accompanied me to the abortionist as a result of that. Ironically in the same time period my sister Hannelore's only pregnancy ended in a still birth. Had I been closer to her, could I have considered giving her my child? Mysteriously, while I had less in common with David E. the young math professor (one year younger than me) whom I had met in the first months at Berkeley through friends at the international weekly Folk Dance, which I really loved to participate in, was my real love of those years. He was a prince.

It was Lenny, a painter and a warm wonderful human being, living with his wife, Esther, and babe, in the basement apartment of the Woolsey house, who told me I needed a prince as we dug, planted and cultivated the vegetable garden. David was Russian Jewish, set to wed, someday a Jewish virgin. Eventually as we met again in Amsterdam (by then he was a tenured professor at Stony Brook, New York) he asked me to marry him. But by the end of the weekend I knew I could not; this indescribable sense of void gripped me. Later I understood all that much better and the blackness lessened, becoming the cloud of (relatively normal considering the circumstances) anxiety.

Before finally leaving California for New Mexico, one more relationship was necessary to send me/place me squarely on my path to being an artist. A couple of friends and I began visiting other friends in Mendocino, California where we met Bill G., an artist and teacher at the Rochester School of Photography, living there while recovering from a nervous breakdown. I felt immediately drawn to him and his plan to start an artist's community in North Carolina, near Ashville, where he owned land. Bill was eight years older than me, talented, charismatic and inspiring. While he was not yet divorced from his second wife, Rita, a former student of his, our relationship had her blessing. Over the months, Bill introduced me to Baba Hari Dass and MaRenu who would become a source of spiritual growth, guidance and comfort for this period and for many years. Perhaps together, I could help Bill achieve his goal.

In the Fall of 1972 we left California together for New Mexico, which was known for its mysticism: a good place to meditate, and for its lure to artists, though not yet run-over by them. I had already hitch hiked there twice and had been planning to return permanently. For me this trip would an exploration: of our relationship, (to me we were a couple) and of the possibility of a true community. First we would spend time in New Mexico where Bill had several long term friends at Lama Foundation and La Cienega, as well as knowing several well-known photographers, among them Beaumont Newhall and Paul Caponegro. I listened to a lot of conversations about Minor White, their mentor and teacher, before continuing the drive to Rochester via North Carolina.

At Lama we visited with the founders: two couples, Siddeq, then divorced and remarried, and Asha, his sister, married previously to founder Nur. Ram Dass (Richard Alpert), formerly a Professor at Harvard had also been involved. I still have the large, wonderful, hand printed at Lama, edition of *Be Here Now*, given to me. I am drawn to children so I immediately befriended Siddeq's young, ex-model wife and helped her with their infant son. Later when I again spent time at Lama, she had left to study with Trungpa; eventually Siddeq married Sakina, (another more mature resident) and they moved to a suburban house when he became a Tutor at St. John's College. I always had great respect and appreciation for Siddeq and what occurred later only increased this. The other couple we visited also had roots in Rochester, in this case, through the Gurdjieff Movement; John March's mother had been an important figure in it. Judy March, a weaver with three children (two from a former marriage, Mariam and Jacob) and Wolfie, a toddler, with John, who was also artistically creative. I still remember the cartoon she drew that humorously expressed her life: a mother chicken with the barely hatched eggs, running after her. Judy and I hit it off and she told me: "If things don't work out as expected in New York, come back and stay with us." It turned out the invitation was a godsend.

Bill and I stopped at the land in North Carolina and met the couple who were already living there and exploring ways to make the land sustainable; one idea they were considering because it was a cash crop with a lot of demand and profit, was growing tobacco. They were willing, as was

Bill, but I was horrified. What a way to start changing society for the better. In Rochester, Rita greeted both of us warmly; I liked her and their two boys immediately, feeling sympathy for her decision. Rather than staying at their house, I stayed in a loft in the barn on their country property, leased by friends. The barn had no heat of course, and while the water in my glass froze every night and the snow fell outside, I was toasty warm in my sleeping bag. I saw quickly that this divorce was in the messy stages, and would take more time than I felt I had.

But in the meantime, two opportunities that would affect the rest of my life were available. The first was attending a session with Jane Roberts, the medium for Seth's appearances. For the last year in Berkeley I had immersed myself in the *Seth Material* and *Seth Speaks*, later reading the other books as they were published by Roberts and her husband. The idea of visiting an actual session (live) was exciting. Bill and I entered the living room where the session was held and sat down with the others around Jane Roberts. She and her husband chatted with us for a few minutes. Then it was time: everyone waited quietly. When Seth came through, Jane took off her glasses, which she wore all the other time, and after a while took a sip of the beer (that Jane doesn't drink) and slowly began speaking. Amazingly, his first remarks were addressed to Bill, looking straight at him: "Trust yourself." What Seth said beyond that all fit to Bill's circumstances. My spine vibrated madly during the whole session. Jane and her husband recorded all sessions, so this is recorded somewhere, possibly in one of her books. Later when I returned to New Mexico I became a member of a Seth group reading and discussing their work and our experiences in relation to it. Over the years I have continued to explore this phenomena of mediumship and see it as an avenue to a higher perspective.

The second was an appointment with a psychic known to Rita and Bill's friends. As a human being he exhibited what I would call a moral flaw, however his words to me were fitting and helpful. "For at least two years put your artwork first in your life, and relationships second." I decided to return to New Mexico and follow that advice. On the way back I made one more detour, spending the night on the North Carolina land, and then heading straight for Judy and John's in La Cienega. I remember one night on the trip back I was tired from driving. It was dark and late and I had found no camp ground. I prayed to the Universe for help, finally finding a place that I felt I could stop for the night: it was quiet and isolated enough to unroll my pad and sleeping bag. I slept soundly. When I woke up and looked around, it was just getting light, I realized I had parked right next to a garbage dump. I thanked the Universe for my safety, packed up and got back in the car. Finally I got back to New Mexico and camped for a while in the March's metal Tipi set on a platform some distance from the house.

When I came into the house to use the bathroom early in the morning (I always awaken long before dawn to meditate),Wolfie was awake, standing in his crib, crying, cold, wet, with snot running down his face. I always picked him up, cleaned him up, cuddled with him for a bit, give him a bottle and he would usually go back to sleep. It was good to feel needed. Later, I moved to Albuquerque for a while, lived and worked in my sister's garage. Wanting to be helpful, I volunteered to weed her vegetable garden; I'm still embarrassed that I mistook her huge watermelon plant for a weed, and pulled it out. Thankfully that was not one of her complaints against me in our last conversation, two years before she died from breast cancer.

I did not try to communicate with Bill in those months, figuring it would complicate things for him, nor did I hear from him. I had assumed since he had never actually committed himself to our relationship and Hari Dass made clear to me his ambivalence, that I was free to be open to another man I had met through my sister's friends at a party. Todd was an artist who had been in the Peace Corps in South America, and only recently returned. We were attracted to each other, spending time to get to know each other better. It was clear to me Todd was ready to settle down. His studio and home were in the northeast quadrant, in beautiful Corrales, New Mexico. Todd had invited me to dinner one Friday night at his place; we talked for several hours, feeling intimate. Just as we began to make love for the first time, the phone rang. It was close to midnight. Astrid: "Bill is on the Freeway waiting to be picked up by you." I couldn't believe it; I felt I had no choice. Todd, who was older than me, was quite a reserved and traditional man. That phone call ended our relationship. Of course, I could not just leave Bill on the freeway that night. But he could have planned it better. I share this because I see the humor in it. Later I could see Todd was not the right man for me, and this saved me from another detour.

Nor did I automatically pick up with Bill again. It was presumptuous of him, to assume I was just waiting for him, not even a word on his coming (no cell phones yet), nor how he was traveling. Bill did not own a car. Though he was glad to see me, I think he did love me as far as he was able at that time, or believed in love, but as it turned out, not in monogamy.

The struggle over divorce, especially how it would affect his fathering his two boys, and the probability of losing the community land, weighed on him. Meanwhile I took him up to Lama, where he wanted to be, at least temporarily. I loved Lama also and had spent many weekends there in his absence, but while I believed in communities and was drawn to the idea, I knew it was not easy to make them successful.

At Lama Foundation (its name already makes its function clear) there was a core group: it's leader, staff and a few residents and retreatants. Lama was not a residential community but a teaching one. Nor could Bill have taken over its leadership, even if he had wanted to. He wanted to found an artist's community; his mother had given him the money to buy the North Carolina land. It was his inheritance. It had never occurred to him that Rita would demand, as part of the divorce settlement, that the land be sold and she get half the proceeds. That is what happened; it played itself out over a number of years. For myself, I knew I could not live at Lama, or even in Taos, New Mexico which I also loved, and focus totally on my art.

I moved out of my sister's garage and rented a studio apartment near the university, belonging to Wally's father. She lived with her two daughters in the main house. Wally's and my path kept crossing. Every time I moved I would find her nearby.

Later when she married Grady, they lived in Taos next to my close friend Ranna, who had bought a property with Jeremiah, east of Taos toward the mountains. They were not on good terms as neighbors as Jeremiah had built a small guest house initially, planning to build the main house later. Grady built their house, not knowing about Ranna and Jeremiah's plans, right where the view of their perspective house to the mountains would be cut off. This was unfortunate; closer communication could have helped? The main house never got built in Ranna's life, as she died early and I've sadly also lost touch with Wally. But first back to Bill, who would come visit me.

One afternoon the three of us were together and I was disturbed to note some electricity (even flirting) between Wally and Bill. From today's perspective Wally and Bill had a strong physical resemblance. Both were large boned, muscular, medium height, and beautiful in the same way, with striking eyes reminding me of my father. I'm rarely a jealous person, but a few times, my feelings surprise me. I spoke to Wally. Normally I wouldn't be able to do this but due to the circumstances of each of our lives I told her I was uncomfortable. Her answer was, "Monogamy does not work. Forget it!" I decided to move. I had originally intended to live in Santa Fe, but could not afford a place of my own there, but now I could and would.

I found the first place of my own in Santa Fe off of San Francisco Street, a converted adobe garage behind the main house. Bill came to stay periodically, but still unsettled. He criticized what he called my "coolie consciousness." I have thought of his term occasionally over the last almost fifty years; he was right and I like that quality in myself: doing things slowly, humbly sometimes, paying attention to detail. Egg tempera demands that. Relations and community building need it also. He was discontented with my little apartment; he wasn't contributing to the rent. It was what I could afford. We had made love rather unenthusiastically on my part; I probably should have refused.

A young woman, Juniper, was pregnant at Lama: Saddeq admitted he could be the father; Bill claimed innocence; but the infant at birth looked exactly like Bill. Nature is known for that. Juniper later moved to Mount Madonna with her daughter. Bill and I argued over this and other things; I had asked him to repair something for me. In his anger, Bill threw the hammer he had in his hand against the wall. It scared me. I told Bill: "Go to California where Rita was by this time, finish your divorce, and then we'll see." Some months later I met Bill at Jacqueline's, a dear, close friend of mine who had given dream groups attended by many of us, including Bill, with a new California girlfriend. To me, Blake seemed harsh to him: "I'm giving Bill seven years to get his act together." He had given up on community, turning back to his photography career, showing in a Los Angeles gallery. Well, I thought, perhaps he needs this type of woman, not me.

About two years later, after I was married to Dan, and Sean our son was three months old, I decided to go to Mount Madonna to see Hari Dass and Ma Renu. Bill and I met one last time. I did not ask if he was happy, nor did he ask me. But again he left me with the impression that he was critical of my decision to marry and have a child: "You will raise him to be a consumer." I felt he meant a normal US citizen, not growing up in a community. In that he was right. There was no community I knew of. Both Lama and Mount Madonna were places for retreat. An artist is immersed in life. I chose that.

Dan and I live conscious of energy use and close to nature. Anyone I have ever truly loved, I'd love to know they are well and have succeeded. I heard Blake gave up on Bill. Hari Dass had mentioned to me: "Bill has the suicide line in his palm." I imagine losing the land broke his heart. Years later I searched the internet and found no Bill Giles, though there is a Josh and a Brody. Hari Dass had told me: "You need a traditional kind of man." I think he meant, one who can commit to one woman. He had met Dan: "He only wants to love you." That love has lasted almost half a century. Ma Renu urged Babaji to give me the advanced meditation he was teaching at that time. For many months I got up at four in the morning to practice this powerful meditation; I loved it and felt its impact on my spiritual growth, but without a Sangha in New Mexico, much less closer to home in Santa Fe, it was too difficult to sustain this rigorous schedule. By six in the evening, making supper for my small family, I felt wasted. My labor of fifty hours, emergency C Section and subsequent infection, as well as caring for an infant, to say nothing of continuing my art making practice, was too much. Everyone doing this meditation had moved to Mount Madonna. It was a difficult decision. I knew I benefited from the practice. I never stopped meditating, but for now I had to move back to a less demanding stage. Babaji understood; art, he knew was my path. A year later which I devoted to learning etching, I could again see how my concentration had grown from Babaji's meditation practice. I felt my art had risen several notches.

My black sheep reputation with two of my sisters and Riner was almost as if, in our family there had to be at least one around whom criticism could collect. It wasn't always too serious, often more like a joke. And since there were so many of us, both Ralph and I could share it. Hans and all three of my sisters married in the normal course of things and were duly critical of what they perhaps considered my promiscuity, but it was not. I think perhaps Hannelore enjoyed exaggerating my faults. For example, repeatedly talking of all my engagements, as though there were dozens instead of two, or of the time I left my husband alone with her for three days. This never happened. On a visit to introduce Dan and our infant Sean to her, I was an hour late from a visit to Berkeley. I do have trouble being on time, but nothing like this. It's clear: some in my family needed a scapegoat. However our aunts in Germany loved this quality in me: "Kontaktfreudig," the joy of connecting one aunt told me. Dr. Offman had said: "Monika, you don't need to get engaged every time you want to make love." Psychology has a different perspective than Christianity: "It is better to be married than to burn in Hell, of course." My husband always likes to say: "You needed each of those relationships." I too am grateful to them.

"Grace of God" Movement / Yogi Bhajan

In the sixties with its free love and revolution we women needed something like this. I had met young students who used abortion as a form of birth control, having four or five of them. At the ashram along with the rule of celibacy, Bhajan introduced the "Grace of God" movement for the ladies. He told us that women in American society did not respect their bodies or themselves; so thinking of ourselves as Grace from God to society and to ourselves, had profound implications for how we viewed ourselves, versus men in our lives as well as to the "Divine." The Berkeley Psychic School also contributed to female self-respect: Women are superior to men because they have the "baby making machine." I loved that. A couple of months after our only biological son Sean was born in December of 1977, I visited the Quimby Center, a psychic school in Alamogordo, on my father's 70th birthday, due to my first of many serious "carpel tunnel" syndrome episodes. They told me that I was a "Walk-in" and also that I had been buried alive (accused of practicing witchcraft) and had died of fright rather than from suffocation. Unfortunately, I did not ask the psychic when the first occurred, but have pondered it throughout my life and felt a kinship with Linda Durham who had also been told that she is one. It could explain my total lack of memory of my first five years and the second could explain my claustrophobia which my older sister loved to exploit. From my Jungian friend Jacqueline, I learned the concept of the "Ice Queen" and added it to my repertoire of ways to handle being a double Libra (wanting to please everyone) with Virgo Rising (learning discrimination rather than judgment).

3 / THE YELLOW PAGES

I found the following writings in June of 2020, a day with a grand square (Virgo Moon sq Sun in Gemini; sq Neptune in Pisces sq Jupiter in Sag). At first, as I read them, I did not know who wrote them, nor when. The answer to both questions was in the text. I wrote them on a retreat at the Lama Foundation, seventeen years into my marriage. I felt the writings to be real, the beginning of my memoir.

§

Here I sit with Sufi Sam, telling who I am from the point of view of my spiritual quest. Sufi Sam had been one of my teachers; he was not actually there. He was deceased and had been buried at Lama. I think it was suggested we use an imaginary listener.

I was born during WW II in Germany to a rocket scientist and his wife who believed there was no creativity in that family, our family, as that was as it should be because the healthy mind is a well ordered mind, following already established ideas, not looking for anything different and, God forbid, unique—a good person followed the established authority, be it Hitler, Eisenhower, Nixon or Reagan. I was the third of seven children. We were all told many mixed messages and contradictions, such as, the third is the healthiest child, the most normal, while in reality they all treated me like the most abnormal. I mostly disappeared into being good and obedient, often disappearing altogether. After an M.A. in literature from UCLA, another way of learning while I disappeared, I went to Europe for a year. Independent studies it was called, and it was there that I learned the answers to some burning questions but learned many more questions. From there I went to Berkeley to do a PhD which I never finished because I woke up—woke up to the fact that most of my life I had been "asleep."

I had already had lots of cues that all was not as it appeared—that my life could not follow the map drawn by my parents when I broke my first engagement, then broke the second one a year later. But my path was unclear; I stayed on the literature path because it was easy from today's perspective, not a waste of time at all. I have continued learning, reading, enjoying literature as essential as music, dancing, swimming and dreaming, i.e. art. A Teaching Assistantship paid me to continue, but more than that I learned what I needed to know through Rilke, Kafka, Thomas Mann, Gertrude Stein, and others what the creative mind is like and I decided to risk being creative, rather than study the creativity of others exclusively.

To get back to where I was born, Carlos Castaneda talked about something stopping one's world. I think all those bombs dropping between my first and third birthday made an impression of the fragility of life, the illusions. After we came to America, a door to the past closed which never opened again until I had a Jewish roommate at UCLA. From then on I took peeps through the forbidden door.

Life goes in cycles. Here I am back to Lama after twenty-one years; I see what a different person I am than I was, partially because someone, one person, has loved me or tried to for seventeen years. Or perhaps because I've followed the same vocation, calling, for twenty-four years I'm still not sure I'm on a spiritual path—a specific one. I've tried several.

I sure am glad you all love me because I need love. I'm trying to find God but he has disappeared further and further. I see him in the people who love me but in the silence there is nobody there. A body is no body unless it is loved and love is hard to find.

My heart pounds so loudly with anticipation because god is under the rock with the centipied and caterpillers and all the grasshoppers I've cut in half.* Half, half…it sounds like laughter but it's course and awful. Awe full, full of awe. Half a grasshopper hops, but the flowers are left alone.

*There was a tremendous grasshopper/locust invasion one summer. They came by the thousands, one could not see the plants, rose bushes in this case in our Lejano Street patio. I had asked Burk Denman, a good friend what one can do, what he does. He told me: "I just cut them in half." I was horrified but desperate to master this terrible, this biblical, apocalyptical problem, and I tried it.

The blood is sweet. I can taste it from my pricked finger, prick, pricked, pain…deadness, swimming…not in a pool but in the waves, gigantic waves swallow me. I gasp for air. I pray then float to safety.

Emptiness...fullness floats, above the empty water. Waste knee deep in garbage a little dove comes to collect it's young, they gingerly step around the plastic; one cup becomes a boat that avoids the snake.

I saw a red rose in the blue sky as I leaped across the empty sand...dust blew and the rose joined a cloud that poured it's tears into the dry ocean bed on which I roller skated with rusty wheels stuck on a rock.

Seafoam green where lemons are lollipops for old tongues and sea horses ride through the city streets "bearing lilacs from the dead lands" for the babes deserted by angry fathers and 4th of July firecrackers stay up forever. Ending the endless words....

Dreaming of White Sands when I was fifteen and thought the solution lay in growing up. Finding love in the right man, not knowing about the bombs behind my father's eyes who was fearless with his hammer in hand.

My mind flows like a river raging and peaceful in turn...too cloudy to see, too muddy to swim in / yet I swim anyway...will shower later...the water cooling my mind flowing with the current watching for the rocks beneath my feet...

Pooh pooh head you're dead—this is supposed to crack the cement of my youth—where poop was never mentioned and silence buried all laughter except among the children far from adults. My father tracking mud and smelling of cow dung on his clothes.

I'm coming home dear, I miss you...that's logical she must have a husband we all have a husband or lover or friends or a cat a dog to go back to but let's change all that let's not go back to things as they were, let's be magical and alive...

Remember it's a mystery, dreaming on dream after dream, what is real, my feet, my ankles, my knees – from there we jump to my neck, skip the nose, eyes, hair, now we have to start down again, anus oh oh dirty fingernails

Slowly the Gorilla opened his huge fist and held up an ice cream cone. I was afraid to lick it because I'd have to get close and he might playfully grab me by the neck, swinging me up into his tree and showing me what the world looked like from there. Stars and Stripes forever.

Aggressive wanting mind...my mind's wanting is unclear, my heart's wanting to be alive, to feel everything, not shut it out, to leap with feeling, tremulous, before the flower opens in the bed, mind not distracting, mind not over matter…seeing.

Go down stream to where the fish hatch and the sun warms the water, put in your feet, watch for the glass, step carefully until it's deep enough to float, swim, let the stream carry you, water caressing your soul the soles of your wounded feet...

If you ask me I will say yes to all your questions. There I have said it. I have seen your heart when you speak of Sean I feel your heart when you speak of Paolo I see you struggle to love Melissa; where is your heart when we love? Oh Shit! Synchronicity! What is that smell? Oh my god! I forgot...I put the plastic honey jug in water to warm it enough to put the honey in a container where from the honey can be retrieved...I've melted the plastic and boiled the honey, now ruined! to continue.

Peanut Butter Parfait has 71 calories – the peanut butter lady, mom-cookies and apron...where are the dirty dishes and the moldy food in the frig...I see his heart in his eyes when we sit across the table eating out but over the dish filled sink I wear handcuffs and think about the dust on the dresser...

Sometimes I miss Scotland like I miss not having stayed in Germany, having been more secure—aunts, uncles, grandparents, an old culture, even the rubble would have been grounding, no doors to shut on it.

This is not my favorite picture nor is this a succinct little Haiku. I could have chosen Van Gogh's "Starry Night" and told you a lot of art history or revealed my own madness. I almost took the picture of the woman in black and white, dramatic and bawdy, lots of make up sexy dress, dance hall atmosphere, actress. Do I want to reveal how at thirteen that I was afraid I might be a whore and so did not touch a man until I was twenty?

Always had stage fright, can't catch my breath, all out of breath, forgetting to breath. No, I chose, there were so many I could have chosen, reluctant to pick one, this strange image, like something out of a holocaust...

This woman from another time, distraught...a kind of vacant yet concentrated other worldly expression in her eyes. Her arms, one beckoning or offering something. Oblivious to the figure behind her, or because of the figure behind her...an Angel? It's feet do not touch the ground...or someone who died turning golden in the flames...alchemy of the Soul...your pen turns you to gold...arms out stretched—flying away or coming to help..."

Getting lost in the swamp of uncertainty, powerlessness and isolation... that's why I returned to Lama after twenty-one years, to regain my inner strength and perspective.

Life seems to be a race to recover whatever we knew as children before we become too old to experience it and die.

The Kinkiness of a person who chooses creativity as a role in society.

I am embracing my own body's love of movement, my heart's response to music, the pleasure and dedication I give to a visual expression of my exploring life and my relationship to it.

I know "attachment disorder" and "sanctuary trauma" (not just through my daughters..it's due to them that I've learned the terms) but from the inside also. Years ago when Yogi Bhajan stated in a teaching at the Ashram: "I am a hammer to the ego." I knew my ego did not need that. Later I learned more specifically how much hammering I had already received. The inner prison walls versus freedom...how much of our freedom we give up voluntarily: "look what I'm doing for you to prove we love each other..."

I give away a lot of power and then am amazed and feel betrayed when it is not reciprocated. Felt lowering of self-esteem in relation to T/C.

POWER STRUGGLE with kids. H & M are constantly trying to manipulate me.

See how dumb you are. Am I controlling? My need for order in the kitchen.

Creativity, Truth, product, money.

Left Berkeley and arrived in Santa Fe with literally ten cents in my pocket. Pact with the Universe: I will trust that You will support me as I am doing what I was sent for. Did a Fair at Taos Pueblo; the ladies loved my Batik clothing. Earned enough to live off it for two months.

Sean: "I'm completely normal, Mom leave me alone! Dad makes me feel like a dumb kid."

Desire to be seen, to be understood...

As a child I repeated the prayer of St Francis over and over...as an adult I still do that at times but I also acknowledge it's opposite in myself.

Children are a mirror. You want to like what you see. Very few people don't like their biological children. It's real common with adopted older children. I wonder about that.

As I read the "Yellow Pages" to see what to include in my book, I saw that the need to be alone in Nature, my camping trip just finished, had the same basis, only now there seem to be no retreat places that do not sport wireless. Really troubling. I will keep seeking.

4 / MATURE PERIOD

In the European tradition in which I was born and which I continued to study, traveling in foreign countries was considered a prerequisite to artistic maturity. Luckily I married a man who loved Germany and wanted to travel to Germany even more than I did, always saying he could relax better there. While he loved the beer, even when he later gave up drinking alcohol in the Covid period, he missed traveling even more than I. Mostly Irish with a little Chek and Slovac thrown in, he couldn't drink with the restraint natural to me. At seventeen, leaving his family as quickly as possible, he had joined the US Air Force and ended up in Berlin as an Air Traffic Controller, and when he got out couldn't wait to get back. So being German I had an extra advantage on the road to his heart. I had just had a serious talk with the "Universe" that I am okay being alone, but would make a great wife for someone and a loving mother for a kid or two. Shortly after, my friend Ellen L. told me: "Monika, you've got to meet this guy I work with; if I were single, I'd go for him." (I didn't know of course, Ellen was already having an affair with their boss). So she set up the meeting with Dan. My first impression was: "Oh he's got the same profile (a prominent nose). That made me comfortable. And I didn't marry him for his money; he owned a bicycle and a Taos chair, a trade for some law work. He missed passing the Bar by a quarter of a point so when the methadone clinic closed I found him work with some friends. After a few months, since two can live more economically together, I invited him to join me in my little Sosaya Lane house where the living room was my studio. The Taos chair fit in well, but the bicycle was stolen when he forgot to lock it because he was preoccupied with his first important law case.

So while later his ability to generate income far exceeded mine, for a while and off and on, my income supported us.

In order to be both a mother/wife and artist, I have often felt I had to be "super woman" as well as "Olympic trainer" mom. Many women give up child bearing and focus totally on their career. But there are many more who manage both. Even male artists have been role models for me. I looked at Arthur Haddock's career. He was a full time railroad employee all his adult life, and only painted on weekends (must have been hard on his wife, at least if she wanted some of his attention!) but created a substantial body of work. But mostly I had woman artists as models.

One of my favorites has always been Kathe Kollwitz, whose museum I have visited many times in Berlin. She not only had two sons, one of whom died in WW I and her grandson died in WW II, she was one of the first to address the suffering of workers in her art, at the same time as writers were beginning to do so. Carol Hurd, my friend and contemporary, had three children but did not paint until they were grown. Both Georgia O'Keeffe and Frieda Kahlo wanted children. The latter tried several times to get pregnant but due to her serious internal injuries from a trolley car accident, failed each time. Stieglitz, of course, talked O'Keeffe out of being a mother, convincing her that being an artist demands single minded focus. I assume this worked well for her. But for me, being an artist is exploring life deeply; being a mother, experiencing a life growing inside of you, and giving birth, is an experience that changed my life and gave it much more depth. For months, even years I would look at someone in awe: this person was inside a mother's belly. Raising children, far from being a distraction is also a part of waking up, becoming more human.

Eventually, unexpectedly, and yet in an appropriate way, my father came around to supporting my being an artist. I had settled into beginning my real art career, different from my transition to art by doing Batik and mostly fairs like New Mexico Arts & Crafts, a high grade juried show for a couple of years. I had done my year of etching, practiced with water colors as a transition to painting, and had already begun to establish myself in an area of oil painting that no one in Santa Fe yet pursued at that time: figurative interiors such as Santa Fe restaurants and hotels.

When my father approached me about doing a bust of his friend, Werner von Braun, I told him no, I am busy establishing myself as a painter. Sean, our only birth child, was about four at that time; we owned our own home on San Francisco Street, an 110 year old adobe that needed much renovation and I was planting fruit trees and a substantial vegetable garden. I was very busy. But he kept asking. Finally I said, okay, Vati, if you pay me by the hour, he had already told me he would fund the bronze, and I had done quite a few portraits by that time and was confident I could do a good, accurate likeness. Also, sculpture seemed easier to me than painting in which you had to create the illusion of three dimensions, instead of actually working with them. A figurative wood sculpture I had done in college had been in a show in the Cincinnati Museum.

NASA sent me a mailer containing dozens of photos of Von Braun covering many years, from his time as head of Peenemünde until close to his death from cancer. Visually I was fairly familiar with him, as I had seen him several times over the years. Since he could not sit for the portrait for me, the photographs were essential; I studied them and made drawings. I hired David Pearson, who was just beginning his own sculpture career to help me with logistics of preparing the clay model. I learned what I needed and we soon parted ways in that Pearson wanted me to be more modern while I was seeking a recognizable likeness. At the same time I did a clay bust, for practice, fun and relaxation, of our son Sean and later one of Paolo, that I am sill proud of.

My father who looked a little like Einstein, with his shock of white hair, took the bronze under his arm and caught a plane to Washington, walked into the Smithsonian and told the director: "You need this; it's the best likeness of Werner von Braun there is." This was completely unorthodox. Over the months that followed, the committee of forty researched, debated and finally voted my bronze in. Being accepted into the Smithsonian Institute in Washington, DC brought me some success.

My etchings also did, though I was chided by another etcher of hubris to plan some editions of 60 to 100. To me it seemed that since etching plates are so much work, larger editions made sense. I print them like Rembrandt did, as needed. I was getting portraits commissions through Jamison Galleries; even one of a house, Don Meredith's family. This brought other wealthy well known people for portraits; some were particularly challenging, such as one of a whole family from Dallas, Reagan's Comptroller of Currency. When his daughter commissioned one of her mother as a gift, the latter told me, make me look twenty years younger, as I will after my face lift. I felt sure her husband loved her as she was, but I requested she send me some photos from twenty years ago. She did and I painted the portrait. I had noticed how fond the mother was of her dog, so for fun I painted a portrait of her dog, putting it on the wall behind her in the painting. When I explained this to her daughter, she was worried she would not like it, so I said don't say a word, see what she says, but she loved it.

My "Interiors" took off, six of La Fonda, two of De Vargas Hotel, two of the newly renovated St Francis, Grant Corner Inn, one of Pasqual's with my family plus my model Cindy all at the Community table. In the last one of La Posada I put the artist nude in the foreground because as I would sit in the lobbies and restaurants, I always felt somewhat exposed. The owner of the hotel loved it and bought it. And until Elias Rivera and one female artist, who did not stay long but returned, came from New York, I was the only artist who did interiors with people in Santa Fe as a full body of work.

Then I did my first poster in an edition of two thousand of my most popular La Fonda painting, followed by commissions for other posters: The Legal Tender in Lamy, the newly renovated Plaza Hotel in Las Vegas, the Cloudcroft Lodge, even up to Durango with the Strator Hotel. I would have had a lot more success if I had continued this genre. I went from there to doing Indian Market, exteriors with people, then briefly the Balloon Fiesta as well as continuing etchings. But once I had mastered these realistic paintings and had reasonable amounts of success, I knew I needed to move on.

This was only the first stage of my painting career, preparation for more challenging work. Synchronistically, when I brought in my self portrait "The Yellow Apron" the owner commented: "That's really a bright yellow" instead of "What a beautiful painting" or "I like your self-portrait." I wondered if my star in this gallery was falling. I had had a ten year retrospective at the gallery at St. John's College and a private conversation with the art critic from *The New Mexican*. She told me: "There is a lot of intensity hidden in your paintings. I would like to see it come out more directly." Simple enough! At the same time I was in a Master Class with Henriette Wyeth that I had assumed would bring my work to a higher level. Well it did; to an entirely different level. Not simple at all. I had accomplished what I had set out to do: learn to paint well and produce a body of work that would establish my career. My name was recognized and I was considered an important Santa Fe artist. That done, I was ready for a greater challenge, working from my imagination, making up paintings. Scary.

That night alone in my studio, the interview/talk with the critic seemed almost like an acid trip. I feared I would be crucified—an exaggeration of course. Certainly I would leave Jamison since my paintings began frequenting the basement. I knew the owners were less exited about my work. Henriette did not consider me her best pupil either. I had asked her:

"Is there any role for the imagination or accidents in painting?" "Absolutely not." I was friends with her daughter, Carol, who though also trained in art school, did not begin painting on her own until after her divorce from Peter Rogers, and when she did paint, her style was closer to Peter's "magic realism" rather than her mother's more realistic and conservative style. They later resumed their marriage. In the evenings after Henriette's class. I would start exploring my imagination: starting the "Journey of the Fool," close to home.

A couple of years into this transition another occurred simultaneously: my change in medium to egg tempera, which I was already aware of through painters like Peter Hurd and through Robert Vickrey's book *Artist at Work*. Eli Levin suggested I look up George Tooker as my work reminded him of his paintings. I was immediately fascinated by Tooker's subtle, surrealistic, dreamlike paintings and his incredible craftsmanship; they were absolutely beautiful. I decided to take a six week break from oil, to try egg tempera out. When I returned to oil it seemed so much easier.

While oil painting is easier, I realized it made me sick. My already normally hypersensitive liver did not respond well to the solvent, any of them, needed for oil as thinner. This helped to encourage my self-apprenticeship to Medieval religious painters like Fra Angelico and Fra Lippo Lipi. Before the development of oil painting, which replaced egg tempera entirely, it had been the medium of the 13th and 14th centuries, But, aside for being healthier, it is superior in some respects in that it does not darken or crack the way oil does. I also do not varnish the finished painting for two reasons: needed repairs are much easier and quicker and secondly, one needs a space absolutely free from dust, difficult in New Mexico. People always ask why I did not switch to acrylic which is so much easier. The idea of painting with plastic basically, is unappealing if not abhorrent to me; a nightmare of bad paintings that won't deteriorate! Over the next decades I did have to admit that acrylic can be just as beautiful as oil and egg tempera but I still prefer a natural medium. Of interest, Yale University demanded that each art student enroll in one course in egg tempera, which led to the revival of egg tempera across the world, and especially in Santa Fe.

Copying masterpieces, or anything for that matter, was not only not encouraged, it did not exist in the classes I had enrolled in. Over the years of being primarily "self taught" as I tried to find my way, I started secretly longing for the centuries ago practice of apprenticeship. How wonderful that must have been. But like anything else the system probably had its own problems, sometimes or often. I decided I could do my own apprenticeship. I had been to Berlin's Dahlem Museum many times. I would always visit the medieval section, spell bound by the beauty of the paintings. I decided I would copy some from the beautiful reproductions in my art books. It was challenging but wonderful: what a way to learn the principles of what makes a master piece. At UCLA in painting class I only learned how to stretch a canvas, being told "If you are an artist, just do it!" There are principles of balance, order, rhythm, color that can be taught. If, having had twenty-one years of classes was not enough, I'd have to teach myself. I also gave myself many other classes in many subjects: Spanish, Russian, Tibetan language, and others, but all on my own.

After a year I had my first show of my new series: "Journey of the Fool," still in oil, at Edith Lambert Gallery. Unfortunately, the opening was the night we started bombing Iraq and the opening was a bust. But I continued the series and stayed with her for the rest of the year. When the next year's show schedule came out and I was not on it, it seemed time to move on. We remained friends, Edith lived next door, but I was welcomed by the newly opened Peyton Wright Gallery, where I soon had a solo show with substantial success. The owner was ambitious, moving, expanding the gallery and impatient to sell, so that often work that had been chosen to hang in a show, was not there.

When another gallery approached me about joining, I thought it could be a better fit, but to my disappointment, it didn't turn out well. Ah, the illusions. We, artists and gallery owners, were all learning the ropes, sometimes with success sometimes through mistakes. The relationship between artist and gallery owner(s) is a delicate one. The gallery survival depends on sales unless there is independent funding from another source, and even then the profit motive is usually if not uppermost, certainly present. I've observed that in many cases the better galleries from my point of view, meaning also the least mercenary, with the highest quality art, have not survived in Santa Fe as well. Trust, essential in all relationships, was an issue for me in these gallery relationships.

I've learned a lot over the years. First I have to trust my own worth as an artist, which has become more solid through experience, and then trust the world outside myself: that it will treat me fairly. On a conscious level I tended to see myself as optimistic and trusting. But deeper down, and this definitely played a role, coming out of the terrible war experience of my earliest years, trust is difficult.

Nevertheless the 1990s were a heady time in Santa Fe's art scene. Later, through my spiritual friend Craig Liebelt, who was a loving, unmercenary soul, my best period started. In his Lya Gallery, my main collector, Dan Lynch, found my work when he stopped in for a meditation evening. My solo show dominated the gallery and Lynch began a ten year period of collecting my magic/narrative/poetic realism paintings. That really helped my confidence in my art. I had moved on from the more personal journey to social/political/spiritual realm of "Collective Folly," in paintings such as "The Four Horsemen of the Apocalypse Over Bagdad," "Liberty Occupied," "End Game," "Election Year Circus," "Restoring the Balance," and "Rapture Anyone?" In my solo show at Hand Artes Gallery, the owner, Bill Franke decided to include my earlier Ballet paintings. Lynch bought almost all of them. Rickey Medlock, an Arkansas eye surgeon and friend, also bought many paintings over a decade or more. There were many collectors who bought only a few or one or two; Dallas Denny, sometimes after a longer break, reappears to continue collecting my work.

Starting in February of 1999 the Roswell Museum showed a selection of my mature period in a solo show for three months: "and god gave Dominion," "Forest Primeval/Early Meltdown," "Missile Forest," and others was a high point in my career. To me, Roswell is a long, visually boring road from Santa Fe, and one needs to stay overnight, so I was grateful to the many friends who came to support me. The other high point of the show, next to a fairly modest catalog, was the comment book of which Michael Riley, the curator made a copy and sent it to me. I loved it. Some observers thought, and expressed clearly, that I was the greatest painter they had seen; others were sure I was going to Hell. You know Southern Baptists.

While my work sold well, Lya Gallery, like many in that period, struggled and finally closed. That left Hand Artes, in Truchas, as my only gallery representation in the US. Simultaneously, at the time, my most recent show was at a museum in my birthplace, Peenemünde, the culmination of showing in Germany for more than two decades: first with artists Michael Ginger and Peter Pabisch through the Dallas Goethe Institute, which went from there to Berlin, to Kohnert Gallery. Peter Pabisch was a professor at the University of New Mexico, a poet, artist and the most popular speaker in Betty Jalbert's German Club based in White Rock, but meeting also in Santa Fe.

Normally, I was not interested in any German clubs that I was invited to or that I was otherwise aware of, but after adopting Paolo, which I write about later, overwhelmed by his completely understandable emotional insecurity, I needed a break, and my first attendance met that need. And more than the social, the intellectual stimulation kept me returning. Barbara Haarf, charming, beautiful, brilliant, a teacher in Germany, who visited Betty every summer, always gave particularly challenging, stimulating lectures. We became good friends, visiting her at her home in Germany and every summer enjoying the Santa Fe Opera together.

Pabisch invited Dr. Ulrich Janetzki, director of the LCB (Literariches Colloqium Berlin) to Santa Fe. Janetzki and I hit it off immediately; knowing of my literary background and continued interest in writers, as well as being drawn to my paintings, he invited me to stay at the LCB, which occupies a beautiful 19th century villa on the Wannsee. Writers of note or promise from around the world, received a stipend including room and board in the mansion in order to have space to write. As an artist I was also welcome to stay overnight with breakfast (alone or with Dan) for a modest fee whenever I/we went to Berlin if a room was vacant. We returned to visit him year after year: "Ulrich, Du rauchst zu viel!" I would greet him, before hugging him. I loved the man! He was so warm hearted and enthusiastic; he always visited with us and we also spent wonderful evenings with him and his wife Hannelore over a delicious dinner at their home. In warm weather I walked or biked to the Wannsee Strand as soon as it was open to take a swim.

Once I discovered the nude beach there, I wanted to have the courage to go with my drawing pad. I had to be nude too, to fit in, and did not want to make it obvious I was sketching. It was so humorous to see portly bankers/"Burgers" (conservative citizens) playing volleyball nude. If I were to end up being a totally forgotten artist, this period in my life would make all the effort worthwhile. From Wannsee it was only two or three stops on the tram to the Dahlem Museum. Synchronistically, it was called the "Mexico" stop!

While exploring the region around the Wannsee, I met Frau Hoffman who owned the small "Galerie am Havel Ufer" across the lake from the LCB, which I visited several times over the years because I liked the elegant original gallery and we enjoyed each others' company. Her husband especially respected and loved my work. She included my paintings in a year of four solo shows for non-German (i.e. foreign) women artists. While at the opening several collectors approached me with an interest in buying a painting. I referred them to Frau Hoffman, but she was so busy with her own collectors (she made ceramic sculptures) that no sales were completed.

Around the same period, Daniel Schmalzer, (German born) from Dallas, came to the show at the Goethe Institute, became a friend and supporter of my paintings. He would later bring a famous Mexican artist to Santa Fe to see my work before arranging a solo show with a well known Mexico City gallery. Antonio Ramirez didn't like what he called "the merchants of art" (those who profited from selling it). Nevertheless he was successful, both in sales of his work and reputation, as well as a professor of art at the Mexico City University. During his visit to my studio, Ramirez told me: "You are a better painter than I." While I was flattered, I also pondered the deeper meaning of this and felt I understood what he meant: his work was decorative and appealed to a much greater group of collectors, while mine was more challenging.

As poet David Bell, the first Santa Fe art reviewer and critic of my career said: "You won't be as popular as Georgia O'Keeffe, but serious collectors drawn to your work will continue to support it." This addresses a dilemma: in a capitalist society in which art is not supported sufficiently by government (replacing the church and wealthy patrons of the nobility), the artist must find another source of support, either teaching or producing sale-able work, which is often not one's best. Even my husband, who is drawn to Impressionists like Max Lieberman who owned one of the Villas at Wannsee, regretted at first my change from Interiors: "Why did you change to this, more difficult, work; you were doing so well?"

Because I had to. Creativity has its own energy; one must follow where it leads if one is to be true to it and sustain it. Similar to the Frau Hofmann syndrome, the Mexico City gallery owner had given Schmalzer a choice: pay a fixed price for the show and get 100% of sales, or take 50% and the gallery gets the same. I would have chosen the later but said nothing when Daniel decided on the former. He was confident of sales and felt we would come out better. Mysteriously, the owner sold nothing even though collectors wanted to buy my work. She did not make a secret of her decision to keep the collectors for her regular artists, as she told Daniel afterwards. I was less shocked than my patron, having already had some significant come-up-pens under my belt. Perhaps another show there can happen; the show was a success in that collectors and sophisticated viewers came and loved the work. And I enjoyed Mexico City and showing there; the friendly, supportive translator, half German (like Frieda), who understood the fairy tale (Grimm's Brothers) sources of some of my paintings.

The street food, cactus tacos, I ate every morning was delicious, healthy and inexpensive. And most fascinating: the ancient pyramids were being excavated right in the central square underneath the several hundred years old Catholic Cathedral I featured it in my painting now in the Albuquerque Museum of Art, "Mexico City: El Zocalo." Once when we were having dinner after my show at a restaurant overlooking the square there was a demonstration/protest of the Chiapas Indians with drums and dancing. I thought, one more beer and I'll go down and join them. It was an exciting time.

During the week I was also able to visit the main Mexico City Museum and see two important shows: Frieda Kahlo's and Remedios Vara. Both surprised me in different ways. I had only known Kahlo's paintings in reproductions up to that point. The process of photographing and compressing the work to book form, makes or can make the work look more refined. Like that of Gauguin at the Hermitage, the work looked looser, even cruder than I learned to strive for through egg tempera. Elias Rivera emphasized this: really working the surface to get the utmost perfection, that is the goal I accepted. Their work was more about expression. In Vara's case, the show had a lot of early work, especially figure drawings and portraits. These were refined, even exquisite. Her mature work by contrast was disappointing to me. It seemed almost contrived to fit a particular idea of surrealism instead of being organic like dreams tend to be, intrinsically both coherent and always surprisingly magical. This experience helped me identify where, along the dream like spectrum to surrealism, my work fits.

In 2002 I was invited to show in the first Austrian Biennale held in an old iron smelter in the mountains of southern Austria which had been remodeled at significant expense to become a museum. It made a stunning setting, though a little hard to get to. I didn't mind the long winding road through the forest; it was beautiful and I was moved deeply when around a bend a huge Tara Tanka hung from a high cliff. I had already been practicing Tibetan Buddhism's Green Tara meditation for over ten years, so I felt: "I'm meant to be here." In the handsome large hardbound catalog of the exhibition, I was the only artist who merited a whole paragraph by the art critic. All others mentioned shared a paragraph or even just one sentence with three or four other artists. Unfortunately, it became the only "Biennale" of its kind (fine art) for Austria. The cause of it's demise: the Austrian government had refused to support it financially unless the organizers would move it to Vienna, which they agreed to do for the subsequent fairs, so they would be financially underwritten and be more easily accessible.

However, the art world is crowded with fairs and each country needs to find a niche that is unique and profitable. Sadly, Austria decided "Design" would work best for it. Years before the Museum of New Mexico Fine Arts Museum, had its own Biannuals, open to all artists in New Mexico. My work was always chosen during this period, encouraging to my path. Then suddenly this changed to being run by FOCA (Friends of Contemporary Art with a paid membership and a small selection of artists). Finally, only artists chosen through certain galleries had shows. The museum has gone through various changes of director and curatorial staff; I'm curious what it's direction will be in this new digital world.

In the meantime another art centered relationship occurred near my birth place, in Berlin, with Peggy Lange. Before heading to Hamburg where my cousin, Werner Madee and family now lived and then to Usedom, my birth place where I loved to swim, Dan and I decided to stop by the Adlon Hotel. As I wandered around the already familiar hotel, I noticed a small elegant gallery with windows looking out onto "Unter den Linden" Strasse (as important in the old East as "Kurfurstendam" in the West) and walked in. "My work would fit well in here, " I said without thinking. English or German? I don't remember. Peggy was fluent also in English. The well dressed, attractive young woman with shoulder length dark hair, greeted me with a friendly smile: "Do you think so?" I told her that I was an American artist who does figurative paintings, but was born near Berlin in the East. The Wall had not been down long, and Peggy had grown up in East Germany. From this meeting began our friendship and collaboration. When we returned from the north, I showed her some of the paintings that had been in the show in Kladow. Peggy took several, put them right into the window looking out on the big avenue. Mostly the paintings were my "Contemporary Icons" but also some of the mid-sized (non-disturbing) works; they started selling well.

As the world economy got tougher, so did gallery business and Wallentovski, the owner of the Wallentovski Galeries, took longer and longer to pay for work sold. Peggy was embarrassed, and suggested I might speak to the owner myself. It was pretty cheeky of me. He happened to be at the small bank branch inside the hotel. I walked in and told him publicly that I would not leave the bank until paid. Wallentovski kept his demeanor. I got my check, but it was obvious to me that he did not welcome pressure from an artist.

Peggy still featured my work, but more carefully and not as prominently. Her life also changed. Dan and I used to joke about how her boyfriend, a musician, was proudly living below the poverty line. He was talented, handsome, and a good conversationalist, so meeting them over dinner was always interesting.

Around 2007, Peggy met the love of her life, decided to get married and became pregnant, which eventually ended her career with the Wallentovski Galleries. She moved to Switzerland with their infant son, Erik, to live with Thomas in his mountain cabin. The discovery of his illegal marijuana farm, among other things, was too much for Peggy. She then moved to Dresden where she had grown up, to be nearer her family. Germany has an excellent social safety net: a single mother being paid 80% of her salary during the child's first year and beyond.

Some years earlier we had met her friend and ex-lover, Klaus, a Baron who owned a beautiful resort at Tegernsee. A one person show was planned there of my work. Dan and I were also invited to stay at the expensive hotel for two nights free. Similarly, as has happened in my career a few times, the count became a bit nervous about how his guests would receive my work. As Peggy started to hang the show, suddenly Klaus asked a friend of his living nearby to hang some of her cow paintings. I had seen several hanging around the hotel. He's the count; he can do that. Peggy was mortified, Here I had come all the way from Santa Fe for the show. Well I didn't make a big deal of it. I've gotten used to different opinions about what was important in art.

We were also invited to dinner with the Count at the hotel. Klaus sat opposite me, and in the course of the conversation was expressing a fairly "republican" view of Cuba, criticizing it's Communism (I had not yet been to Cuba, where I did spend a week with Code Pink less than two years ago), but had empathy with the Cuban people and disagreed with our treatment of Cuba, so I argued with the Count. I could tell people at the table were shocked. Germany was still class conscious. How could I criticize my host, a Count? I enjoyed the heat of argument and invited him to come visit us next time his helicopter flies over New Mexico. Perhaps he will. He did buy one painting of each artist from the show: "Goddess as Child II." I was grateful.

Eventually Peggy opened her own gallery in Dresden's Old Town, and hosted a one person show for me. She had continued to sell my work privately in between. It was also the beginning of the "wireless" era; I had discovered that I am electromagnetically sensitive" (EMS). In booking a room for one week at the newly renovated "Kangeroo" I inquired whether they had wireless in the building. In the phone call the staff assured me they did not. It was walking distance from the train station. As I approached it, next to it I saw a converted chimney that looked like a cell tower to me. Before I signed in I asked the attendant about this; she heatedly claimed it is still an active chimney, not a cell tower.

I naively believed her, went to bed that night, waking up a few hours later, throwing up, having "the runs;" and feeling deathly ill. It probably did not help, with the thin walls between rooms, that the four mafia looking Italians seemed to be on their cell phones all night? At six in the morning I got up, went to the kitchen/reception room and looked more carefully at the chimney/cell tower through the large picture window. It was definitely a cell tower. My first encounter with a cell tower had been in Winslow, Arizona about a year earlier when we had driven from San Bernardino. Right out our window I could see a cell tower. At that time I knew nothing about "wireless," but the tower made me uncomfortable. It was just intuition. We changed rooms, but I still could not sleep, the EMF invading every room. Across the world, many traditional hotels were using the money from cell towers, to renovate.

I walked a long time before finding a hotel. Even the best I could find took two internal moves to find a room I could tolerate. It was clear to me, either I trust my own body, or I will end up in a hospital. The old town Dresden five star hotel was acceptable to me because it was far cheaper than a hospital room.

While I had been to Germany alone many times for several years because Dan did not want to fly due to PTSD from his time in Berlin as air traffic controller, my first educational trip was to the Equator, to Forteleza, Brazil, in late May of 1985 where we were adopting Paolo, just born on May 5th. Usually both parents went if possible, but Dan felt he needed to stay home to earn money to support us and the adoption, as well as take care of seven year old Sean. I roomed with another prospective mother in the adoption hotel whose husband could not accompany her either.

Within a couple of days each of us was given the baby designated to us by Rainbow House. One of the couples who already had a child from Columbia was disappointed their child was so light in that their first was significantly darker and they lived in a race conscious area. A darker brother would be preferable I thought secretly: maybe we could trade since our birth son is Anglo, and Paolo first seemed like any ordinary brown baby to me. I never voiced either of those ideas out loud. Soon enough I became totally bonded with Paolo. I wanted to go to his orphanage as well as the hospital he had been in for bronchitis. The staff greeted me with dismay. Osterne, our translator, explained they thought I had come to bring him back. Once we clarified that that was not the case, they relaxed and enjoyed visiting with Paolo again. Another older infant near the entrance had met my eyes appealingly as we entered. I asked if I could pick him up. "No. no, we can't let them get used to being held; we don't have the staff." I was shocked. Not picked up; not held?

This was somewhat contradicted by another incident there. An expensively dressed woman walked in and was greeted warmly by the staff. She walked up to Osterne and me (I was holding Paolo) and asked to hold him, explaining that she knew him from her frequent former visits. Somewhat reluctantly, I started to hand him to her, but to my surprise and delight I have to admit, Paolo's little fist held on tight to me, and I decided to trust that, not force him. I apologized to the rather aggressive woman. I was sensitive to the fact that perhaps we foreigners seemed like interlopers to this wealthy society woman who gave of her time and energy to these orphans.

One reason Paolo became bonded to me so quickly is the natural bonding that happens through nursing an infant. Paolo was nursed by his mother for a week before the family she worked for decided caring for him was interfering too much with her household duties so they demanded he be sent to an orphanage to wait for adoption. I had decided to try nursing him and had ordered supplies from La Leche League. Unfortunately, the nursing kit arrived after I had left for Brazil, thus was forwarded immediately. So since I assumed it would arrive any day I decided to already let him suck my breasts so that my own milk could be stimulated more quickly. I'll never forget what happened, it was so dramatic. When he saw my breasts a look came over his little face like: "Oh my g*d there they are!" And he glommed on with enthusiasm. Of course nothing came out. It usually takes time and the equipment lets the baby get milk through the tube attached to one's breast so that the sucking accomplishes both goals. While it obviously felt wonderful to both of us, it did not satisfy the primary need for nourishment. The LLL came to late and was sent on to Santa Fe after we had departed Fortelza. By then the bottle had become the necessary method.

Meanwhile, the staff showed me around the orphanage. There was a separate room for babies over one year old. That scene was also painfully seared into my memory: the poor babies looked like vegetables, so pale, even gray. No wonder Kosta and Katarina came home with two babies instead of one, unable to turn their backs on the one year old Tulio as he stood in his crib with pleading, intense eyes. Ironically, it was Tulio who made it safely beyond adulthood, while Mario, the seeming easier, healthier child, took his own life on the brink of adulthood , like several other adoptees we knew—a really heartbreaking occurrence. I was really tempted to bring home a second child, but I had promised my husband: only one, only Paolo. Remembering my mother's seeming over-burdenedness, I respected my husband's wise restraint.

When the doctor assigned to our adopted infants in Brazil laid down the law that the feeding schedule of every four hours must be observed, presumably for the welfare of the baby, I did not disagree but thought inwardly: "we'll see." I remember what my Mutti had said about her experience with her first child. Her regret was so poignant I can still hear her today. She was given the same instructions and followed to the letter as the other babies parents would also do. My brother Hans would wake up, cry from hunger every three hours, cry for the whole wait, then be so exhausted he would fall asleep after a couple of sips. He always remained skinny, however maybe better longevity than being obese, which you see so often now. Paolo and the other two babies cried after three hours Sean my only birth child did also; stretching out the night feedings happened gradually. I fed Paolo on demand. When the doctor returned after a few days and asked: "Are you feeding him on the four hour schedule?" I just said yes.

The other two babies were like Hans, except much worse. The one whose mother I roomed with had kept me up at night. I could not bear to hear his pitiful cry and finally said: either I will feed him or change rooms. The former was understandably not accepted. I did the latter, finding a single room. The other three people had enormous respect for the authority of the medical profession. I'm more skeptical. The male and female nurse parents held their baby, not close to their bodies (their heart) but out, away from it, as though they might contract a germ or virus. Paolo thrived, the other two were problematic. One clearly already had failure to thrive syndrome, being terribly thin. One observer said he looked like a plucked chicken. It was really sad.

I still could not sleep enough due to Paolo's crying at night. One night I felt so desperate, I thought if I don't sleep more I'll jump out the window, or throw Paolo out. I prayed to the Universe: I had to not get up more than once a night; I had to let him cry the second time. I woke up the next morning. Paolo was sleeping calmly in his crib. He had survived. Once we were home he became more insecure again. At least in Forteleza he heard the language and other sounds he was used to. I couldn't leave the room without taking him with me. So we hired a young woman to hold him so I could at least go the bathroom alone. Gradually she could be with him as well as do some housework so I could be back in my studio for a couple of hours.

Adoption is both wonderful and scary, especially foreign ones. There is such an emotional element and potential problems are often not apparent. In the second one we pursued, one foreign and one domestic, couples went through even more intensive study, both as to their desires and their capabilities/suitabilities as parents. My sister Hannelore's was the first in our extended family to adopt after her only pregnancy resulted in a stillbirth, but through a private agency where there is less scrutiny. Asperger syndrome, which my father was suspected of having, also was another possible reason of her difficulty adopting a child.

The planet on the Ascendant rules how other people see you as well as your lens on the world. While Hannelore and I were both Libra sun, we were very different; with Saturn near her Ascendant while I had Neptune, the opposite energy, it is no wonder she was impatient with me and I found her too harsh though she had wonderful loyal friends. If we could have understood how those two aspects can and should complement each other, we could have had a more rewarding relationship, an example of possible natural unity instead of painful polarization.

Whenever I am in a scary situation I tend to pray to the Universe. During this time I did so continually: please don't let this be a mistake; please send me someone I can love and be a good mother to. When I got to Rio de Janero and walked into the courtroom where the adoption papers were to be signed in front of the judge, I was handed Paolo's birth certificate. I glanced at it. It had a different date than we were told: he was born on April 19, exactly opposite my birth, Aries (like my favorite and closest sister) a definite message from the Universe that this was meant to be. My Mars was also in my 7th House of relationships in Aries so we were a good match. When Paolo was a teenager, that Aries persona was often hard on me. When he called me "a mean ugly old witch," in response I would shoot back, "If I weren't a witch you'd be a wimp!" (Robert Blythe). That got him. As a toddler and up to four years old, Paolo is in several of my paintings of interiors as well as "Mural of my Life," where later he objected to his nudity.

"The Olympic Trainer Mom" that I mentioned earlier, I learned two things that really help parenting: 1) Never say no unless you're willing to stick by it through "Sturm und Drang" (Knock down drag out fight). On our first Christmas with Heather and Melissa, we took the kids sledding at Hyde Park. Melly was not only not enjoying it but ruining everyone's fun by whining, falling down, and acting pitiful. I took a chance: "Melissa, if you don't get yourself down this hill without crying and complaining, I'm going to take away all your Christmas presents." Thankfully, it worked. It would not have been easy to carry through, though there are always ways. No more complaints; just laughter and fun. It's painful to watch others saying "no" repeatedly, and eventually giving in to a child's pestering but feeling irritated and angry. And 2) Children came to this plane for their own reasons and lessons; doing your best but having no attachment to their success is important. They are not here to make the mom or dad feel successful.

All children are our children, worldwide, black, yellow, brown or white. They come straight from God and are perfect. There is no "original sin." Each child is different and one can't avoid making mistakes. Once when I was driving the kids home, I had to intervene repeatedly in their fighting. Finally I told Paolo, the seeming instigator, "If you don't stop, I will make you get out of the car and walk." He continued and I stopped the car, demanding he get out. He did and I was impressed by the intensity of his anger at me. I was awed by his sense of personal pride and fairness.

For my second trip, my husband treated me, about a year before the Berlin Wall came down, to a week with a German tour group leaving for Moscow from East Berlin in which I did my typical thing of separating myself from the group. It's my temperament to take chances in order to experience more, and may seem foolish to those around me—that's one element of "Journey of the Fool." The "Fool" or "Jester" has a long history in literature (Shakespeare) and politics (the court Jester) but to my knowledge was usually if not always, male. While Frieda Kahlo was my main role model for processing experiences through art, she did it through self portraits while my heroine is more universal, as are the experiences I chose to embody in my paintings. Taking on the mantel of the fool allows me to address topics that are intrinsically disturbing, but yet not intrude too closely. The viewer can decide on her/his own: is there wisdom in this fool?

I'm always for the underdog or the vilified, as well as loving the works of Tolstoy and Dostoevsky so I've always been interested in going to Russia. As my husband's law practice took off, he offered to pay for a trip. He does not feel drawn to Russia. It was fairly modest and set up by my uncle Walter Frahnert, second cousin to my father who had saved his life in the war, with a German travel group. The trip left from East Berlin, still behind the "Wall" at that time. It was a little scary once the door was closed after we entered the East because you could not go back. We boarded the Russian Aeroflot and took off; quite amazing how the plane rumbled and shook. We got to Moscow (participants were coming from all over Germany) in the early afternoon, before any other participants. In our little Berlin group, I gravitated to a young woman who was a student of Russian language, politics and history who had brought her mother to Moscow for her first visit and who invited me to come along as they went into downtown, riding the Metro which was absolutely aesthetically amazing in the beauty of each station. I was thrilled and fascinated, watching the Russian city dwellers, the sophisticated dress and the contrast between the blond blue eyed pale skinned Europeans to the more Asian, and Mongolian. We eventually got back to our hotel, had dinner and then the group assembled in the hotel bar for drinks. I joined for a little while and then thought: I didn't come to Russia to sit in bar with a bunch of Germans. I wanted to see as much as possible. So I left the hotel and walked over to the subway station, wandering if I had the courage to go down the tube alone. As I stood there, hesitating, a young blond man came up speaking in fluent though accented English: "You're an American." "How do you know?" I asked. He said by my clothes and appearance. I responded that I was. He asked if we could talk. And we did: for two hours as we circumambulated the Metro station. I learned that he was a twenty-eight year old medical student who was really curious about America and Americans, like I was about Russia and Russians.

His main topic after lots of questions about American life, was his interest in the predictions of Nostradamus and the Apocalypse in *Revelations* of which I knew less than he did, but shared his curiosity and fascination. On my return I looked up Nostradamus again. When I was ready to return to the hotel he asked me if he could show me around Moscow the next day, enabling me to see things tourists don't get to see. I said yes and agreed to meet him at the distance from the hotel demanded of non-tourists.

Returning to the hotel, I stopped by the bar. The group was still drinking Wandering through the hotel I heard some appealing dance music: a wedding party was going on. I stood for some time on the periphery, listening to the dance band, even wishing I could join in, music and dance being universal, beyond language. In New Mexico before my marriage, and even after, I could often gather the courage to join an exuberant group. But in this foreign city I felt too inhibited. I noticed a man about my age also standing on the outskirts of the party like I was. Soon after he came up to me and asked me to dance, in which language? It didn't seem to matter. It turned out he did speak quite good English; he was a Russian engineer living in Cuba with his wife and child. He was also a good dancer. During breaks we sat with another couple, friends of his who also spoke English. The woman was a sculptor, so we had an added basis of conversation. It was great fun. When the hotel party ended and the band packed up, the three were not ready to call it a night, so the engineer invited everyone to his room for a nightcap and more conversation. When I got there and asked where the other two were, he said there was a change in plans; they would meet us tomorrow evening. He started kissing me and to my surprise, even shock, I enjoyed it and felt turned on, That was not the plan, nor had I felt attracted to him in that way. The next thing I knew, he dropped his pants! I said, I'll see you tomorrow and fled the room.

The next morning as I met the young medical student, he had been joined by a young attractive woman who reminded me of Lara in the film "Doctor Zhivago." With her was a tow headed toddler. My friend introduced us and told me her husband had worked in this hotel; he is missing and she asks if I can invite her in also so she can inquire about him. I said okay and we all had blintzes (the only vegetarian option) together. I don't know if she ever found him but I felt if I stayed there too much longer I'd have a crowd with me.

We only had three and a half days in which I saw the Red Square (Krasnia which means beautiful not "communist") and it was full of a variety of astonishingly beautiful churches from the simple most ancient fourth century to the ornate, colorful "onion" domed churches. Inside I was fascinated by the supporting pillars that each had a full size realistic man painted on them. My new friend explained these were either Russian saints or important financial benefactors to the church. I also was able to buy a ticket to the Bolshoi Ballet at a kiosk for a small fraction of what I would have paid through the travel group. It was a stunning performance. I noted that the street food was heavy on the meat, in contrast to that of Mexico City. I never tried it. The big famous modern department store (Gump) was depressingly empty of merchandise.

The experience of my first night kind of haunted me, .that I had felt turned on. Part of it certainly was the vodka, but I had not felt anything like that all evening. It was fun but impersonal. Nervously, I went to the meeting place the second evening but somewhat late, hoping he would not be there, and relieved when he was not.

By the time we arrived in Leningrad I had gotten a serious cough. Part of it was the smoking in the elevators, but also somehow related to my whooping cough as an infant. A fantasy followed me into my dreams on the overnight train: I had an affair, my husband left me; I regretted it all my life and would die of this cough. The first night in Leningrad I gave myself a dream suggestion. The result: I dreamed I should eat grapes. At a dusty fruit stand I found some pretty unappetizing looking grapes, but when I washed them at our hotel they were delicious. My cough got better.

On my return to Germany I spent a couple of days with my cousin's family in Hamburg. Over a wonderful dinner with lots of wine, I regaled them about my adventures in Russia. My cousin Werner, who married Barbara when they were students due to her becoming pregnant and who perhaps projected a wilder persona onto me in his fantasy: assuming affairs where there were none, was sure my laughter hid the truth. On a later visit when Werner's hospitality pushed Dan to drink a little too much, my husband said: "My wife can do whatever she wants." "Mein, Gott!" he was impressed. I should not have been shocked when one evening, as I passed him on the stairway to the guestroom, he grabbed my breast. I said nothing and just continued to walk up. It never happened again. While I loved him as my dear relative, there were many areas of my life he had no comprehension of or interest in.

In Leningrad, we visited the Hermitage for two afternoons. By the second afternoon I was tired of all the opulence, of the castles and the furniture, rugs, jewelry and other assorted riches on the lower floor, so again I separated myself from the group, found the room devoted solely to Gauguin paintings, sat studying them for an inspiring hour, then decided to practice my Russian by looking for a cafe. The months before the trip I worked hard learning Russian and was able to read the letters quite well but found while I could make myself understood, the replies were much too fast. But luckily there was always at least one person who spoke English.

Wandering down the closest street I soon found the word for restaurant above the door of a basement establishment. I walked down the stairs and into the open door. People were standing in line, presumably ordering their food. I joined the line. When it was my turn I pointed at a pastry and asked for coffee. When I turned back to look for a place to sit, to my amazement a place was cleared for me between two female students who spoke English. The two girls would ask me a question then translate the question and answer for all the other guests. Wow! My trepidation with the language barrier melted to where I felt really at home. When the two students asked to accompany me to my hotel, I welcomed them and we even found a fruit stand on our way.

Years later my husband and I went to St. Petersburg and to the Hermitage as part of a cruise to the Scandinavian countries. Since he is not as comfortable in Russia as I am, I also enjoyed it less (a downside of my mutability) though we did go to a marvelous male choral concert.

In 2007 at the urging of Sam Ballen, the former owner of La Fonda Hotel in Santa Fe, that we take the jet trip around the world, like he and Ethel had enjoyed, my husband bought me a ticket, rather than for us both. He had learned from long experience that "absence makes the heart grow fonder" or more personally, that we both needed a lot of freedom and experiences apart. He had no desire to see the Far East, but I did, especially Tibet and throw in a little of China, Vietnam, Cambodia, Myanmar (Burma), Mongolia, Uzbekistan and Jordan. In each place we spent only two or three days.

Tibet was my main focus. First we did an emergency landing in Kathmandu due to a wing problem, so we spent two days there. I ventured alone out of the back fence of the elegant five star hotel to discover groups of hungry children in rags who were aggressive in their demands for money. I had to be equally aggressive in making them let go of me, literally, and was relieved to get back to the hotel grounds. In Lhasa, the Potala was the main focus. However most of the group were too worried about the altitude to climb it's steep steps. Since I live at 7,000 feet and climbed mountains up to 12,000 to prepare, it was a little like coming to Heaven, all the gold covered Lamas, goddesses and gods, Dakinis, and Guru Rimpoche. I gratefully breathed it all in. In climbing the stairs I had walked slowly, breathing deeply, so I was definitely high when I got there. In Lhasa, as with every stop in Tibet, there was a heavy Chinese military presence that seemed oppressive, especially the street signs where the Chinese hung bolder, ugly utilitarian signs over the beautiful Tibetan letters.

When it was time to leave, there was a delay at the airport. We were told we would not be able to leave for an hour and a half, so I asked if we could step out of the plane. Almost everyone else stayed in to enjoy the cocktails; one or two may have gone out too. I used every opportunity to walk around as my inflamed varicose vein had developed a lump before I left home plus as readers of this memoir know by now, I like to challenge rules that make no sense to me. So I got off the plane and walked around. In the distance but not too far from where the plane stood, I saw a tall chain link fence that seemed to mark the boundaries of the airport. I walked up to where the two parts became a corner without actually meeting and looked through the small space. A traditional Tibetan village. The space was just big enough for me to slip through and Tibetans to slip out? I walked around the village somewhat self-consciously, saying the greeting: "Tashi Delai" with hands folded in the reverential gesture to anyone I encountered. Children seemed to be walking to school, often accompanied by an adult—mostly their mothers. There were piles of Yak dung used for heating. The houses were small, much like the old adobes in New Mexico "barrios."

I always carried my little drawing book in my purse so I found a place to sit down and began making sketches of the charming scenes. After I'd finished several I realized I needed to pee so reluctantly I decided to go back to the plane. As I slipped back through the fence I thought: Oh, oh! A police car stood a few yards from me. The policeman got out of the car, opened the car's back door and motioned me to get into it! Then he drove off, not toward the parked plane, but in the opposite direction! Was I going to jail? After leaving the airport the car went several more blocks, then made two U turns and finally delivered me back to the plane. Was it meant to scare me? It certainly succeeded. There at the plane, several people were irritated, claiming I almost missed the plane, I made the plane late, etc. Well, by my watch I had been gone just over an hour; we were still within the stated time of the delay. Soon all was forgiven; my "eccentricity" was just part of the adventure.

Change is the order of things. The art market not only changed in Santa Fe but worldwide, it seemed. There were fewer art collectors, and less money available for collecting. To adapt, galleries in Santa Fe had also become more commercial. Rather than opening a gallery because one loved art and wanted to support artists, enabling artists to do their best work, profit had seemed to become uppermost—as a trend, not an absolute. Santa Fe's reputation as an art center, it seemed to me, had been over blown for decades, but new galleries and artists kept coming, hoping for success. I knew lots of good, even wonderful artists whose gallery had closed or changed. I love meeting people who love art and am also a good sales person because I know art history, love to share it and have a reliable sense of what is good.

That was one reason I decided to try my hand again at operating a gallery. In the late seventies to early eighties, I had joined a group of friends to open One of a Kind, a co-operative with about ten members. It was successful and I was repeatedly elected as president. After seven years I decided that I was ready to join a professional gallery with my work. None of the other members wanted to take it over, so we decided to sell it for a modest price.

So opening "A SEA (in the Desert) Gallery" (Association of Socially Engaged Artists) was a kind of spiraling back to a familiar place. I had been moved by the Haitian hurricane crisis of 2010 and decided to do a benefit. We owned a house that I could use temporarily as a show place. It was encouraging how many fine artists were willing to donate one or more works for it. Choosing the Friends Service Committee to distribute the funds (I had been a member of the Santa Fe Quaker Meeting for some years, and trusted them) so I was able to be of help. After the show I moved the small gallery into the Arcade on the Plaza. Soon I found that I kept getting headaches and frequented the bathroom too often. One day I could not help noticing that my bowels were black.

Thanksgiving was approaching and we met our son's family in Salida. Stephanie, my daughter in law (the others are daughters in god's law not to say out-laws) had noticed a palm reader, still part of the Halloween spirit; I offered to pay for her. Okay I'll do it too. When it was my turn I told the reader about my concern. Studying the cards, she said: "You must leave the place immediately or become ill." One day earlier after I had learned about scrolling down on my laptop, I realized my computer picked up twenty-one different signals, eight of them full (five bars). I also noticed several quite ill occupants of the building. The book store above my space whose owner and I talked about the effects of wireless, told me his acupuncturist said his nervous system was so stressed he needs to not use his computer for a time; the guy across from my space who had an appendicitis attack and left for surgery; the vendor opposite to my right who had irrational outbursts of anger and whose family would rescue and take her to the mountains to recover, and so on. I had learned from Quest, the phone company at that time, that the owner had had fiber optic lines laid throughout the building at considerable cost. Every vendor could have had internet and phone connection much more cheaply and safely. But this is true throughout the society. People are not informed on how the technology works and its hazards. I made a flier, distributed it or put it under doors, even under the owner's office. I got an email reply: "If your body does not like the building, take your body out." No discussion, no listening. I moved out.

After a break of a few months I found a Santa Fe Railyard space suitable for a gallery and reopened the gallery as a co-op hybrid with a few artist friends. Sales were not easy, so members dropped away over the first months, but some artists wanted me to represent them and I generated enough sales to keep the gallery going for nine more years. The eight months of Covid ended my Gallery.

PART 2 / THE ART

Paintings

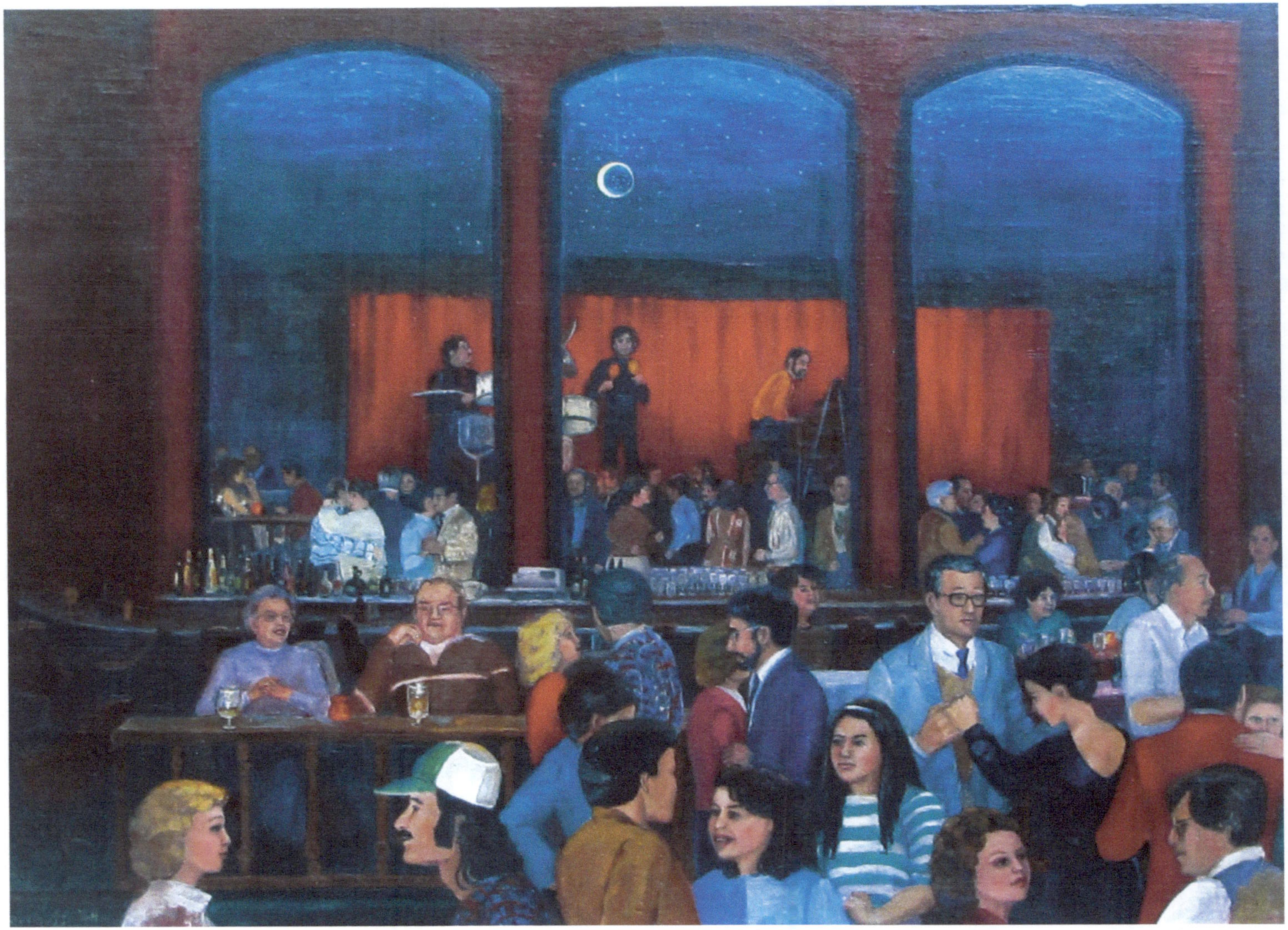

Father Frank Pretto

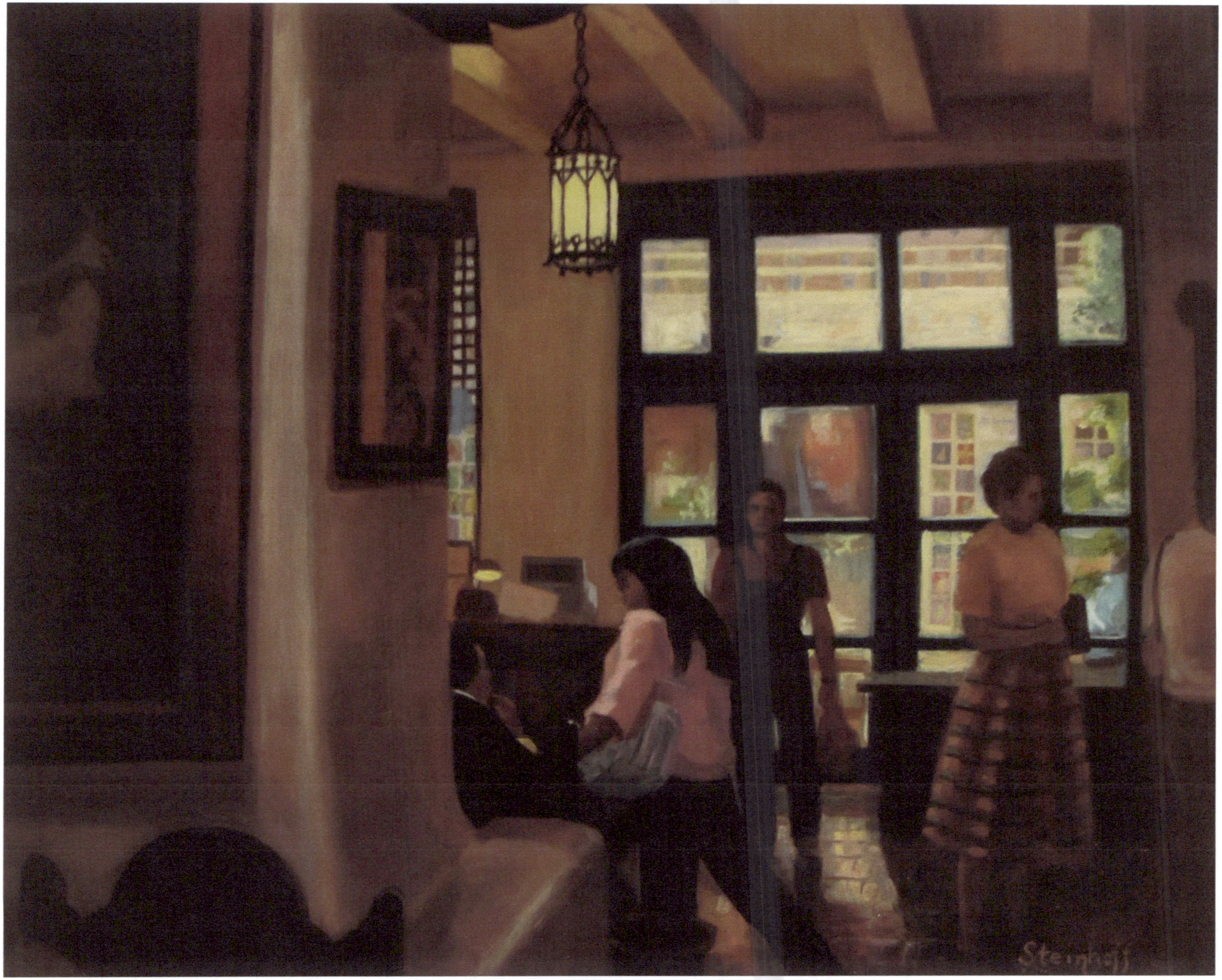

La Fonda V detail

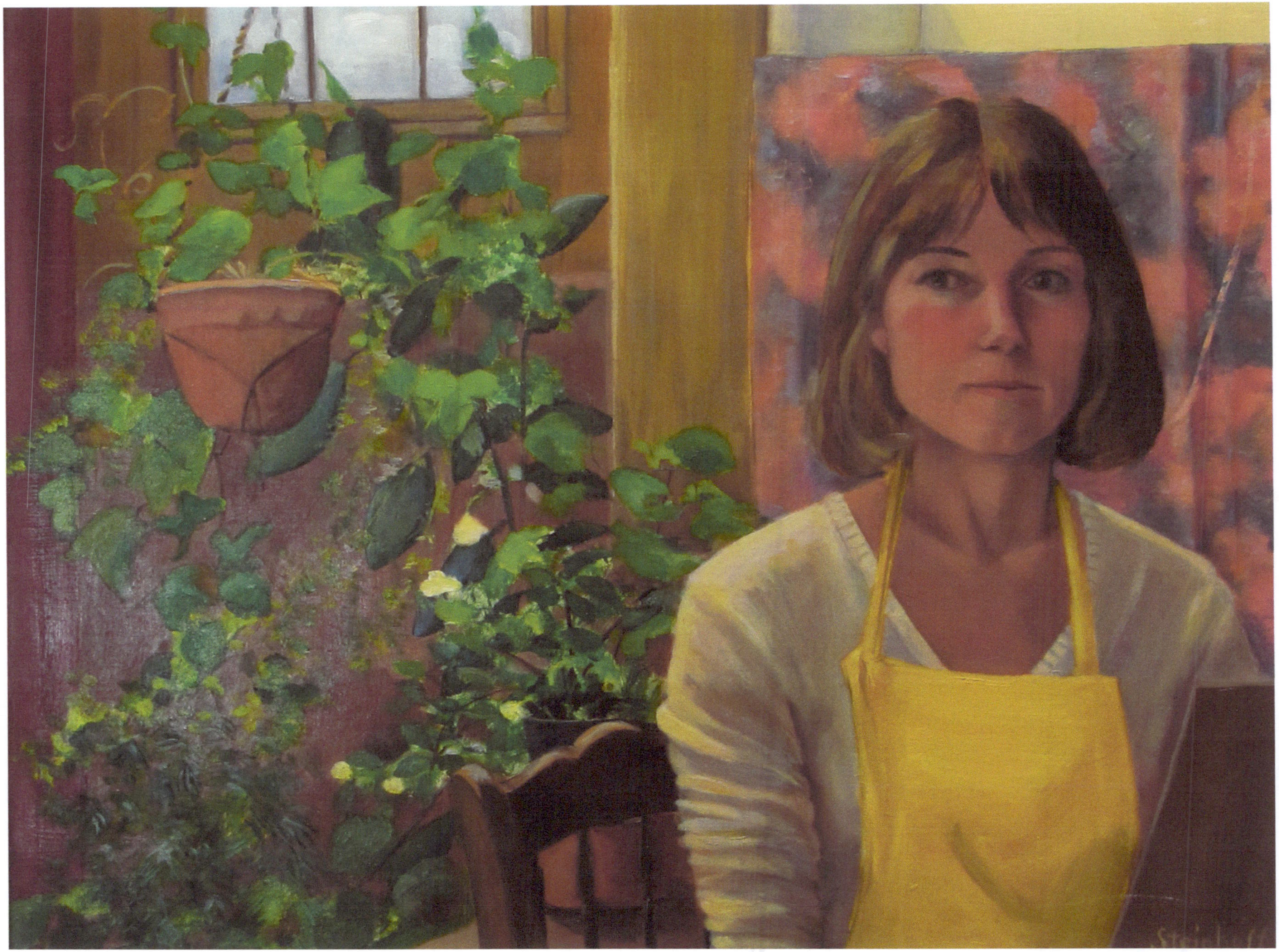

Yellow Apron

Bridge to Unknown

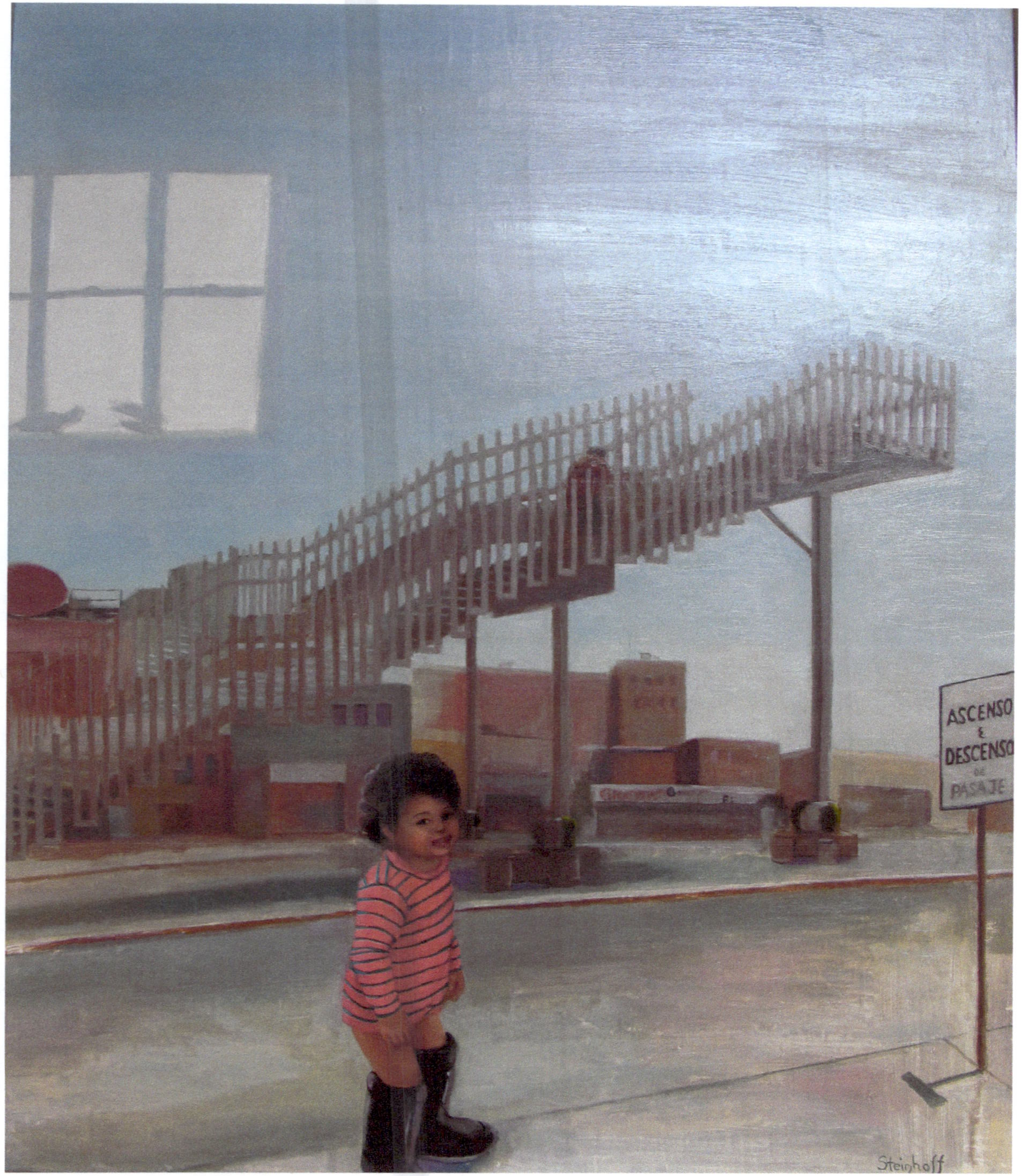

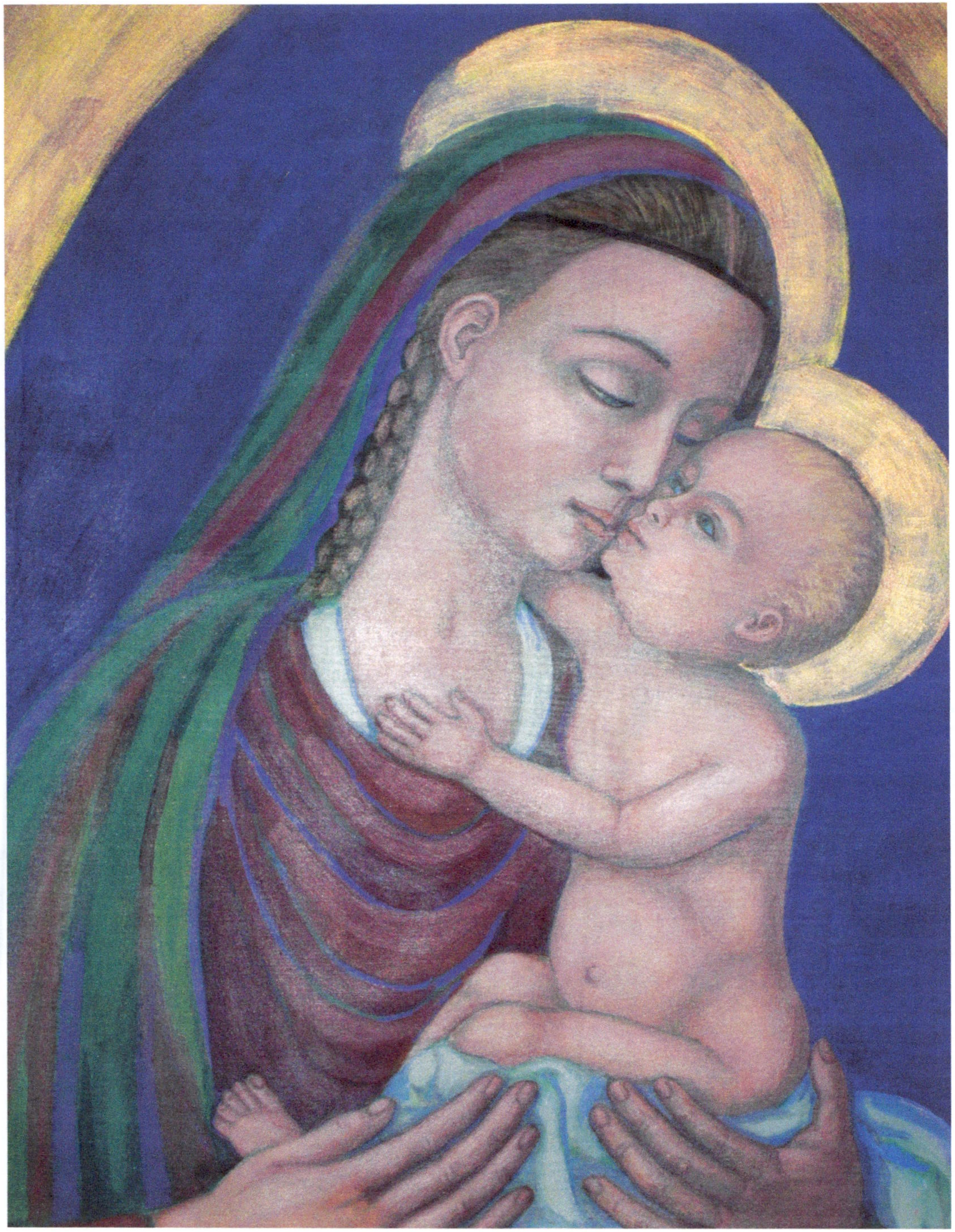

"Artist self-apprenticeship"
Madonna after Boutes

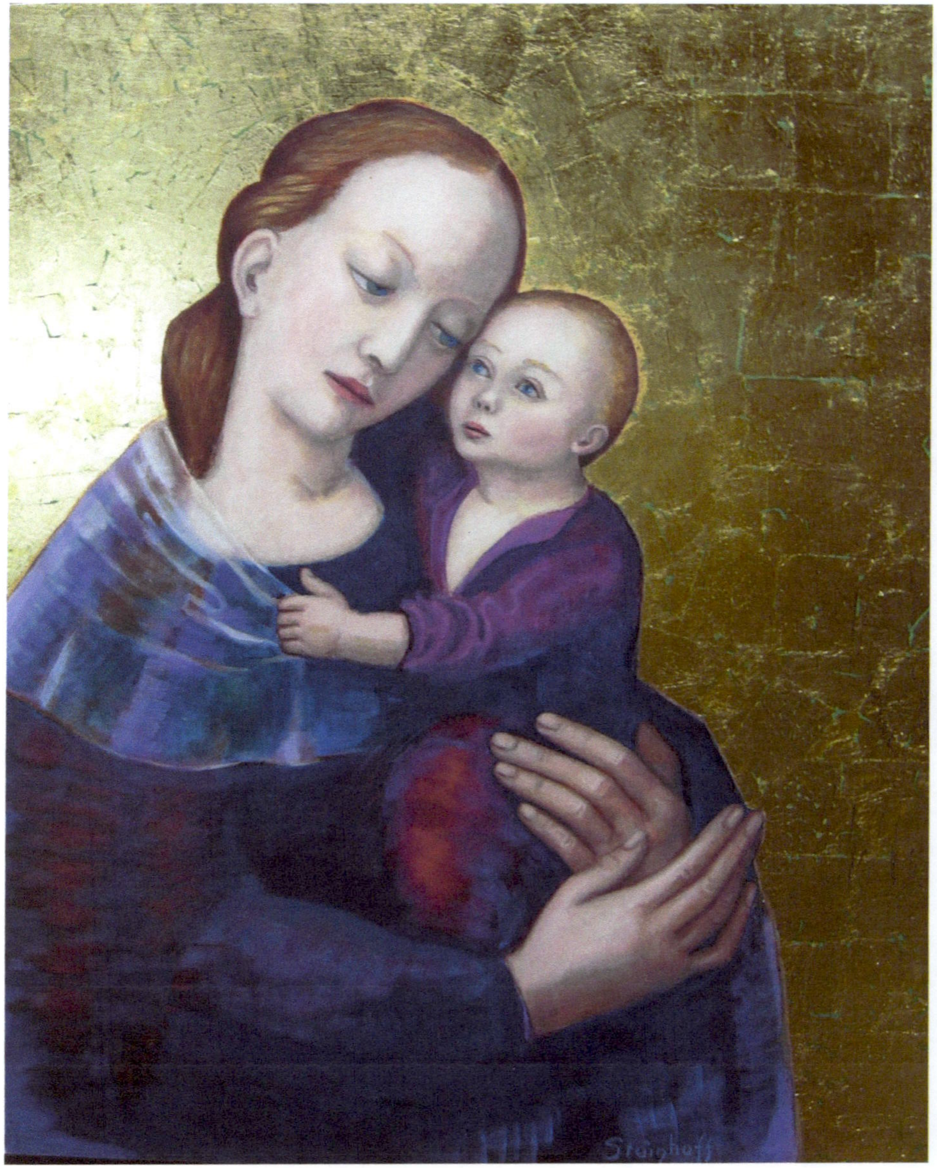

Madonna #3

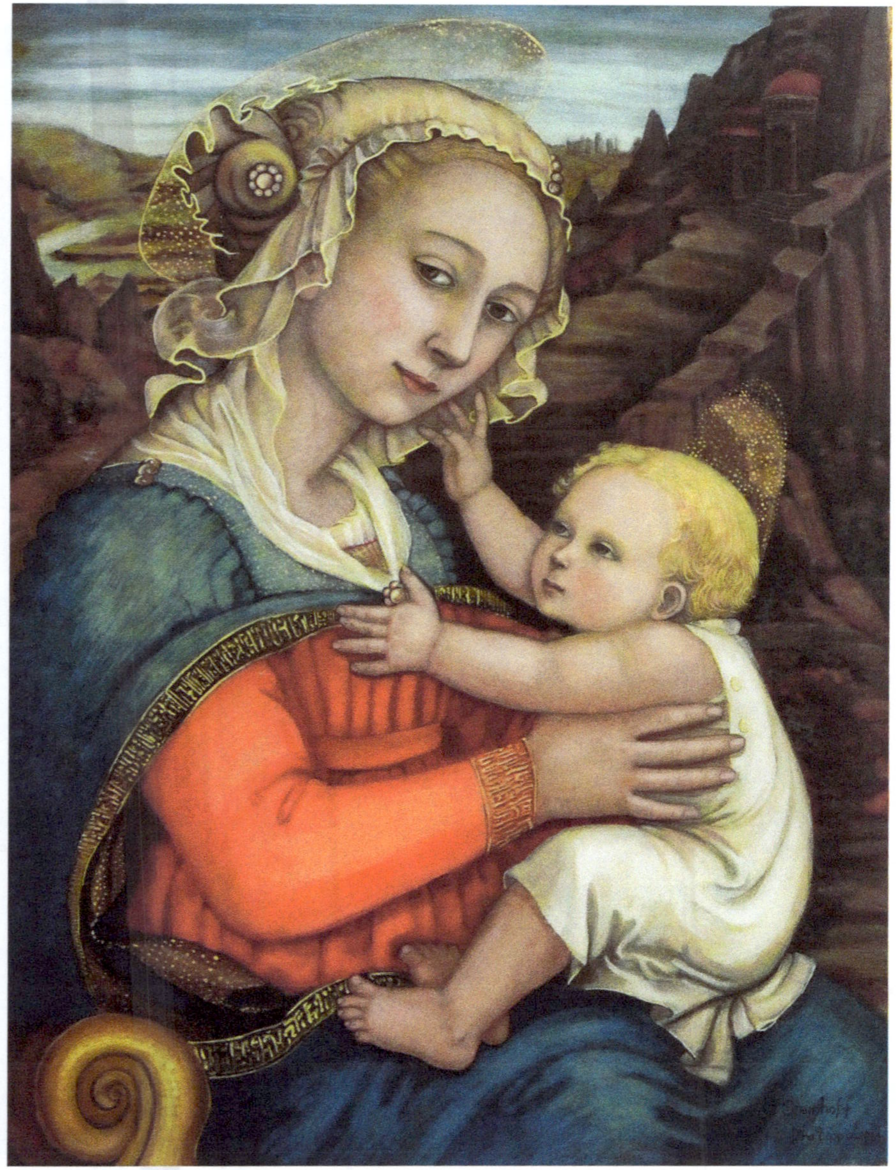

Madonna #4

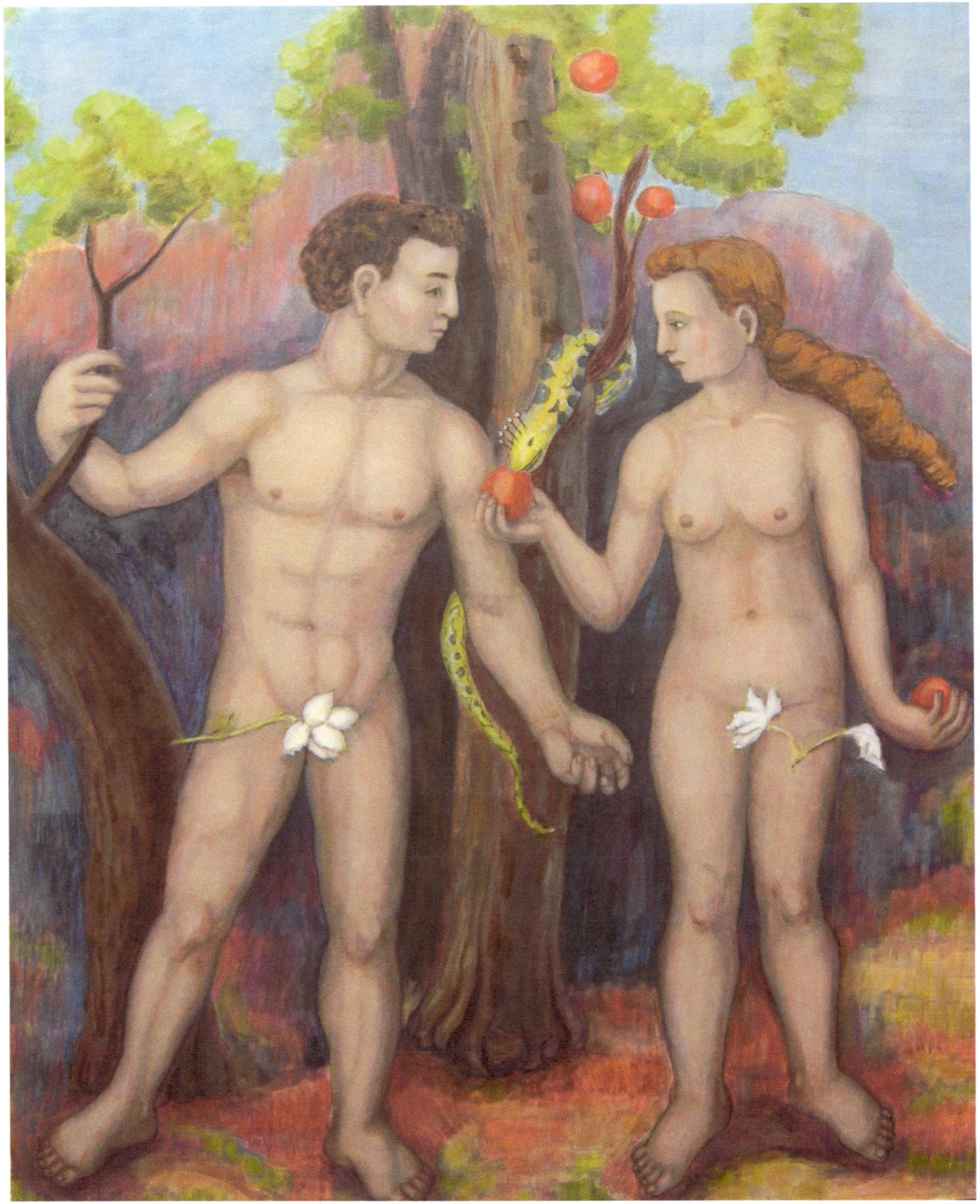

Eden after Dürer

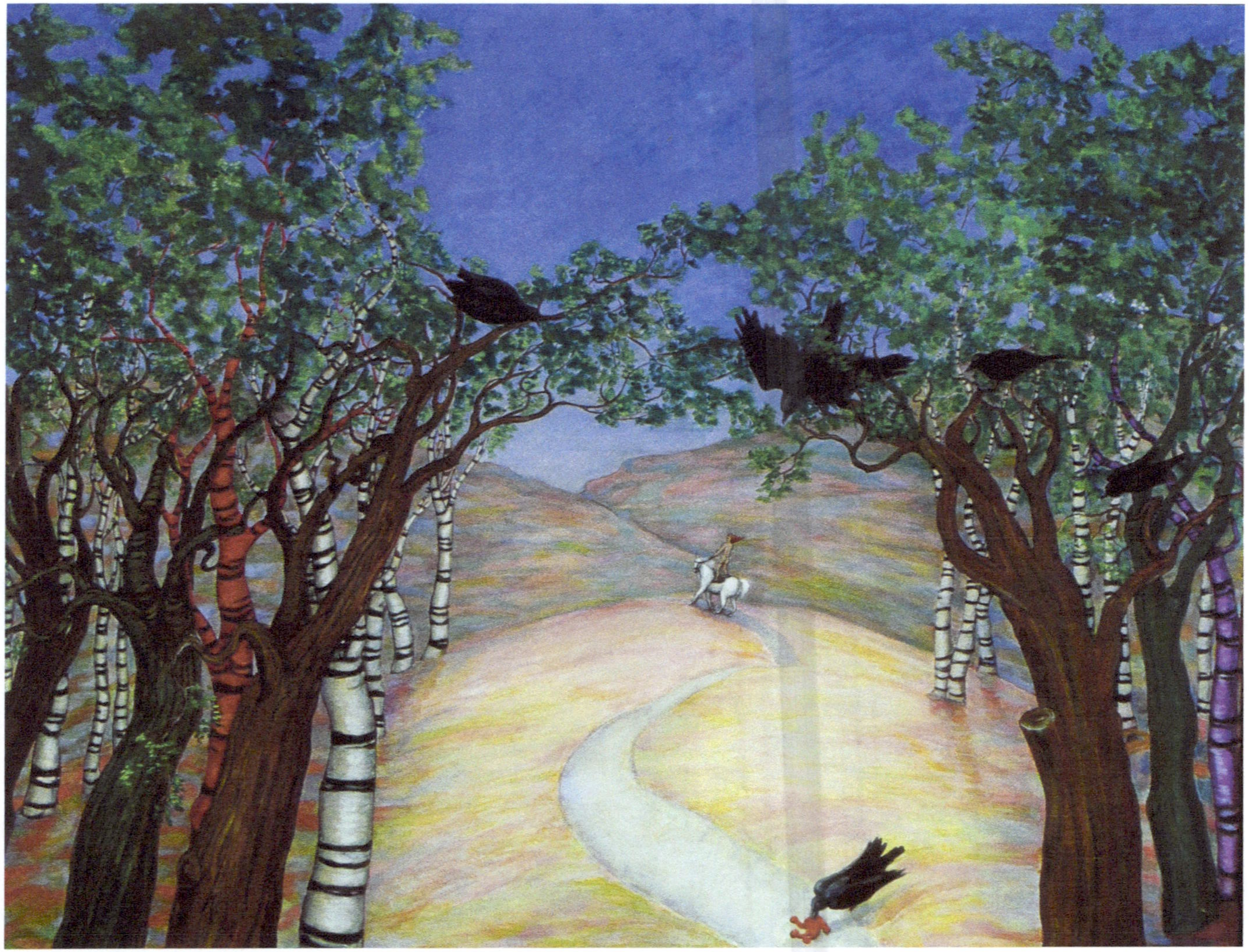

Journey Begins

Earth Occupied

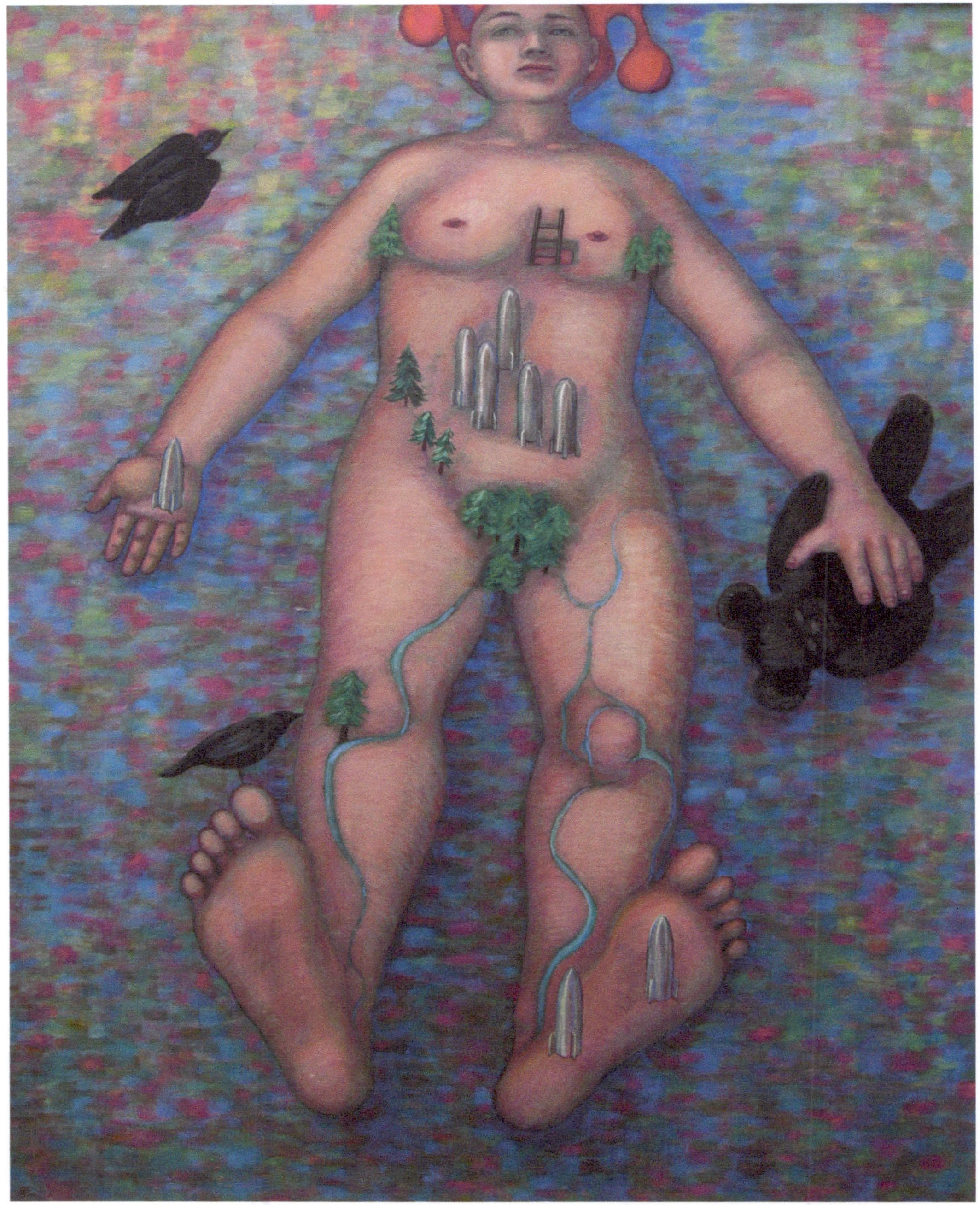

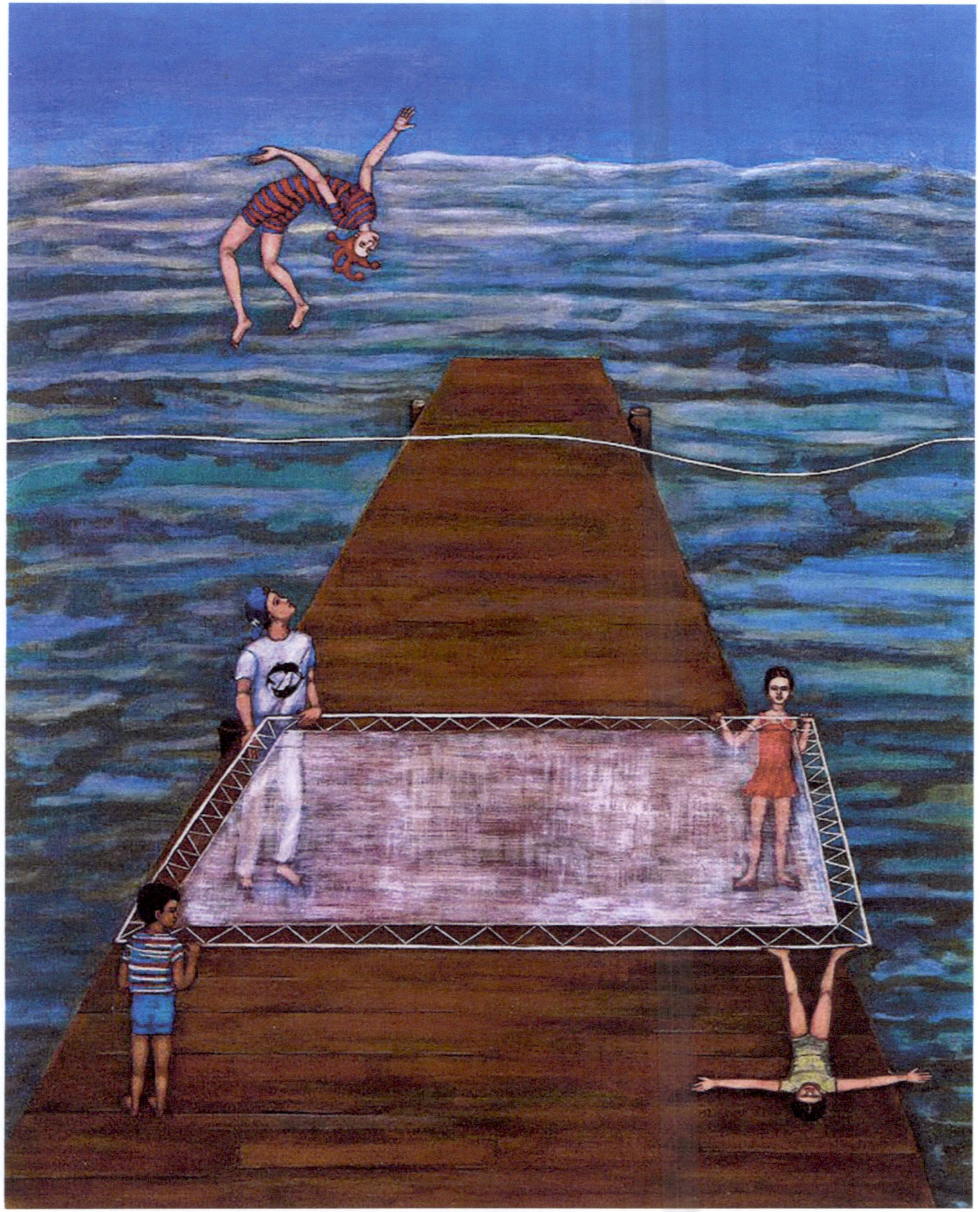

Support System

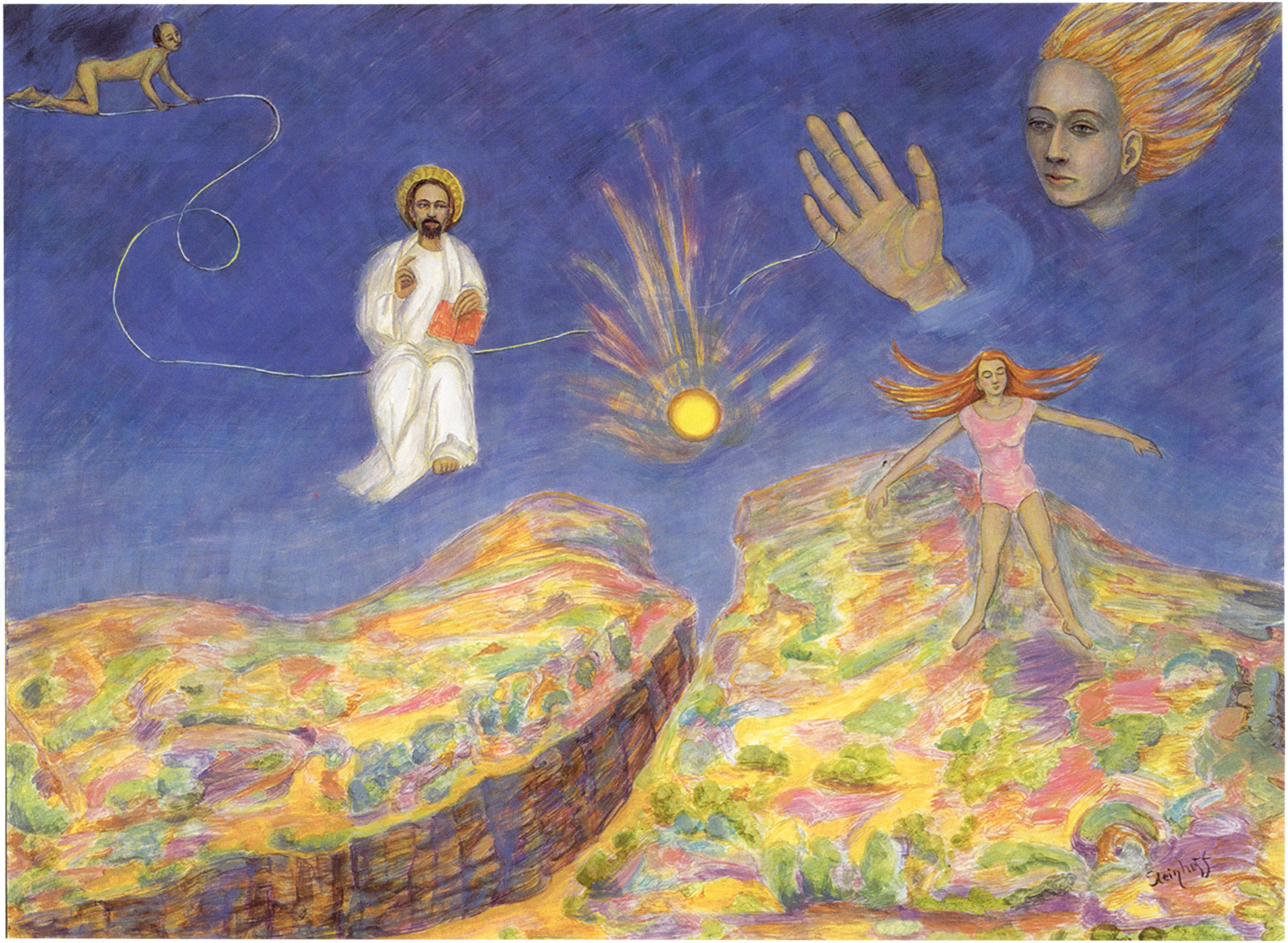

String of Time

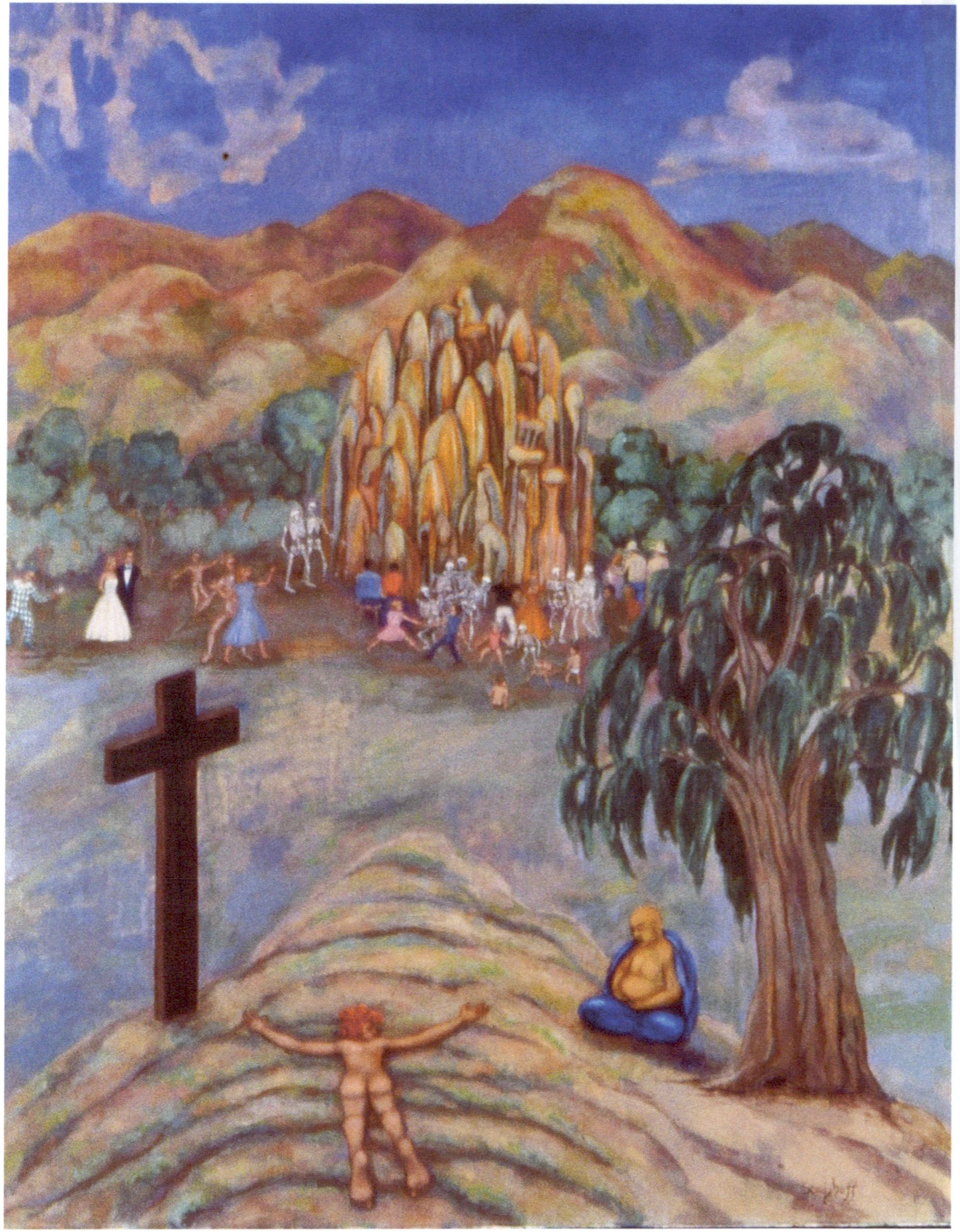

Ritual of the Unlimited II

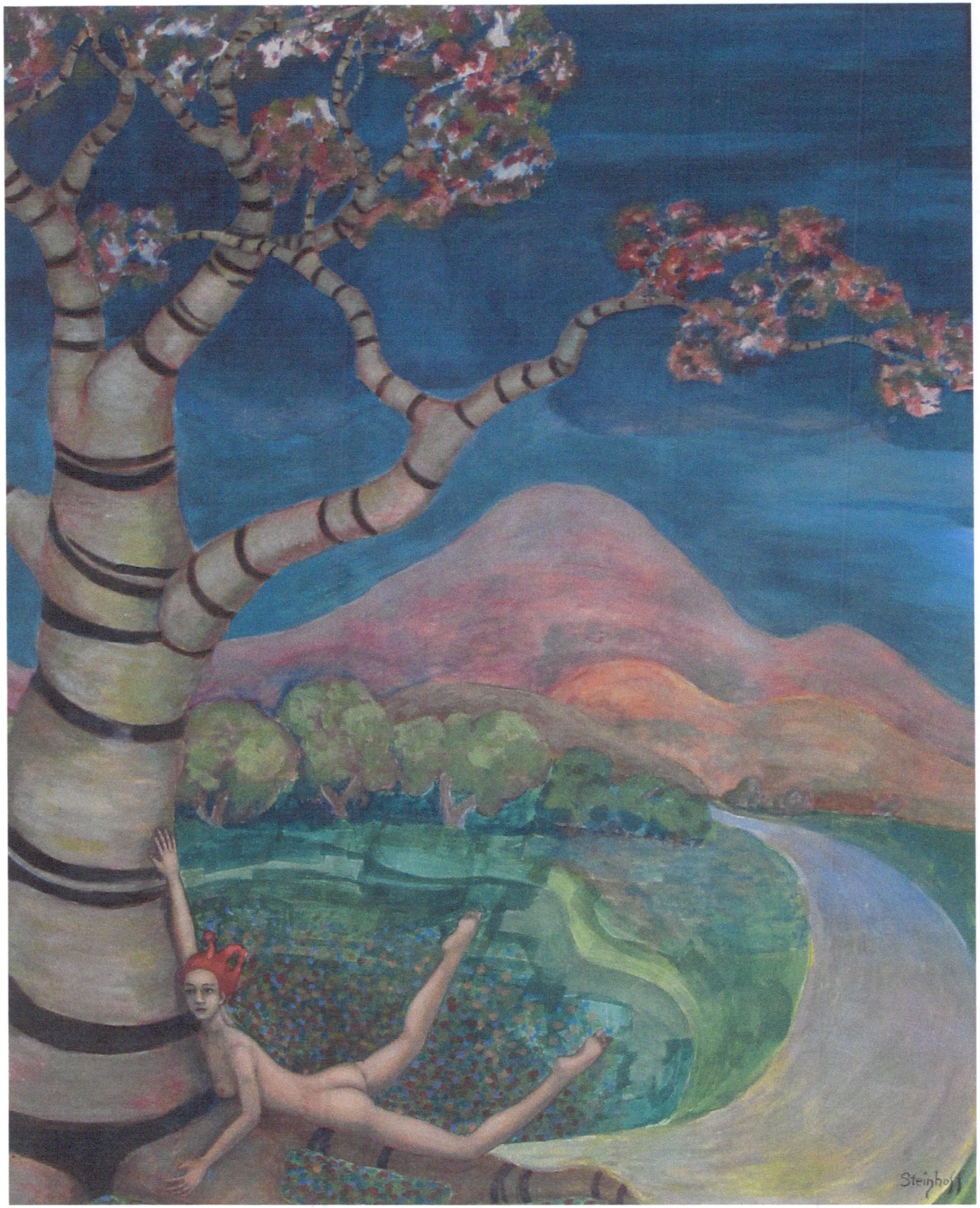

Seeking Wisdom

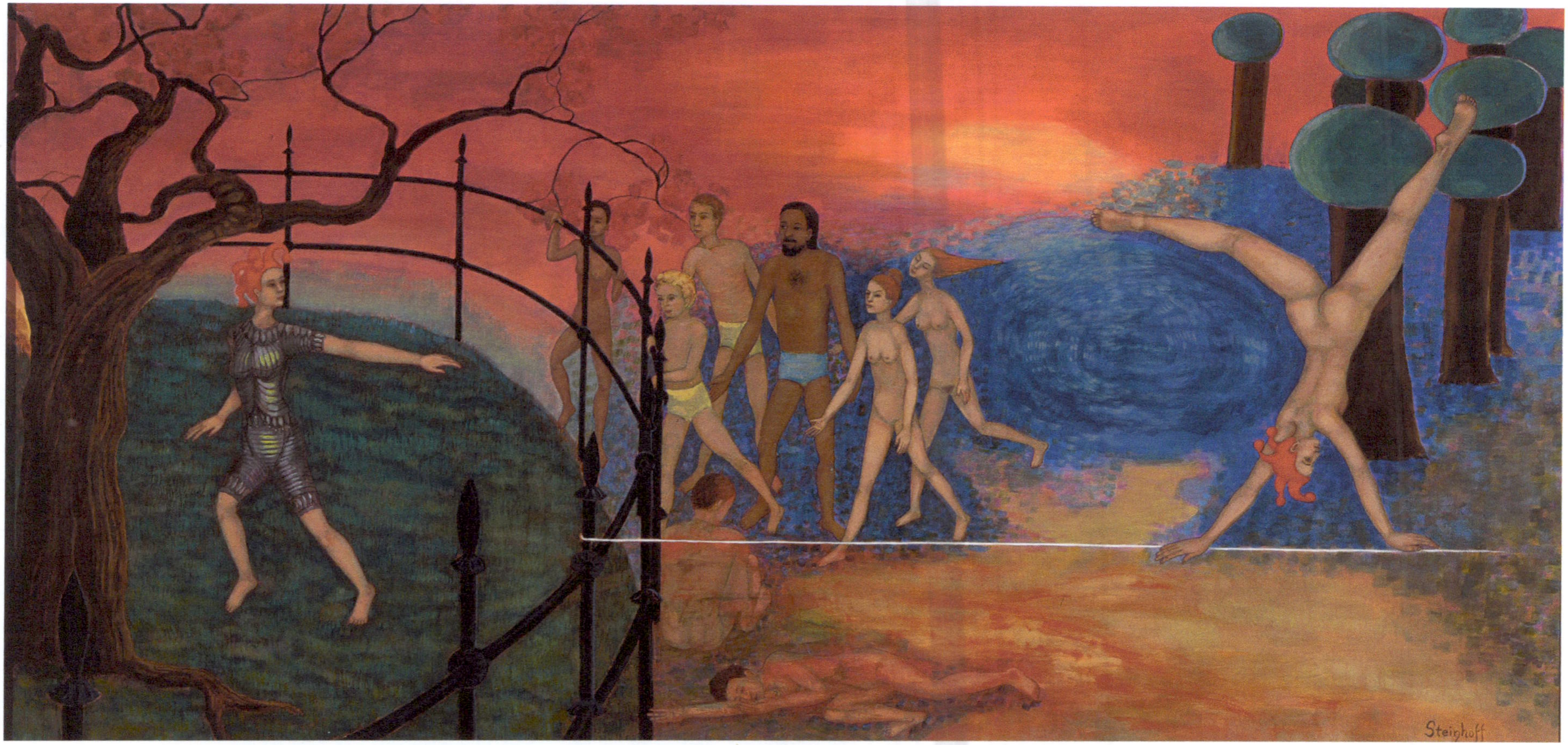

Berlin (after the wall came down)

ICONS

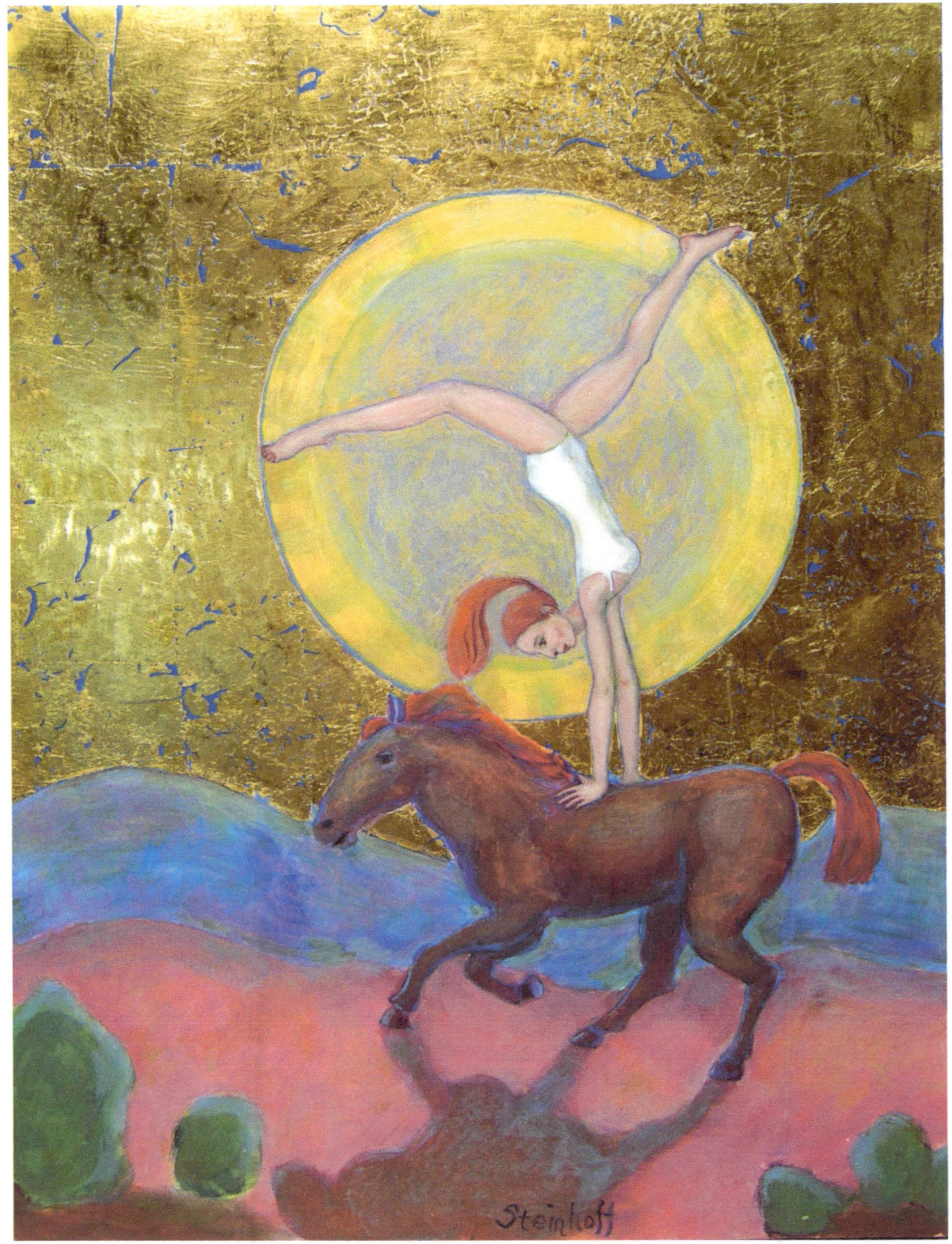

Icon: Acrobat

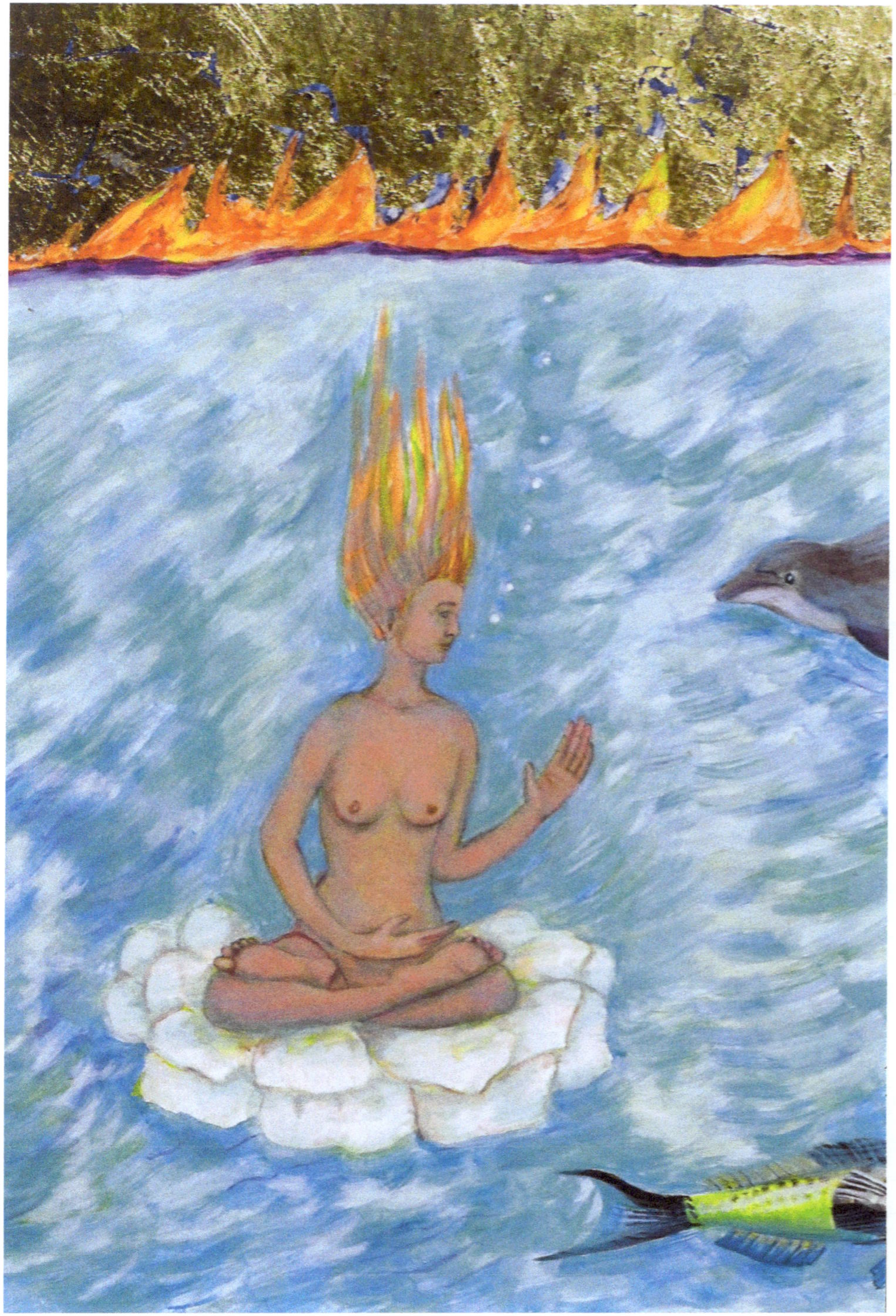

Icon: Fire Over Water

Icon: Dolphins

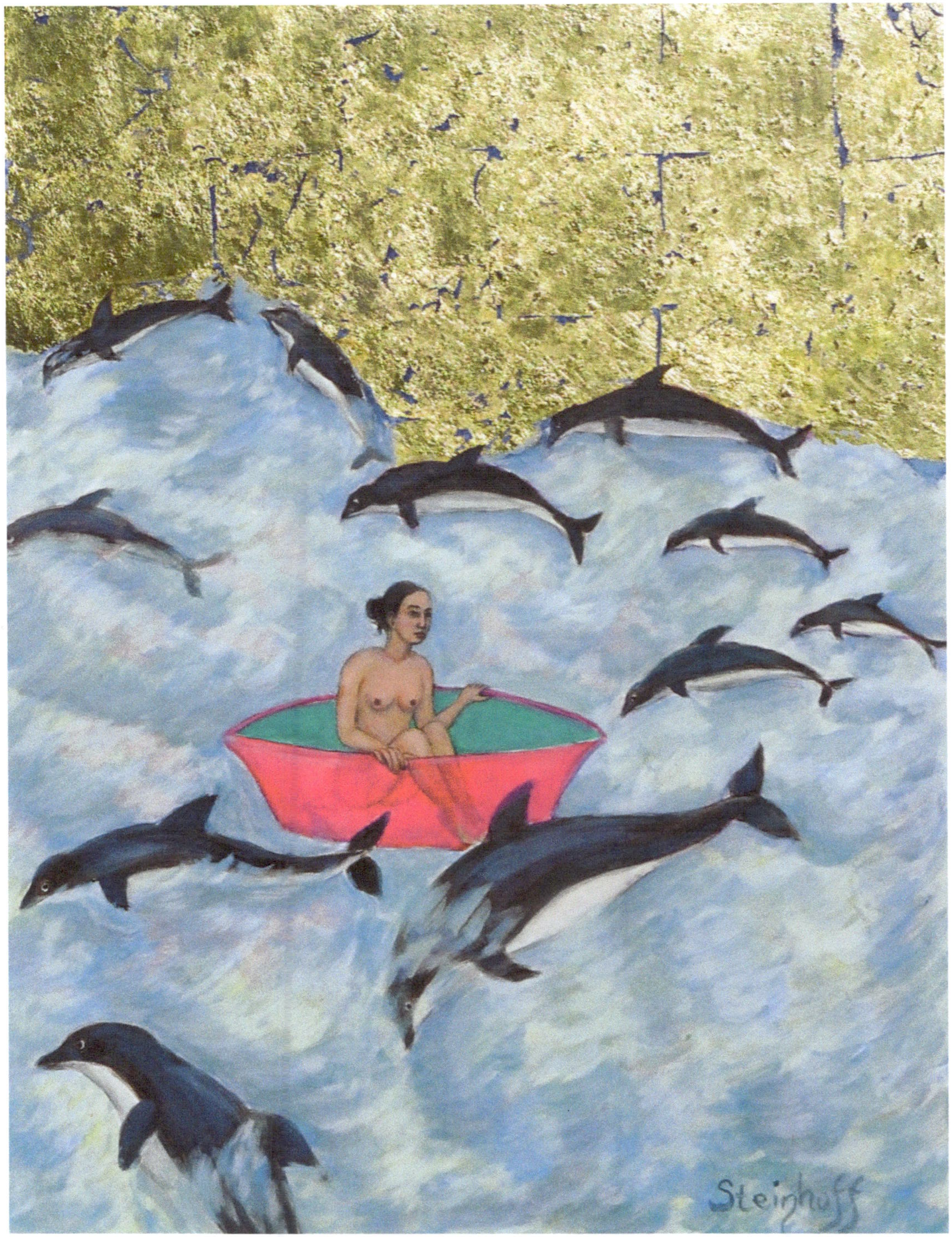

Icon: Go For It

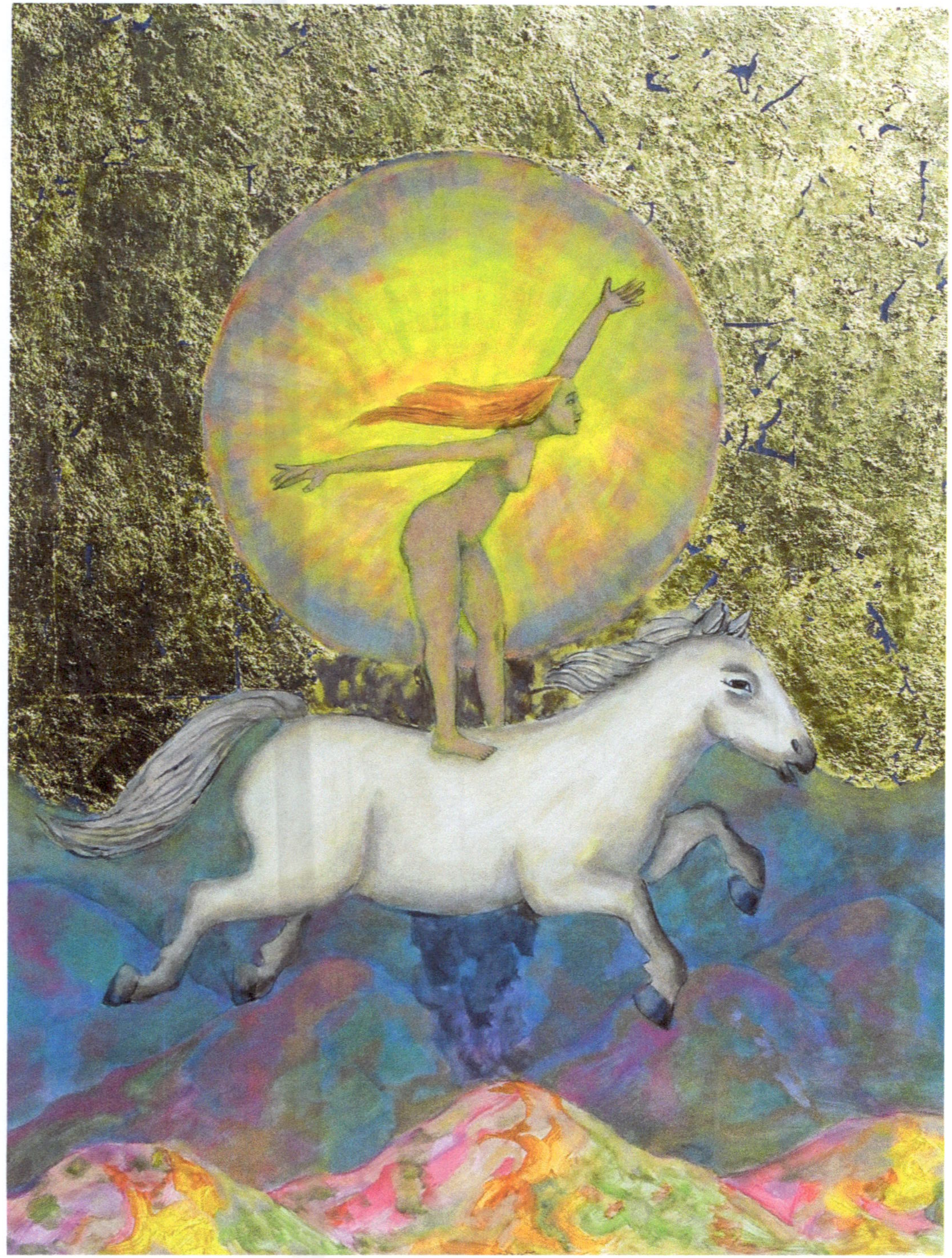

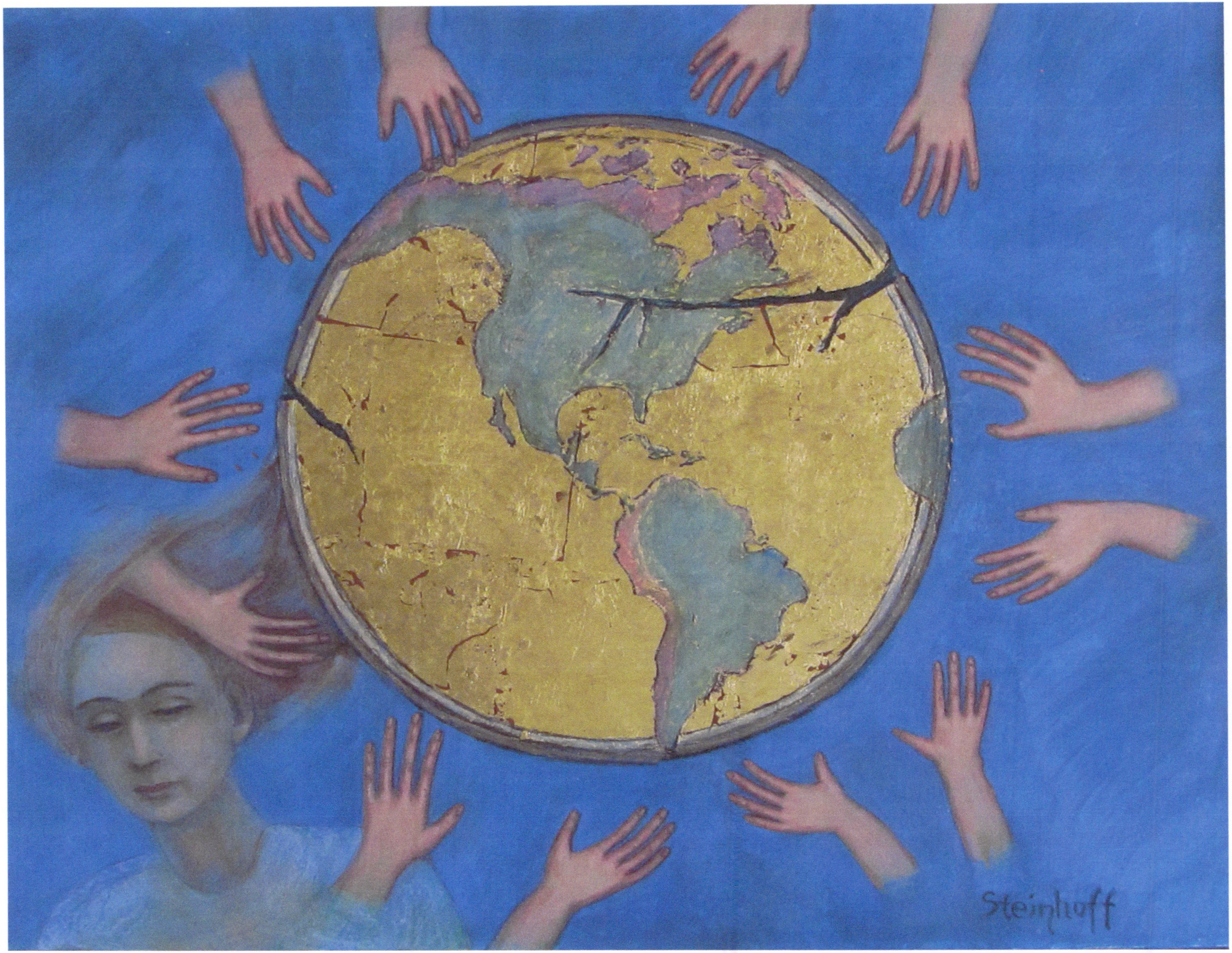

Icon: Hands Around the Earth

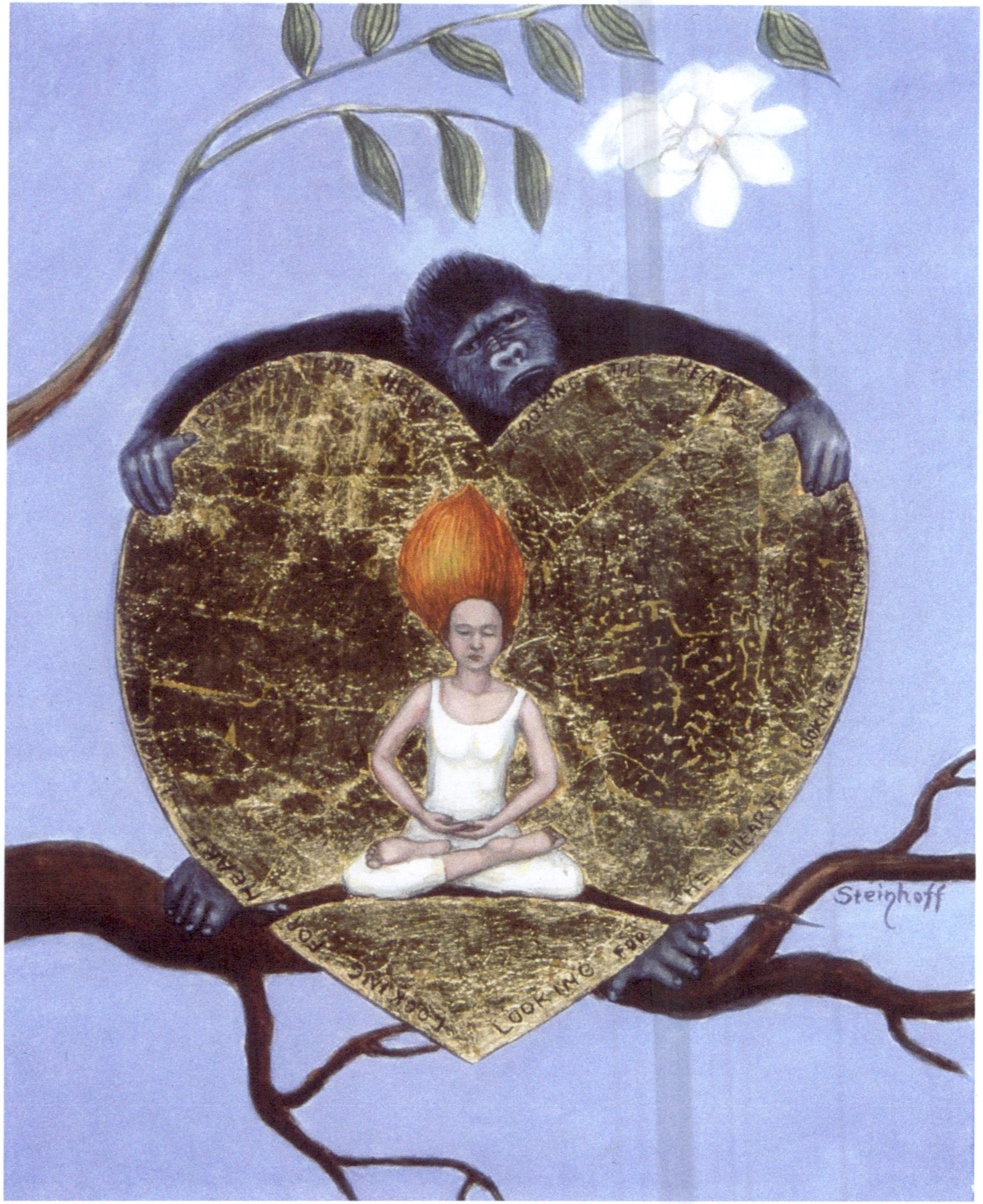

Icon: Holding the Heart

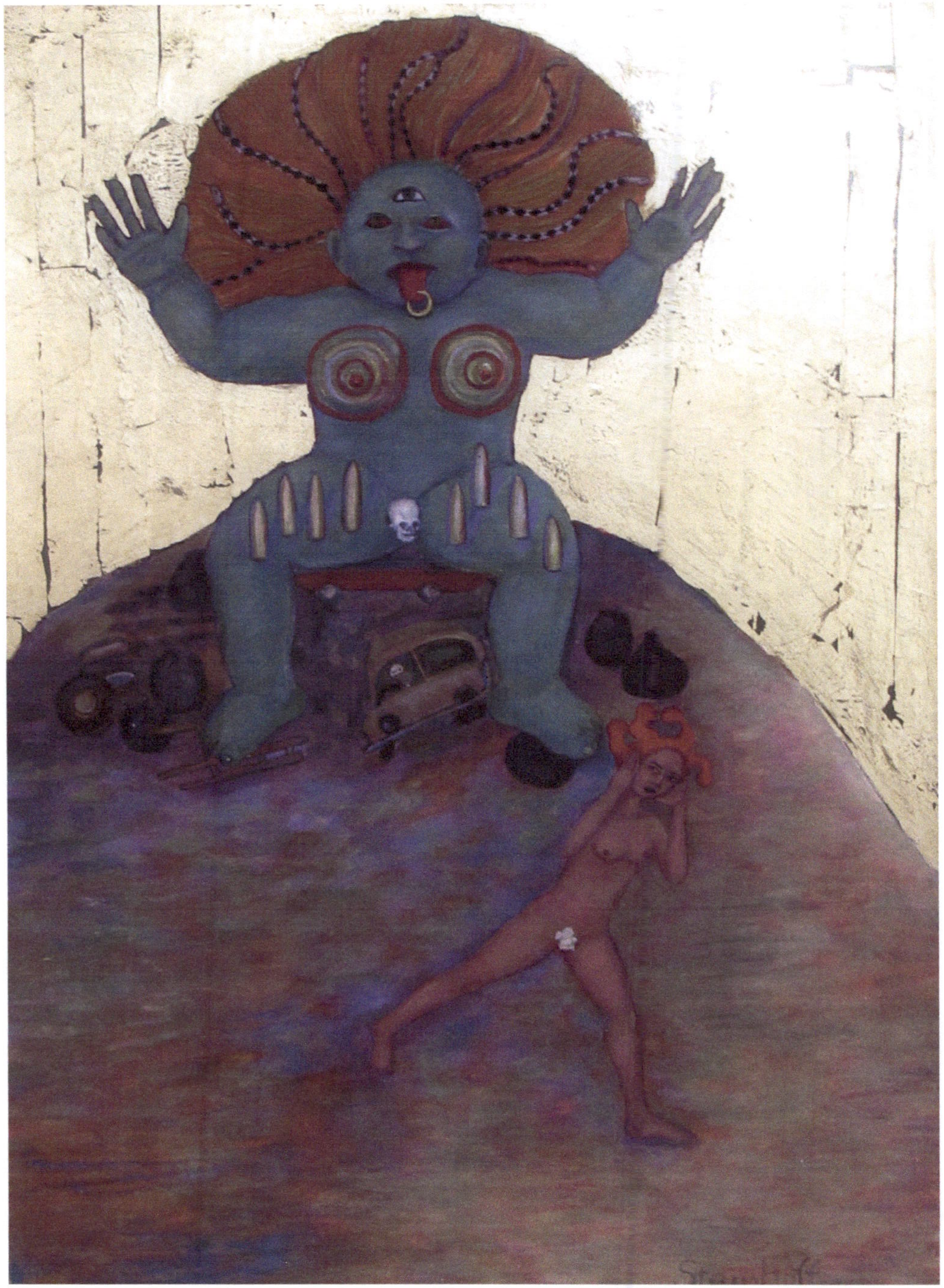

Icon: Kali

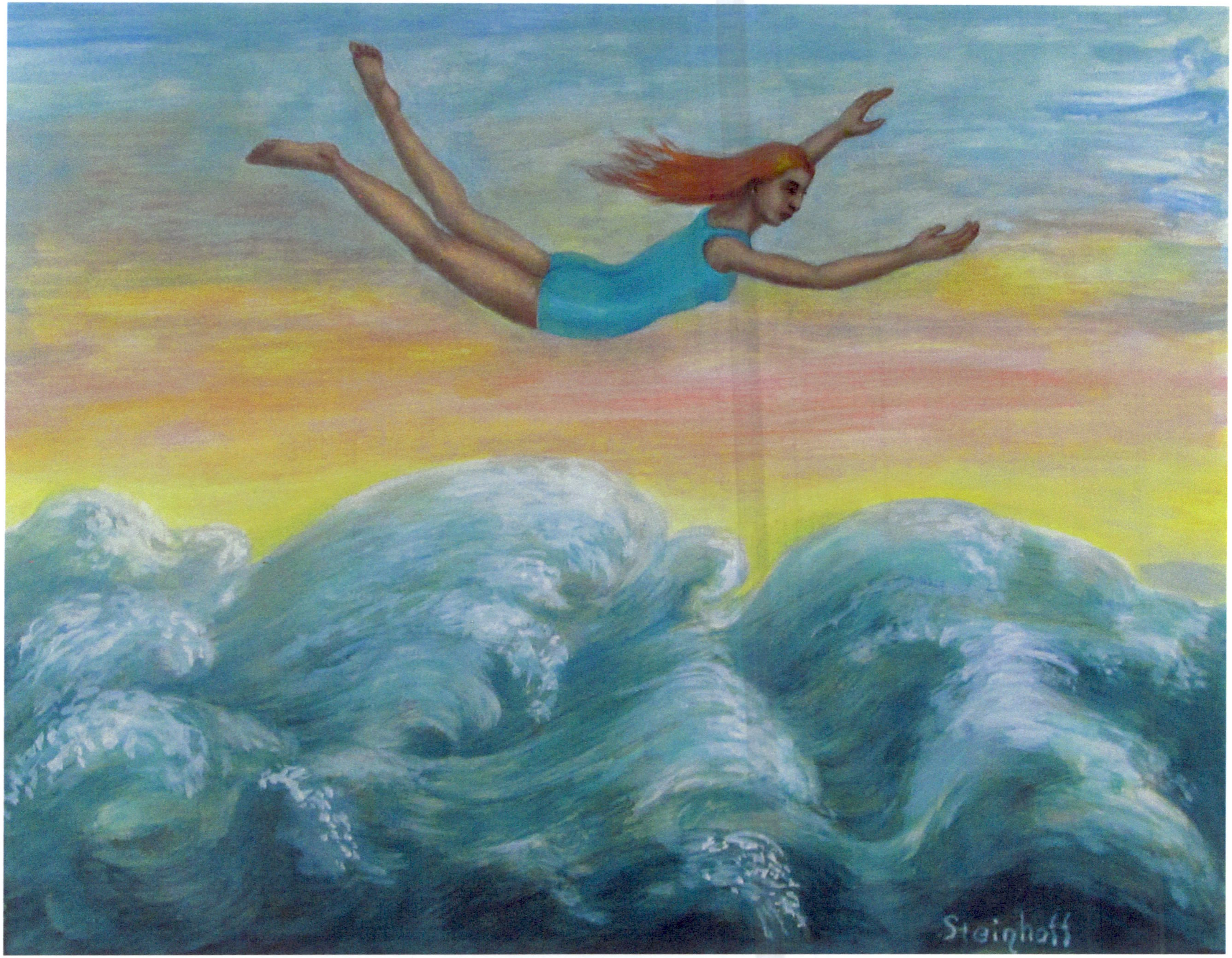

Mind over Matter

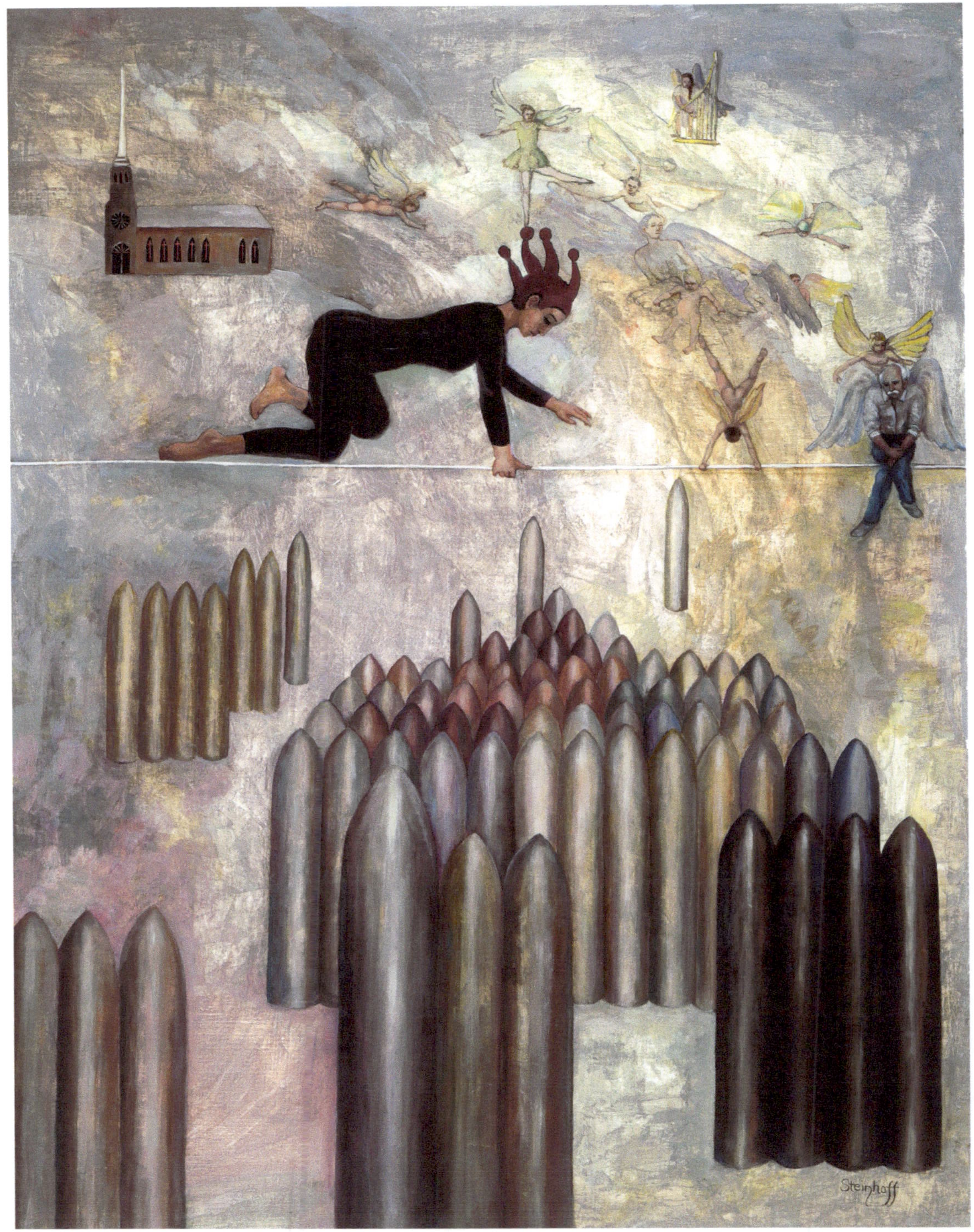

Missile Forest

Icon: Up from the Deep

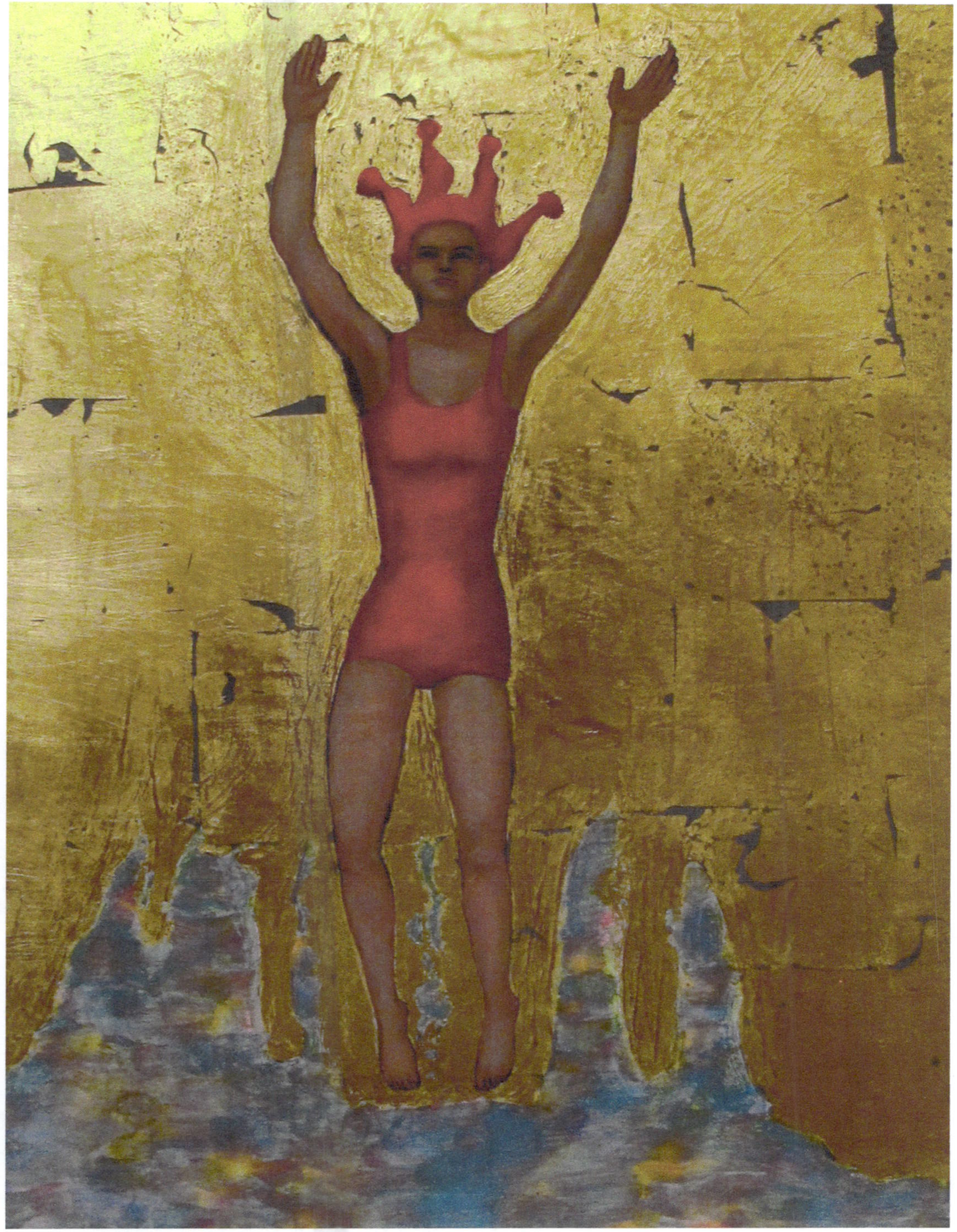

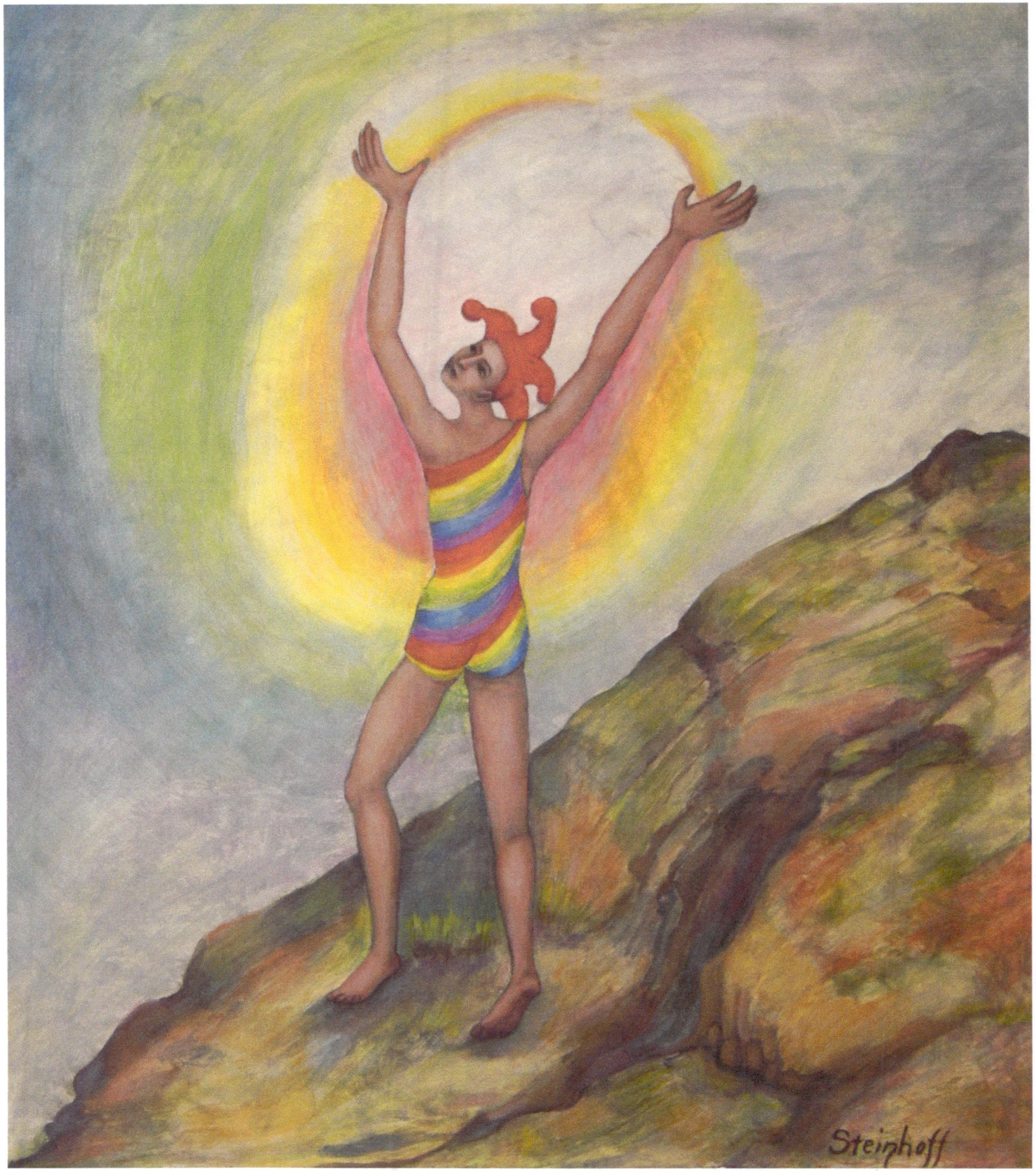

Icon: Rainbow I

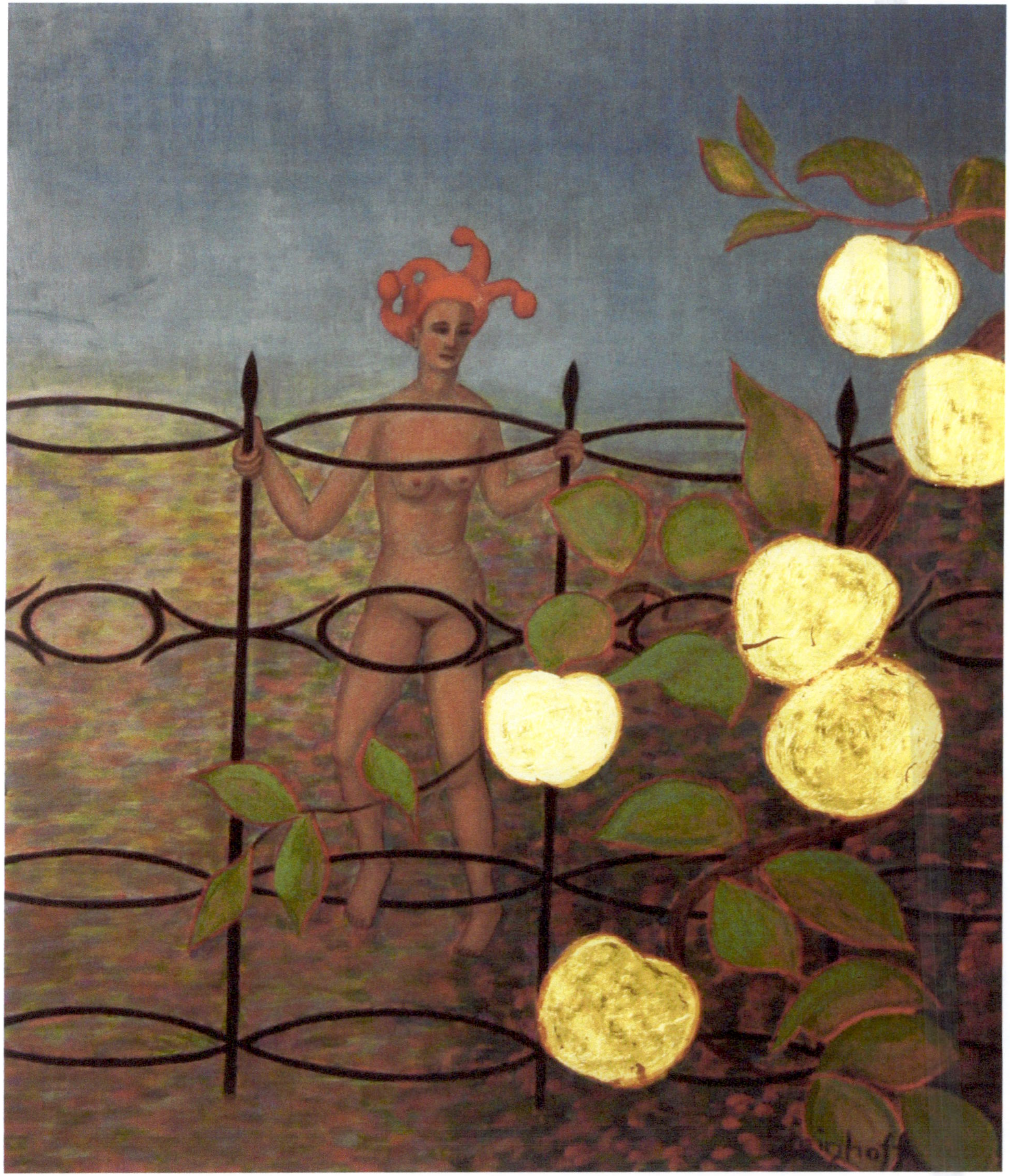

Forbidden Fruit

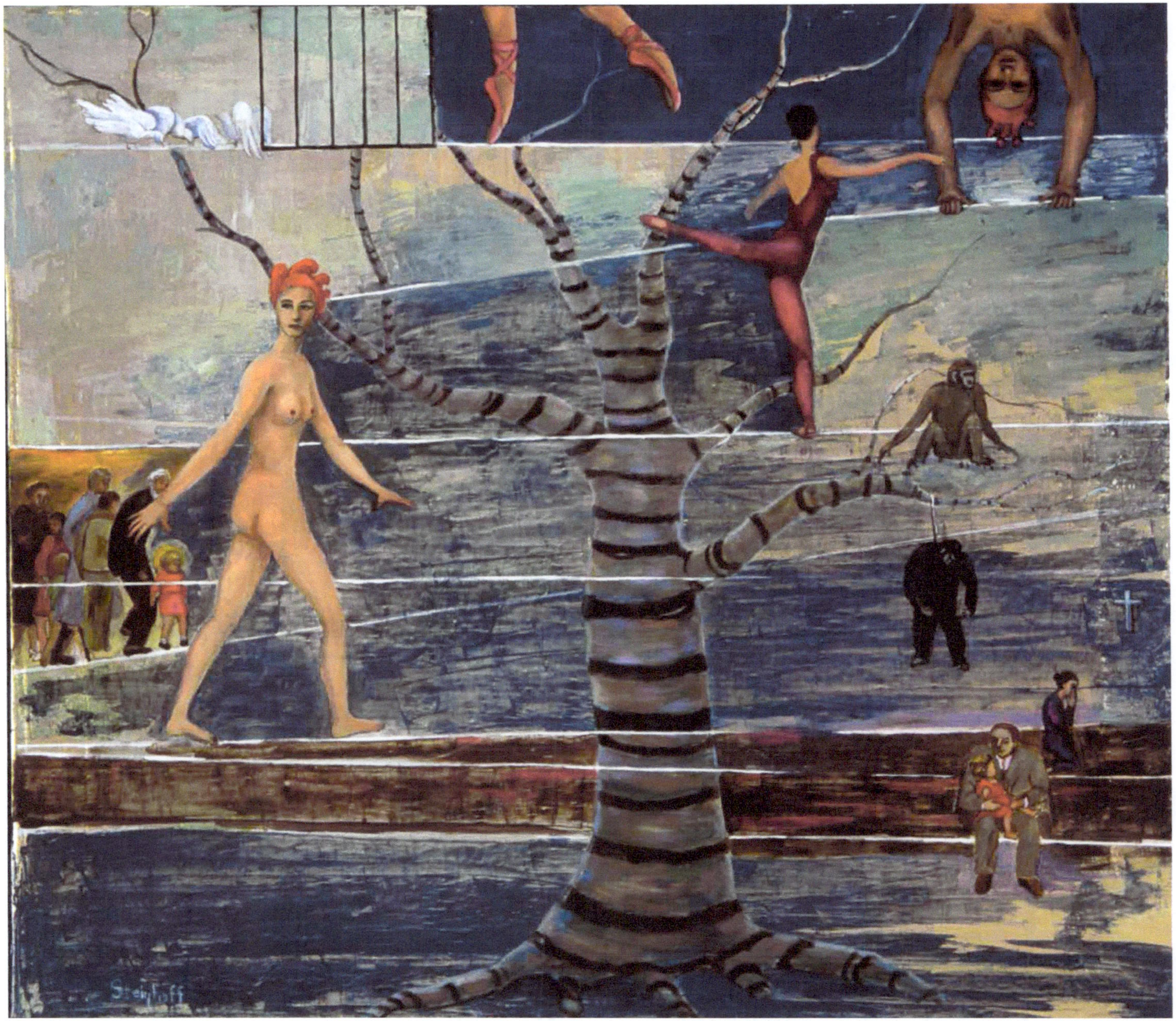

Sins of the Fathers

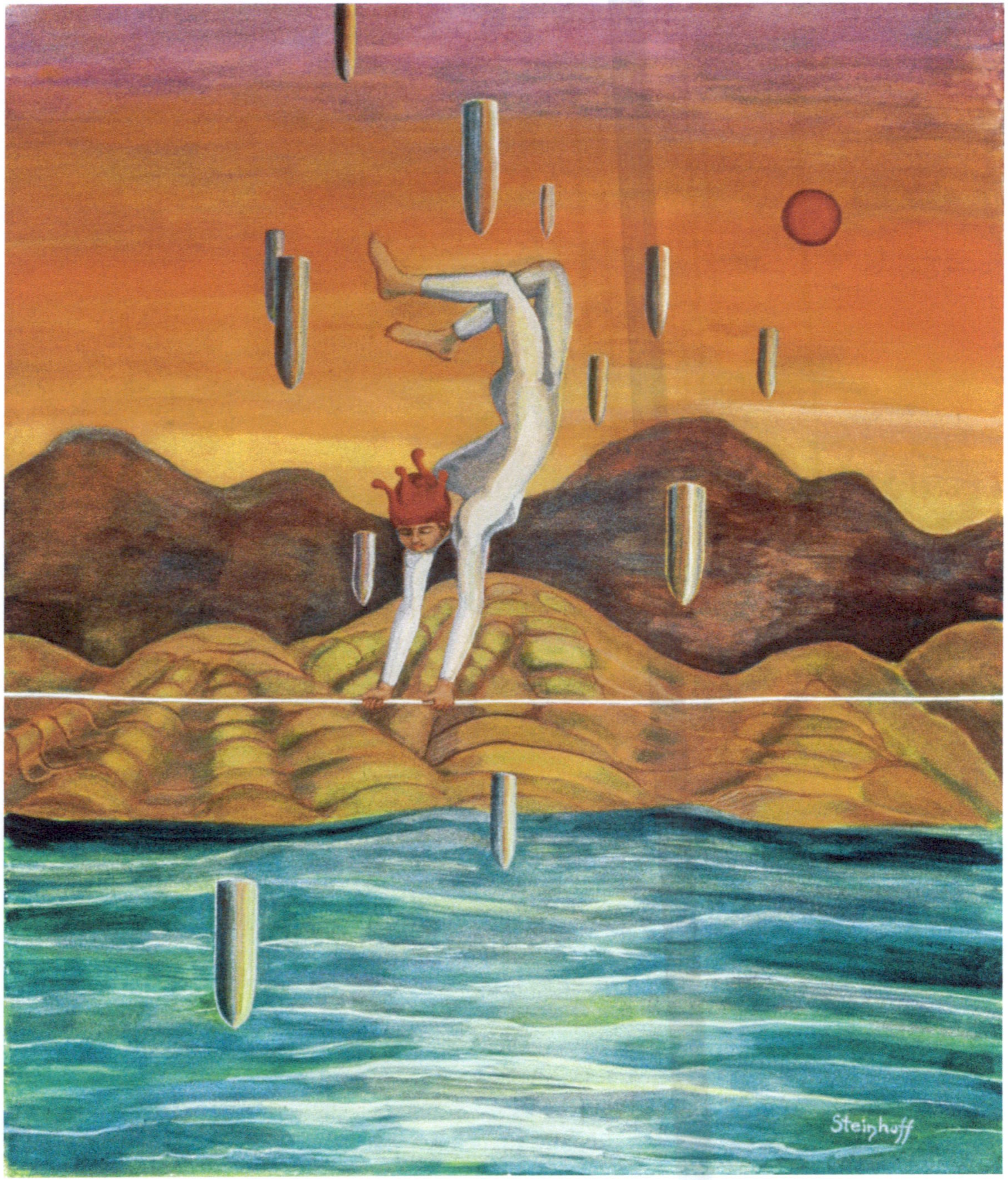

Losing the Balance

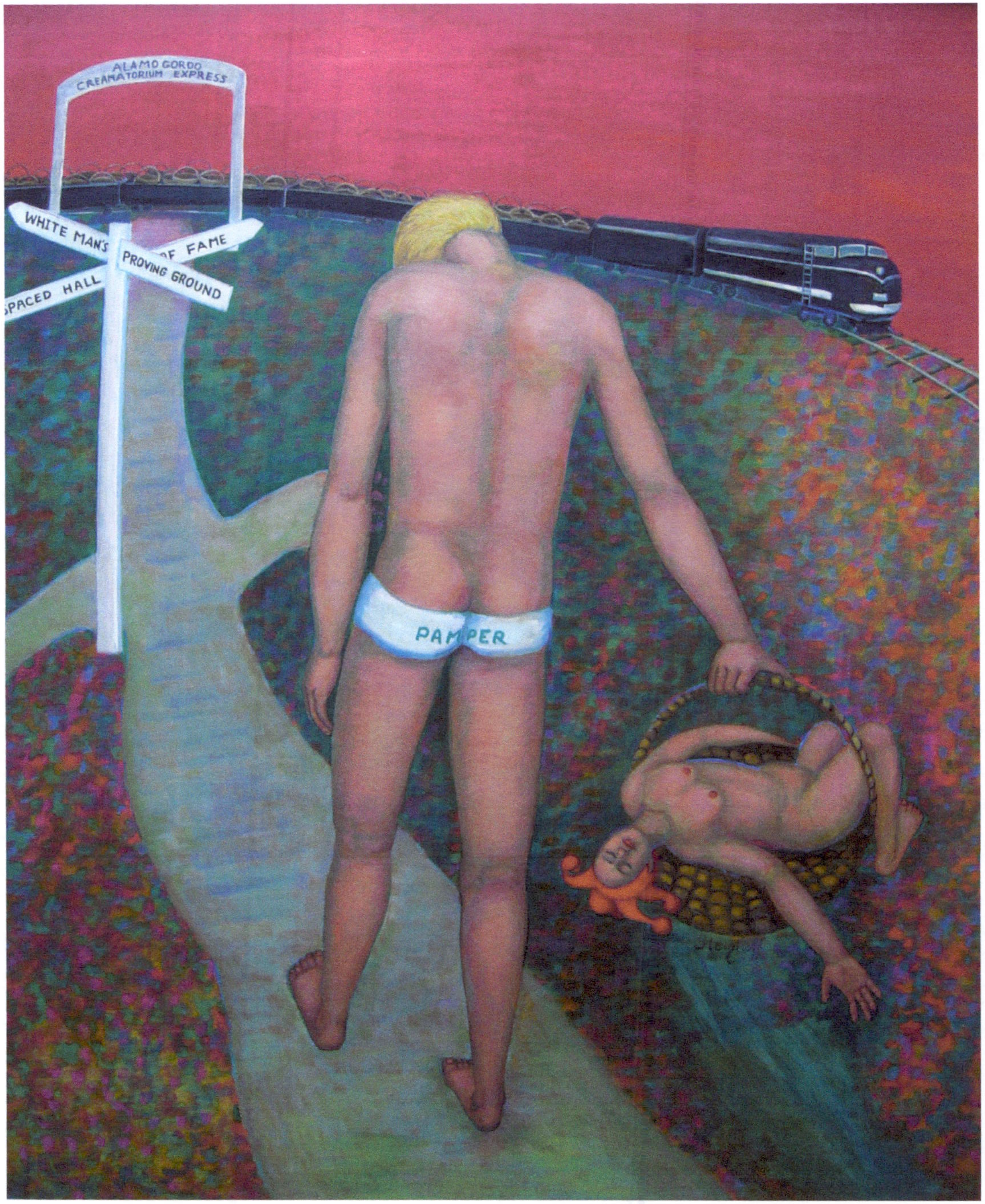

Case of the Basket Case

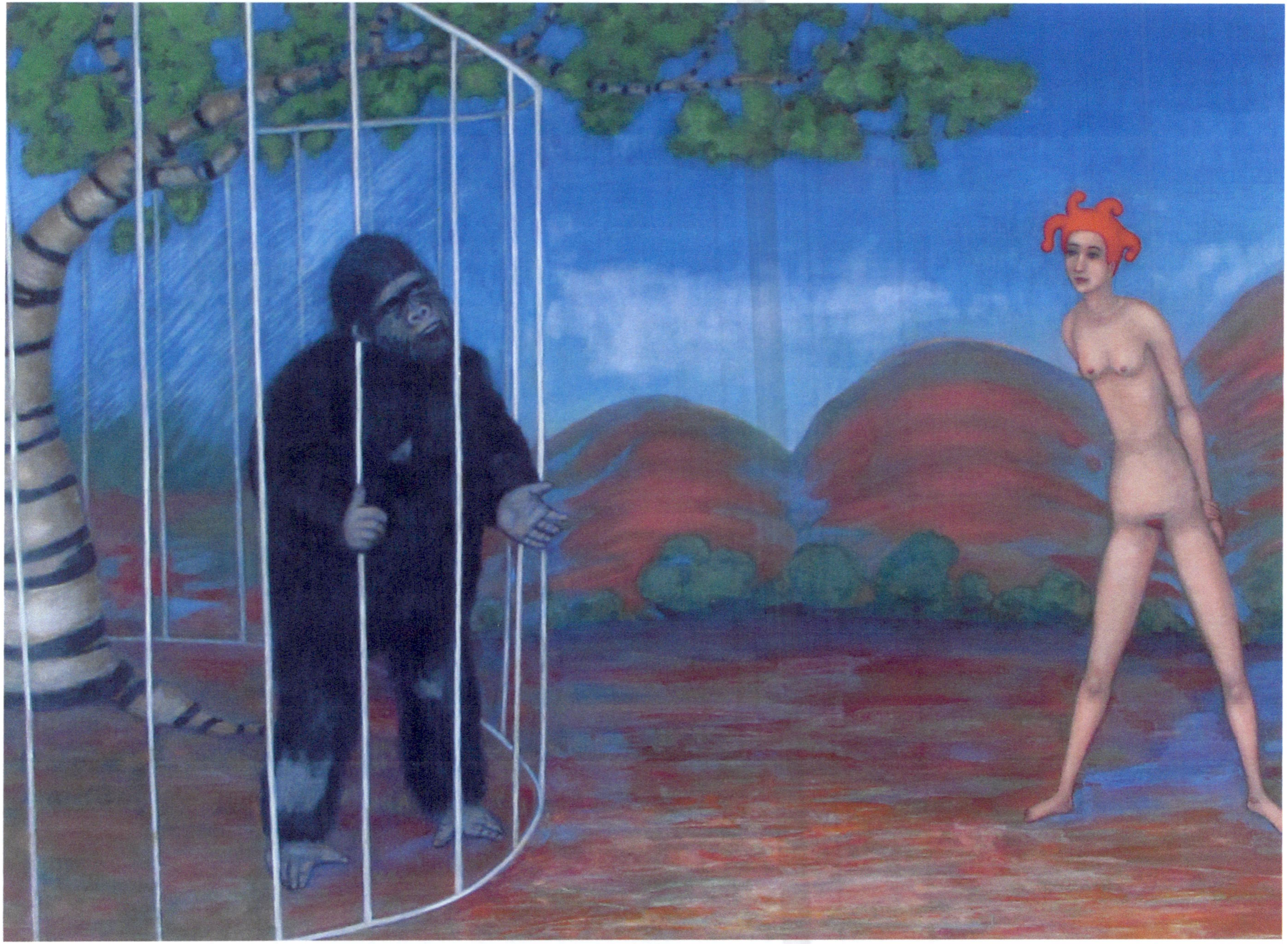

Beast Within

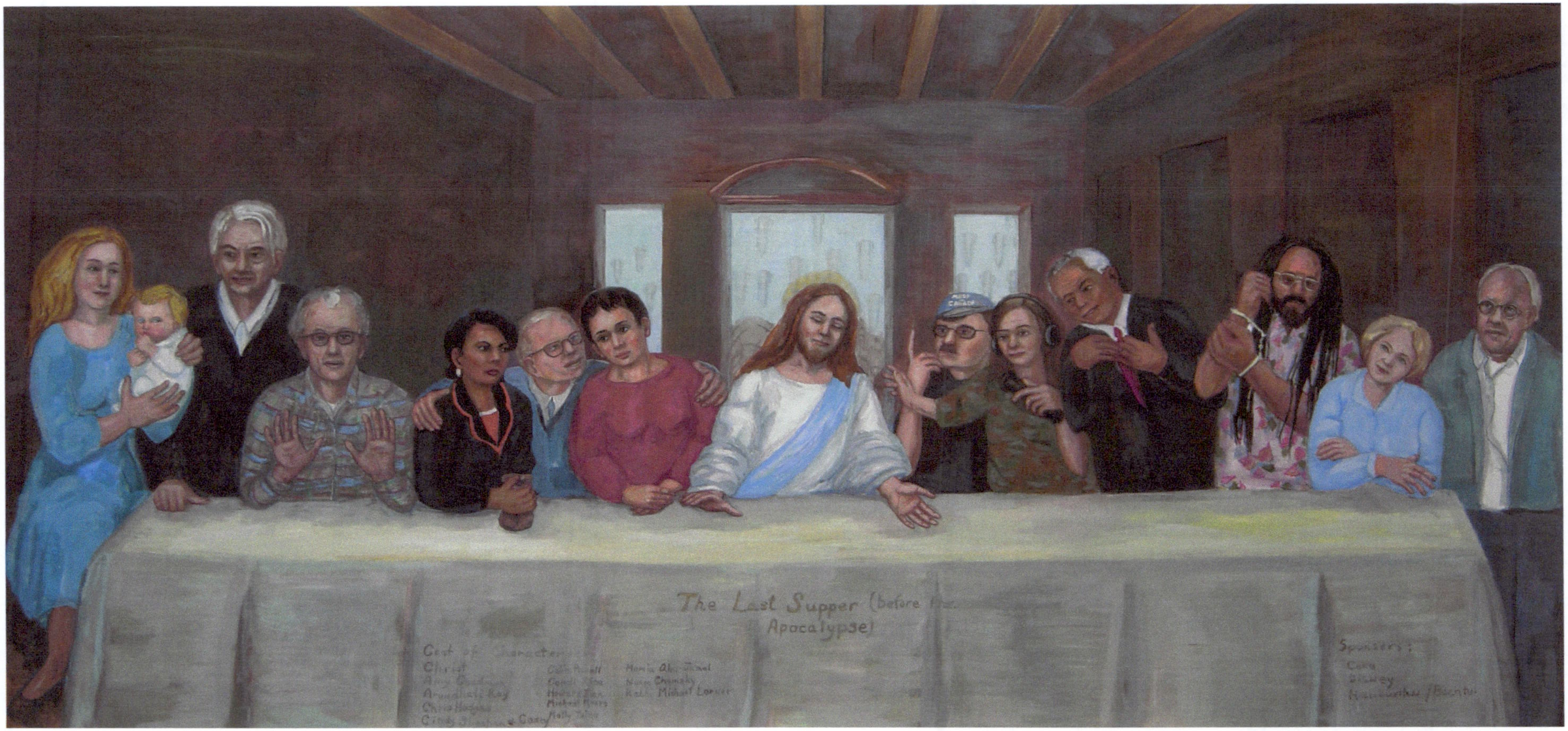

Contemporary Last Supper

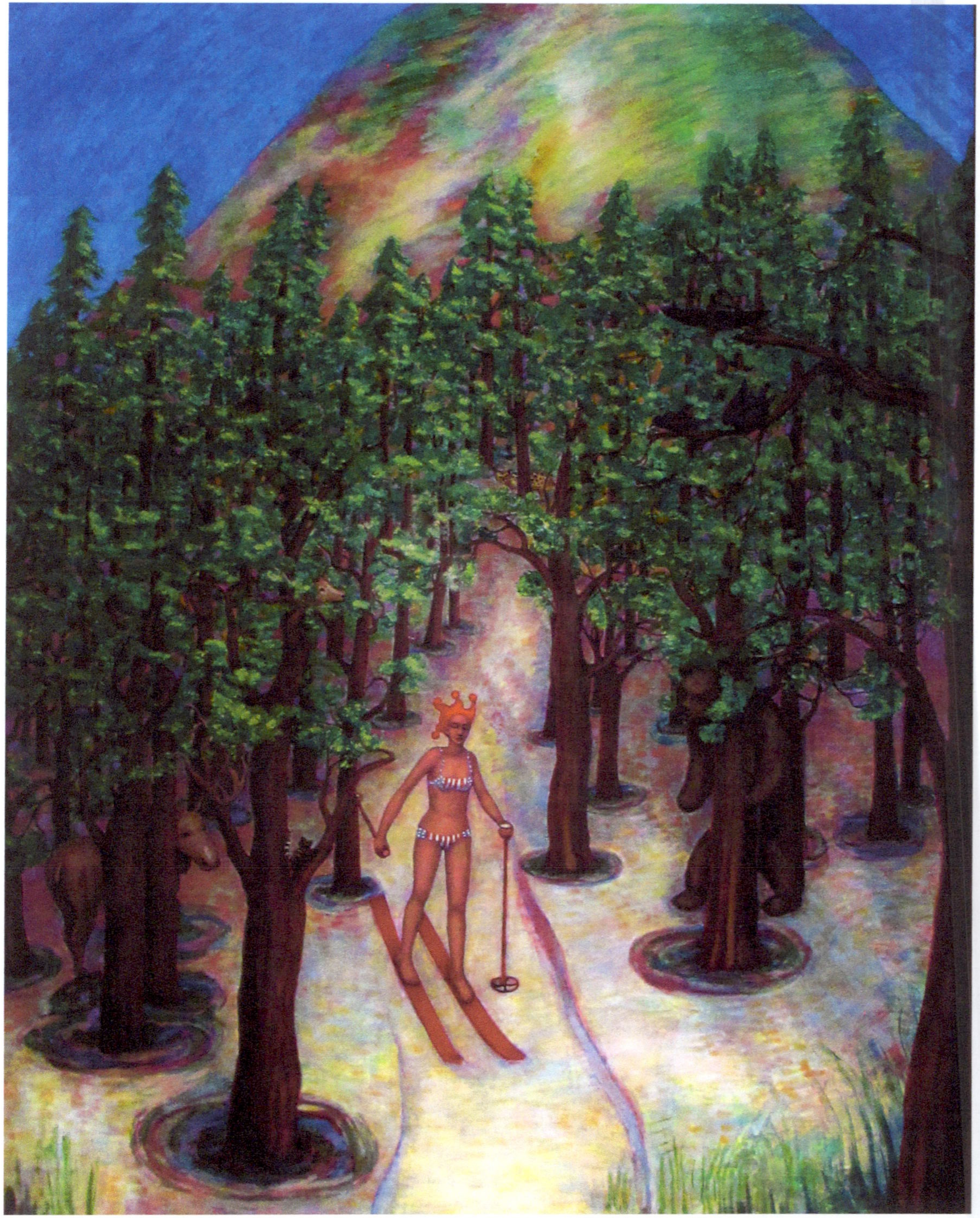

Forest Primeval Early Meltdown

Cage of my Heart

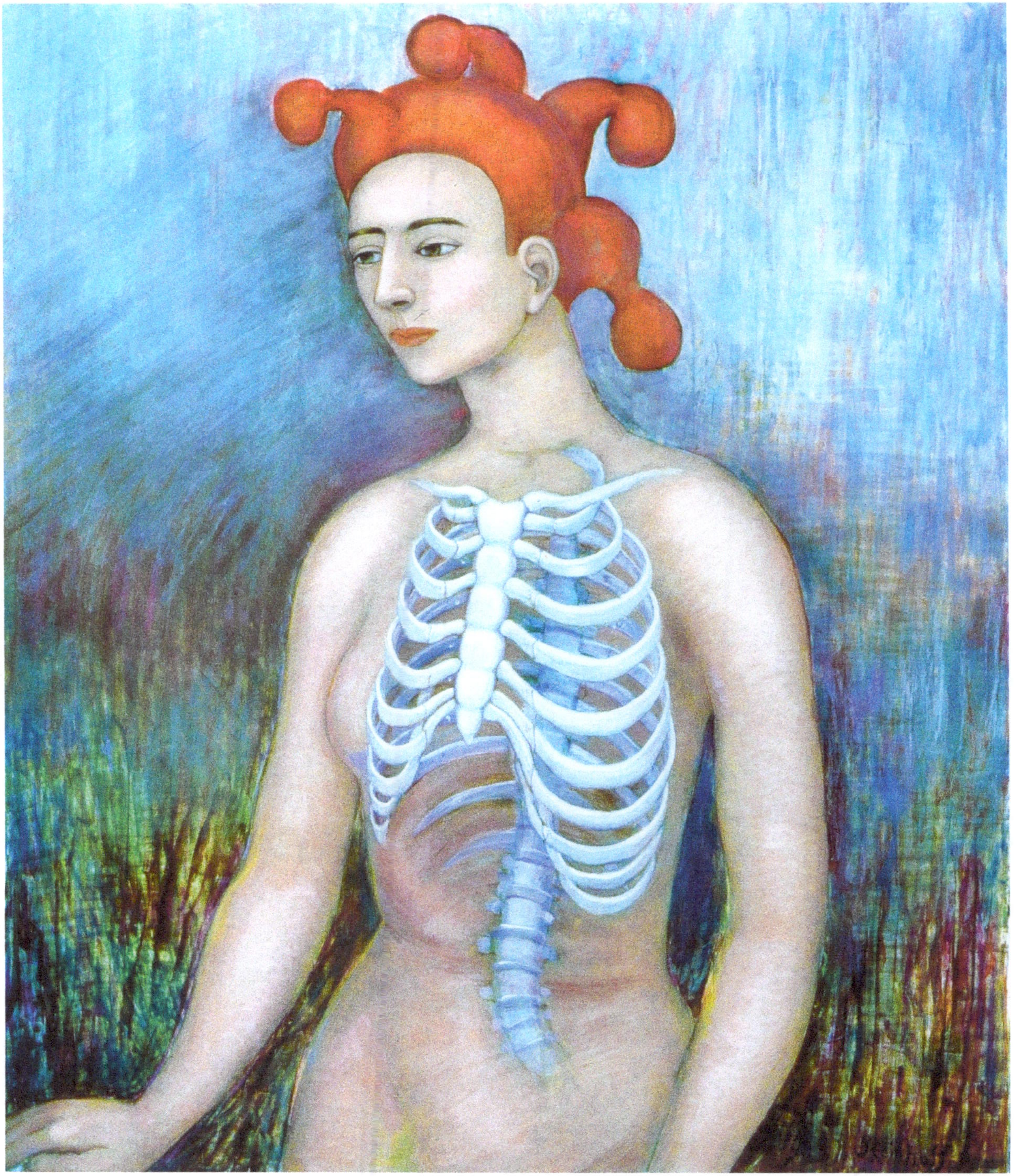

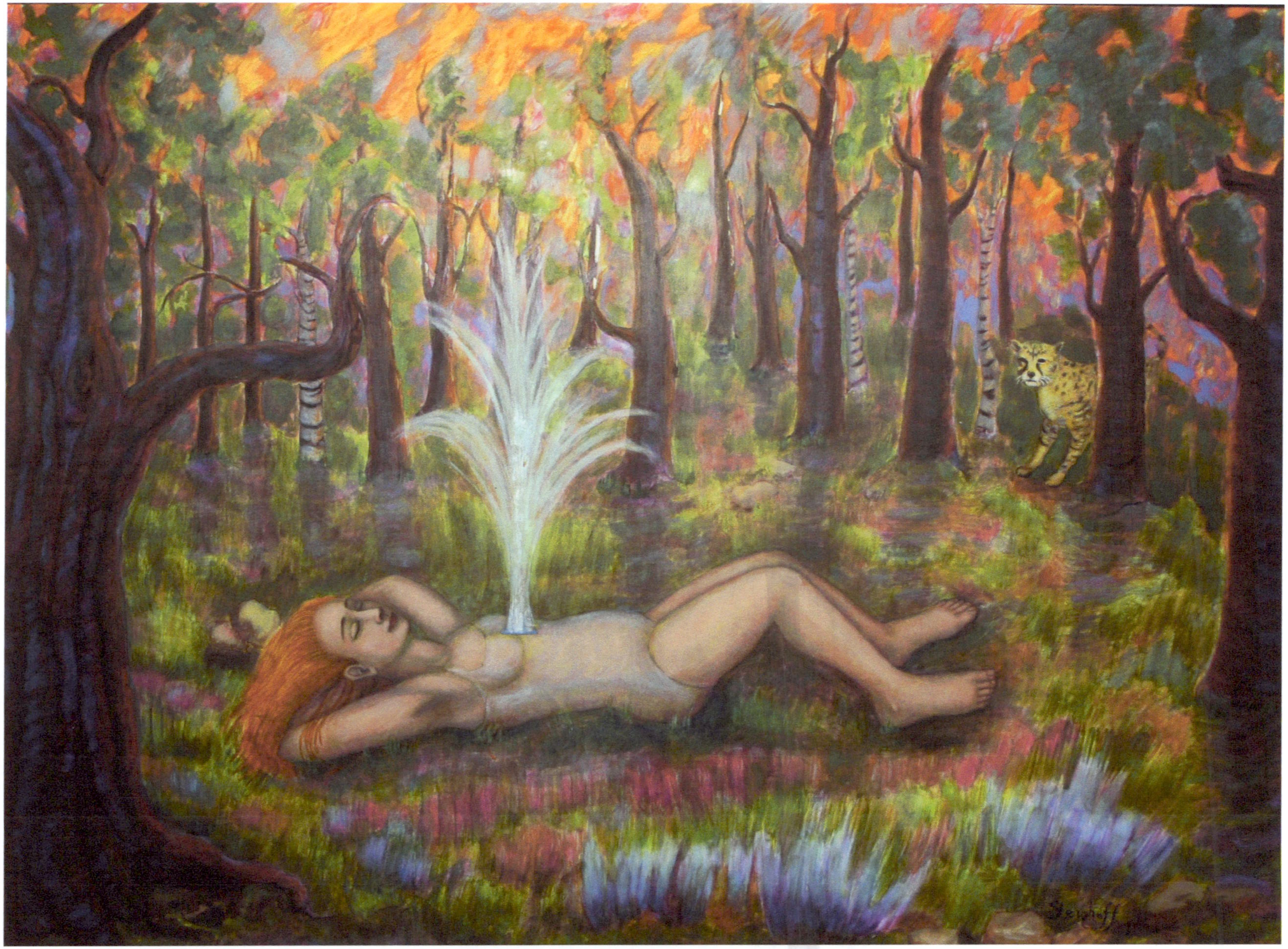

Millennium II Healing the Earth

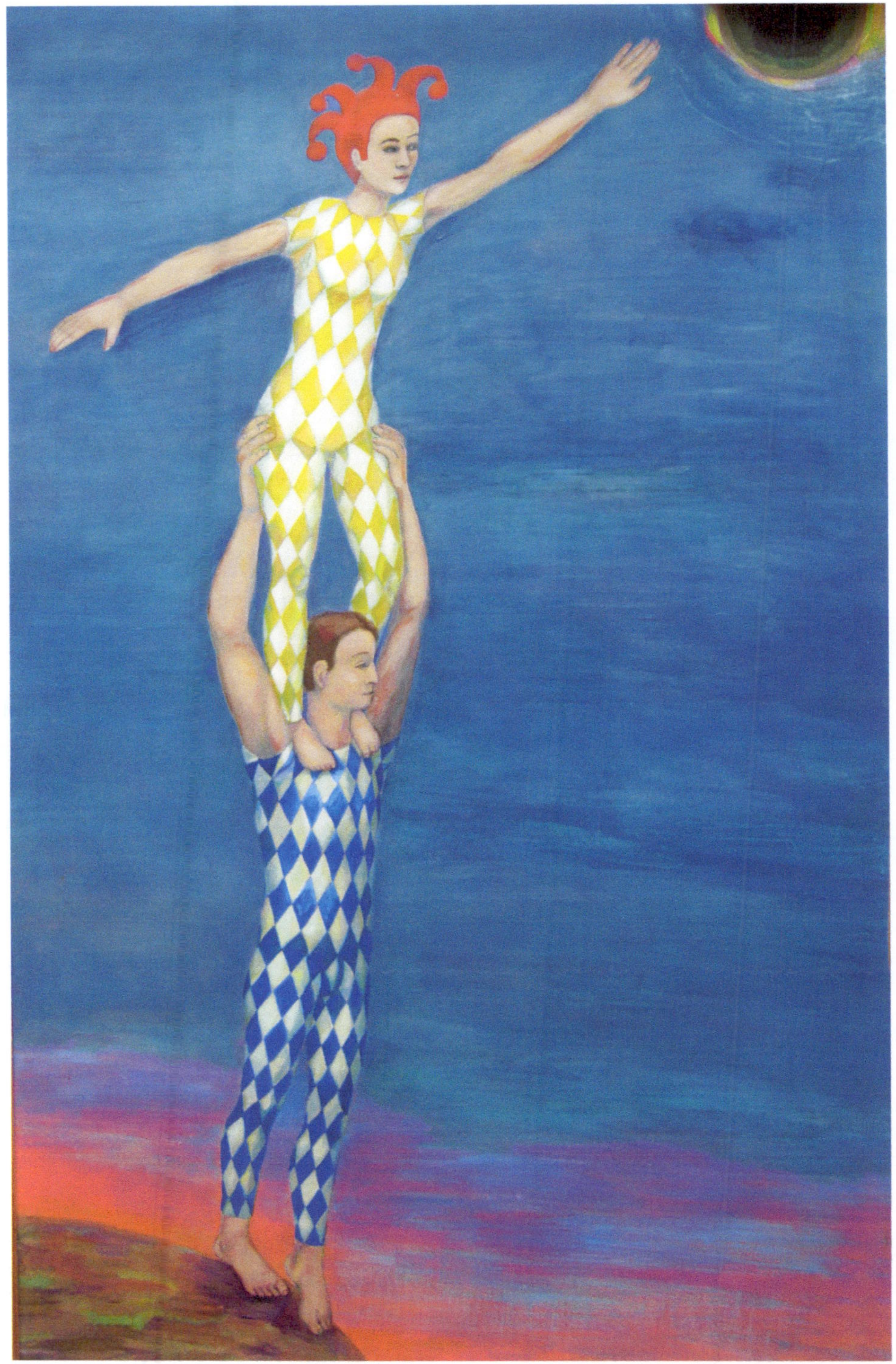

Hole in Sky

Gates of Wisdom

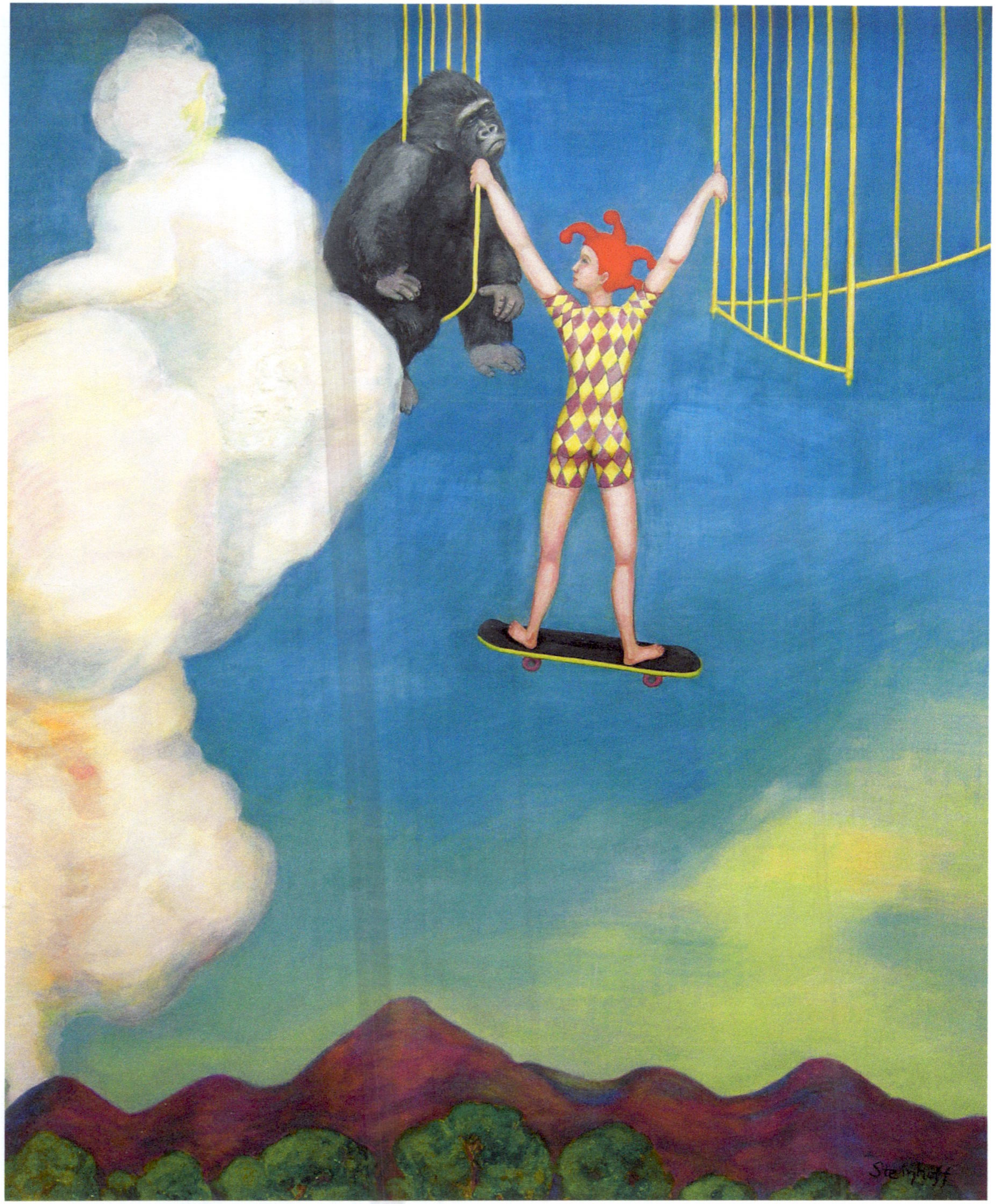

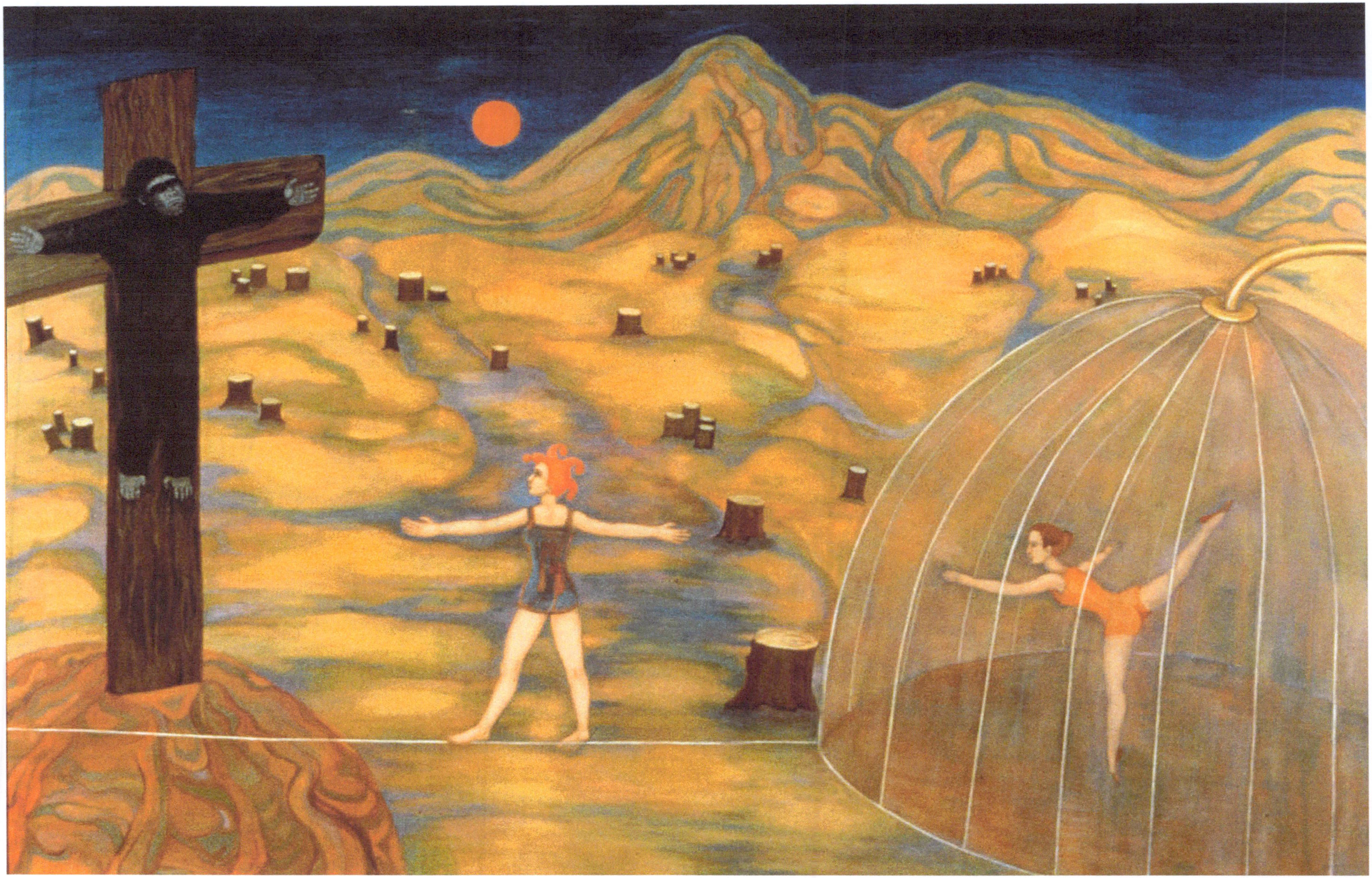

"...and God gave Dominior."

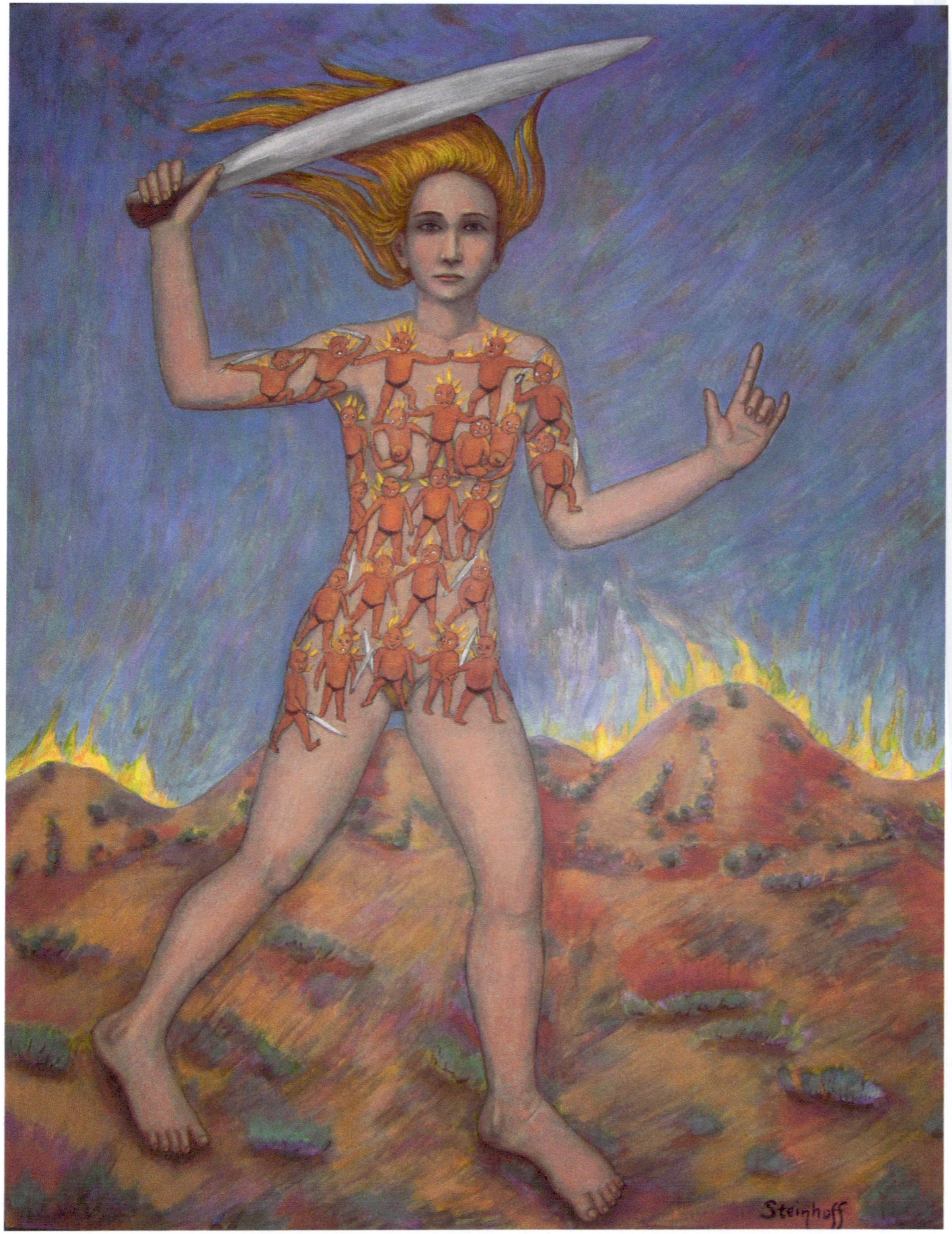

Warrior II

Dance Beneath the Diamond Sky

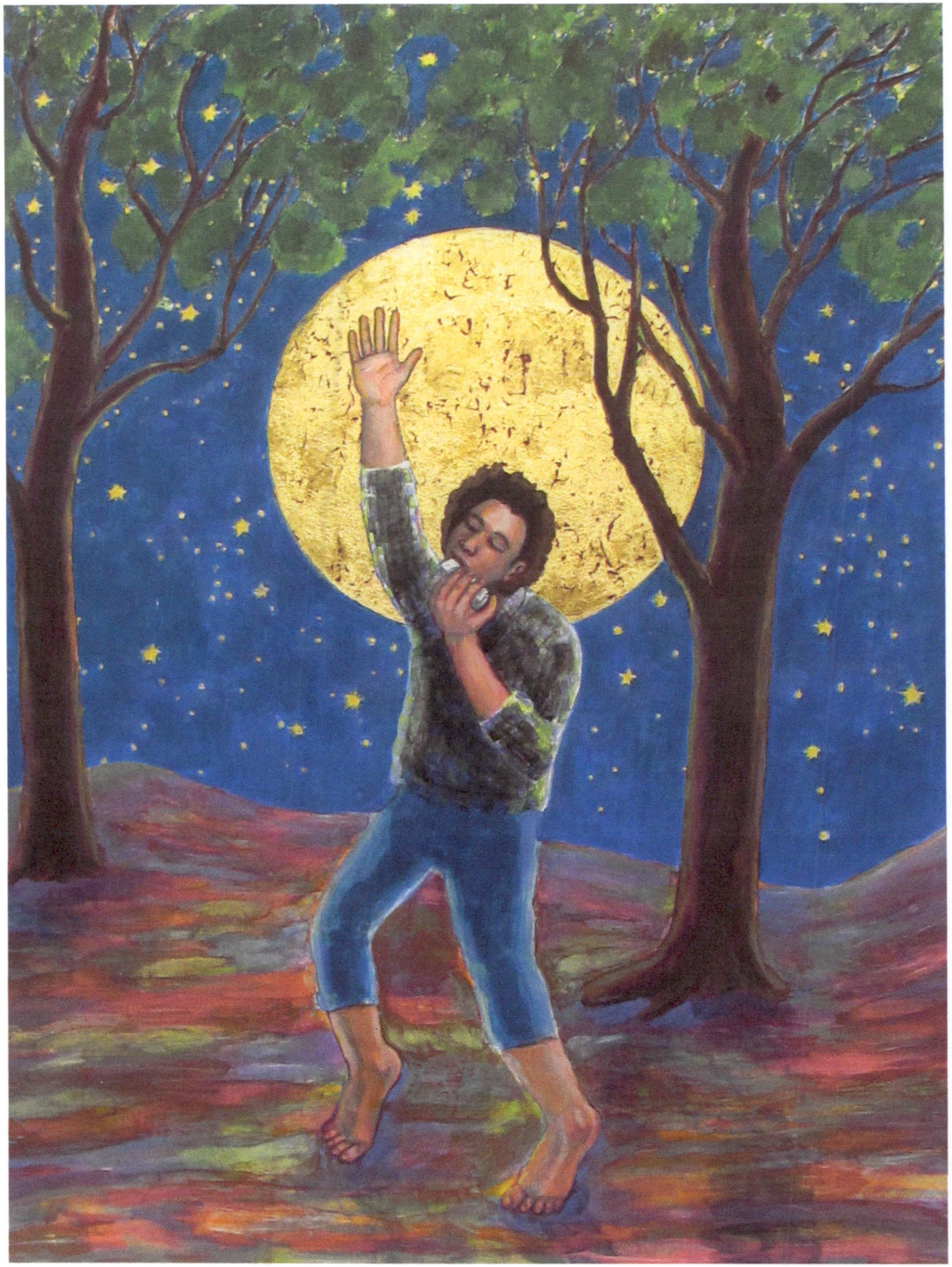

Healing the Earth

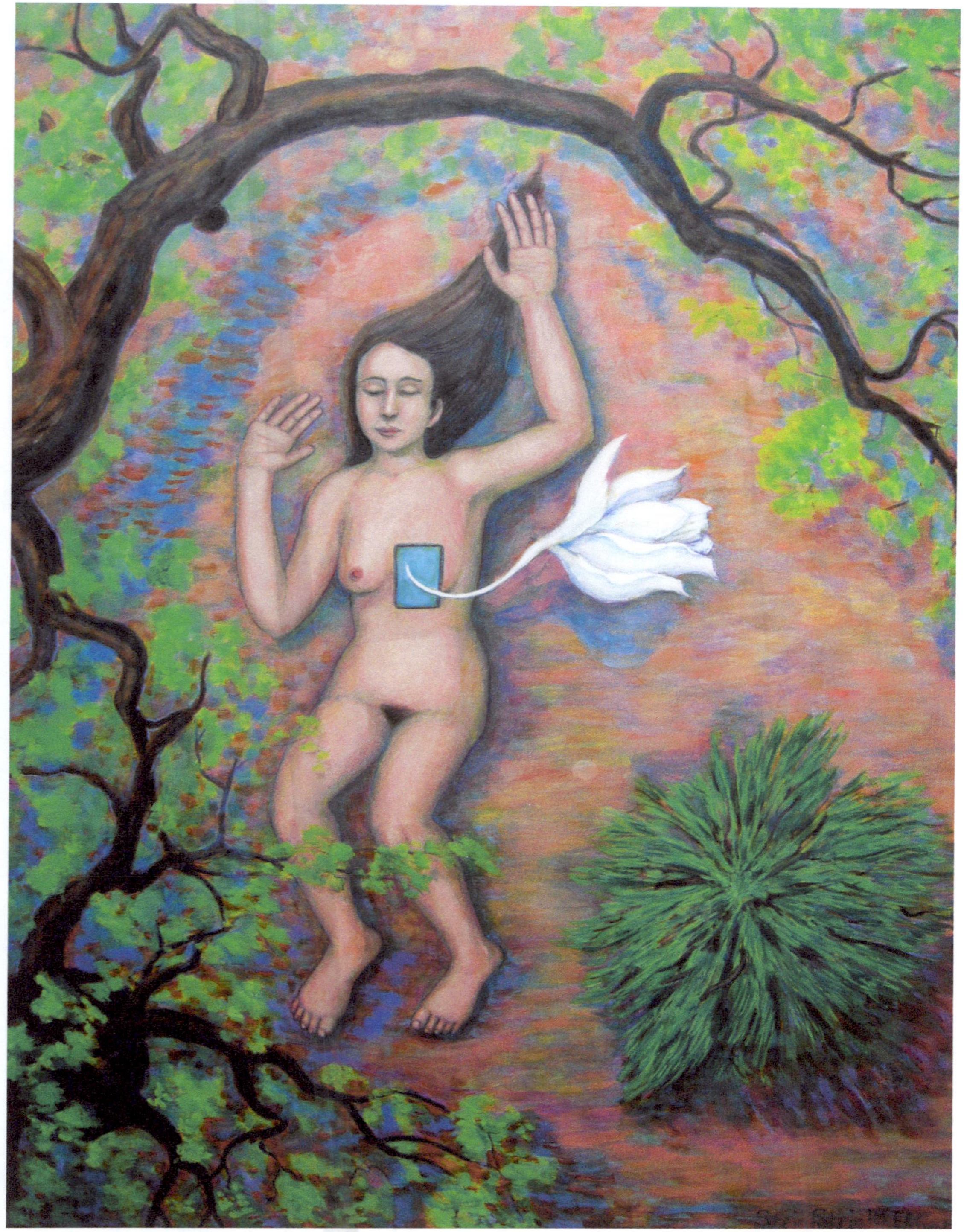

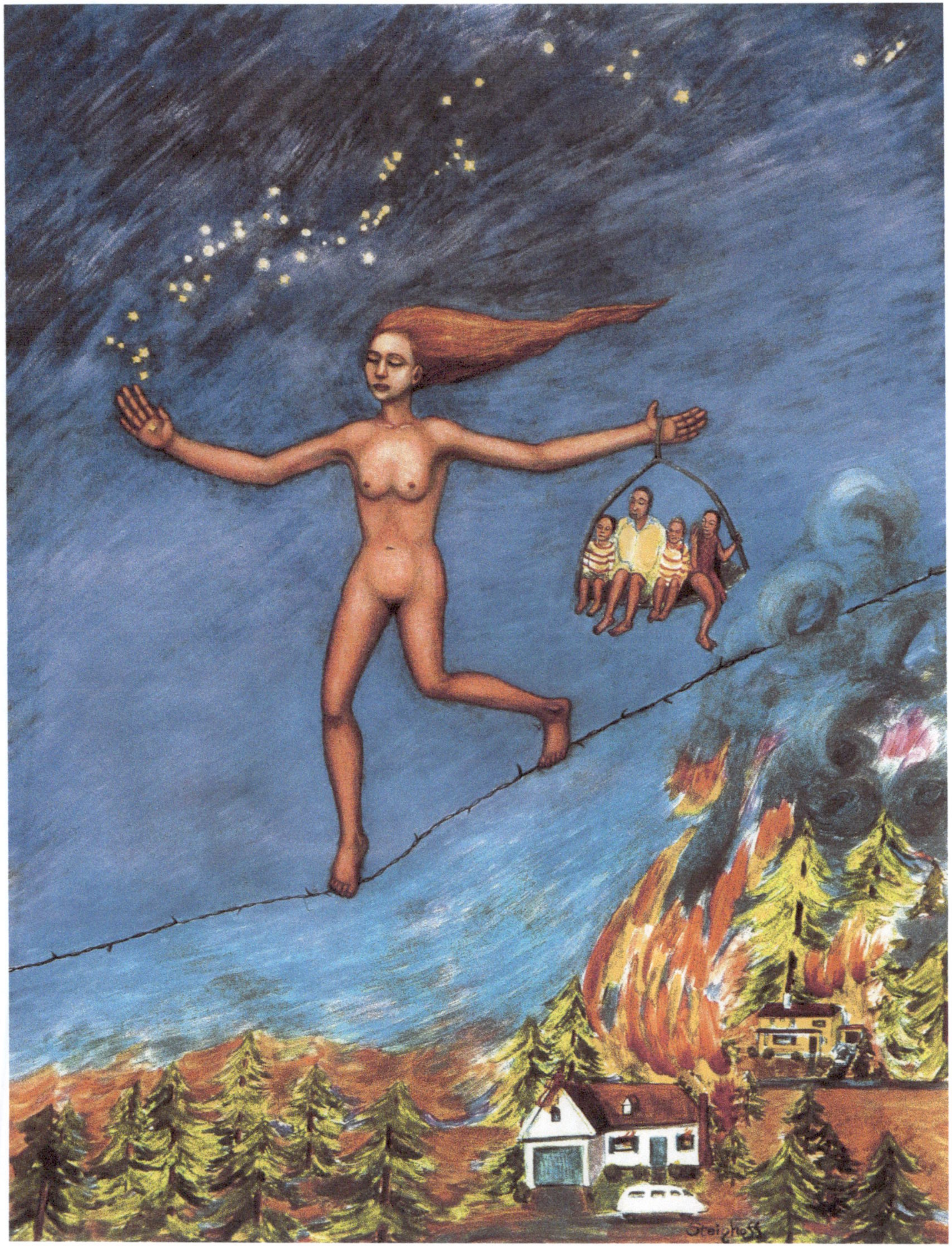

Fire

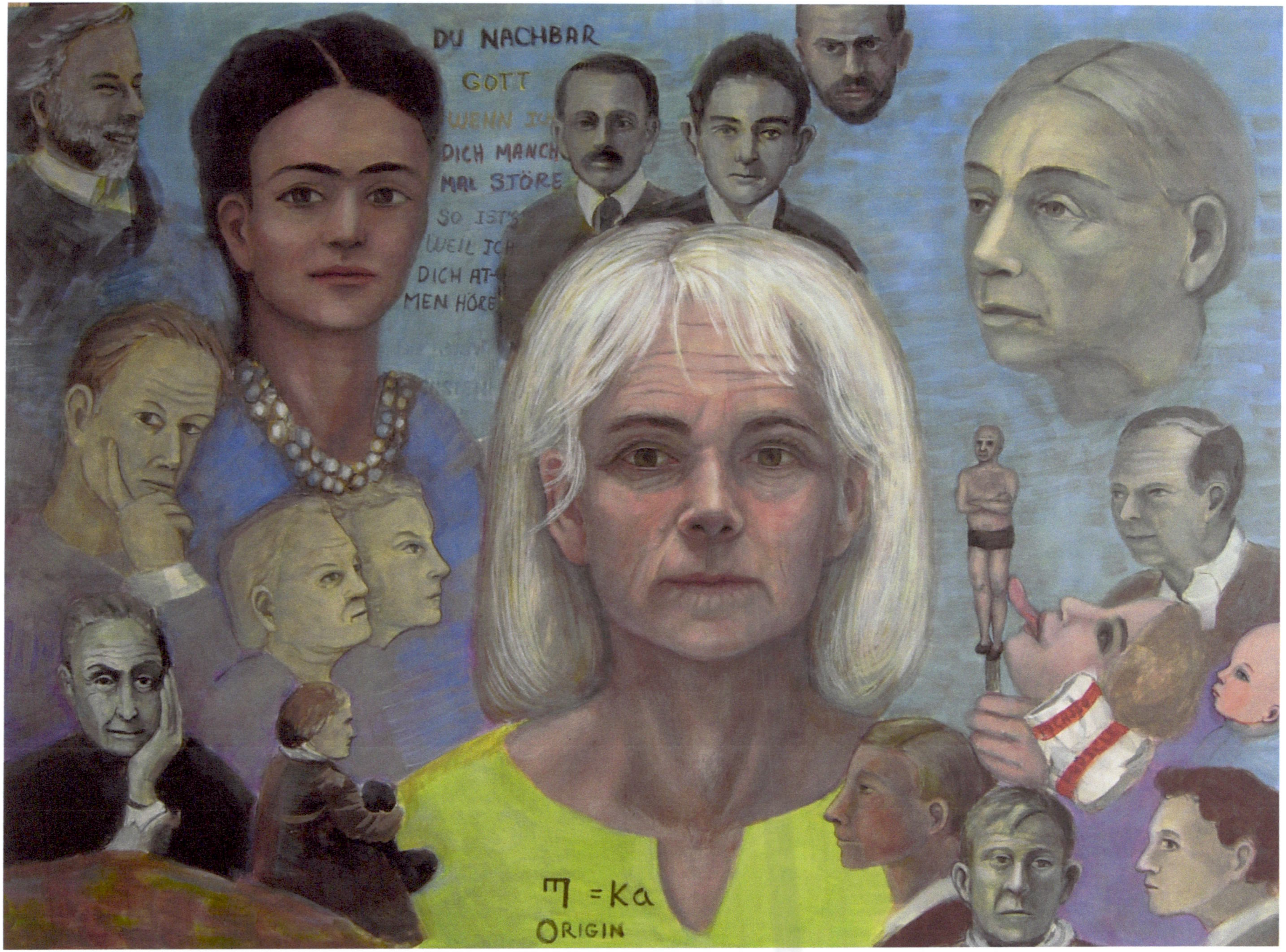
DU NACHBAR
GOTT
WENN IC
DICH MANCH
MAL STÖRE
SO IST'S
WEIL IC
DICH AT-
MEN HÖRE
= Ka
ORIGIN

K Factor

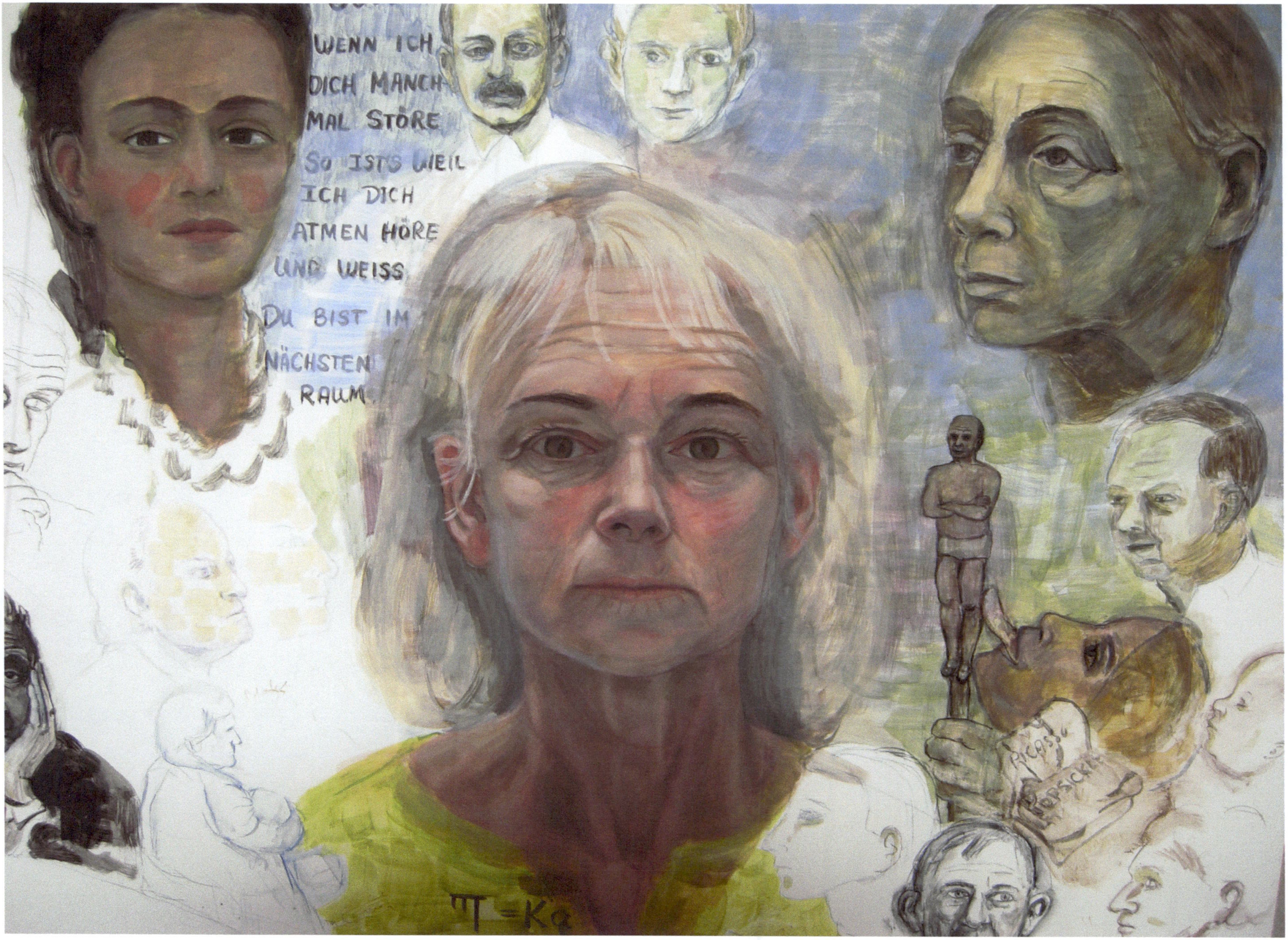

K Factor detail of earlier stage

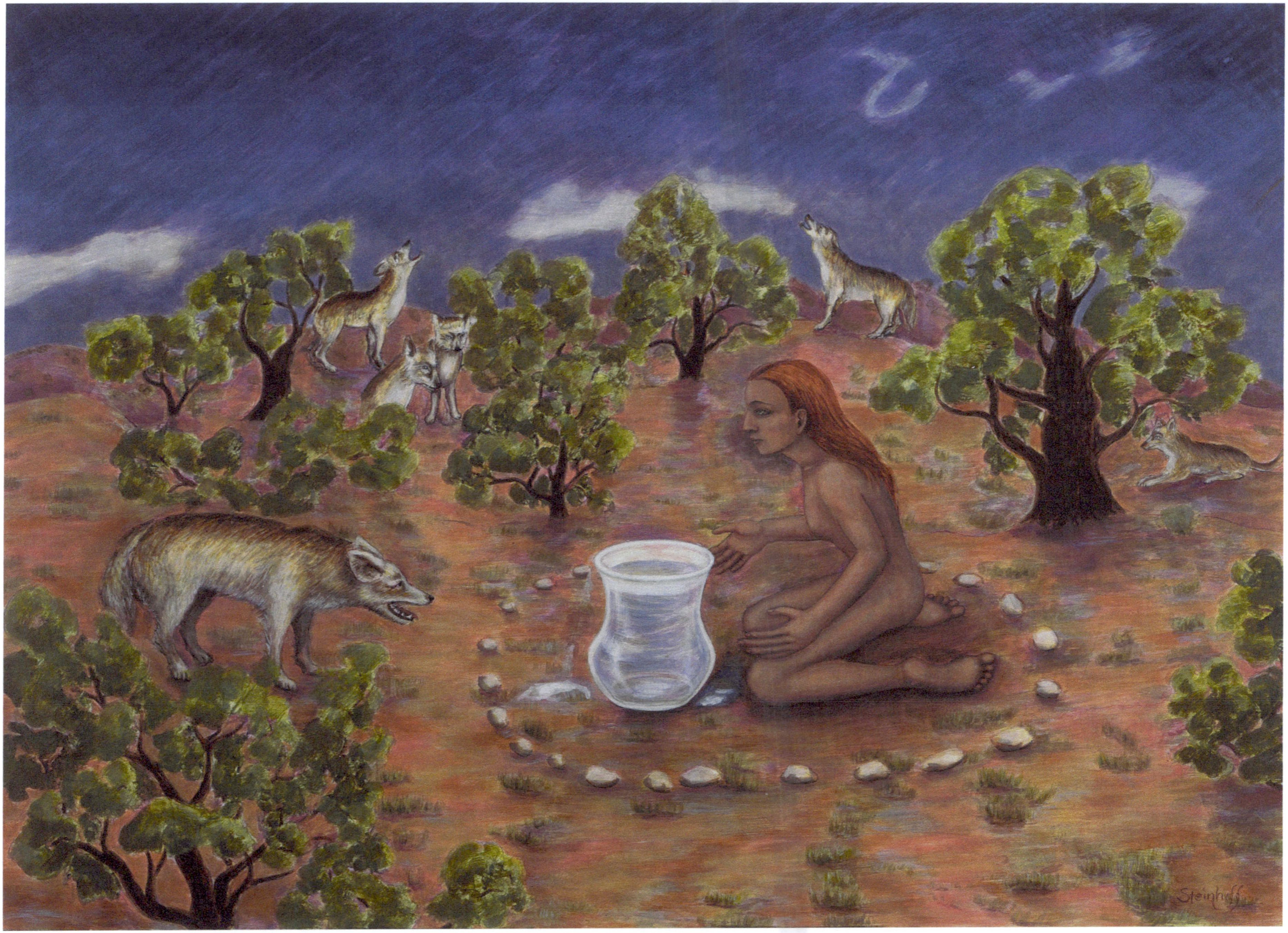

Drought

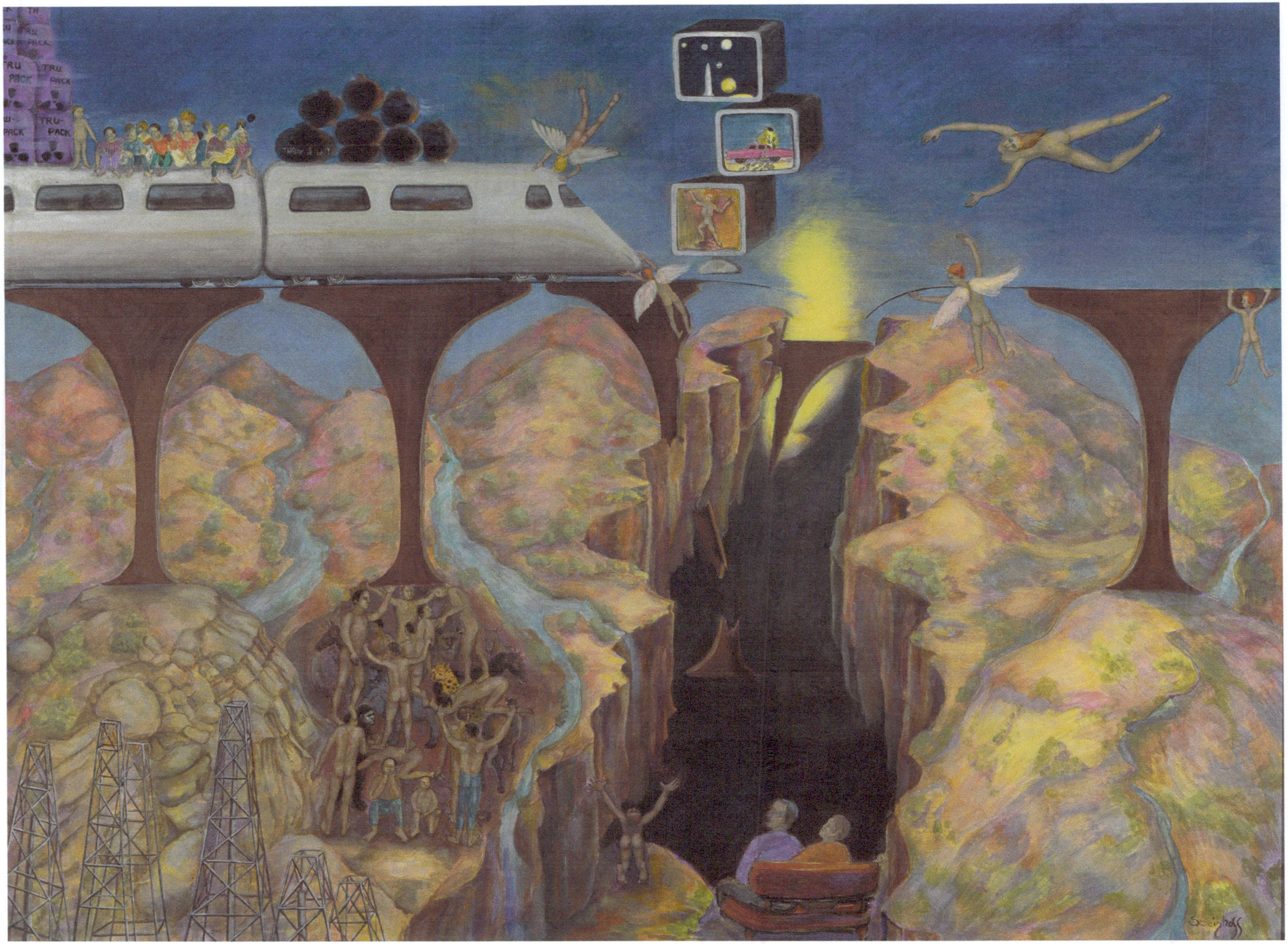

Civilization Express

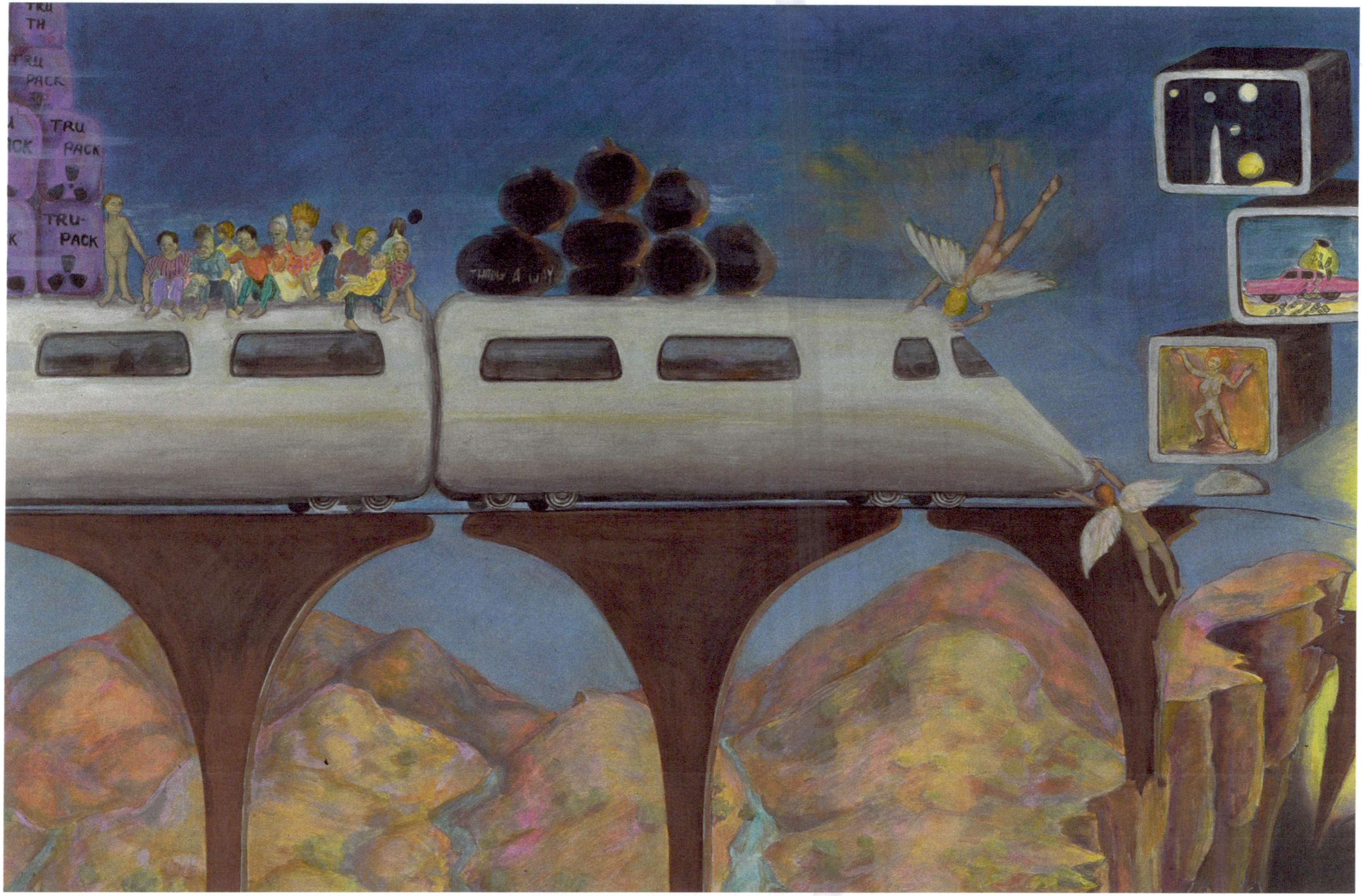

Civilization Express detail

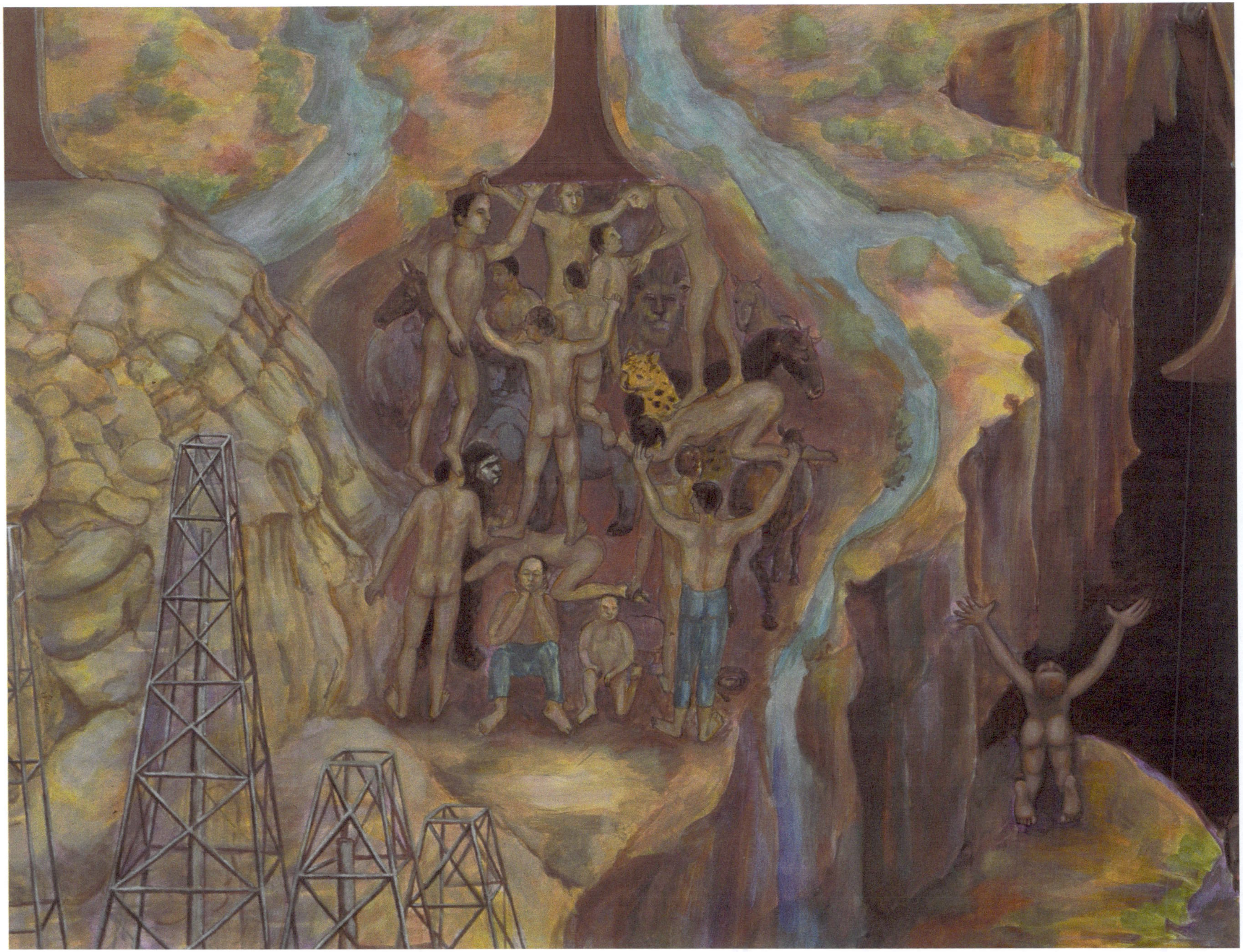

Civilization Express detail

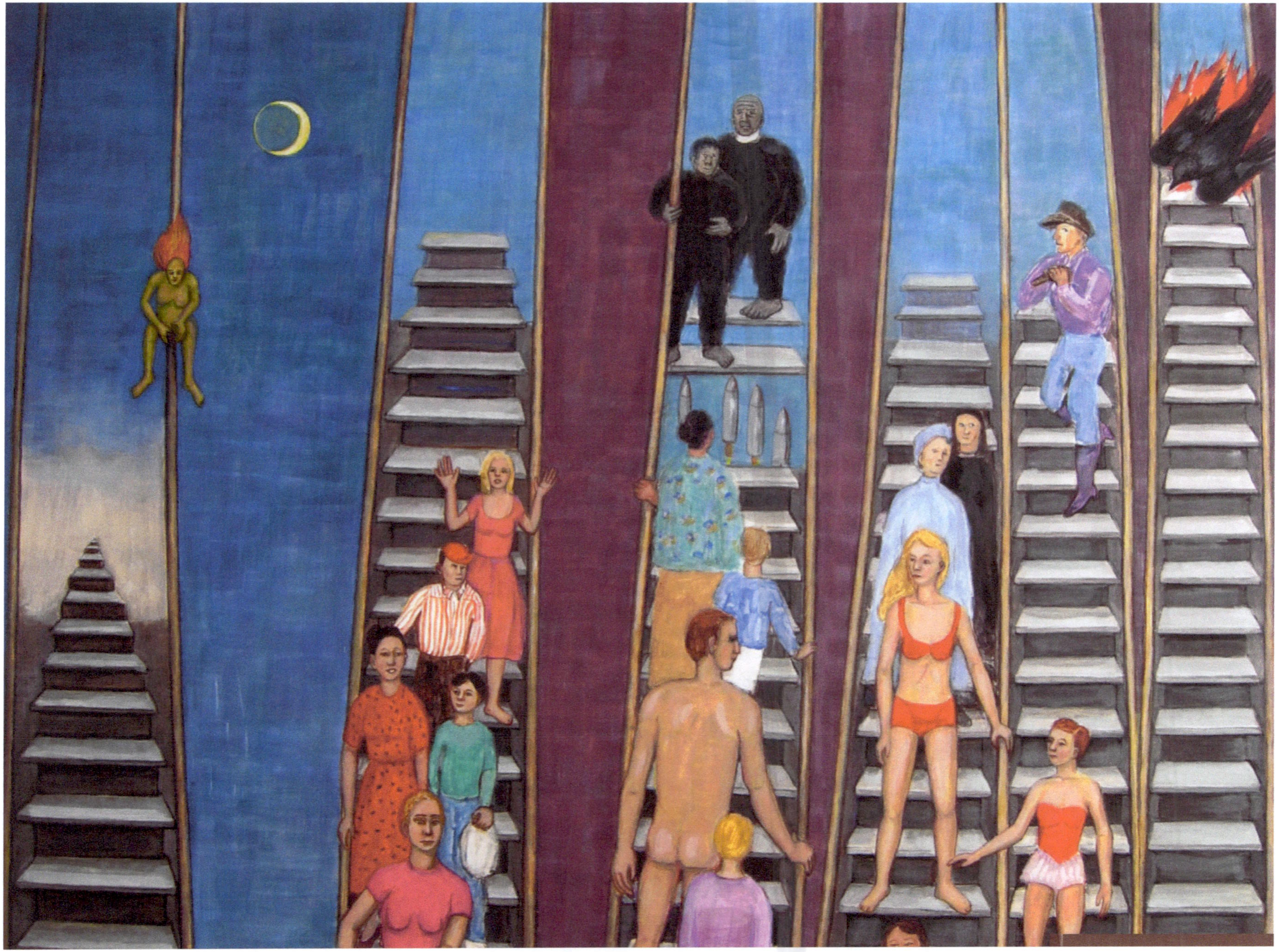

Berlin Alexanderplatz

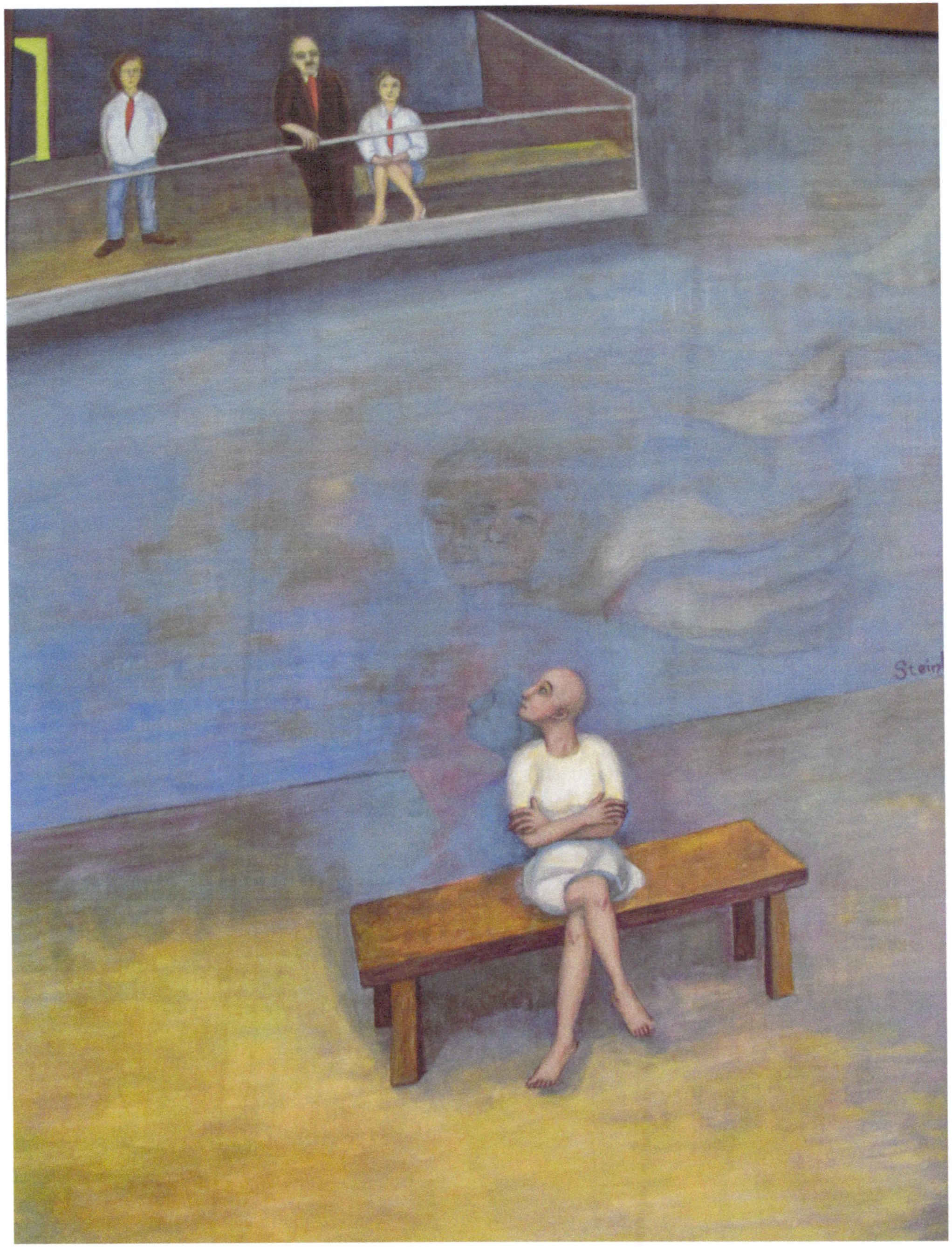

Interrogation

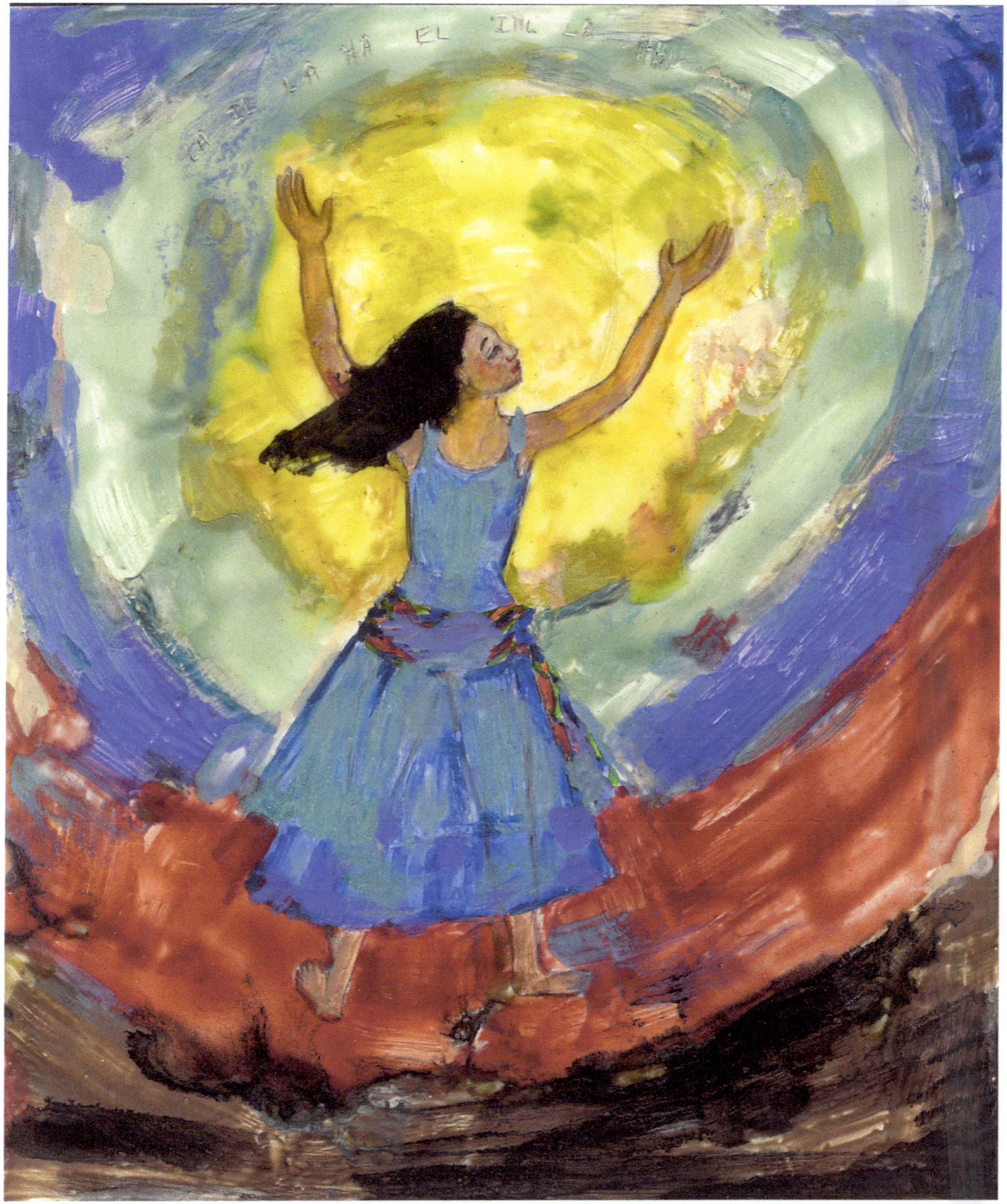

Rainbow II (Icon)

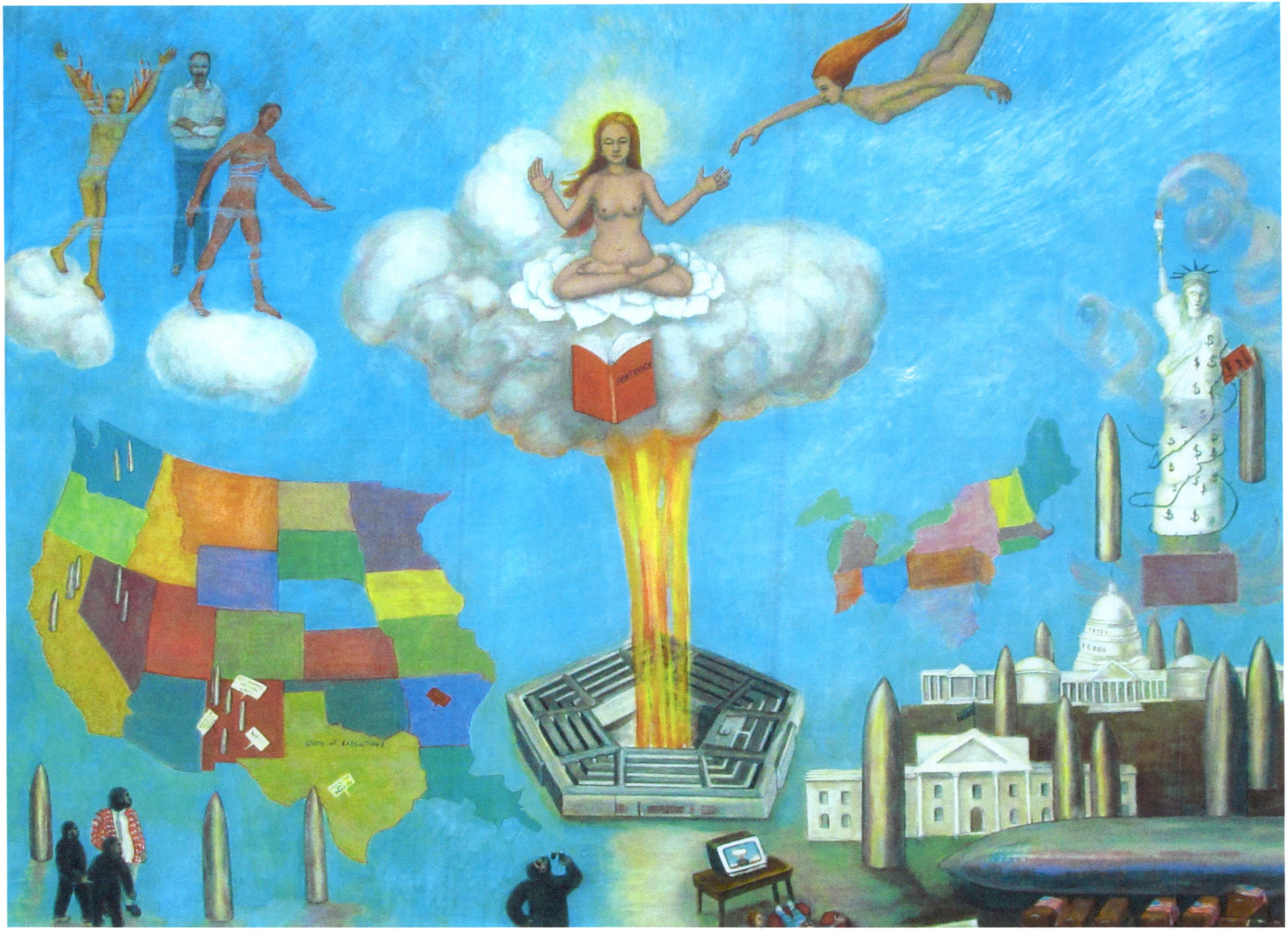

Before 9/11

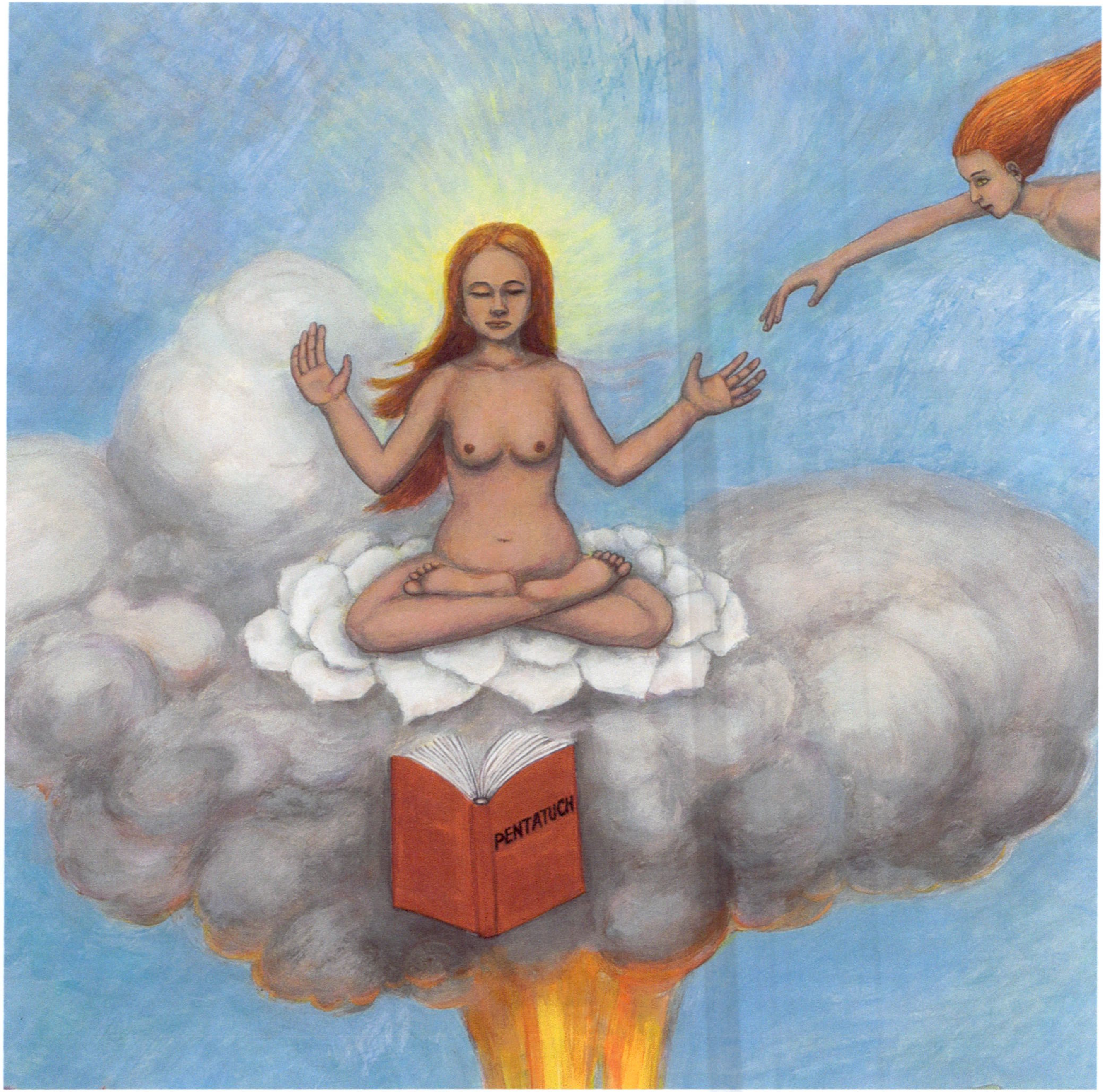

Before 9/11 detail

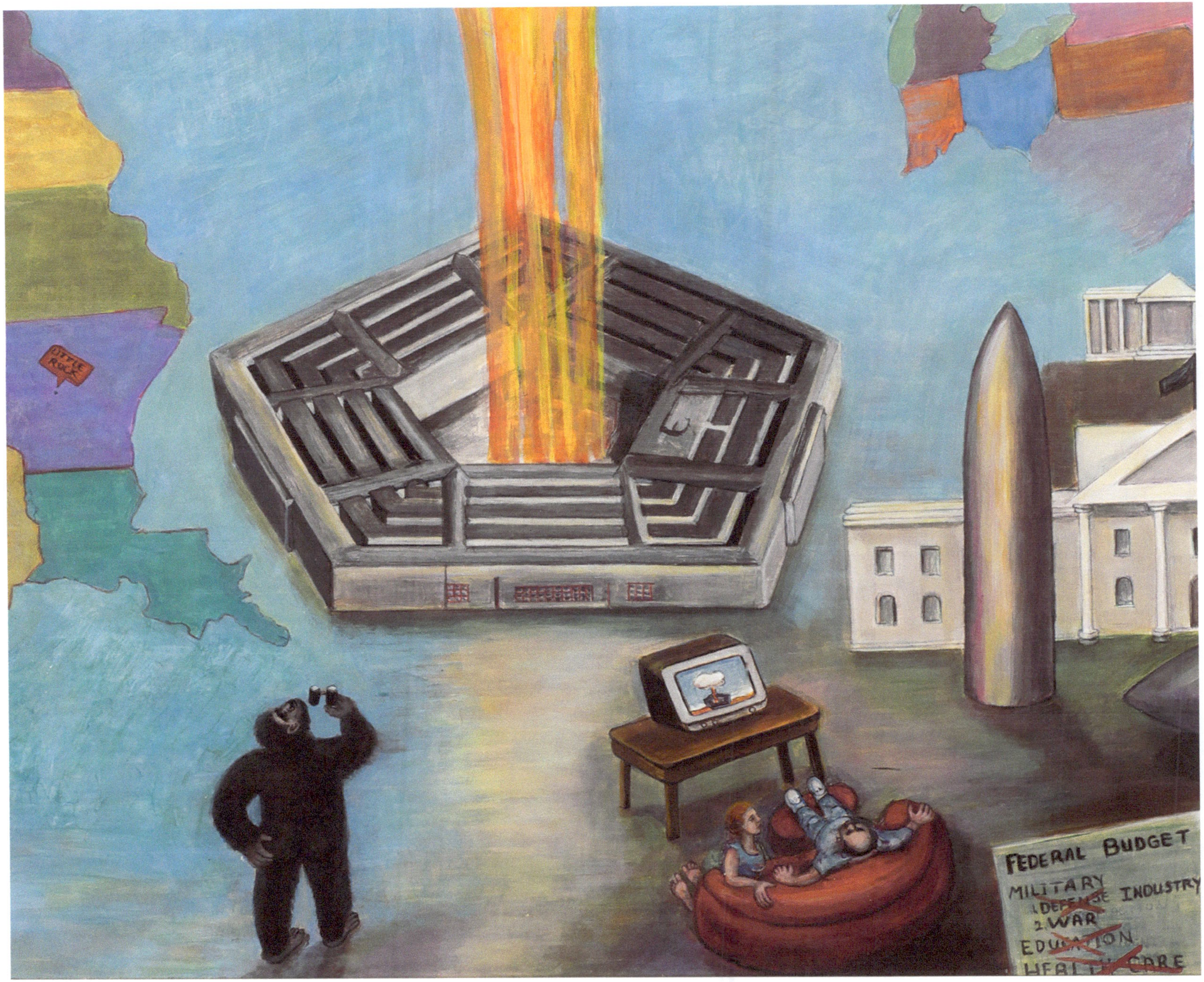

Before 9/11 detail

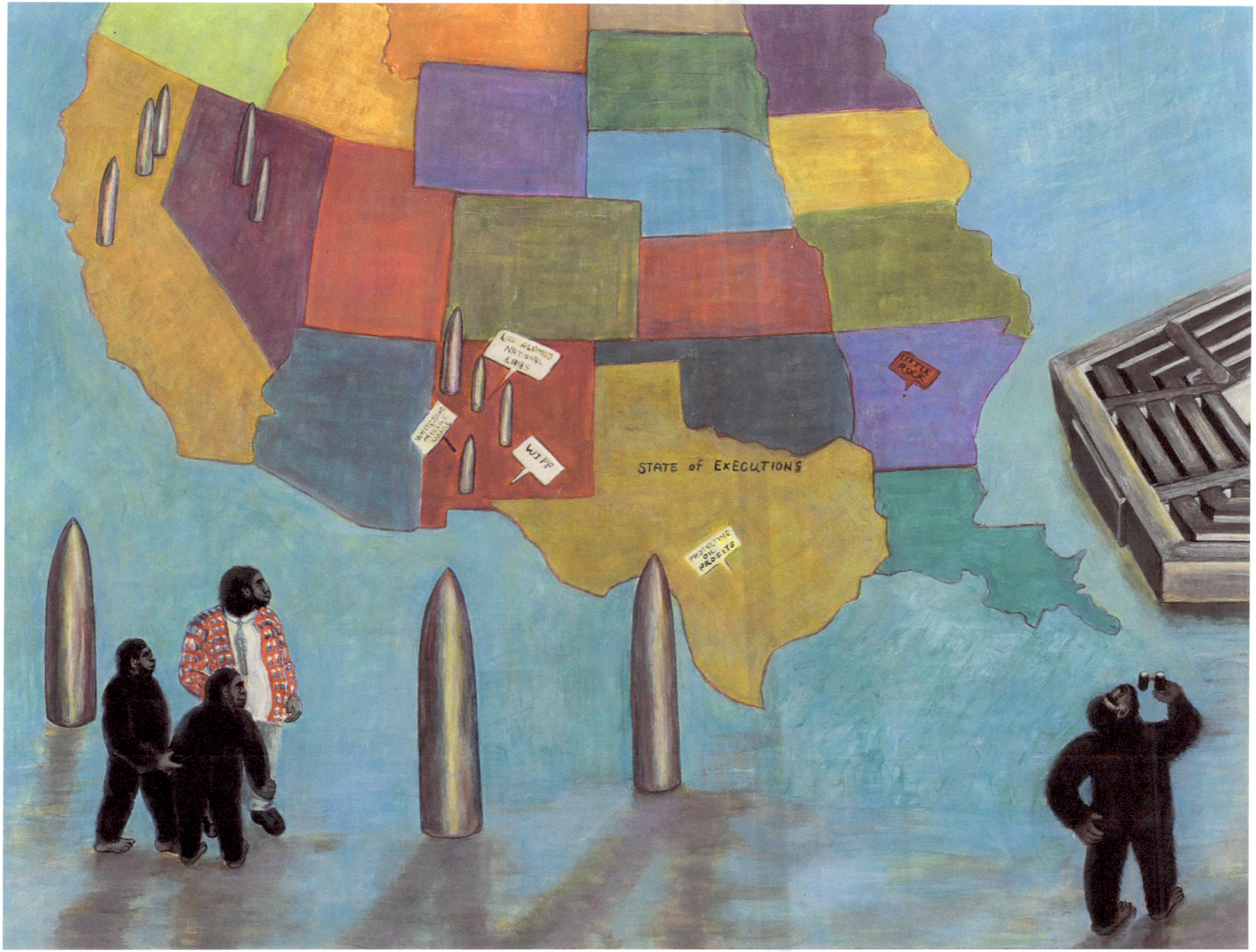

Before 9/11 detail

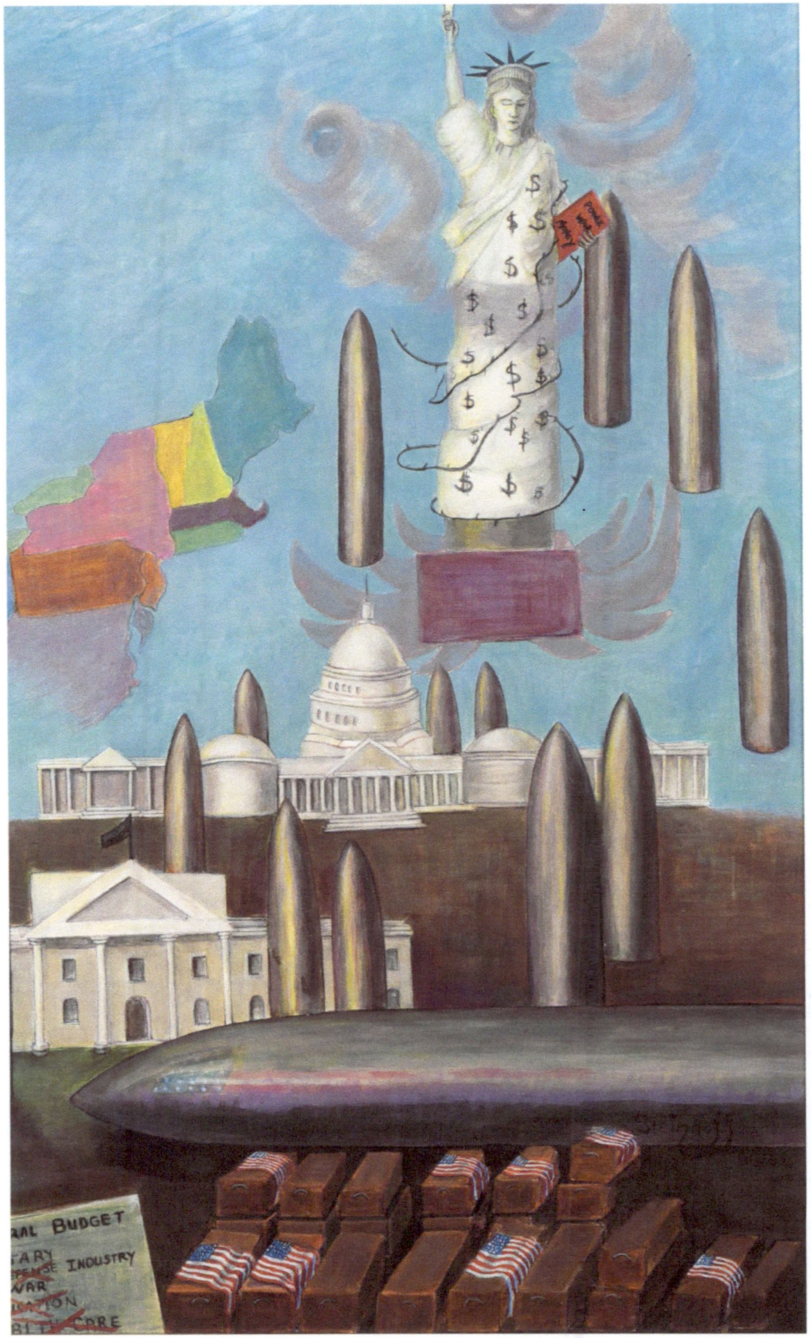

Before 9/11 detail

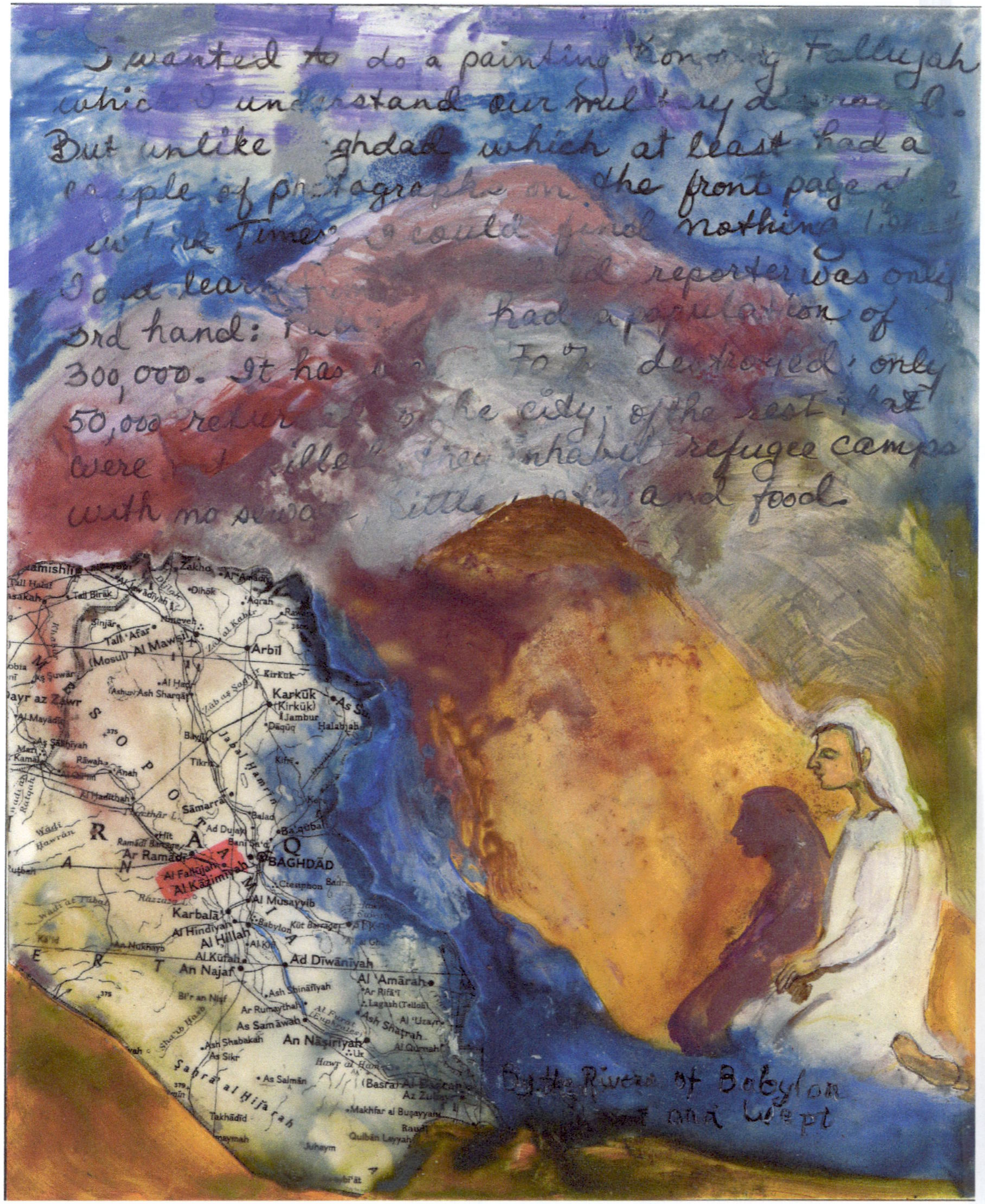
I wanted to do a painting honoring Fallujah
But unlike
which at least had a
the front page
nothing
reporter was only
3rd hand:
had a population of
300,000. It has
destroyed; only
50,000
the city; of the rest
refugee camps
were
with no
and food.
BAGHDĀD
Al Fallujah
Al Kāẓimīyah
Ar Ramādī
Karbalā
Al Ḥillah
An Najaf
Al Mawṣil
Arbīl
Karkūk
Sāmarrā
Ad Dīwānīyah
Al ʿAmārah
An Nāṣirīyah
By the Rivers of Babylon
and wept

Fallujah I

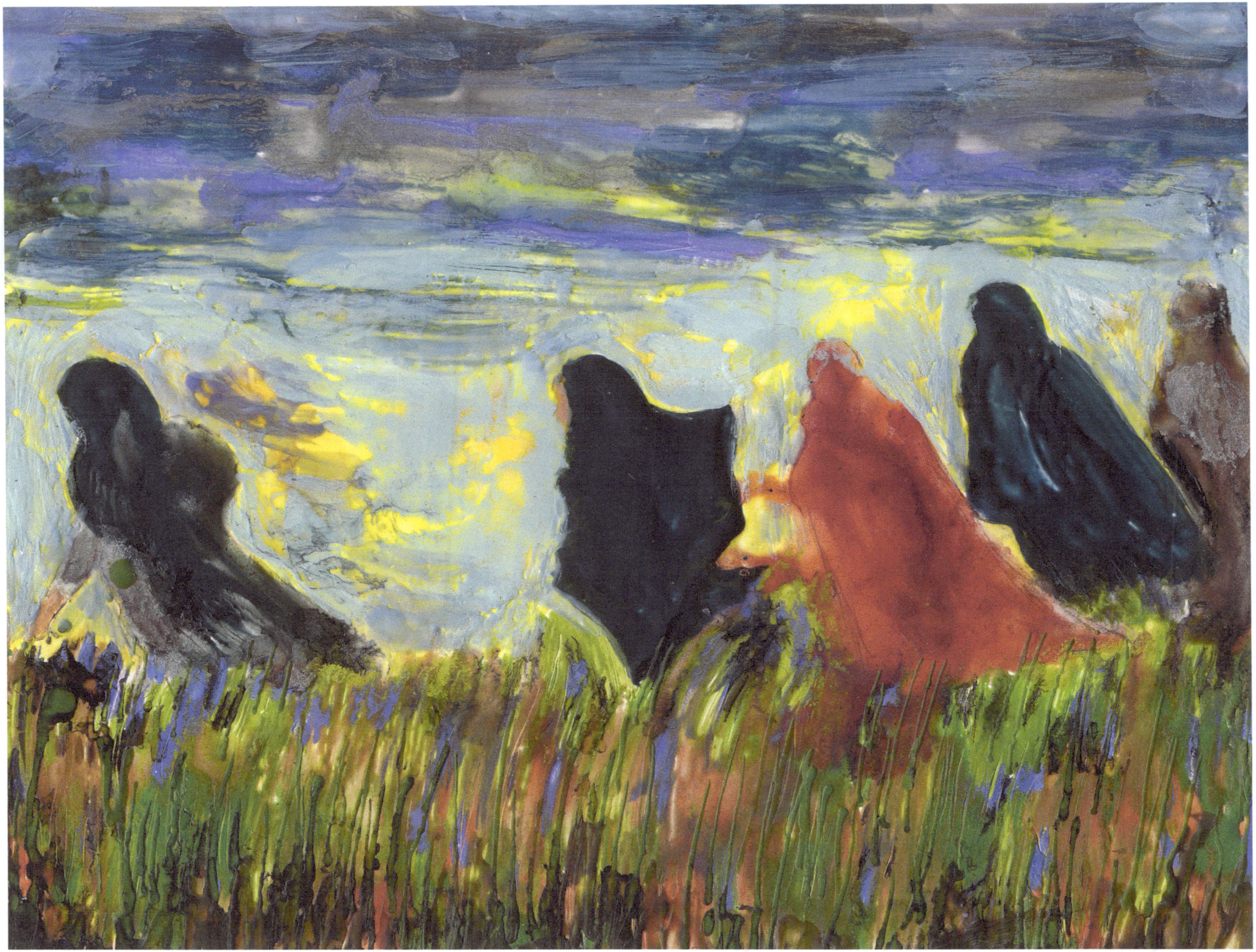

Fallujah III

Calling my Camels
(Looking for Fallujah IV)

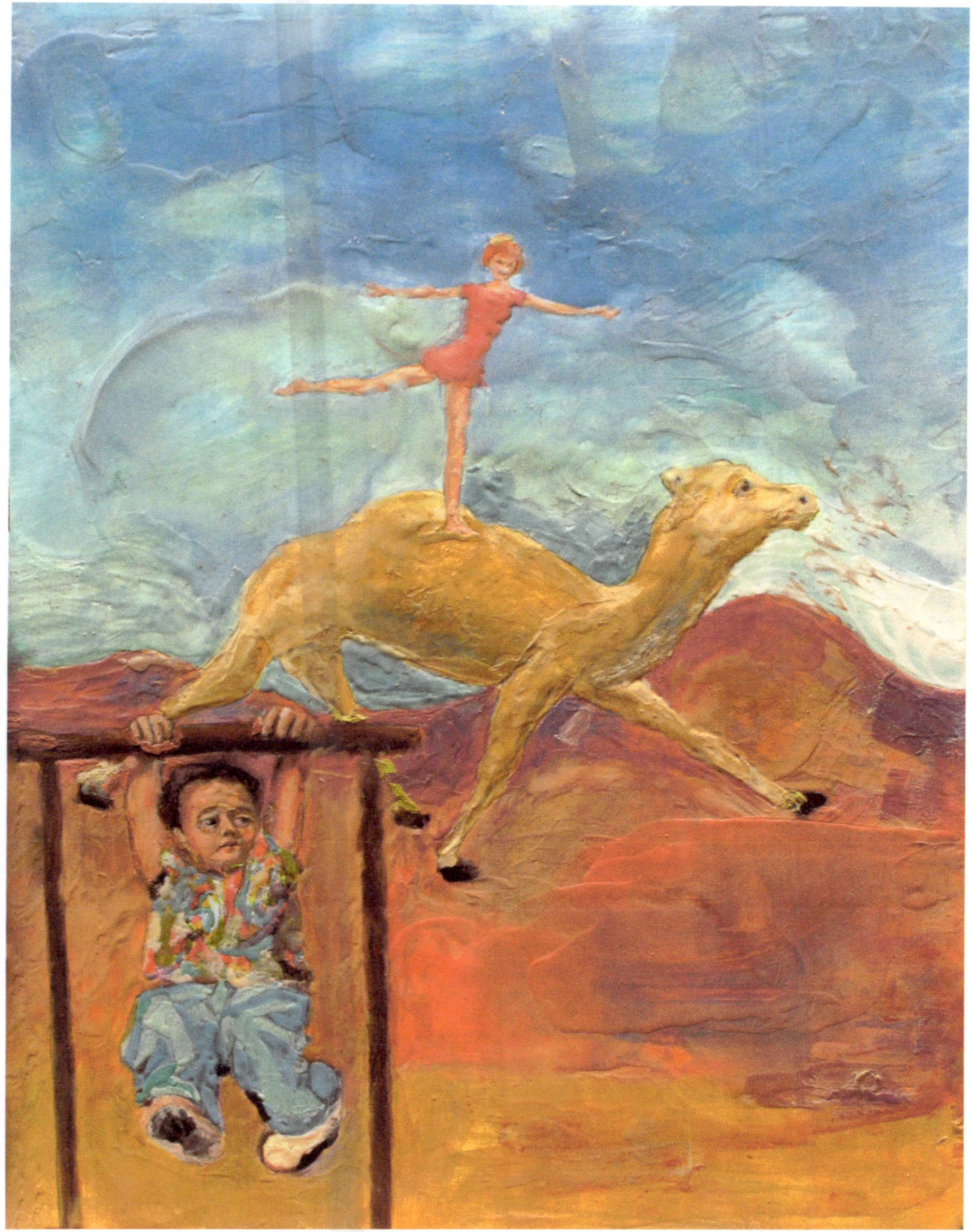

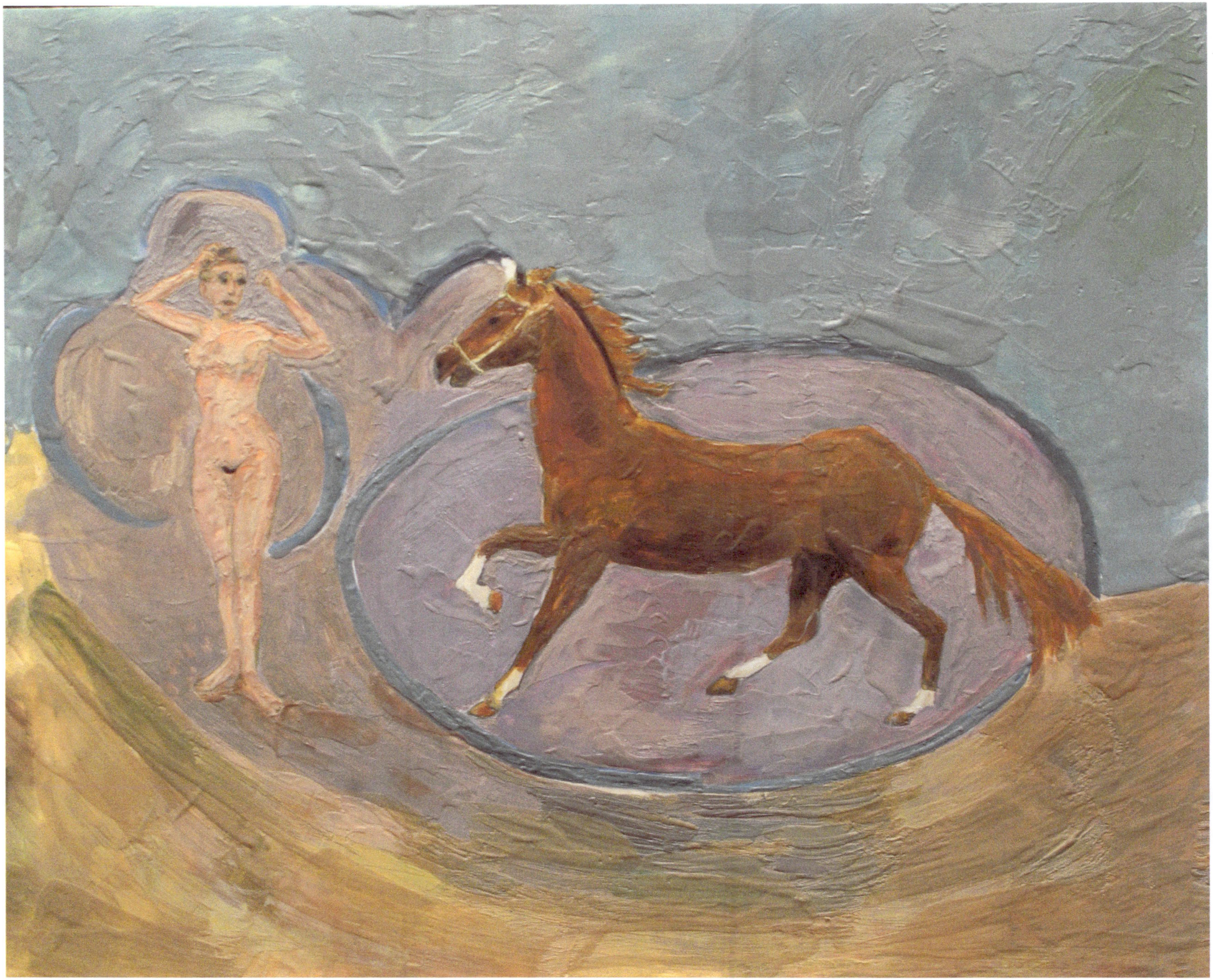

Lady and Horse

Dark Horse, Bright Rider

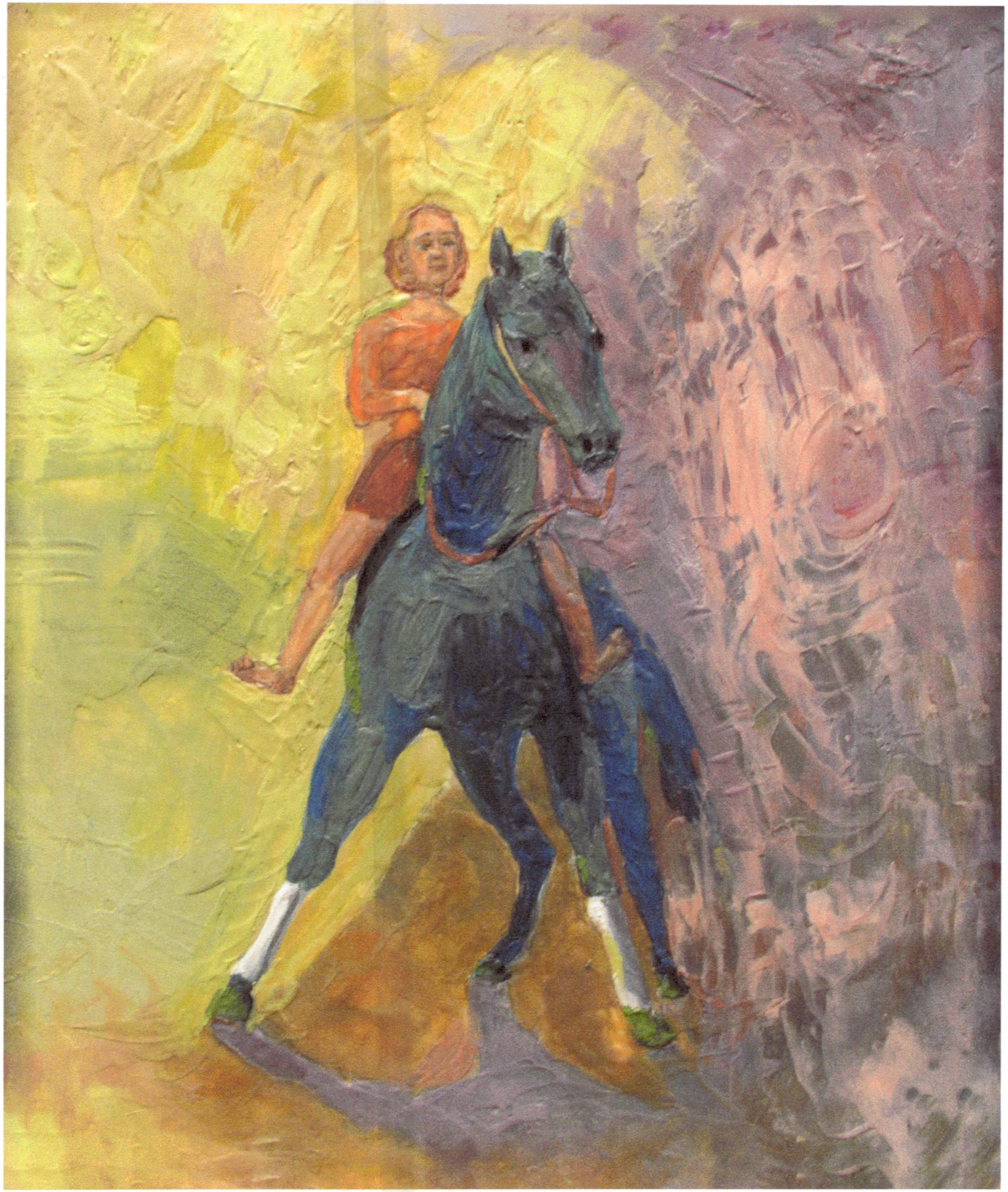

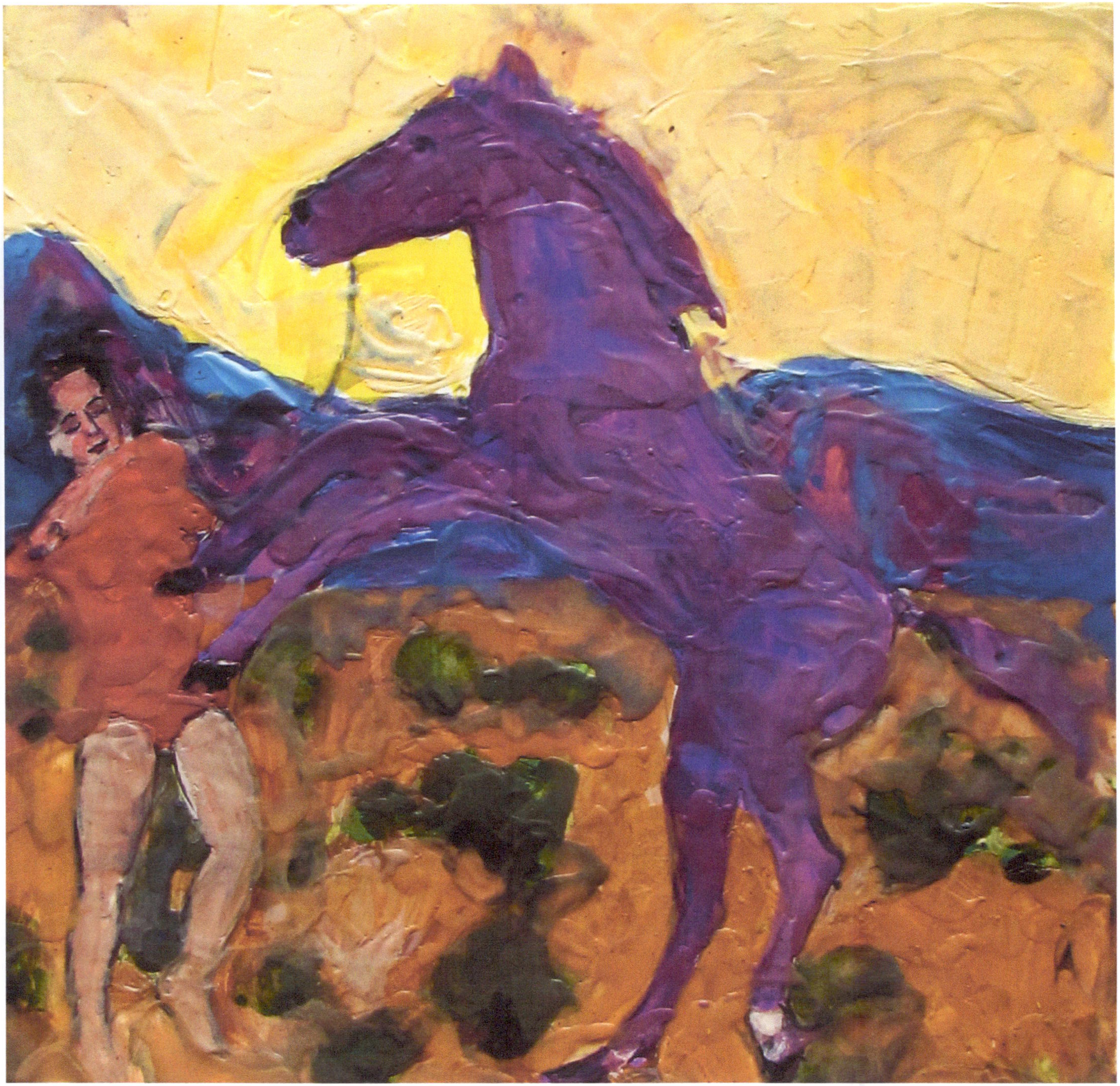

Purple Horse

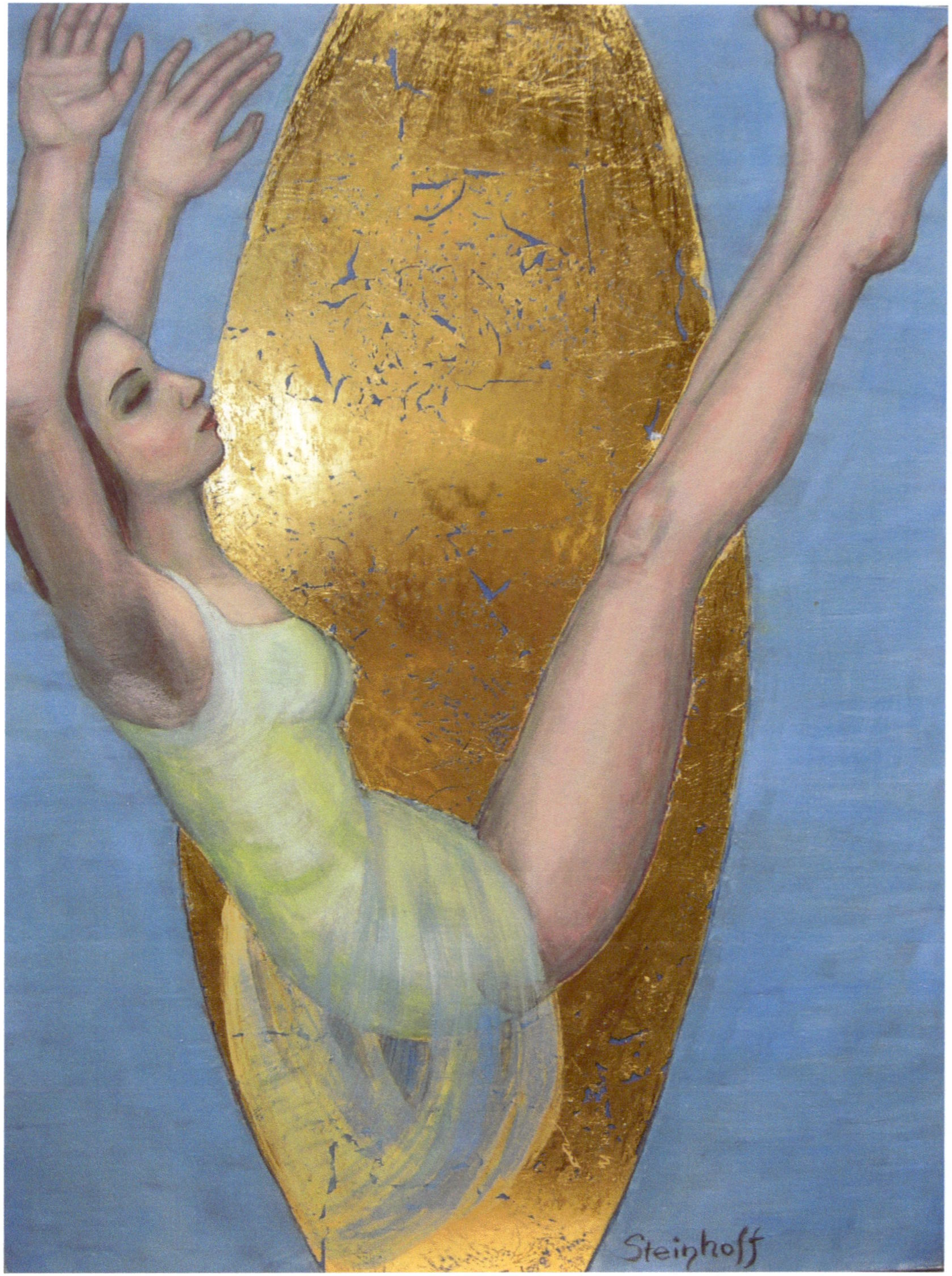

Vase, Container of Life

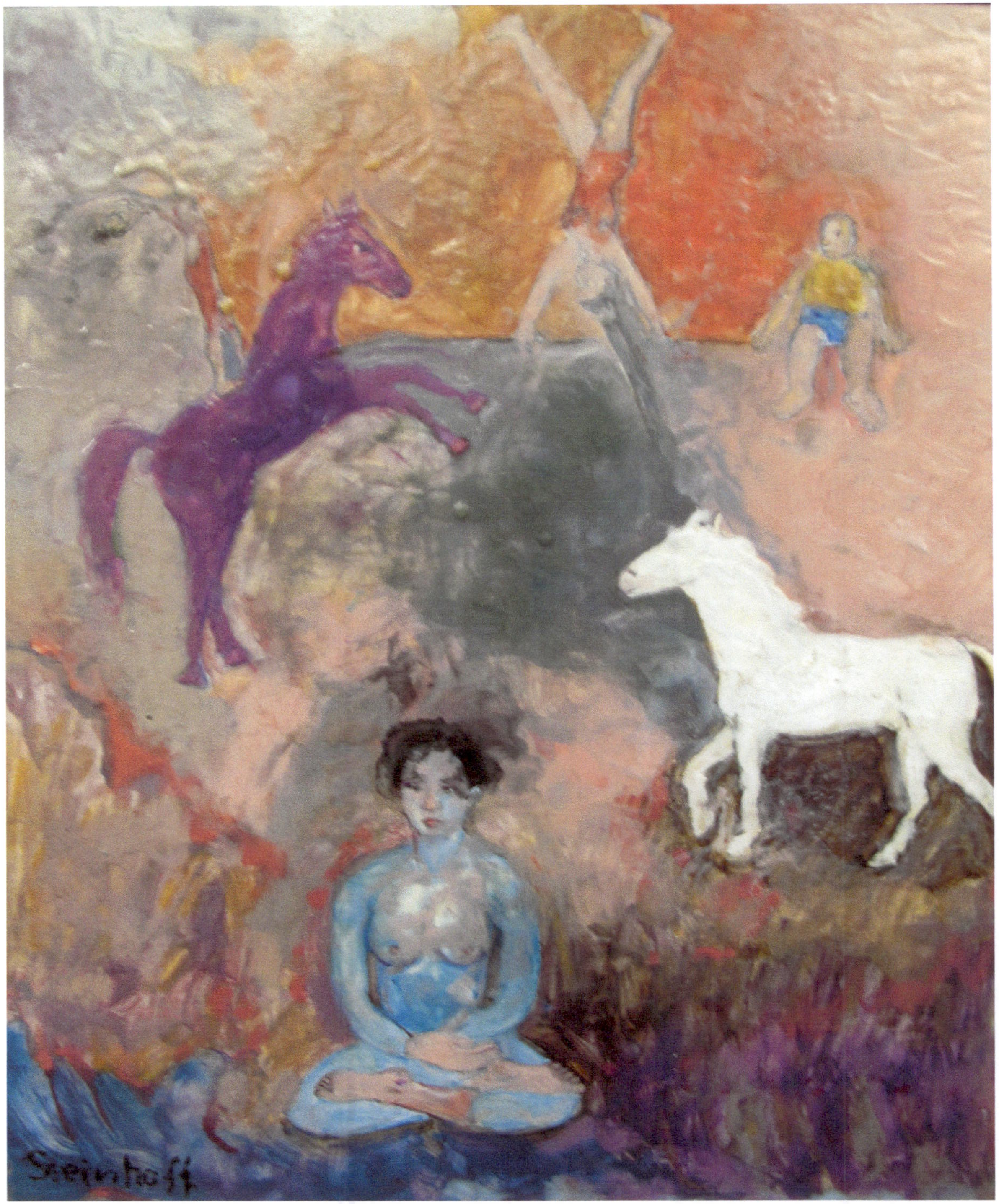

After Chagall

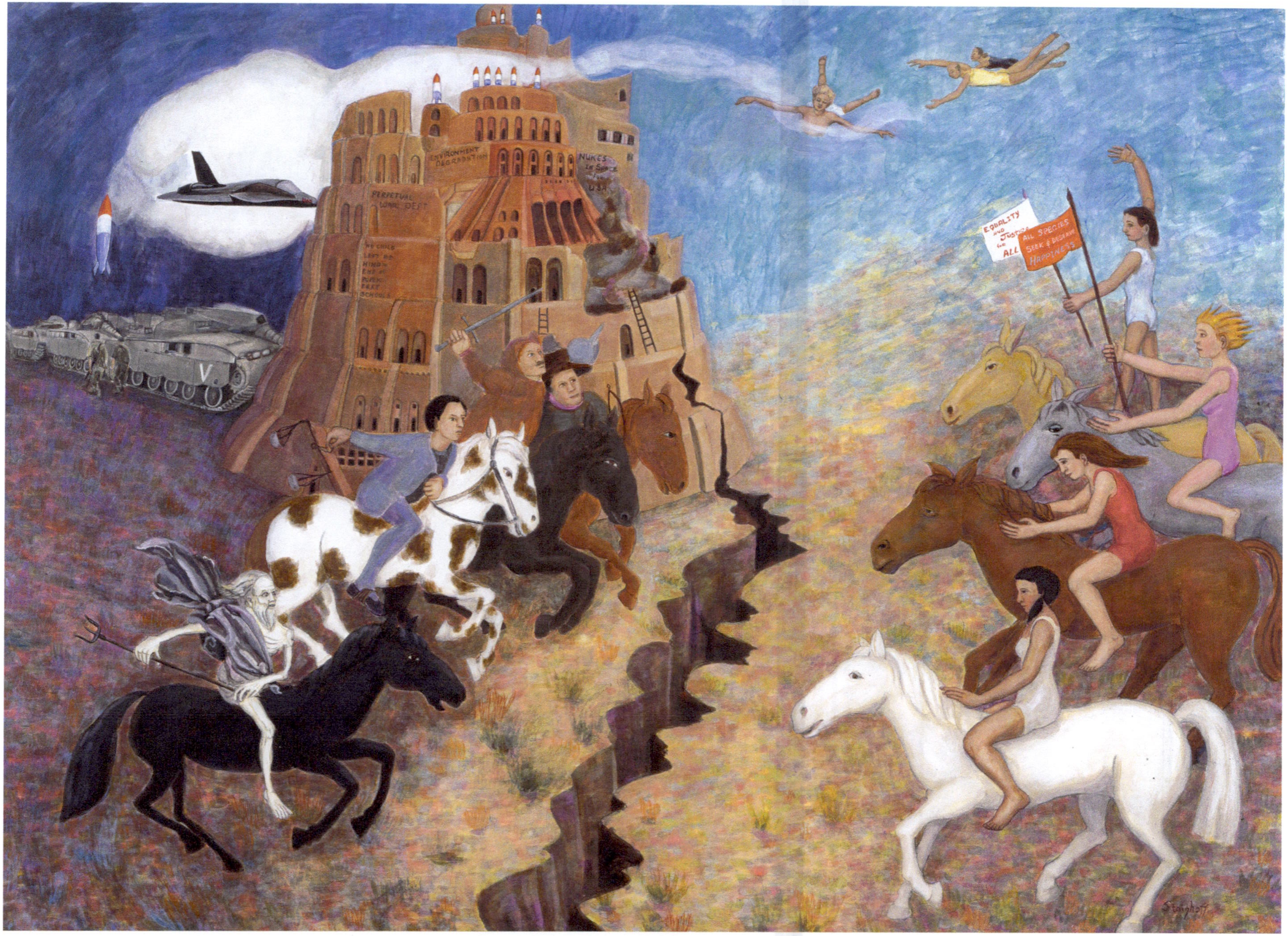

Restoring the Balance

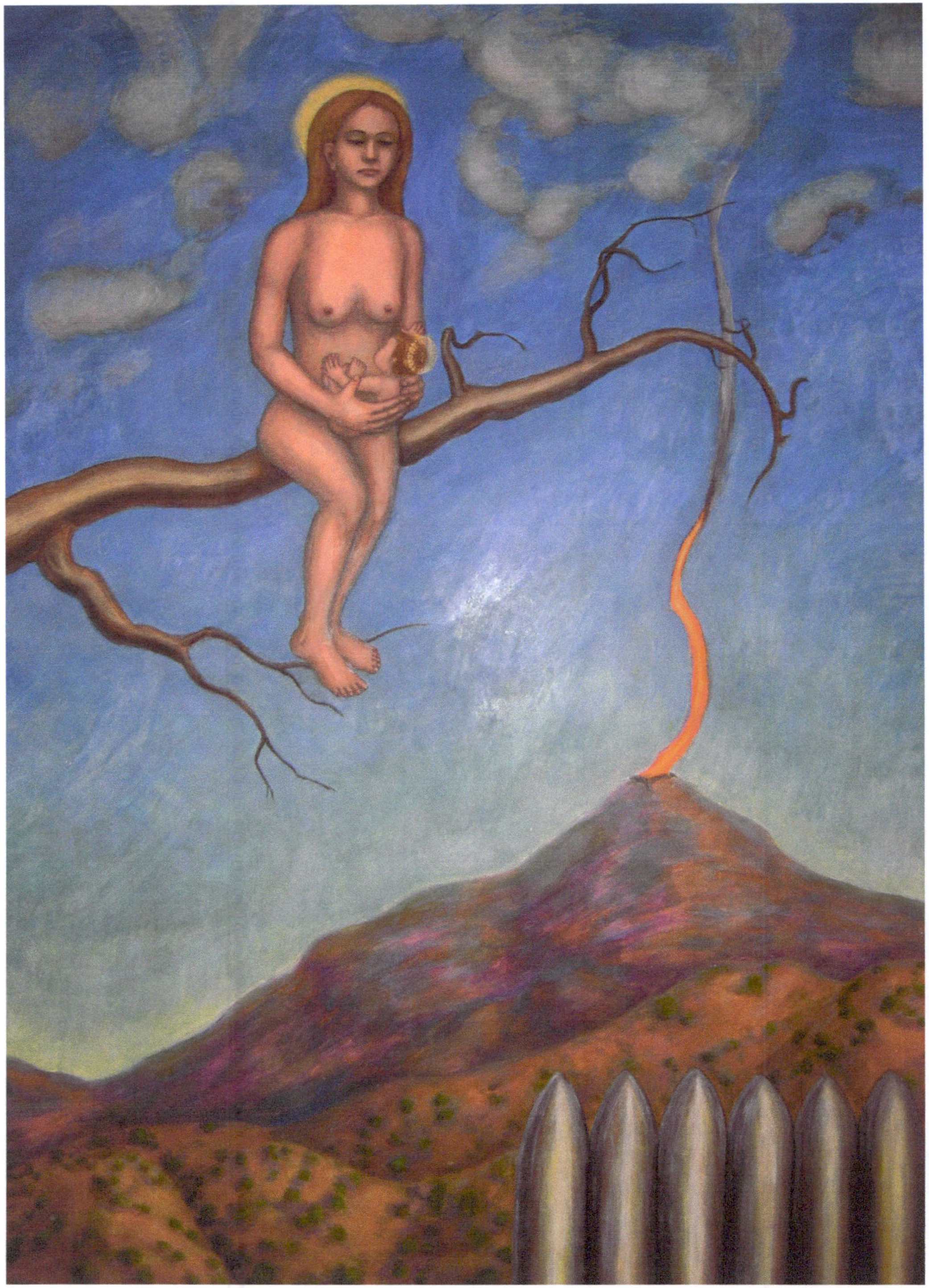

Madonna of Limited Options

Computer Lady

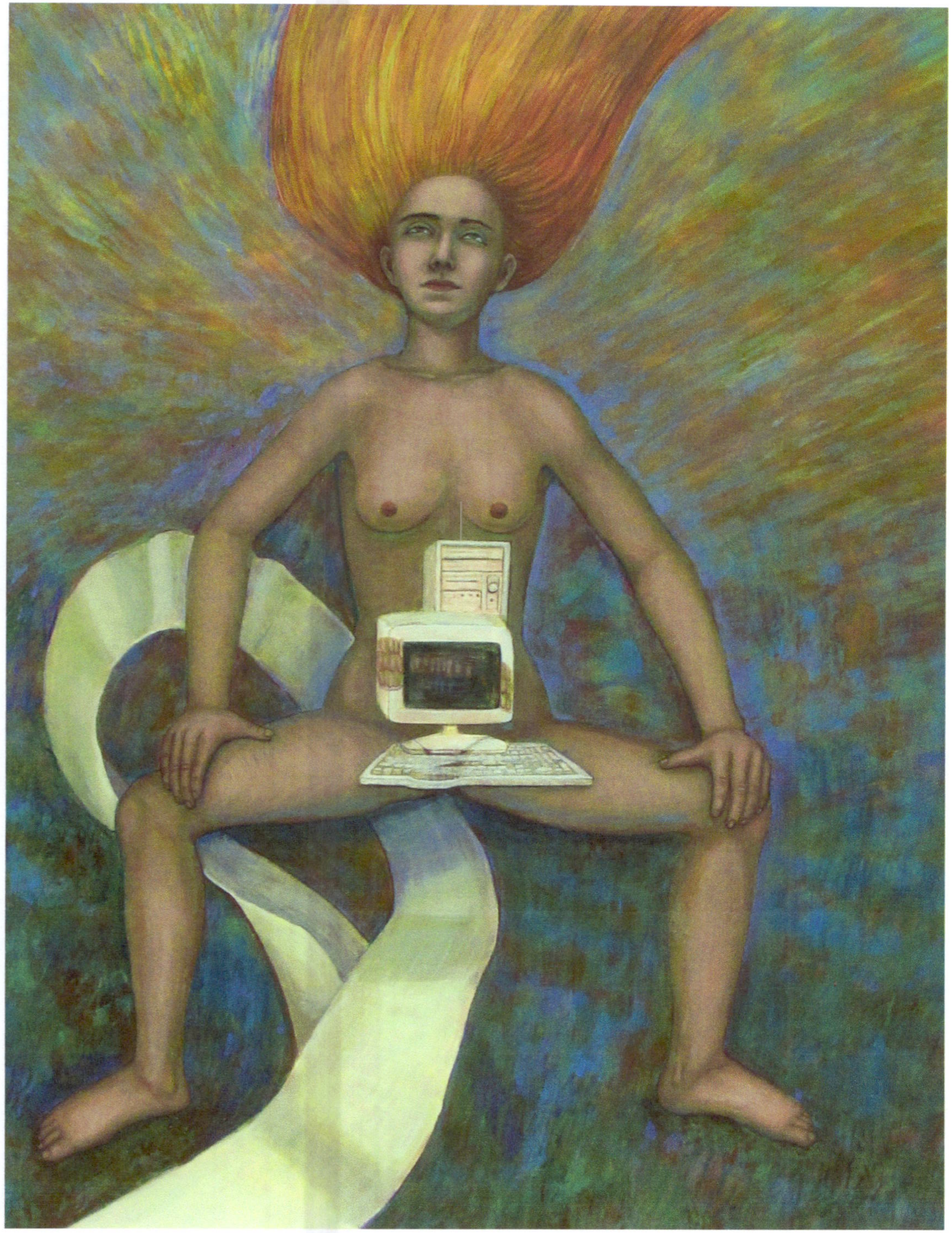

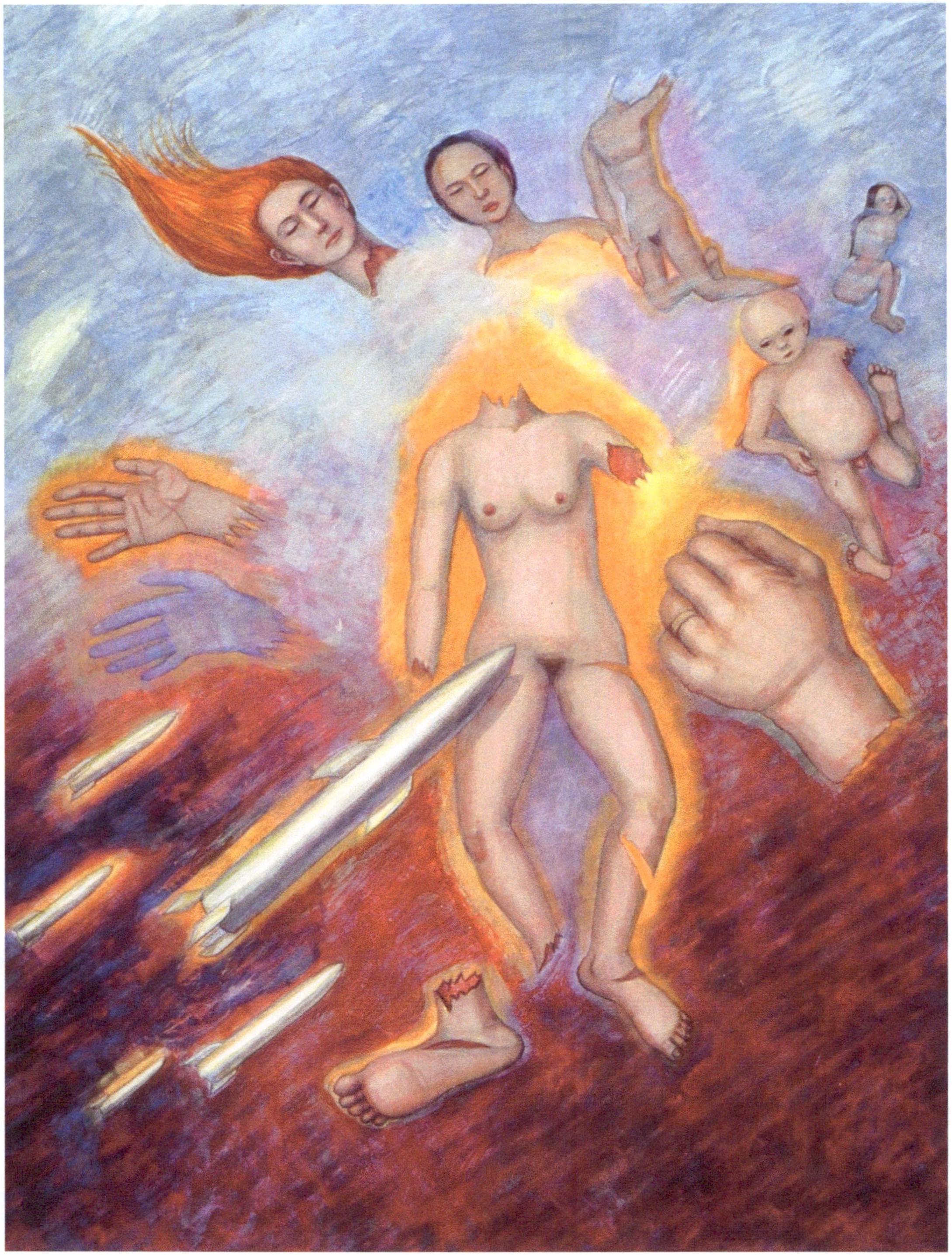

Venus of the Terrorism Wars

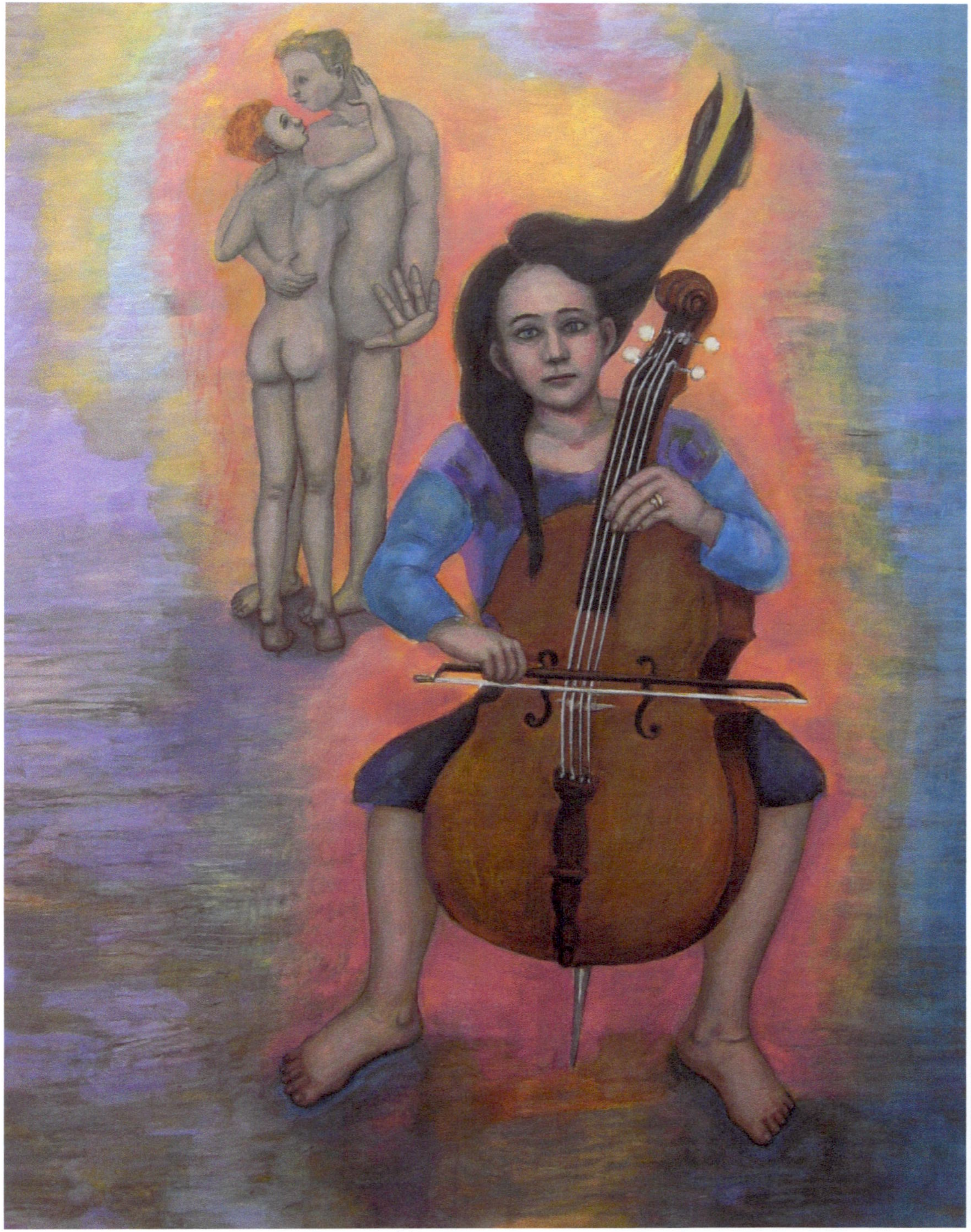

Passion

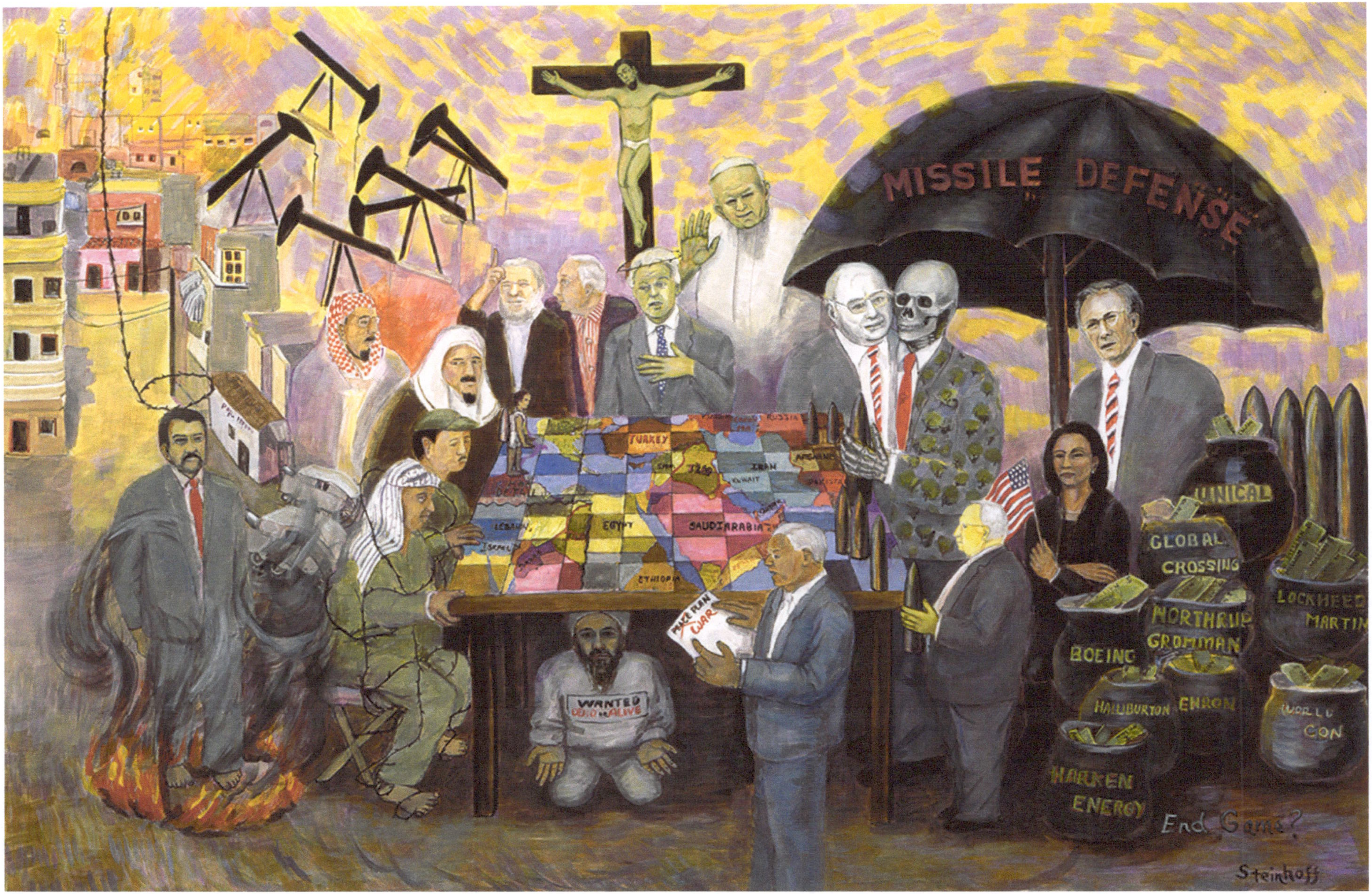
MISSILE DEFENSE
TURKEY
IRAN
KUWAIT
SAUDIARABIA
EGYPT
ETHIOPIA
LEBANON
PEACE PLAN
WAR
WANTED
UNICAL
GLOBAL CROSSING
NORTHRUP GRUMMAN
LOCKHEED MARTIN
BOEING
HALLIBURTON
ENRON
HARKEN ENERGY
End Game?
Steinhoff

End Game

Storm

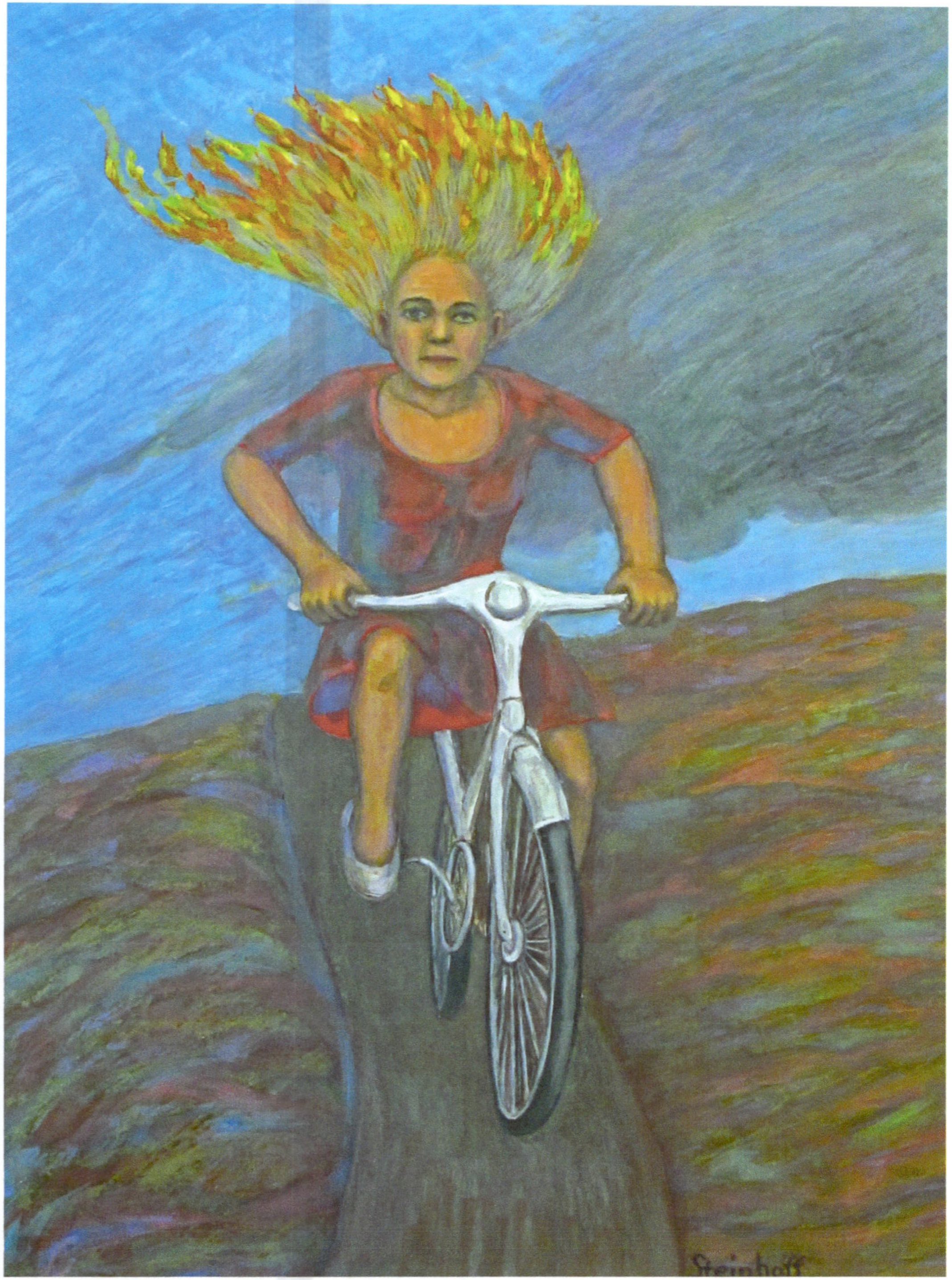

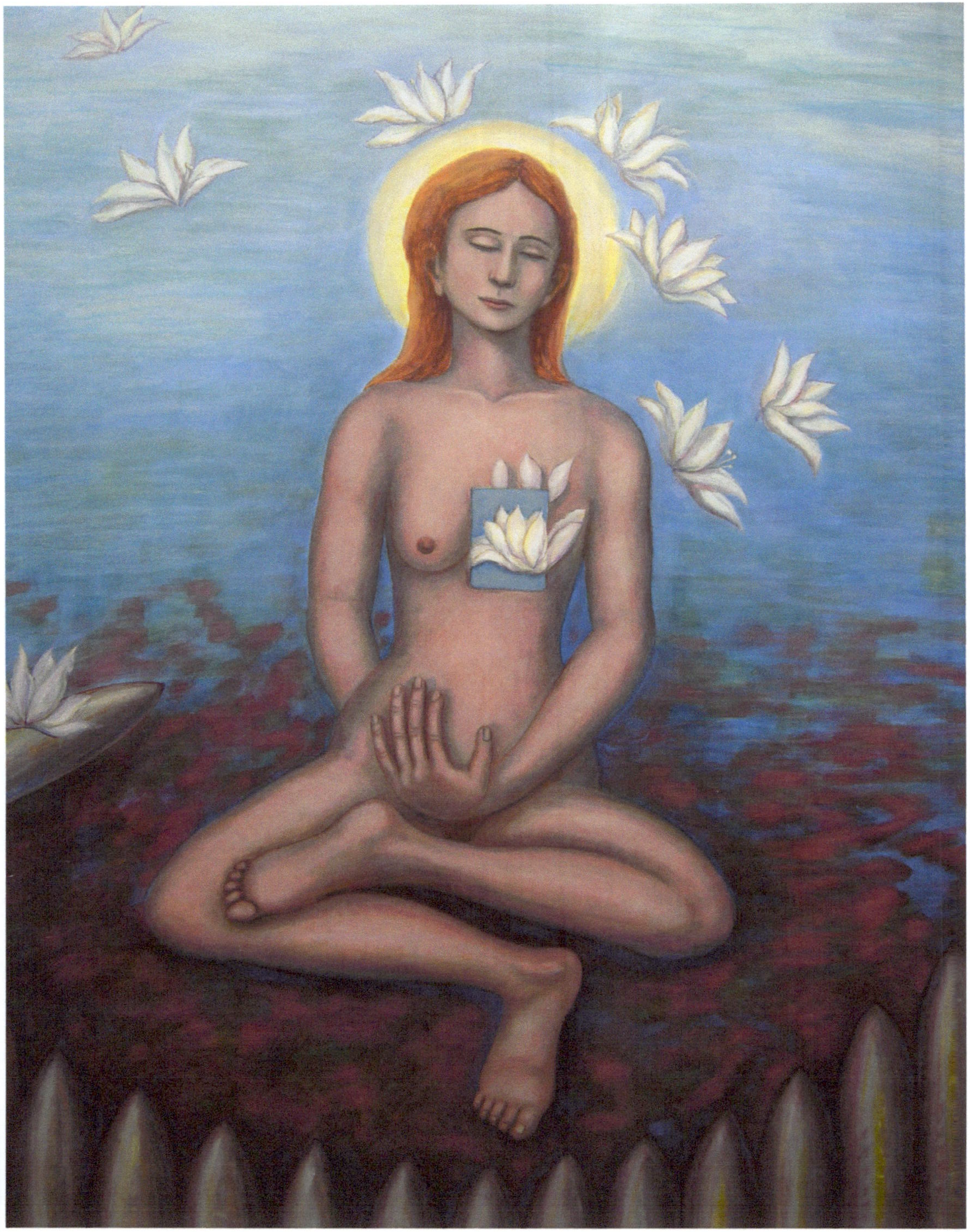

Transformation

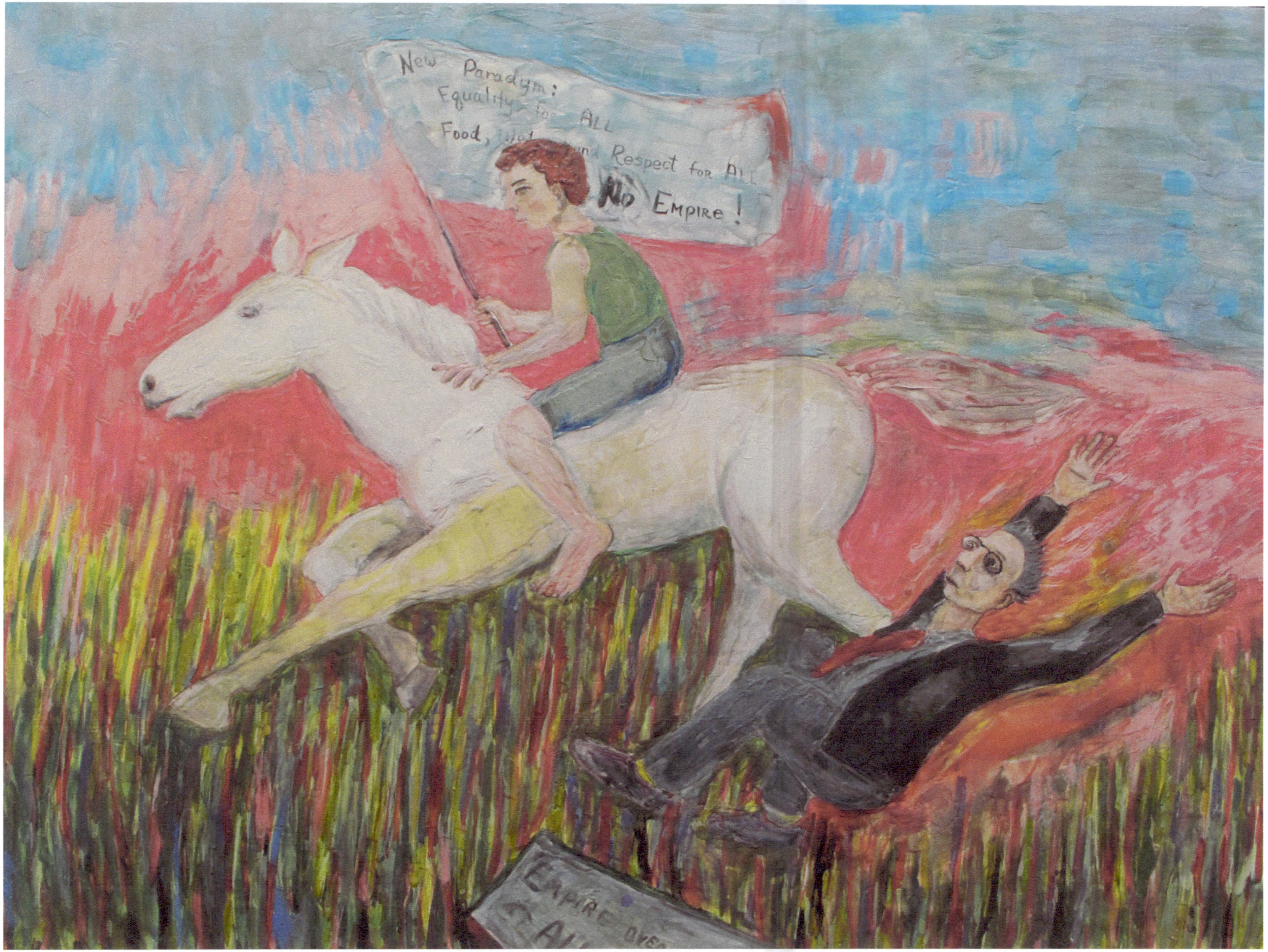

Dumping Rumsfeld

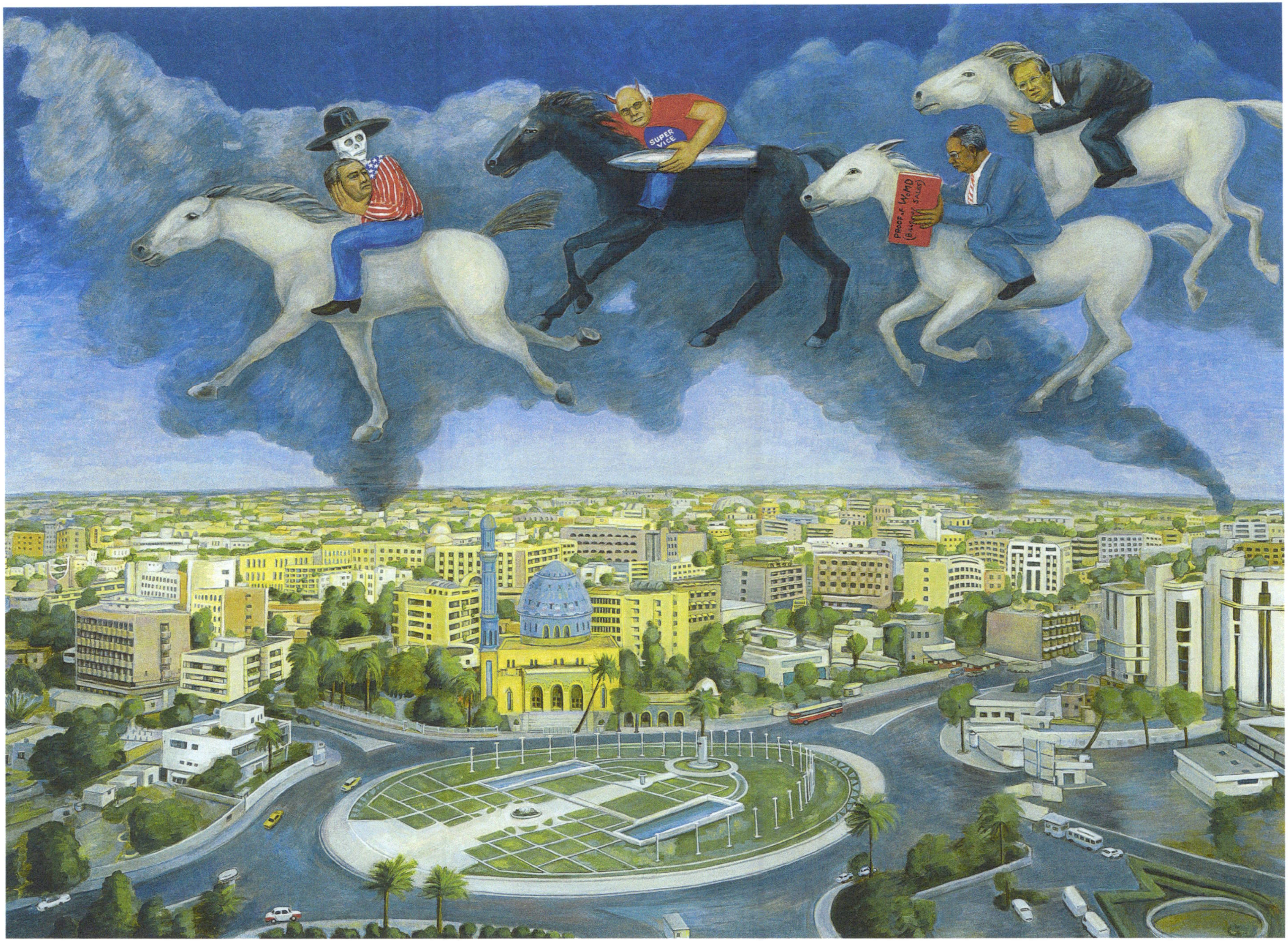

4 Horsemen of the Apocalypse Over Bagdad

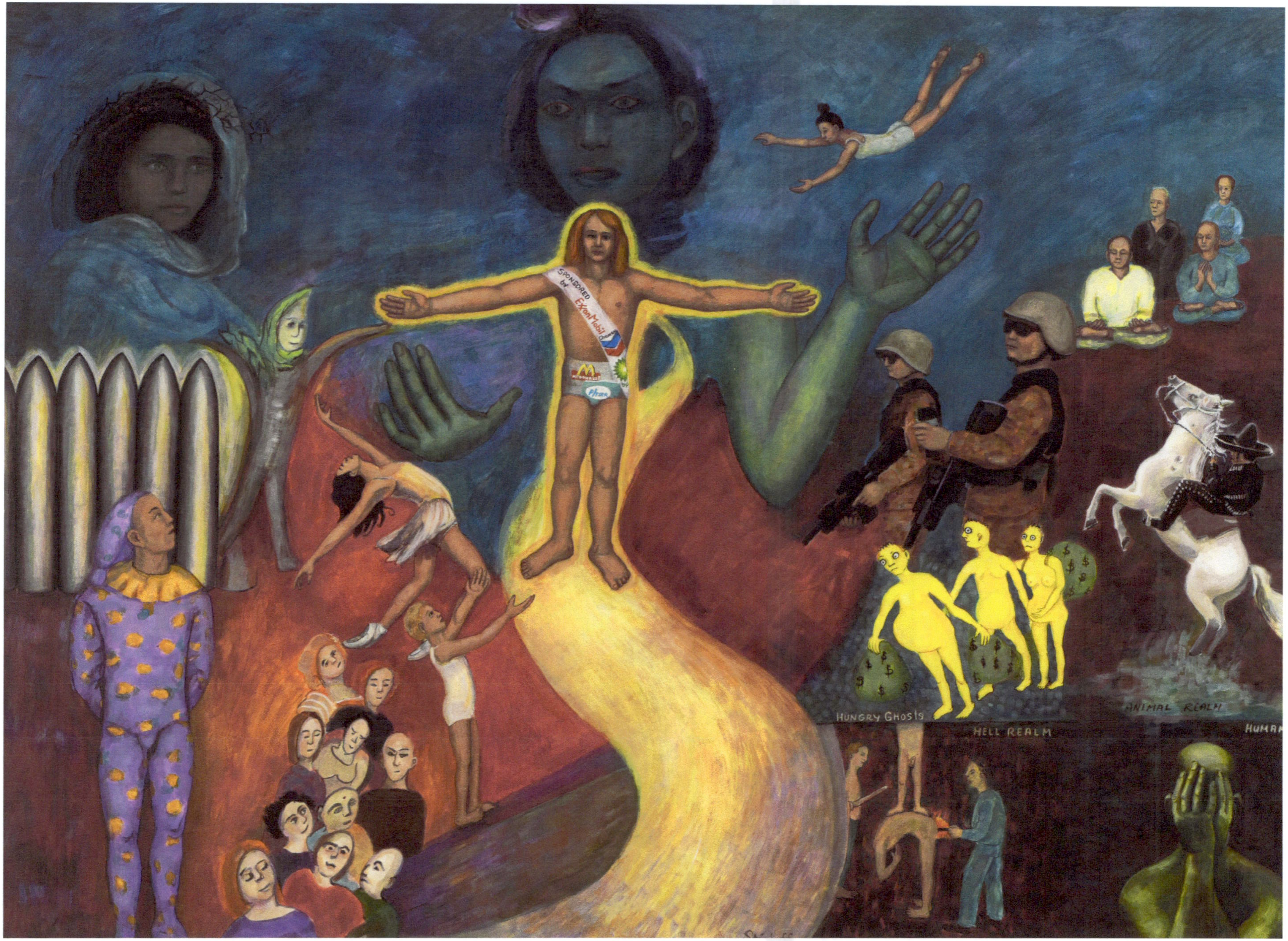

Rapture Anyone?

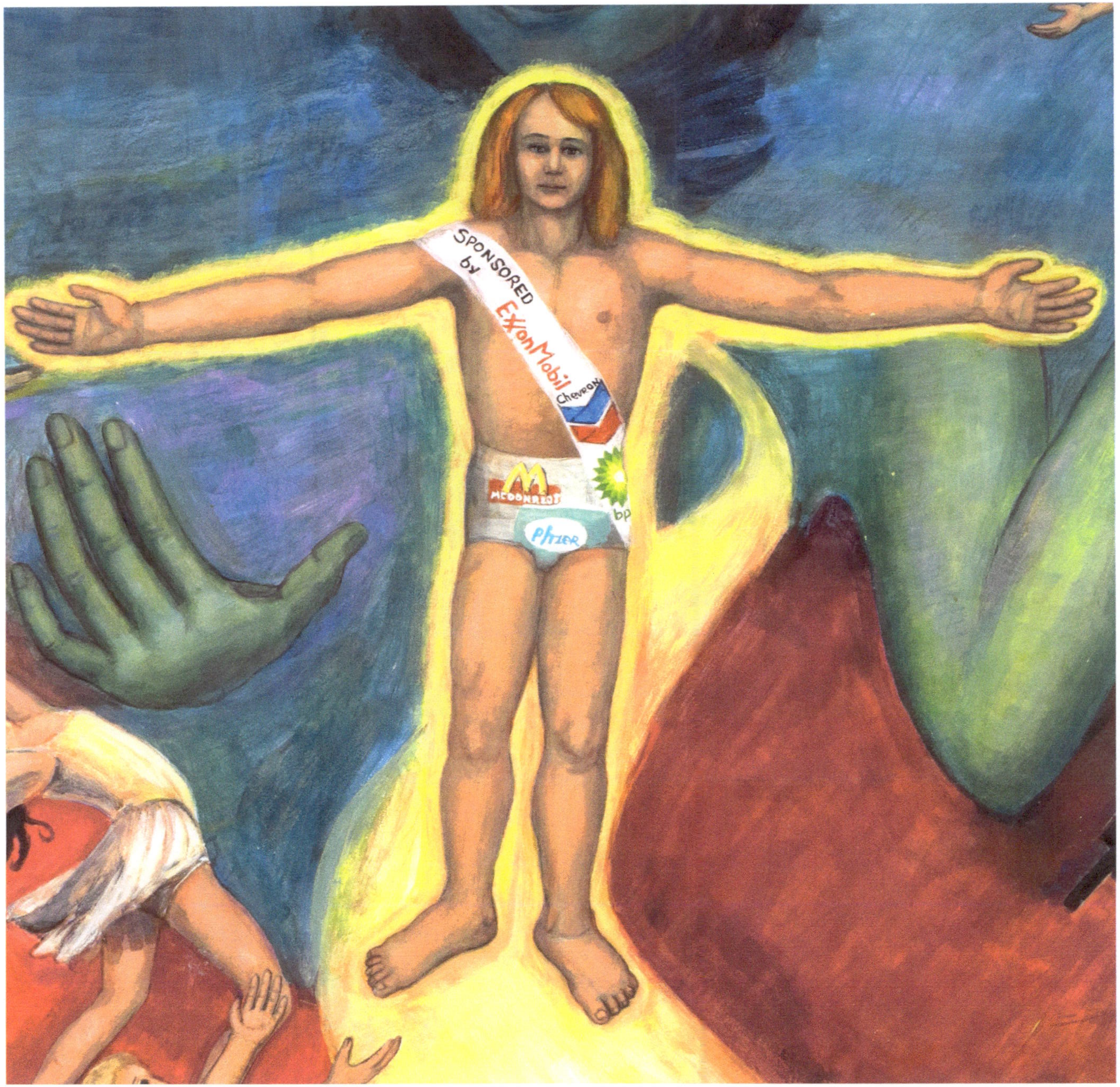

Rapture Anyone? detail

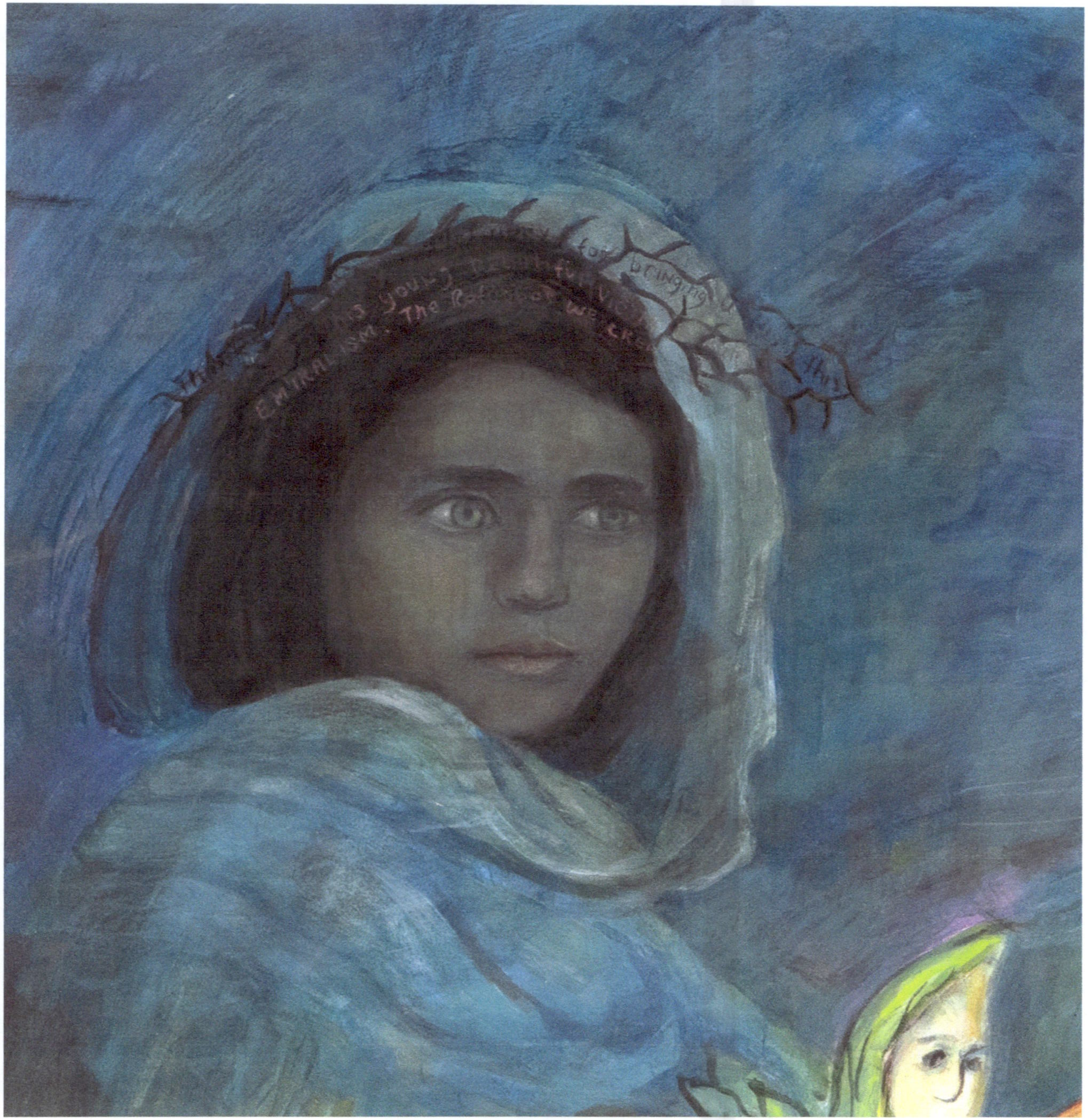

Rapture Anyone? detail

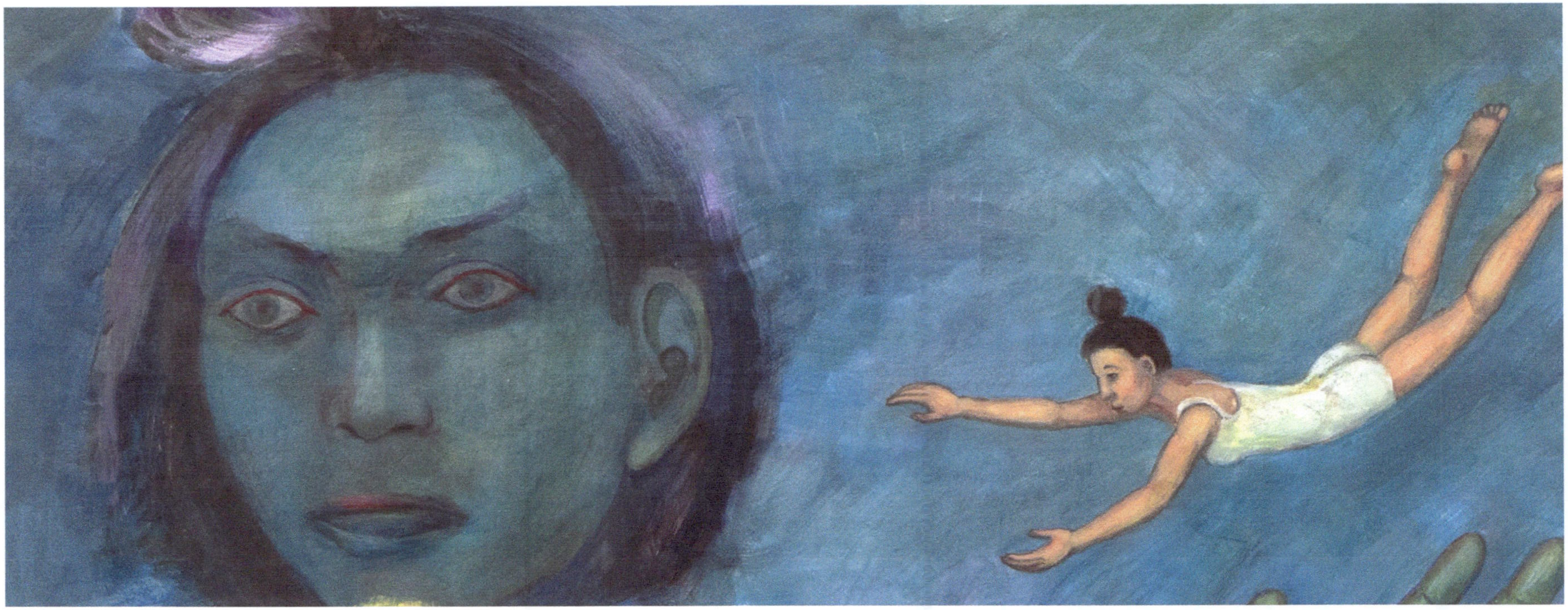

Rapture Anyone? detail

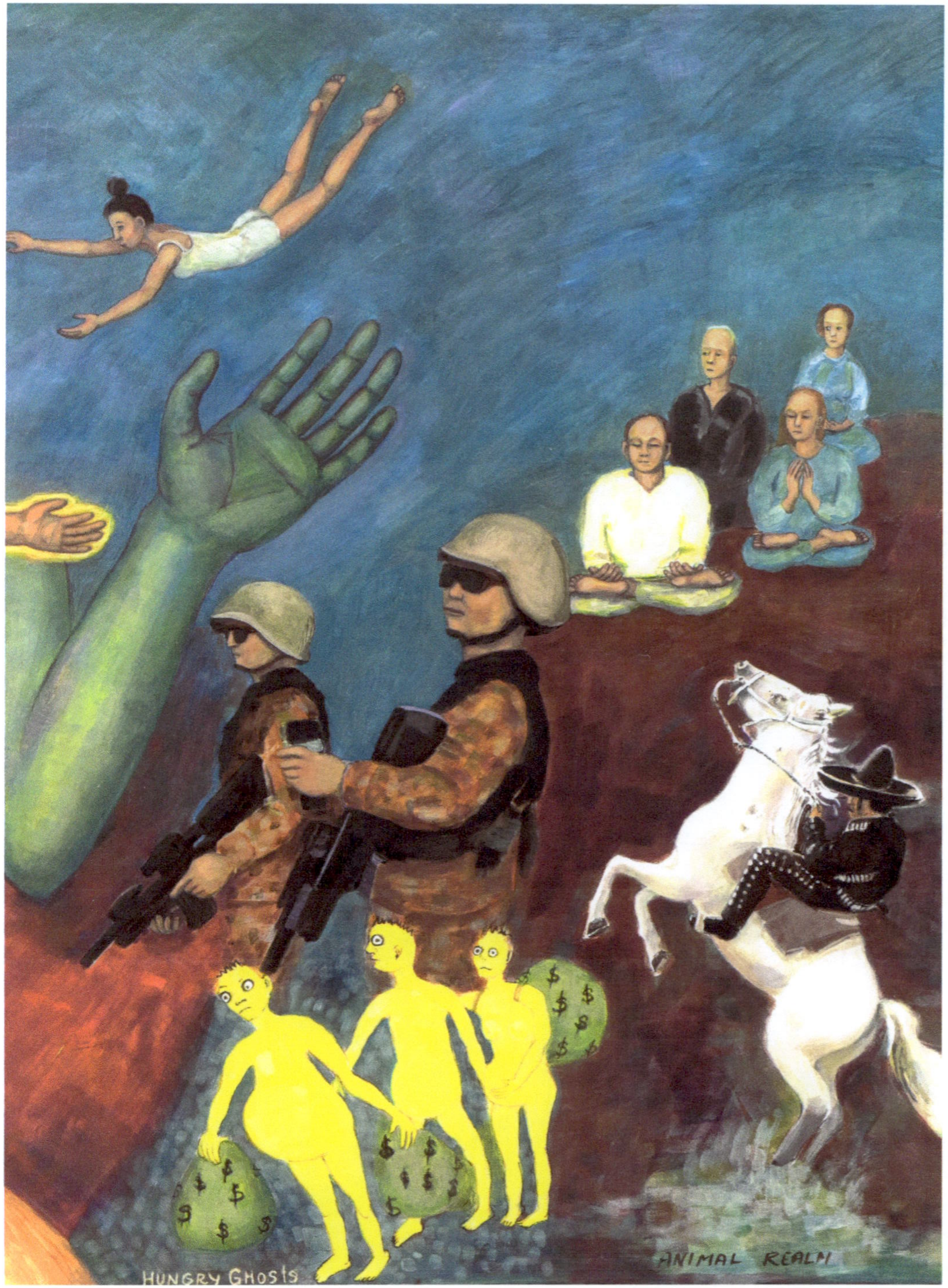

Rapture Anyone? detail

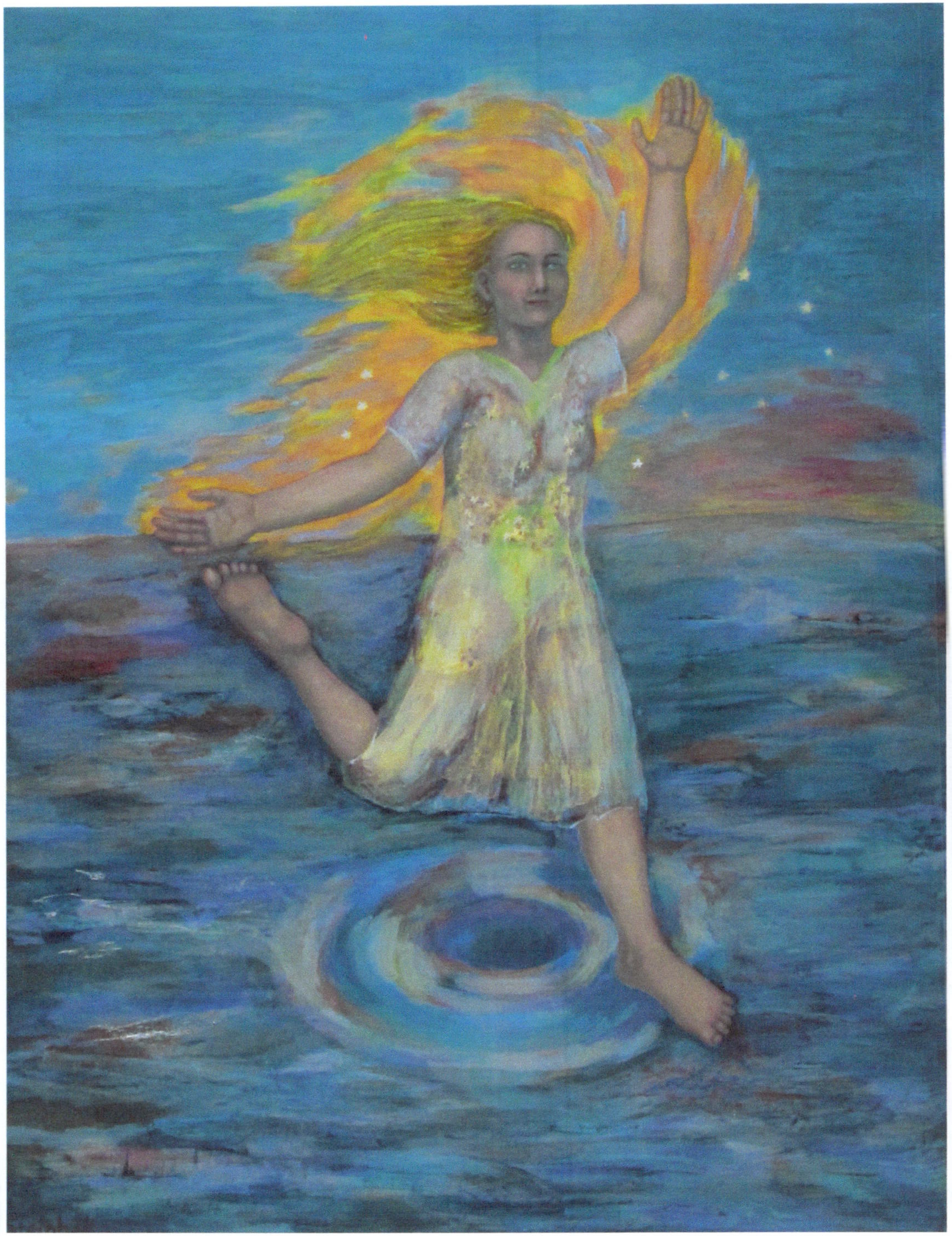

Vortex

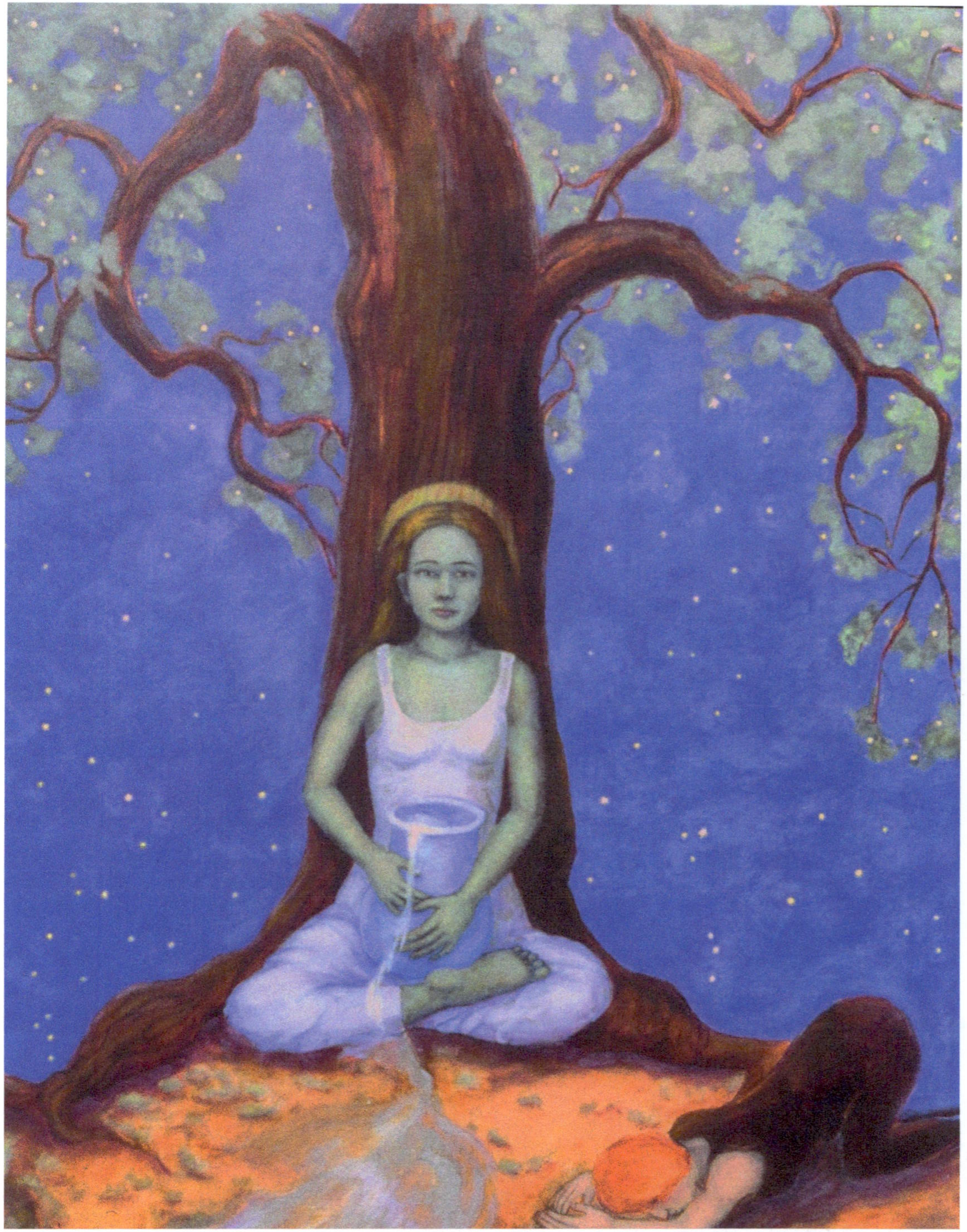

Madonna of the Trees

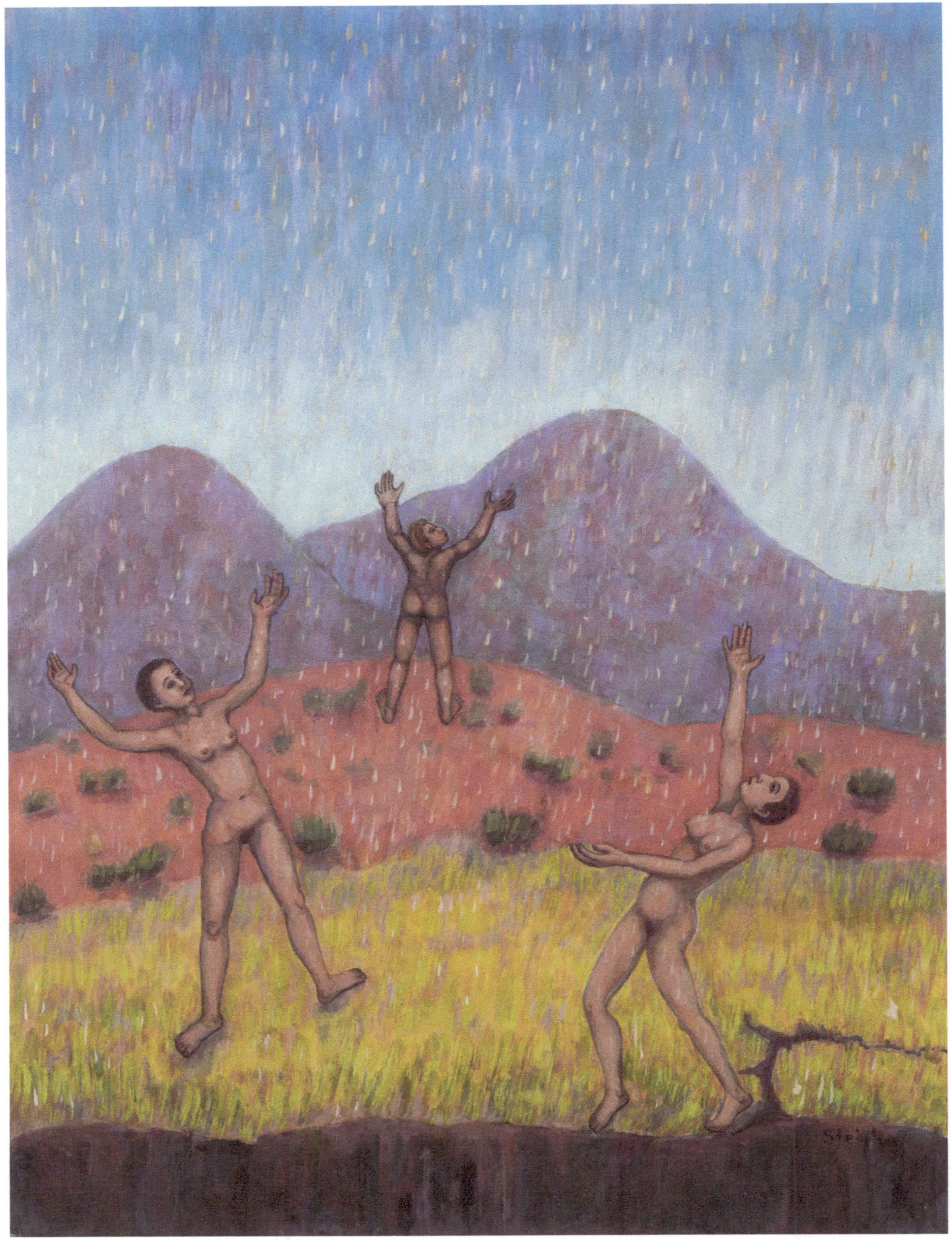

Rain

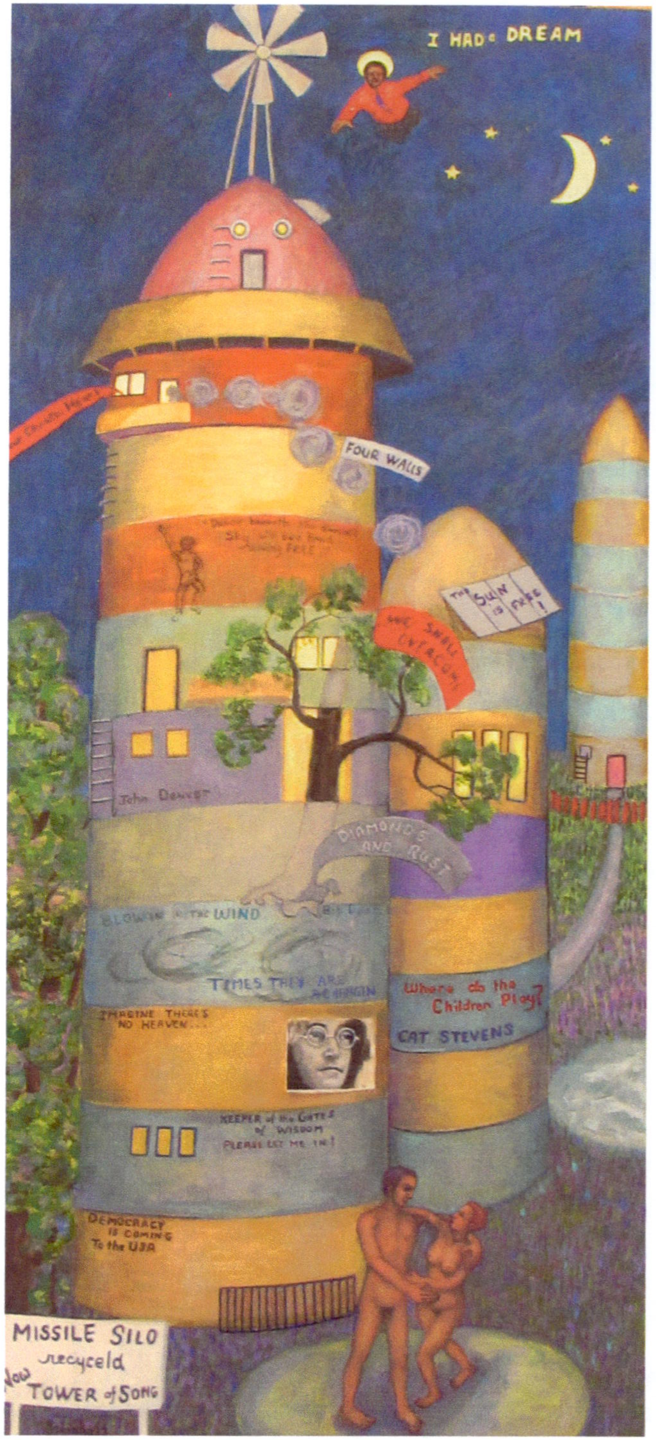

Tower of Song

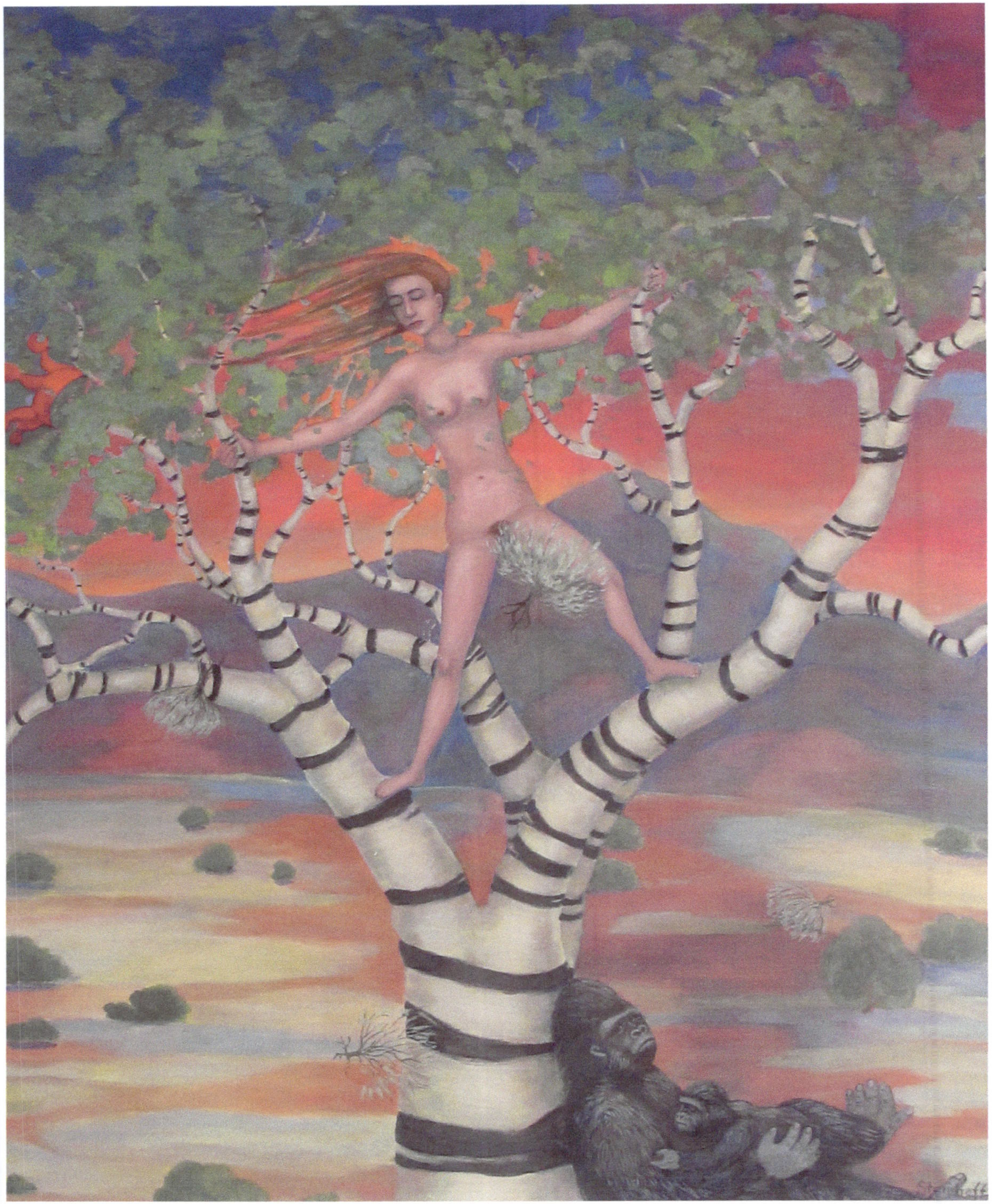

Winds of Change

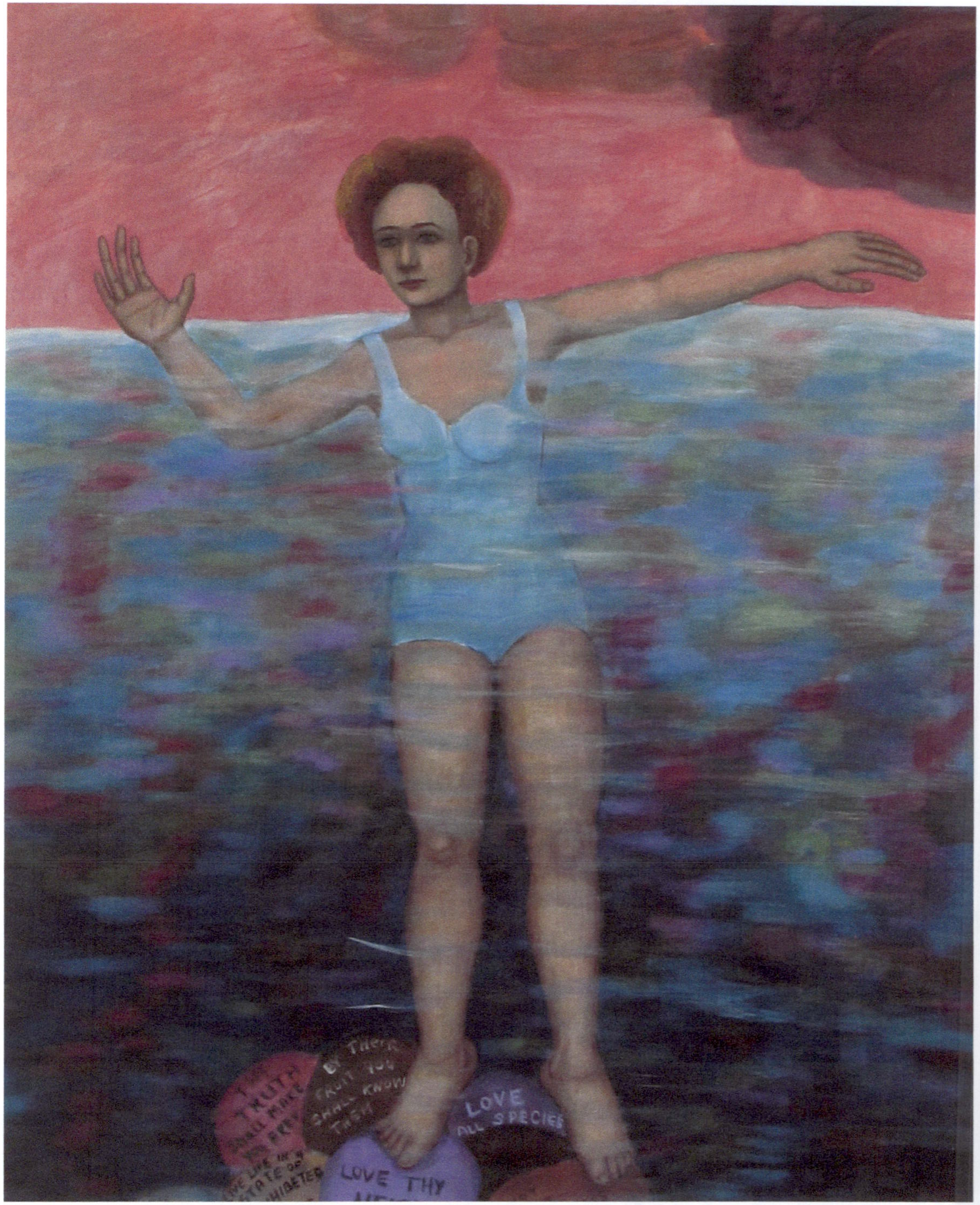

Head above Water

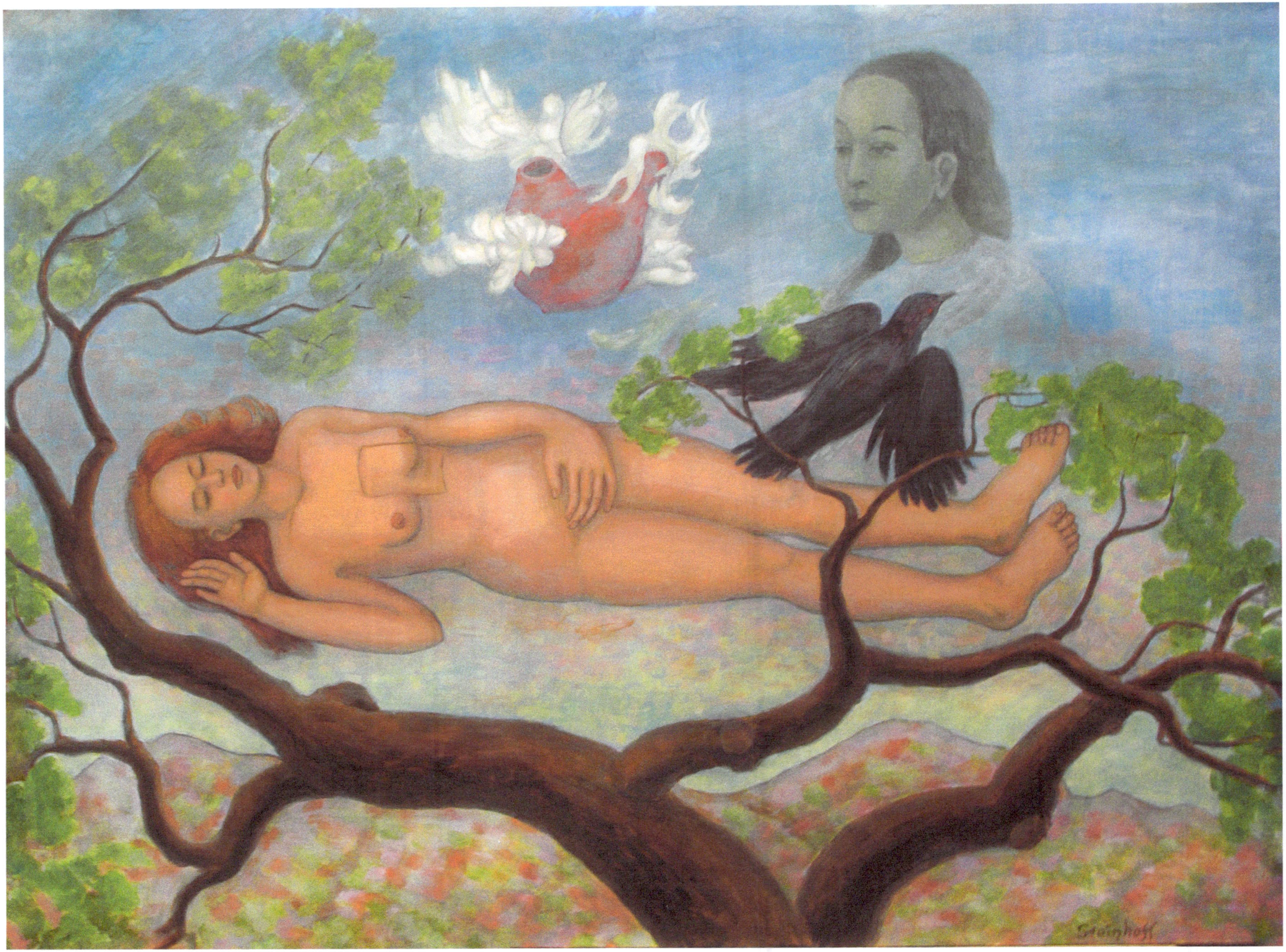

First Levitation

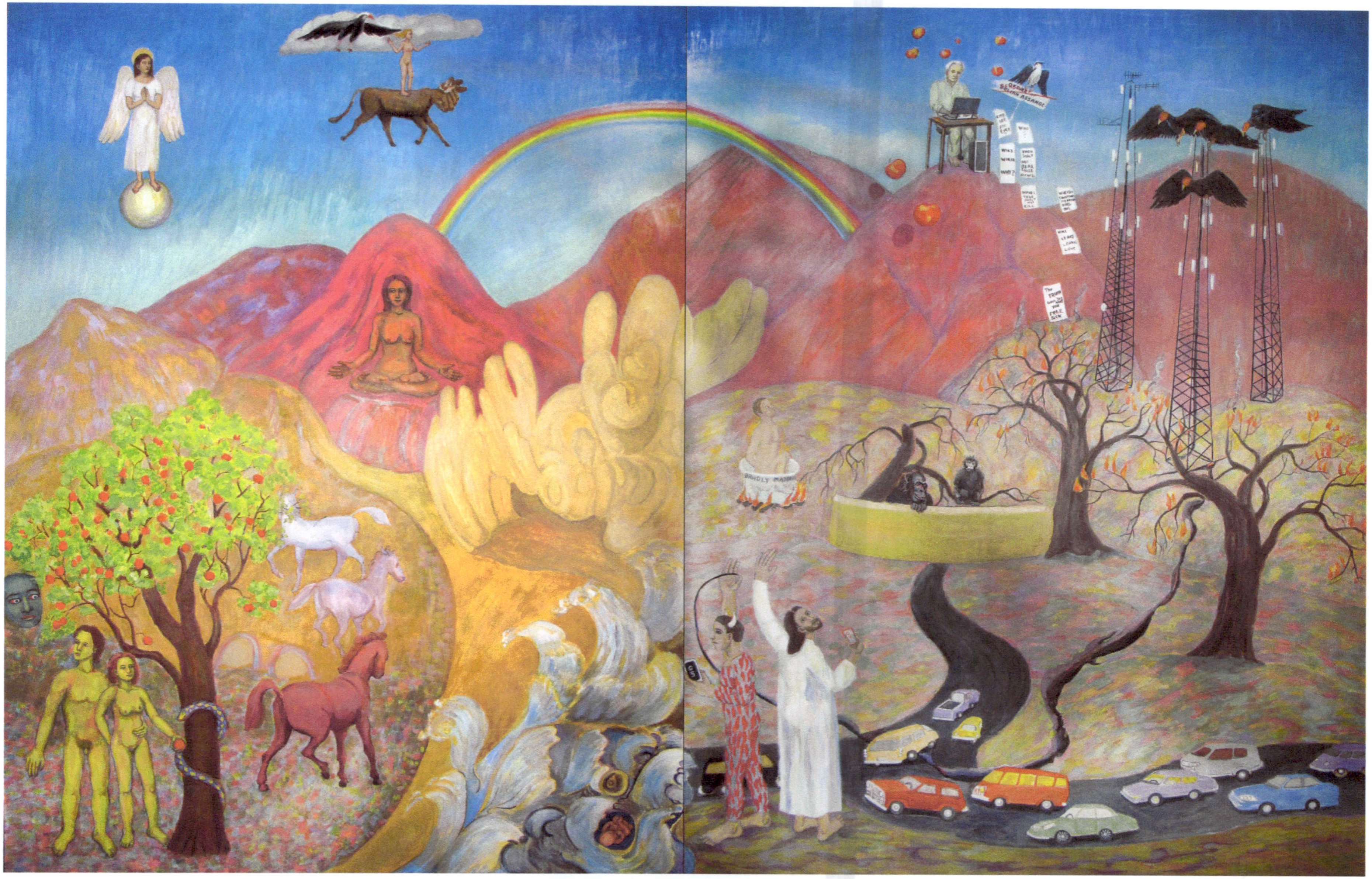

From Eden to Assange

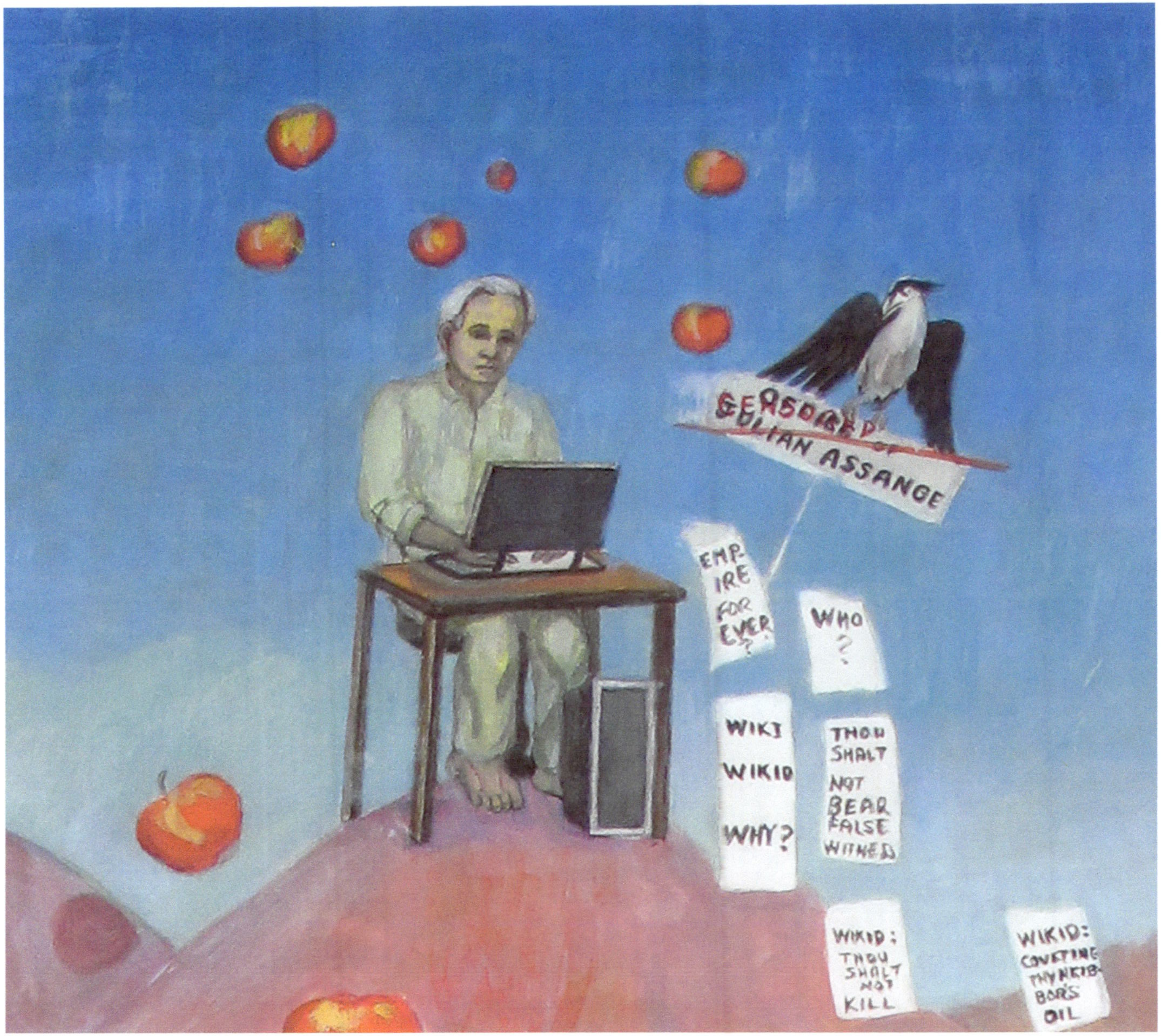

From Eden to Assange detail

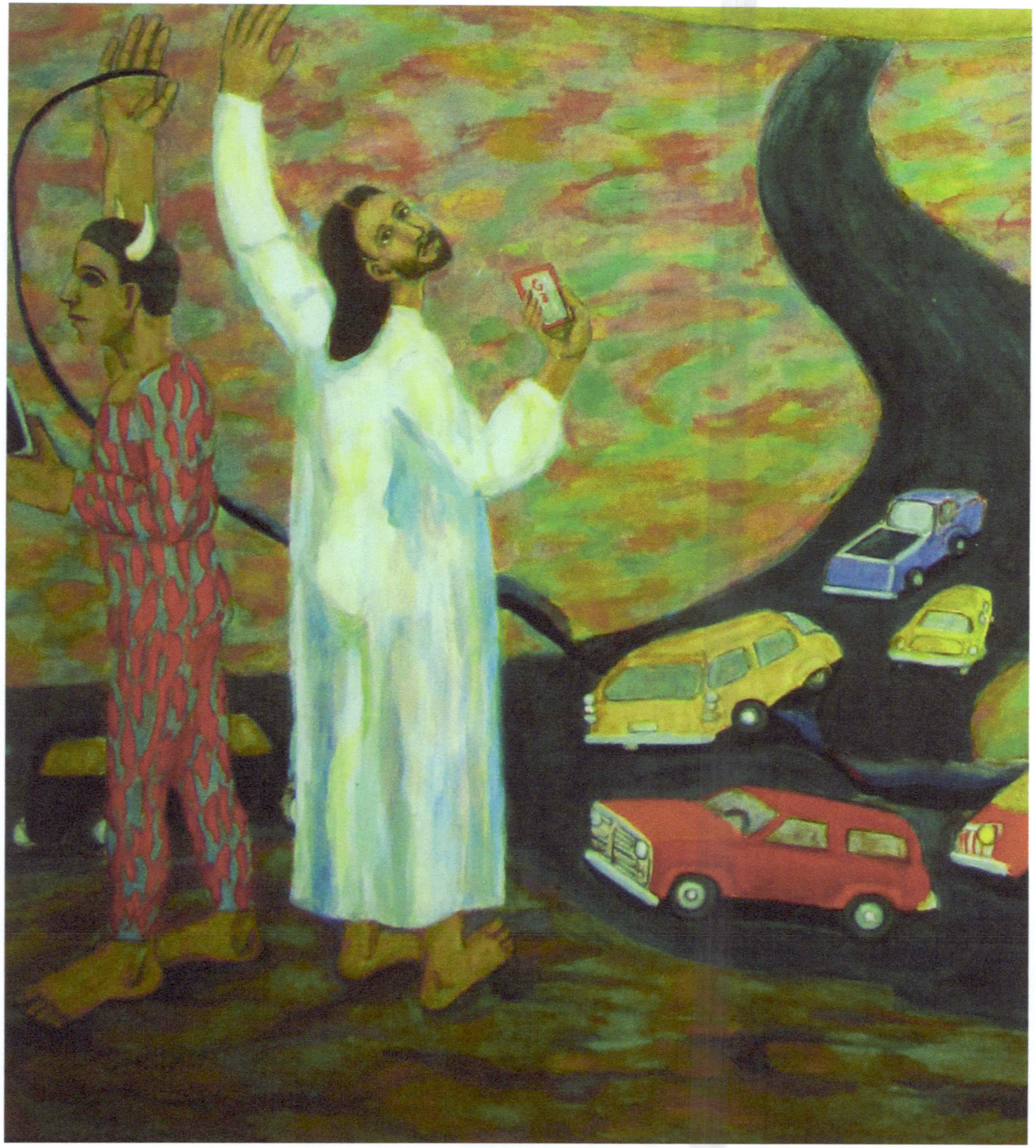

From Eden to Assange detail

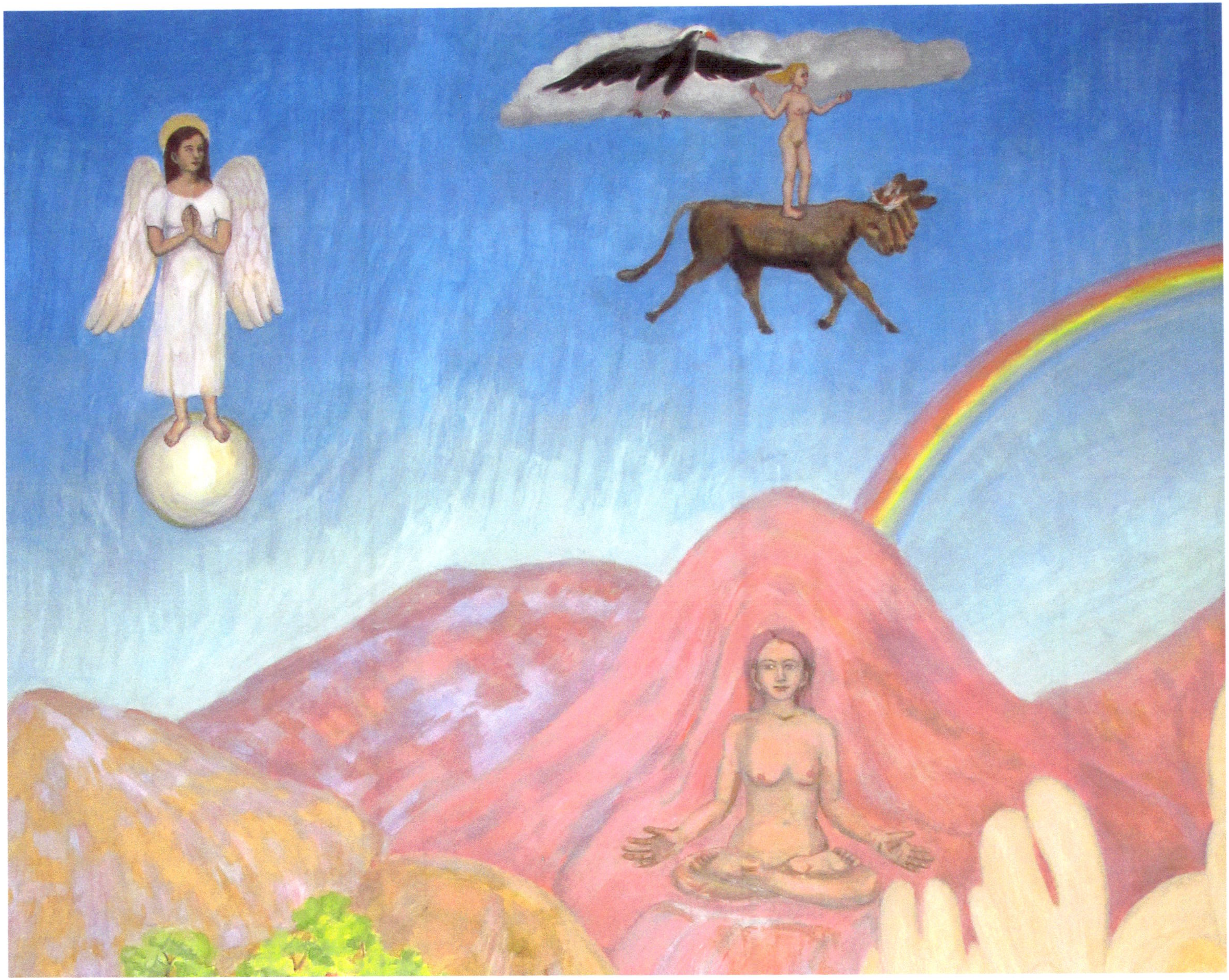

From Eden to Assange detail

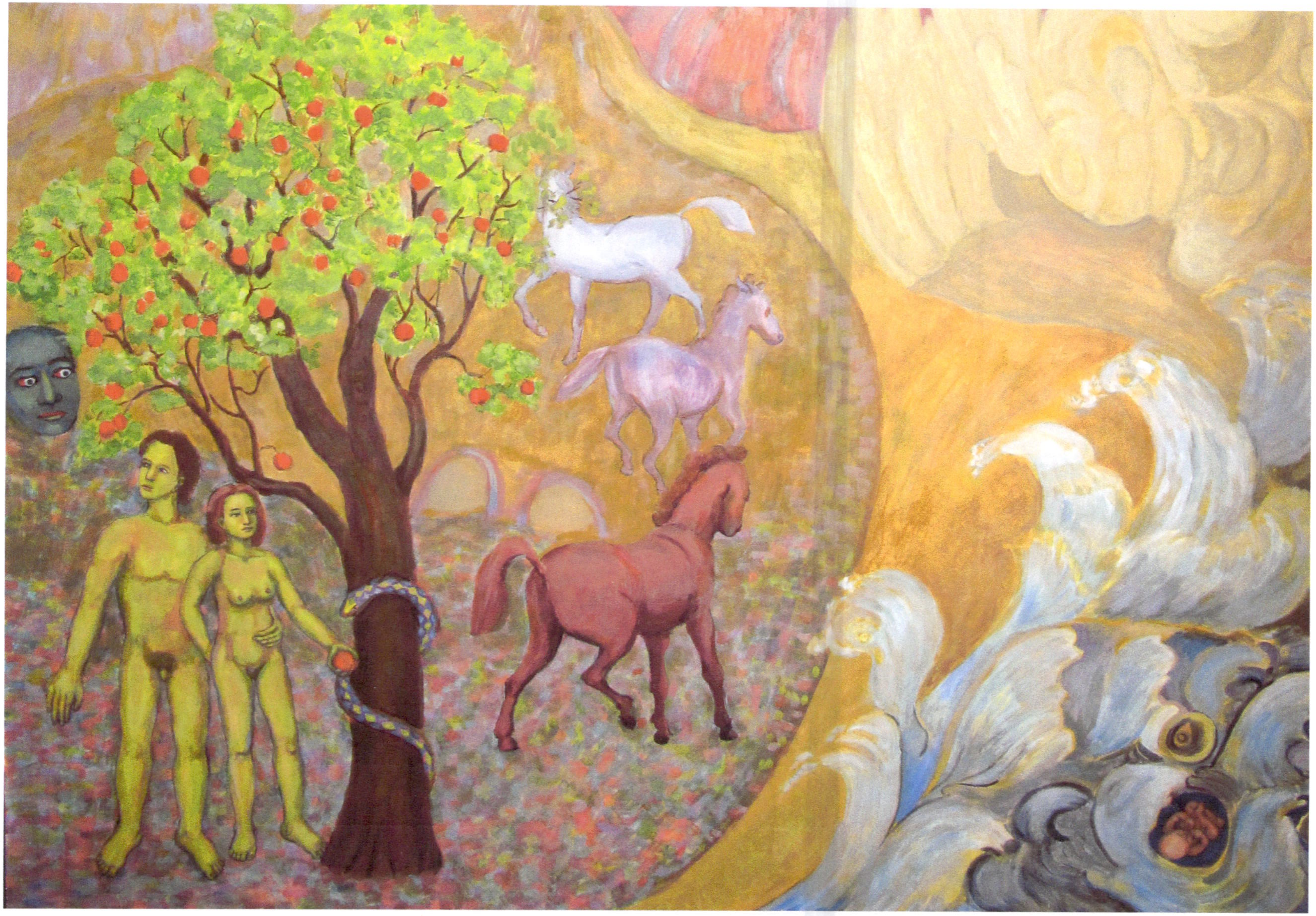

From Eden to Assange detail

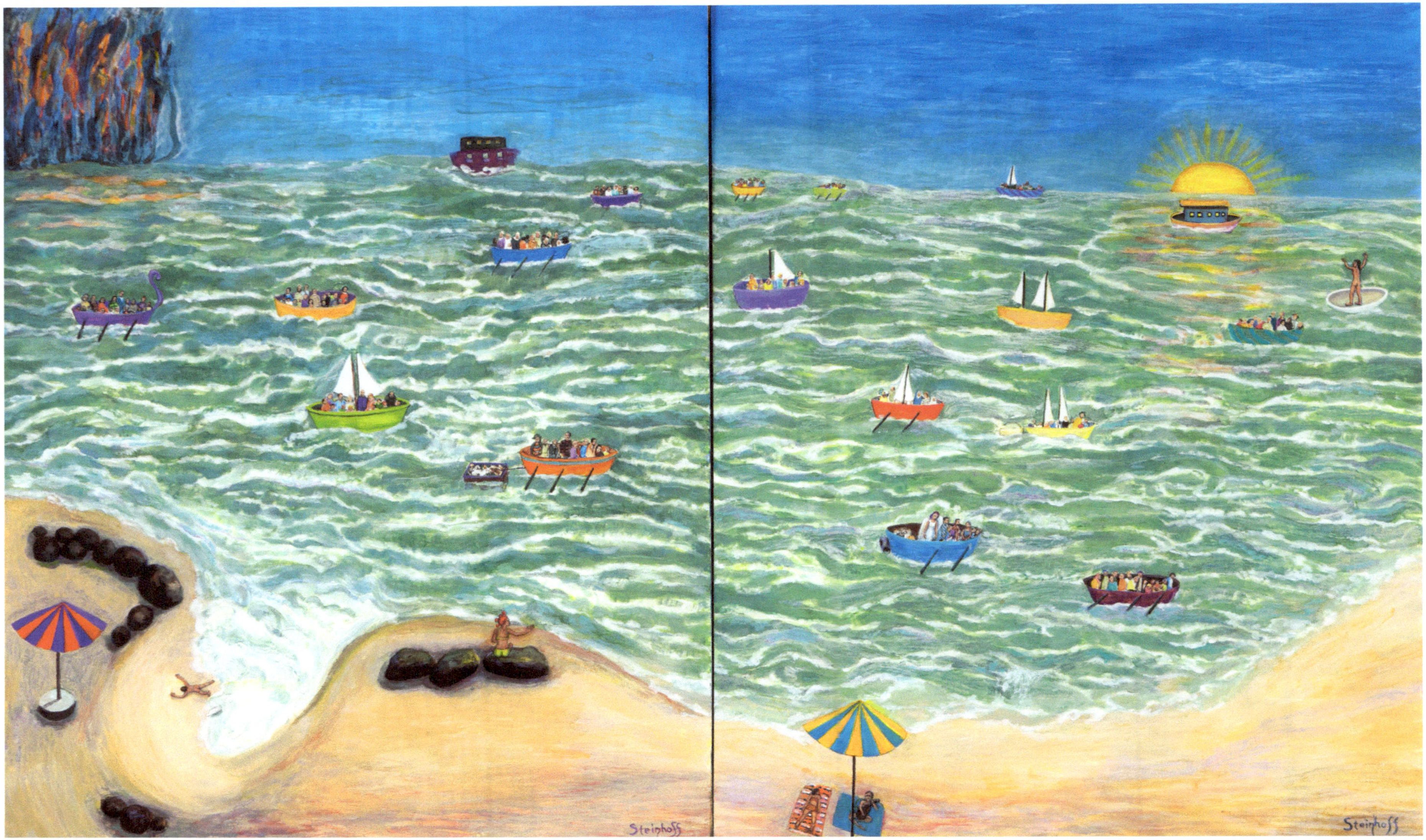

Waves Migration

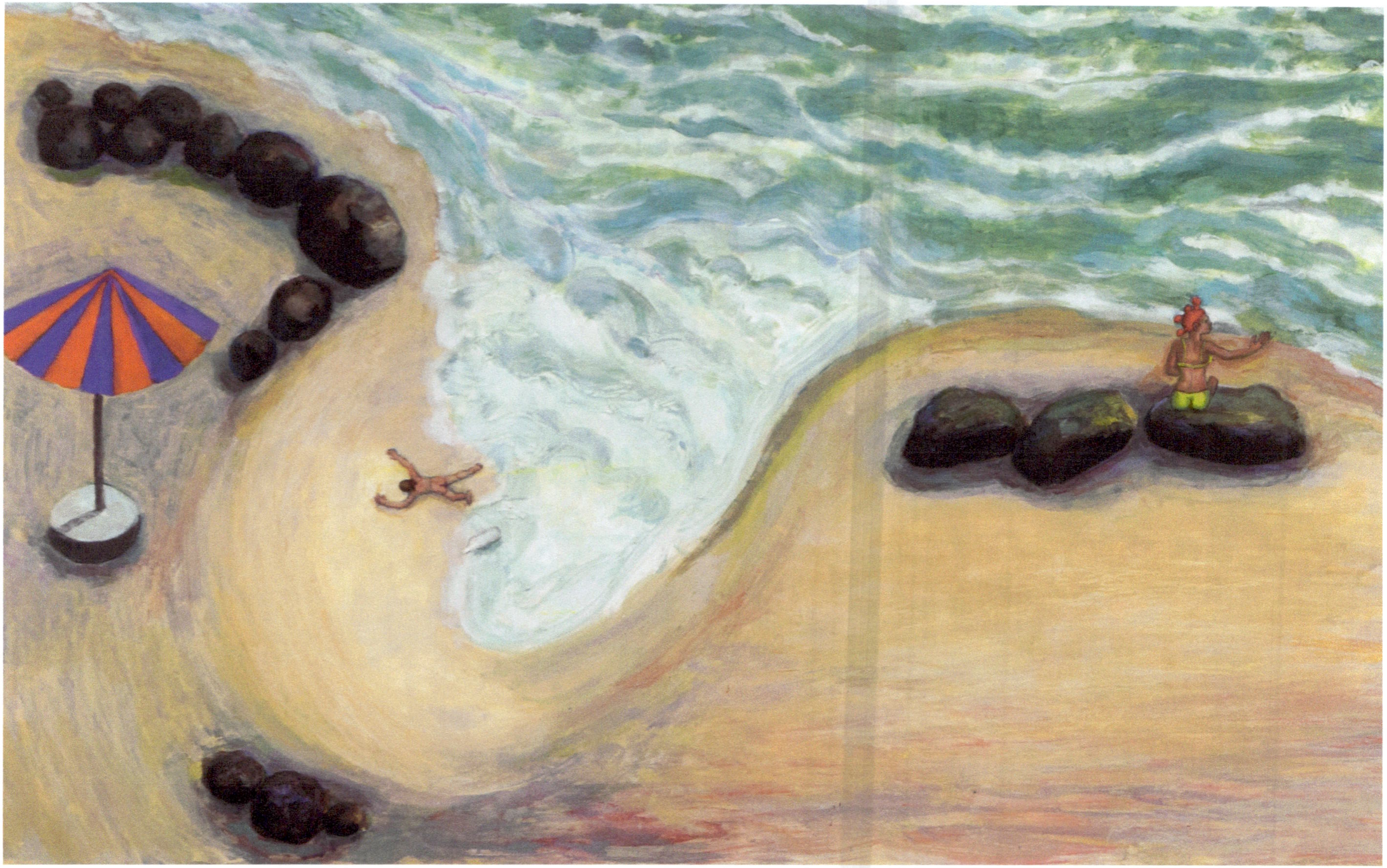

Waves Migration detail

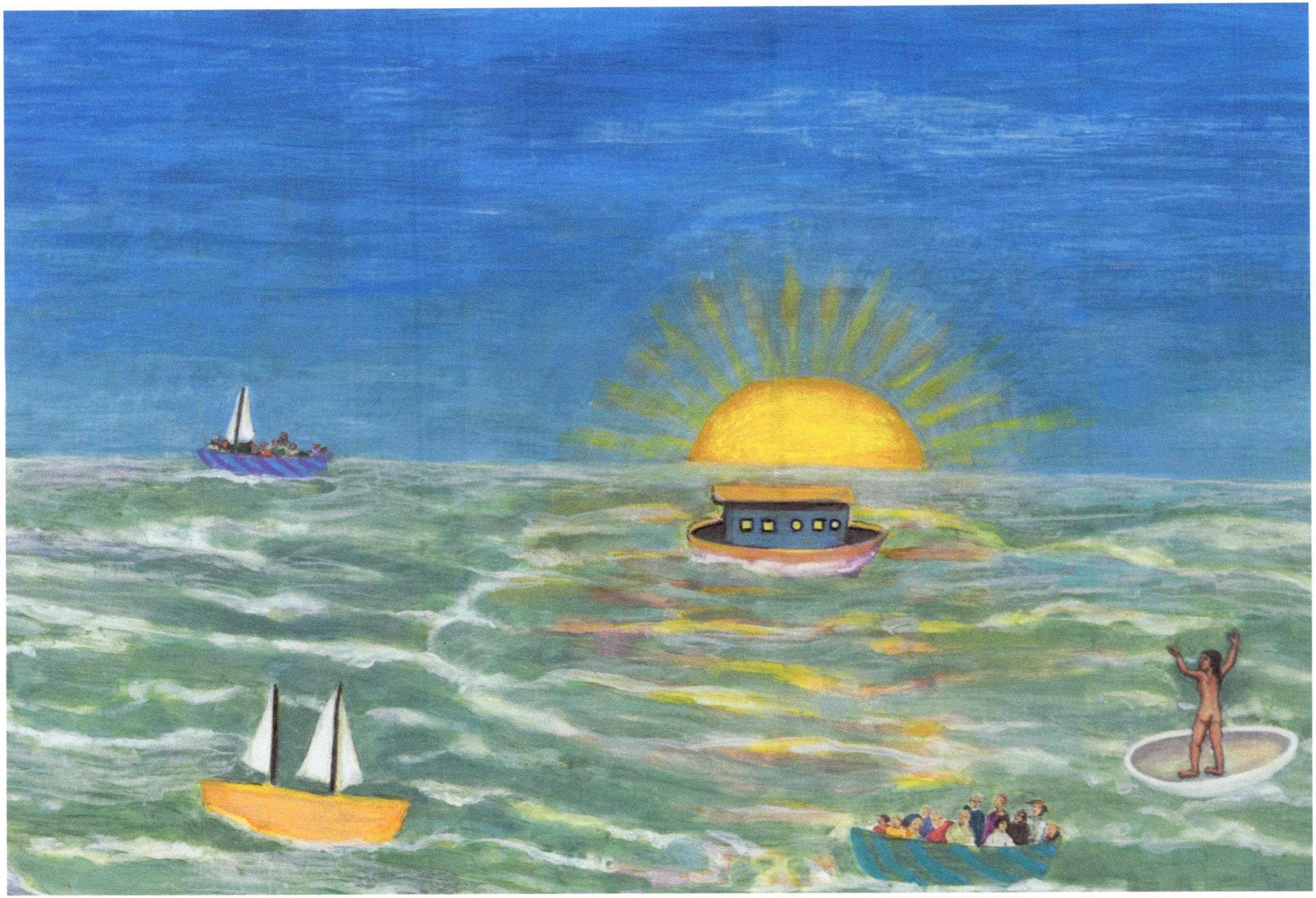

Waves Migration detail

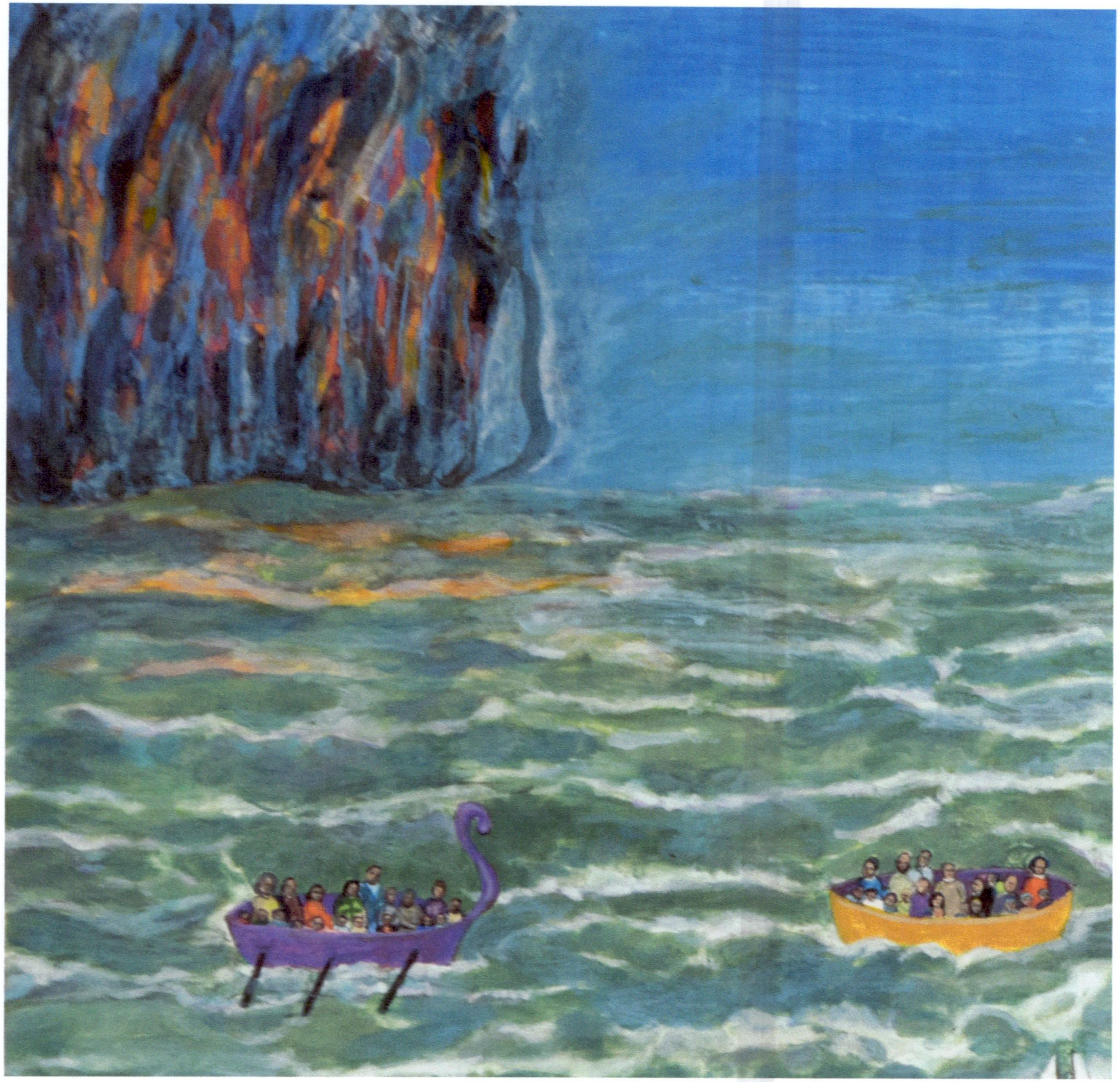

Waves Migration detail

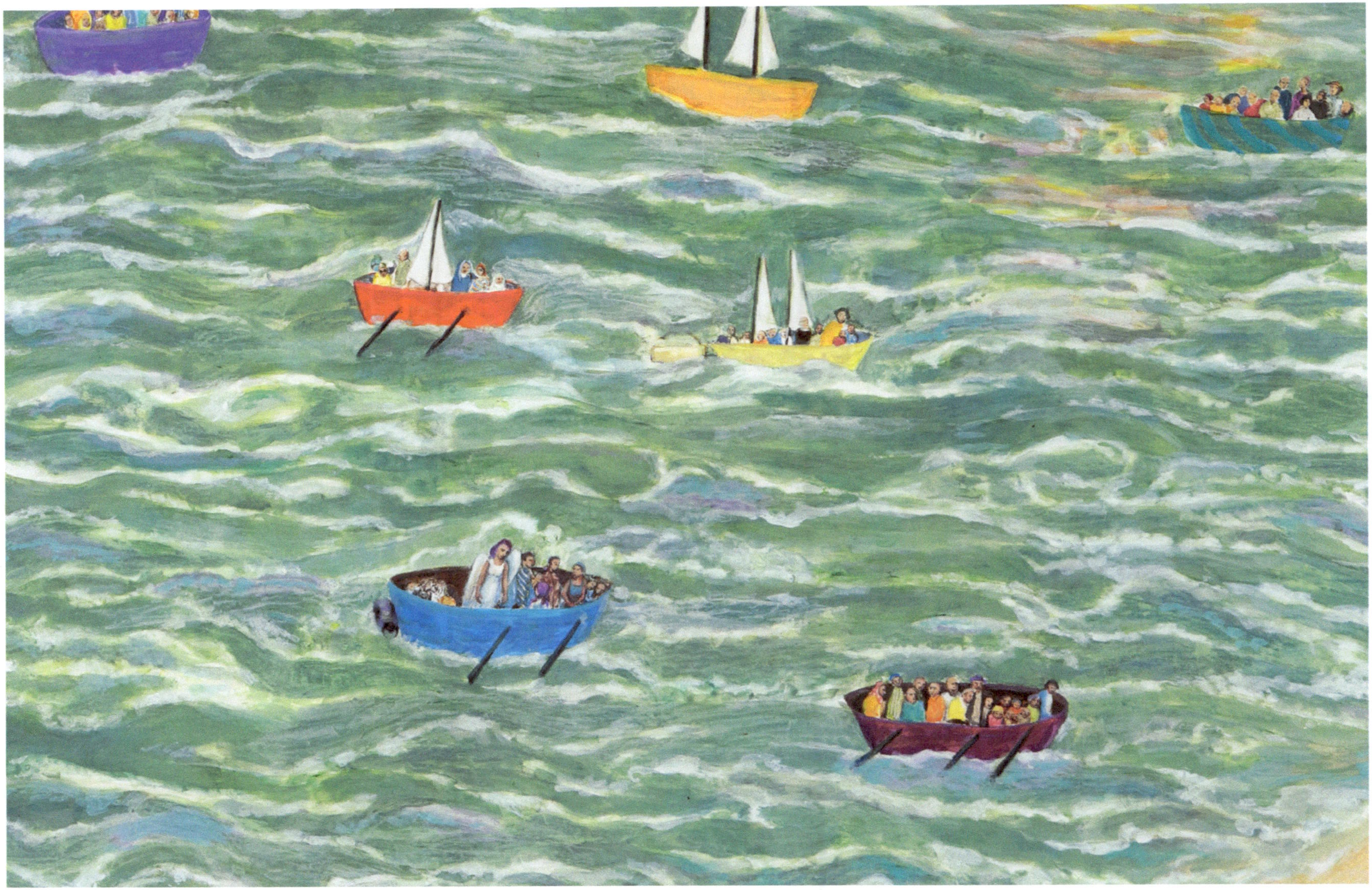

Waves Migration detail

Berkeley

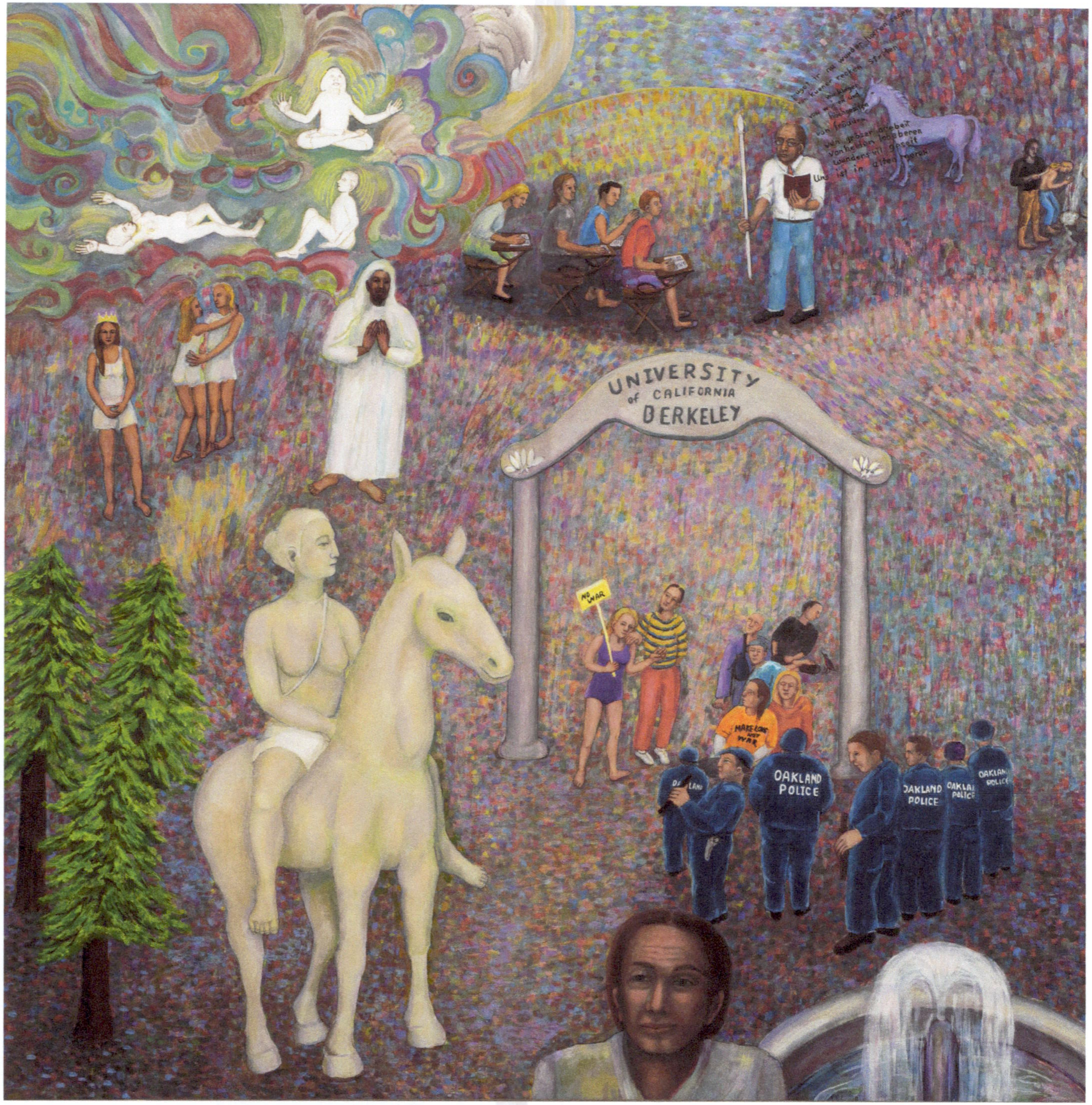
UNIVERSITY
of CALIFORNIA
BERKELEY
NO WAR
MAKE LOVE NOT WAR
OAKLAND POLICE
OAKLAND POLICE
OAKLAND POLICE
OAKLAND POLICE

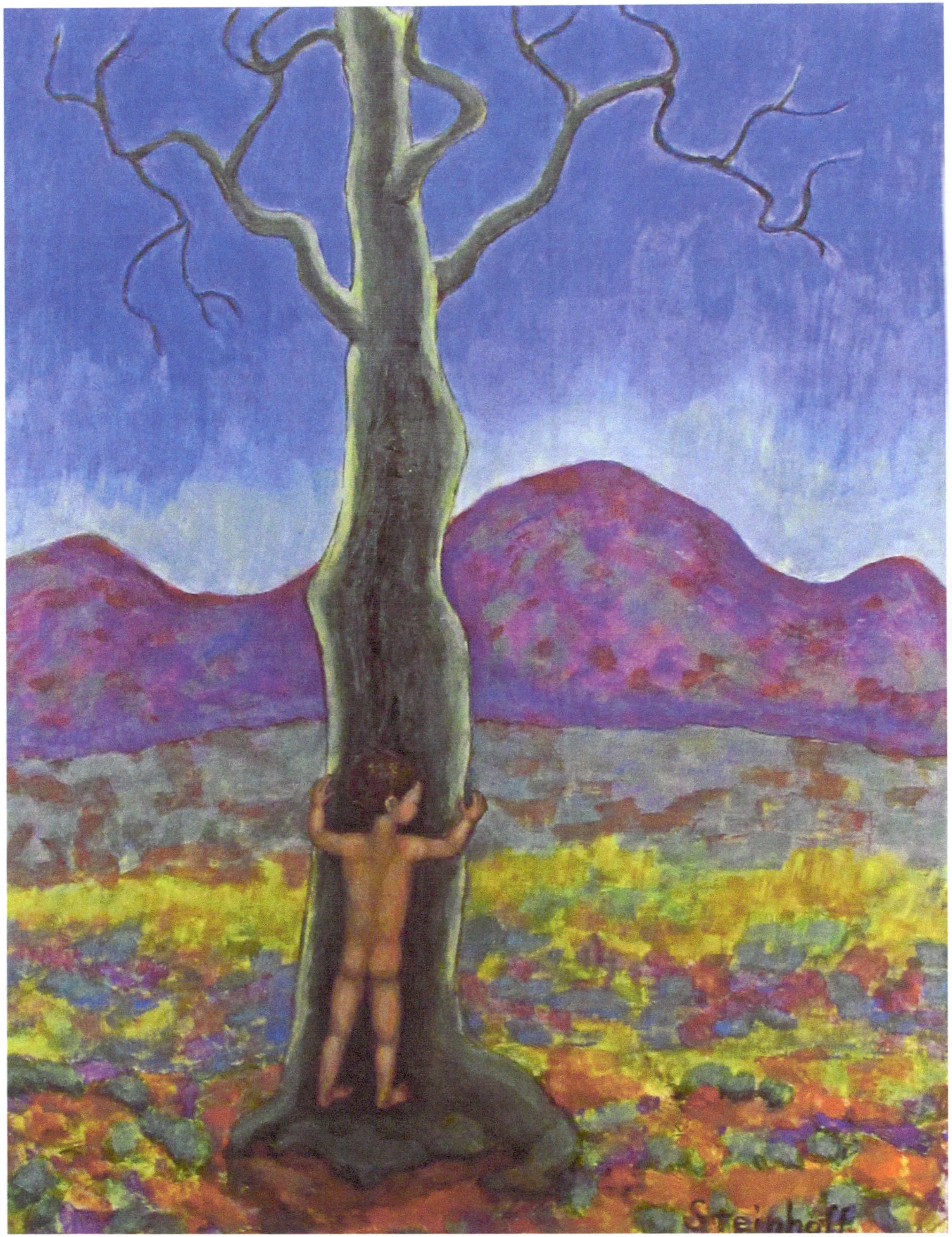

Child and Tree

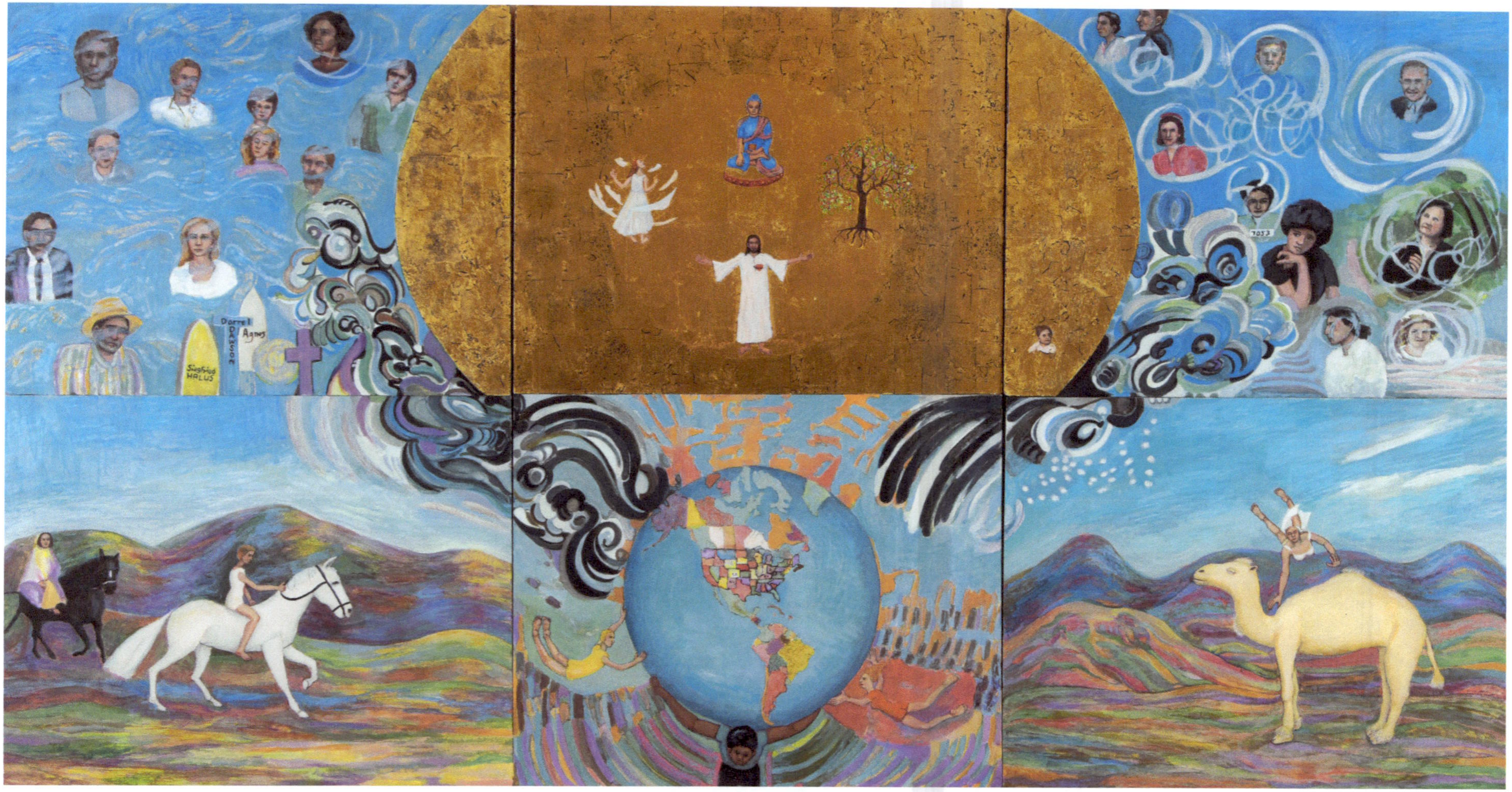

My Cosmology

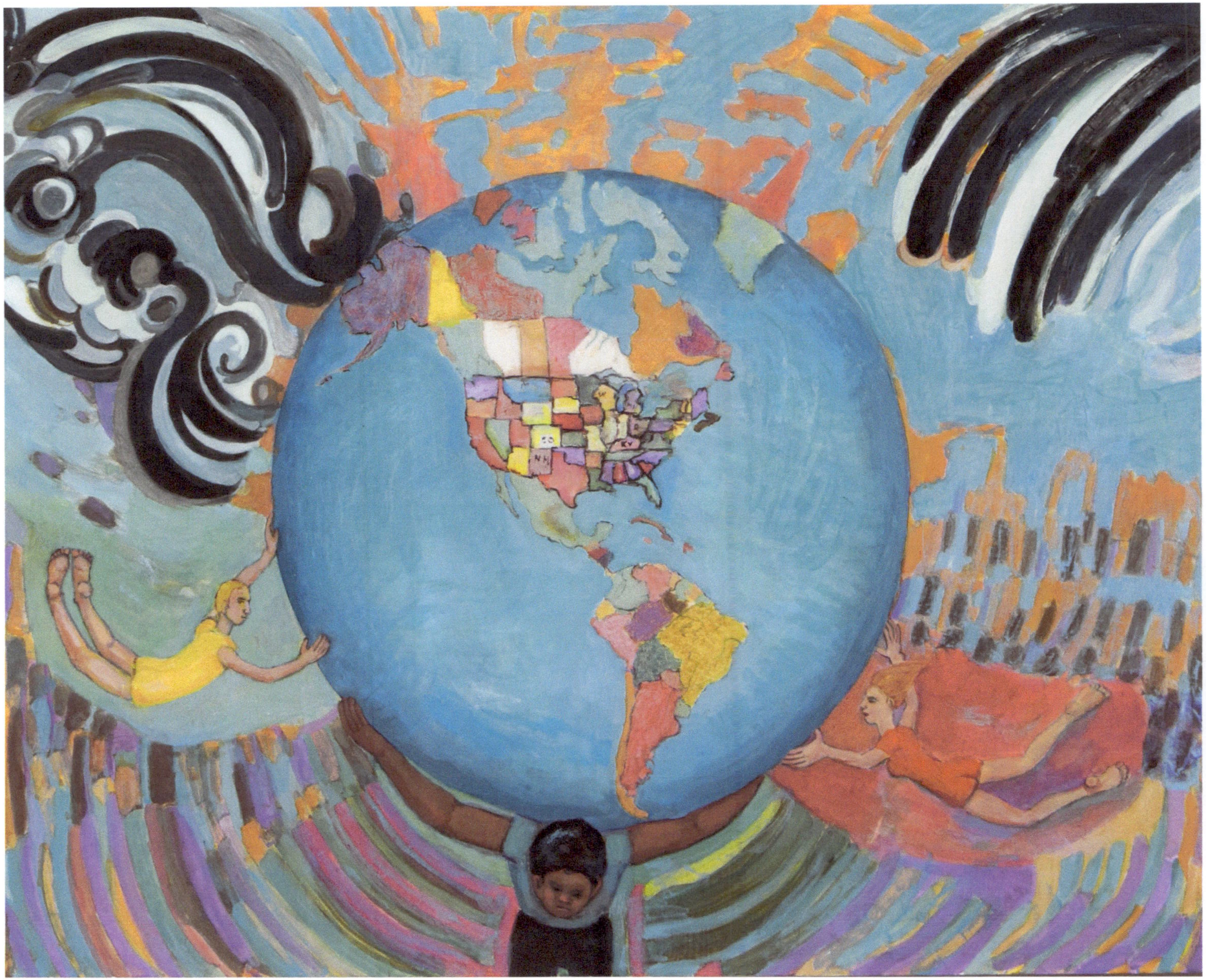

My Cosmology detail

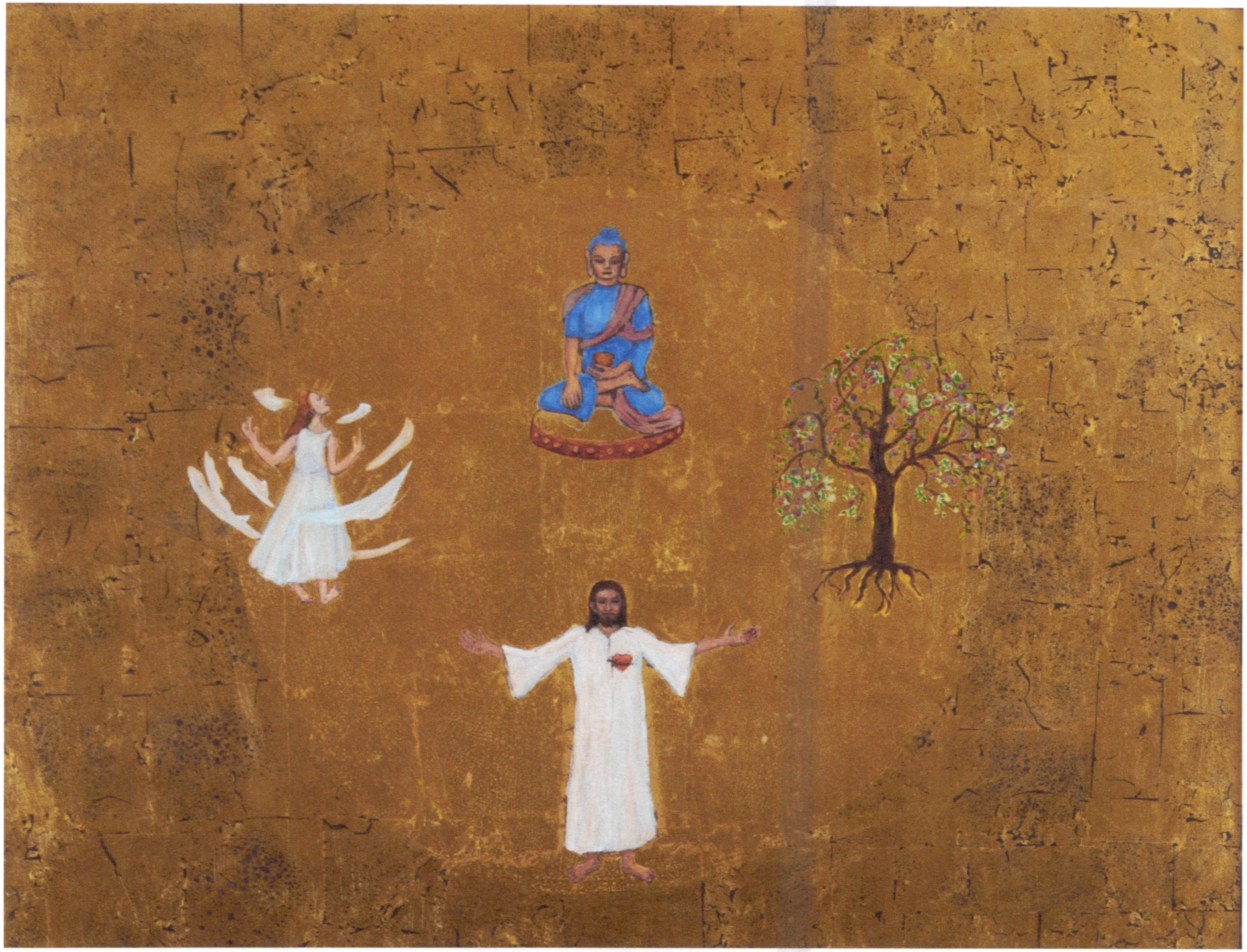

My Cosmology detail

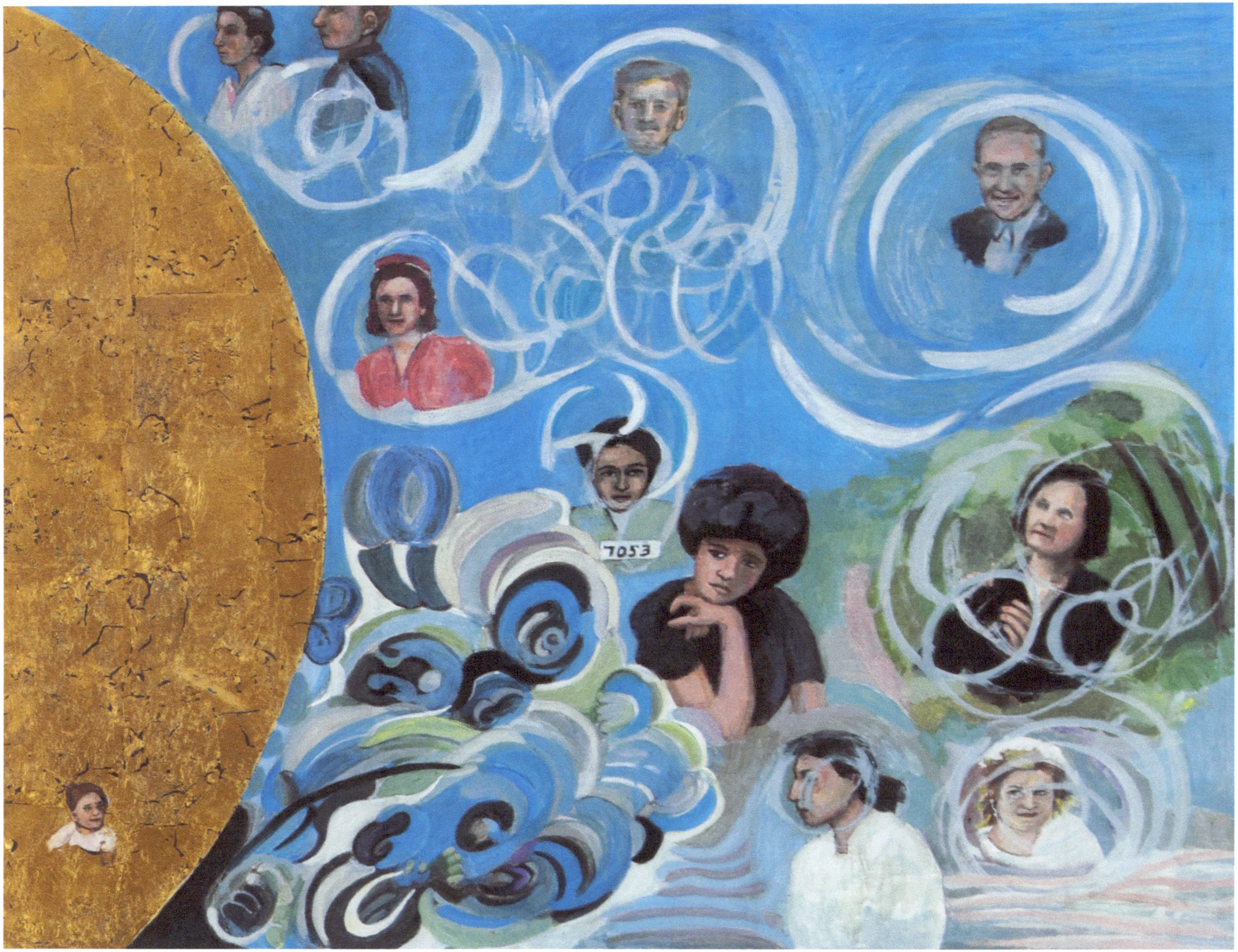

My Cosmology detail

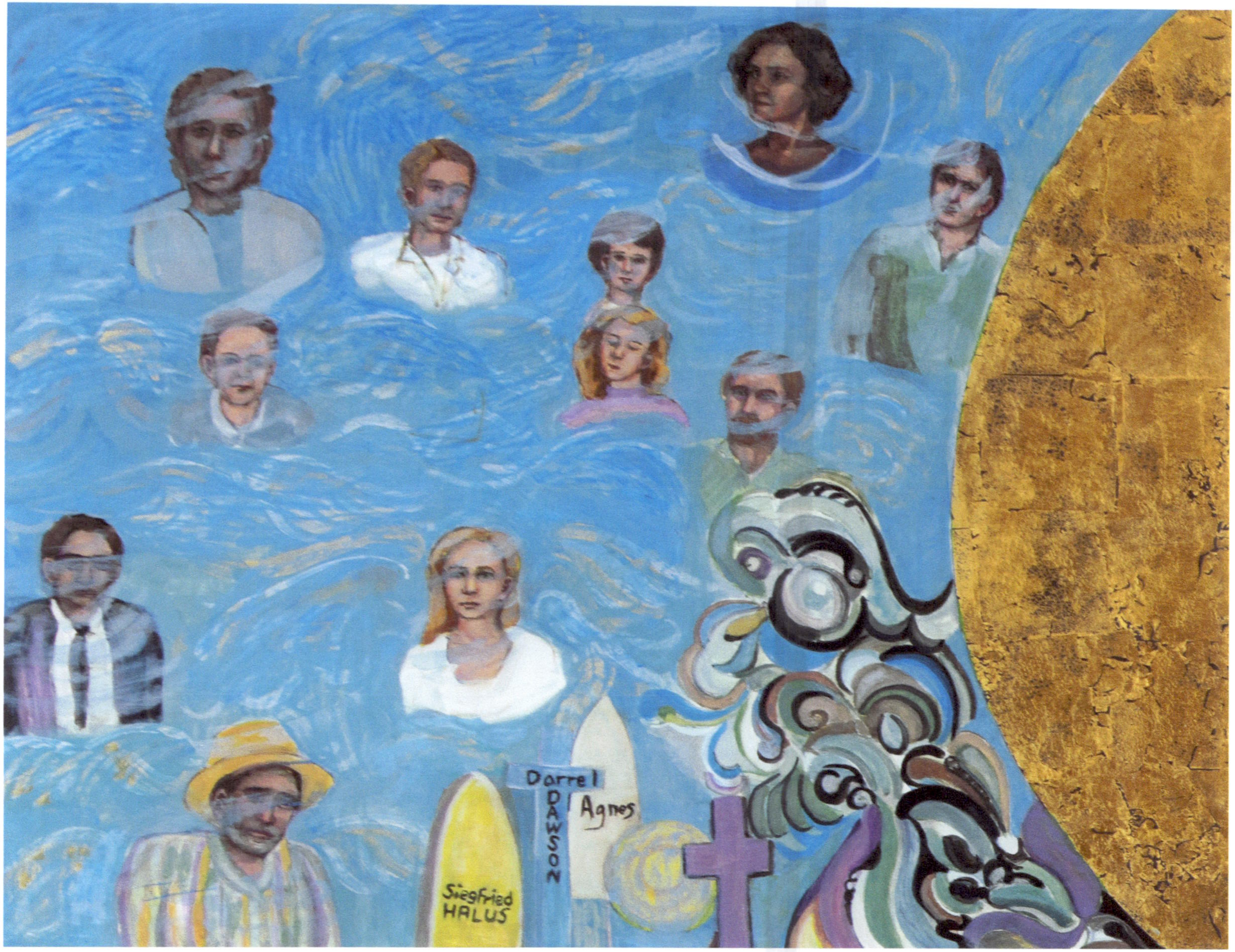

My Cosmology detail

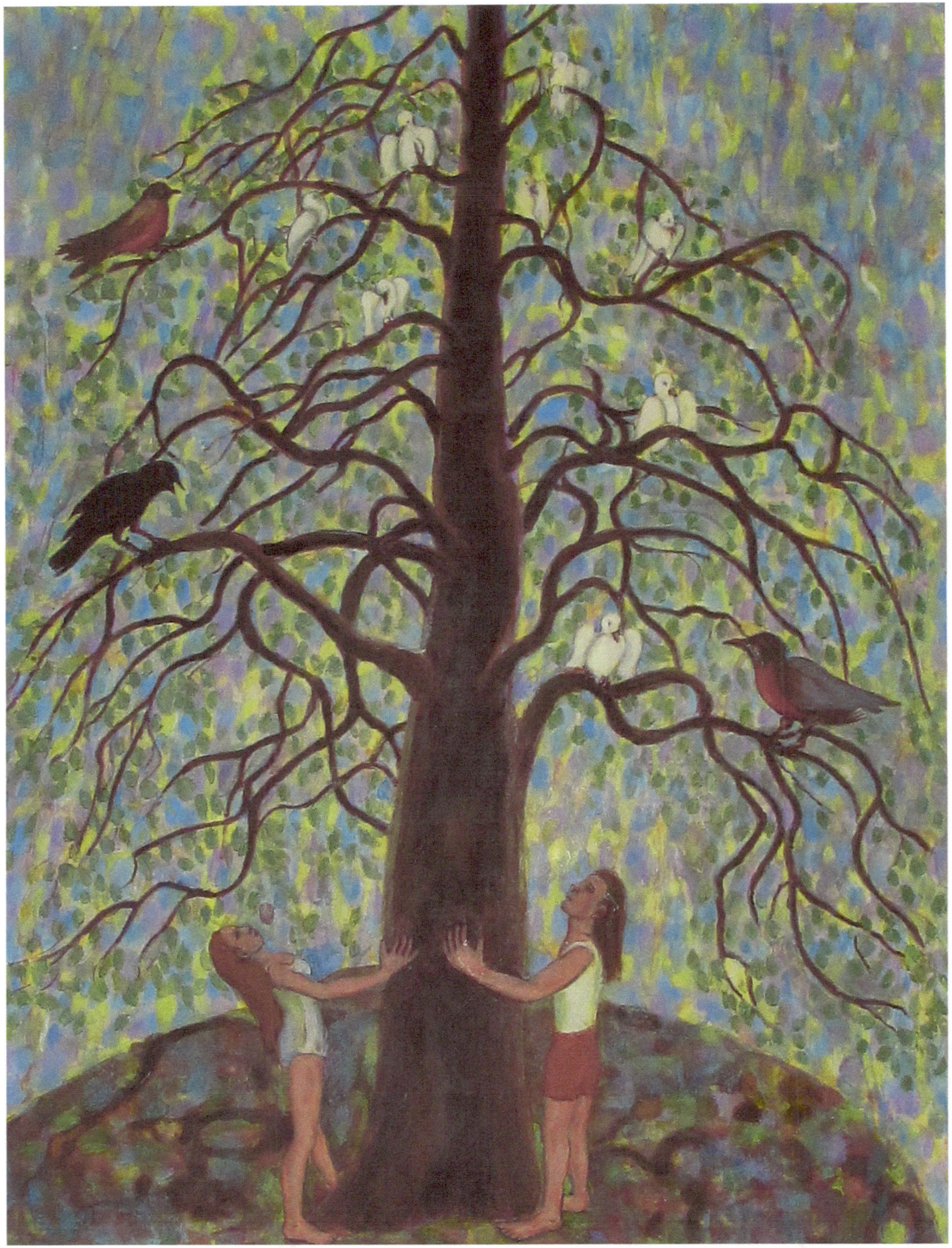

Birds of Eden

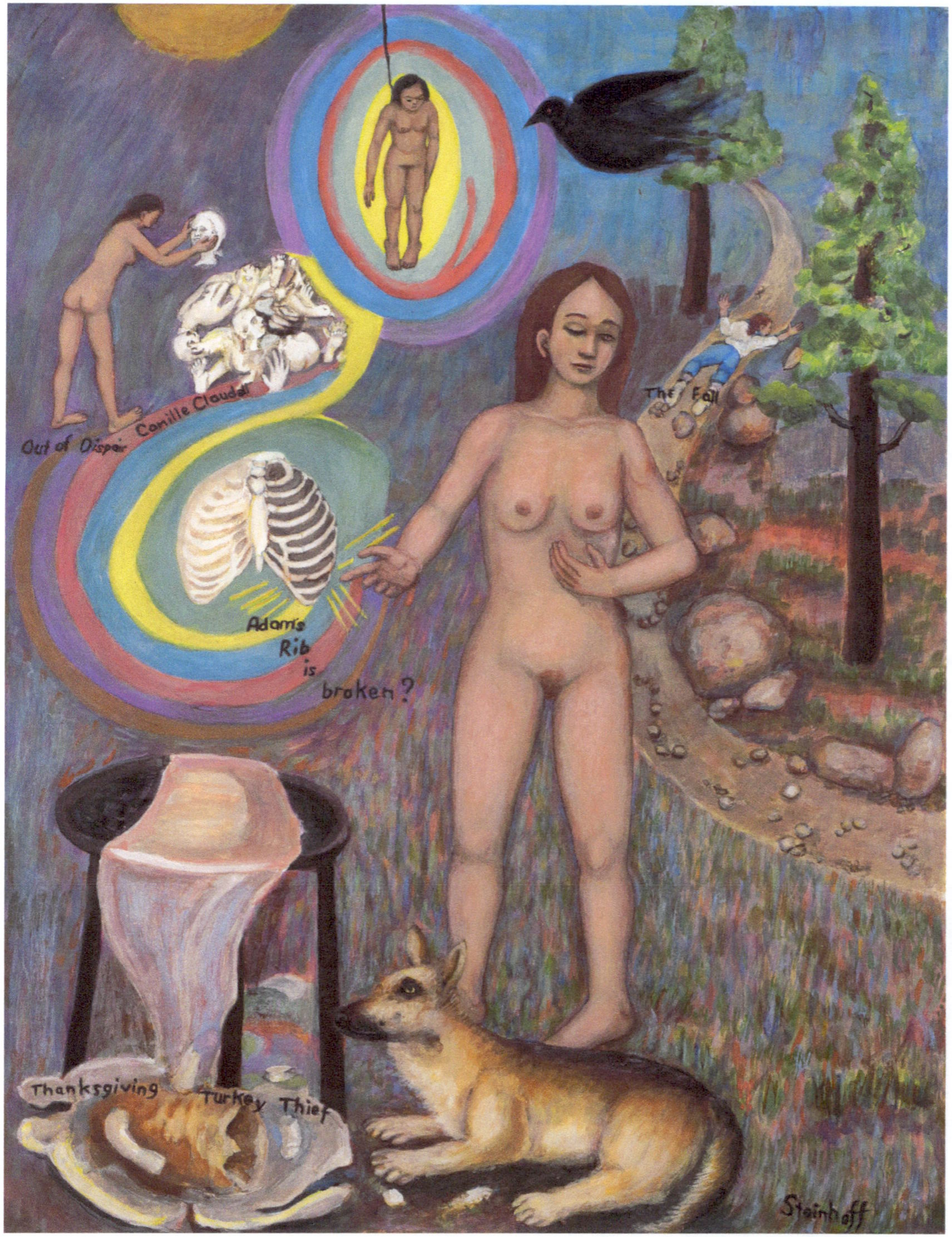

Adam's Rib and the Turkey Thief

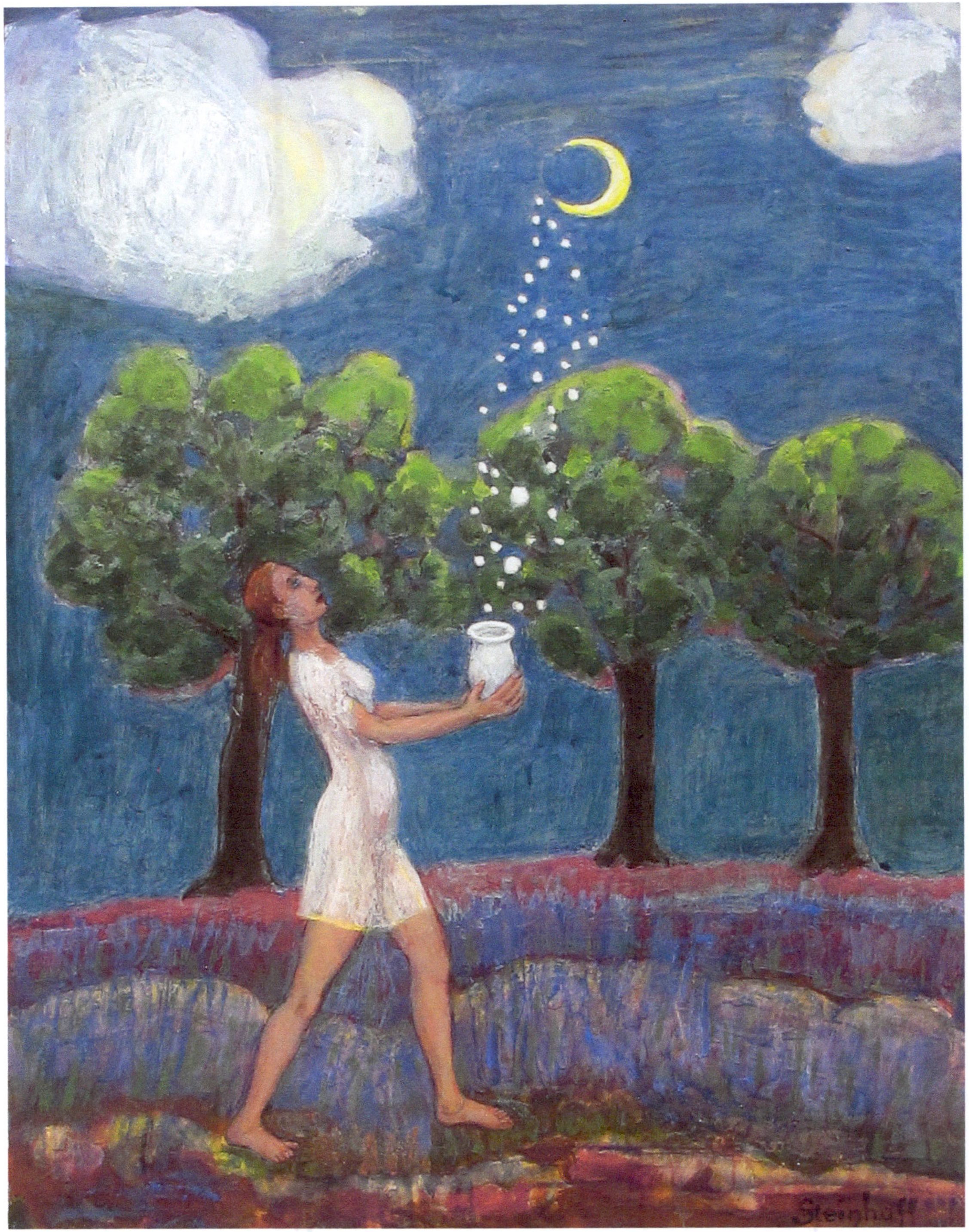

Gift of Water

EXPLANATIONS OF CERTAIN PAINTINGS

1. Ritual of the Unlimited
2. Case of the Basket Case
3. Forest Primeval Early Meltdown
4. "...and God gave Dominion"
5. Berlin
6. Restoring the Balance
7. Computer Lady; or, How to completely recycle a computer
8. Venus of the Terrorism Wars
9. 4 Horsemen of the Apocalypse over Bagdad
10. Rapture Anyone?
11. From Eden to Assange
12. Berkeley
13. My Cosmology
14. Adam's Rib and the Turkey Thief
15. Walking Home

1. Ritual of the Unlimited was inspired by my feelings about the making of the atomic bomb at Los Alamos as well as discussions about unlimited free or very cheap energy, which reminded me of the 60's in Berkeley and discussions about the illusions of the "free lunch." When I attended high school science class in Alamogordo, the faculty assured us that a solution to nuclear waste would be found before its existence in any notable volume. More than six decades later, very little energy has been devoted to solving that problem. There are two versions of this painting; in the second I made the mountain that is being "circumambulated" by the dancers, more phallic as well as more shaped like the missiles than in the first. The radiation is turning them into skeletons as they dance. Overcome with despair, the fool throws herself upon the Earth in the presence of the Buddha, who as in all spiritual traditions, advocates against taking life. After I found the "Yellow Pages," read them, decided to include them in this book and typed that text into the computer, I realized that I had actually thrown myself on the ground like that during the Lama Retreat. After the other retreatants had left the room for a break; in a highly emotionally charged state, I had thrown myself on the ground, charging the Universe: "Strike me dead" if I was not a Jewish inhabitant of a concentration camp in my last lifetime and decided to be born in a German family in this lifetime in order to understand how the Holocaust was possible.

2. Case of the Basket Case is probably the most autobiographical of my paintings. While my parents were recovering from a serious auto accident en route to see Reagan in Washington DC, we siblings had an informal family gathering to discuss our parents' future. Our youngest, Riner, was naturally in charge as he lived on the family property where our parents again occupied the main house and was also emotionally the closest to them. Being an artist and alternative culture oriented, I did not assume much authority in the matter. Nevertheless, I did make a suggestion that my brother disagreed with, and I was shocked by his response: he called me a "basket case," and in subsequent weeks this image appeared before me from my imagination and psyche. When Riner, nine years my junior, was in diapers, I often took care of him and changed them, so there he is an adult in diapers and I, the lady fool, am carried in the basket, as we proceed forward toward our homestead, near and on the wrong side of the railroad tracks. A childhood confusion was resolved when I returned from California to reside temporarily in La Cienega in a metal tent-like structure and realized what I assumed as a child to be the fog horn of our Usedom days, was really the train whistle (the ocean thus was not somewhere hidden nearby). The train became the "Crematorium Express," a reference to my parents' seven-year dairy experiment and our origins from Nazi Germany. Our father, Ernst Steinhoff convinced the State of New Mexico government to create and situate in Alamogordo, the Space Hall of Fame, to honor his friend, Dr. Werner von Braun as well as many others. I, who have always been unenthusiastic of our Space Program, feeling we should first understand, appreciate and protect the Earth, am therefore "spaced out."

3. Forest Primeval Early Meltdown: I was to rendezvous with our oldest and only biological child, Sean, who did not want to fly to Fairbanks to attend the university there, but rather drive all the way from New Mexico because he wanted "to see the ground" (land variations I assume) on the way. I understood that and thus supported his idea, although it was opposed by his father. When I got the phone call from the latter ("Sit down, dear…") that our son was in jail, I felt a pang of guilt. It turned that out all students leaving the United States going into Canada, which you have to do if you're driving to Alaska, get stopped by US officials and their vehicles are searched. The authorities almost always found some "weed" paraphernalia and charged $1,250 for the release of the vehicle ("a profitable little enterprise," the Canadians joked). So with that experience, I was in a bit of an altered state when I went cross-country skiing while Sean snowboarded near Valdez. It was so warm for late January that the snow had melted around the pine trees, creating little pools which reflected the sunshine with rainbows. While according to my senses and compass, the path I had taken had been straight ahead all the way, to my surprise and disorientation, a building just like the one I had left over an hour earlier appeared before me. It took me a while to realize I had skied in a circle.

4. "...and God gave Dominion": During this period my work was represented by Peyton Wright. The gallery owner wanted all artists to create a painting with a wilderness theme, for a benefit for the Wilderness Society. Mine is more a Germanic and archetypal idea of wilderness rather than pristine, untouched beauty. Representing my fear and pain at the loss and degradation of Nature and true "Wilderness," we have "sinned" against that

over which we were given dominion, by clear-cutting, taking the wilderness away from other species, etc. The misunderstanding of this painting by Catholic residents of Santa Fe created a bit of a crisis when some took the cross, which predates Christianity, to be the crucifix, and rather than seeing the gorilla to represent the destruction of any/all species, as an insult to Christ and his crucifixion. I very much revere Christ and his teachings, so that was not my intent, but rather to dramatize the damage we as species and civilization are doing to the Earth and all dependent on its health.

5. Berlin: On my first trip back to Germany after the Wall that separated East and West fell, I had this strong sense that there would be this great crush of people wanting to go West, away from totalitarian governments, and that some Western Germans would feel threatened and want to protect their more affluent, materialistic life styles from too much encroachment.

6. Restoring the Balance: I incorporated Bruegel's "Tower of Babel" as a symbol of the hubris and folly of the Patriarchy's unbounded militarization, as well as Dürer's "Four Horsemen of the Apocalypse," in which the Patriarchy is being challenged successfully by the re-emerging Feminine.

7. Computer Lady, or How to completely recycle your Computer, was born out of a completely sleepless night from a stomach ache due to the worry and discomfort of my decision to finally buy a computer. They are not easily recyclable; in some of our frequent forest fires that encroach on subdivisions, the remains are a toxic mess, very unlike the ancient ruins we have traveled the world to behold. So my stomach ache was metaphorically caused by my "stomaching" the computer.

8. Venus of the Terrorism Wars: The limb-less body of Venus De Milo is very well known and considered very beautiful. Bringing together the destructiveness of war with the beauty of the human body is meant to be ironic and disturbing.

9. 4 Horsemen of the Apocalypse Over Bagdad: I was so horrified when the bombing of Iraq began, having been a victim of bombing as a small child, that I cut out and studied the picture of Bagdad on the front of the *New York Times*, resolving to honor that ancient city that would never be the same. I stared at and studied that picture for hours, and having been a long time student of the Bible, felt it to be an "apocalyptic" event. It took some time to decipher the photo: the park encircled by Baghdad's main boulevard in the foreground, the statue of Saddam that had been beheaded, etc. While recreating the image of the city was hard work, I enjoyed doing the horses against the dark smoke clouds with Bush, Cheney, Rumsfeld and Colin Powell as the four horsemen. Getting a likeness of George Bush (who inhabits several paintings from that time) always seemed hard because he has such a neutral, 'corporate' handsome face (kind of a male Barbie Doll, always reminding me of the "man in the gray flannel suit"), so I resorted to doing him with a skeleton head.

10. Rapture Anyone?: The famous photograph of the young Afghan girl on National Geographic's cover captivated me but I wanted her more as background in the painting rather than a central figure, so I made a lot of effort to "loose" the image. While "rapture" is not limited to Christianity (bliss, ecstasy, enlightenment, etc.) it was also part of the drug culture of the 60's, and in this image it relates to all the ways we delude ourselves with our ideas of saving the world through violence/war, save others "for democracy," and the exploitation hidden in all this.

11. From Eden to Assange: The archetype of the Apple of Eden becomes the Apple Computer: a double-edged sword both for truth, illusion, "fake news," conspiracy theories, exposing corruption, etc. Also, my private ironic joke about Christ using a lesser-G smart phone than Satan (who uses 5G) and who wears a Chili suit because it's very hot where he lives. In the public mind Julian Assange is accused of being a communist, but that has no basis in fact; he is an example of the attack on journalists who are whistle-blowers and, like Mumia Abu-Jamal and Leonard Peltier, I believe him to be a political prisoner, and pray for his release.

12. Berkeley: It happens regularly that when one's mind is occupied by a theme, supports for the theme seem to appear. As I biked in Berlin through the "Zoongartenn", I came across a simple elegant white marble statue in the park I had never seen before: a strikingly strong young Amazon astride a massive, beautiful horse. I thought that it was perfect for Brunhild, the Amazonian queen whom Siegfried vanquished for King Gunther. I got off my bike and made several drawings of the statue to include in the painting. In the very foreground is the narrator whose image I found in a book of

Immendorf's paintings. Beyond him is the fountain and gate to UC Berkeley with the Oakland Police, the "Blue Meanies," confronting the protesters. My visiting younger sister and I had just returned from getting an ice cream cone on Telegraph Avenue. I was totally surprised by the sense of hatred they prevoked in me! Timothy Leary, in an interview, stated that LSD is primarily a visual experience. I took off from there: in the upper right of the painting are some of the people I knew who did "Acid weekends."

13. My Cosmology: My belief is that all major World religions contribute to the Truth, are not perfect nor free from error, but continue to evolve. At this time the Earth is under great stress; the dark brushstrokes represent this energy approaching and surrounding the earth. To understand solutions we must return to harmony with Nature by embracing simpler modes of being, thus the horse and the camel, representing West and East. The right side of the Heavens has my Ancestors, spiritual and physical, and on the left, those of my generation, that I believe did not survive "wireless" (EMF).

14. Adam's Rib and the Turkey Thief: Two seemingly incongruous themes (except that Morgan, the dog and Adam are both males of their species, and theft could be the common thread (the theft of Adam's rib?) or as the dog is 'faulty,' is the rib taken from Adam faulty (in that it bruised so painfully)? Anyway, they are also joined by time in that they occurred in the same time frame. Eden and Adam always evoke the "Fall of Man" theme and the suffering that ensued, in the nature of life on Earth itself (death, illness, hunger, war, etc.) or woman at the hands of men: Camille Claudel who apprenticed with Rodin and became his lover, then separated when she became pregnant. Until recently all her own sculptures were attributed to Rodin. Even worse, her brother had her committed for life, even though the doctors at the Montdevergues Asylum repeatedly wrote to him that she was healthy and should be released. Before he had her committed he told her: "this family has room for only one genius, and that's me." (He was a poet; but of much lesser note than she.) While she died in obscurity, her genius has since been recognized and she has her own museum in Paris. Also in this time period, our daughter in (god's) law, struggling as a single mom, tried several times to end her life.

Thanksgiving: Serving the turkey on my Mother-in-law's one hundred year old platter, I had placed the remaining turkey on the porch table for our oldest son to take home. As we closed up for the night, I saw to my horror that Morgen, our German Shepherd, had pulled the platter off the table by pulling the table cloth, even though he'd been given plenty of turkey to eat already, spilling the turkey and breaking the precious platter beyond repair.

15. Walking Home: In Alamogordo, between the ages of twelve and fourteen, I was sometimes forgotten (maybe related to my, still present, sense of timelessness, focusing too totally on some present activity...which is necessary for creating art, but can be problematic in a "normal" functioning schedule) when my mother picked up everyone including neighbor kids from school, and I had to walk the three miles home. What often began tearfully would become almost exhilarating as "Nature" (the trees against the sunset), my freedom and ability to navigate my own life, comforted me and planted the seed to my becoming an artist.

ETCHINGS

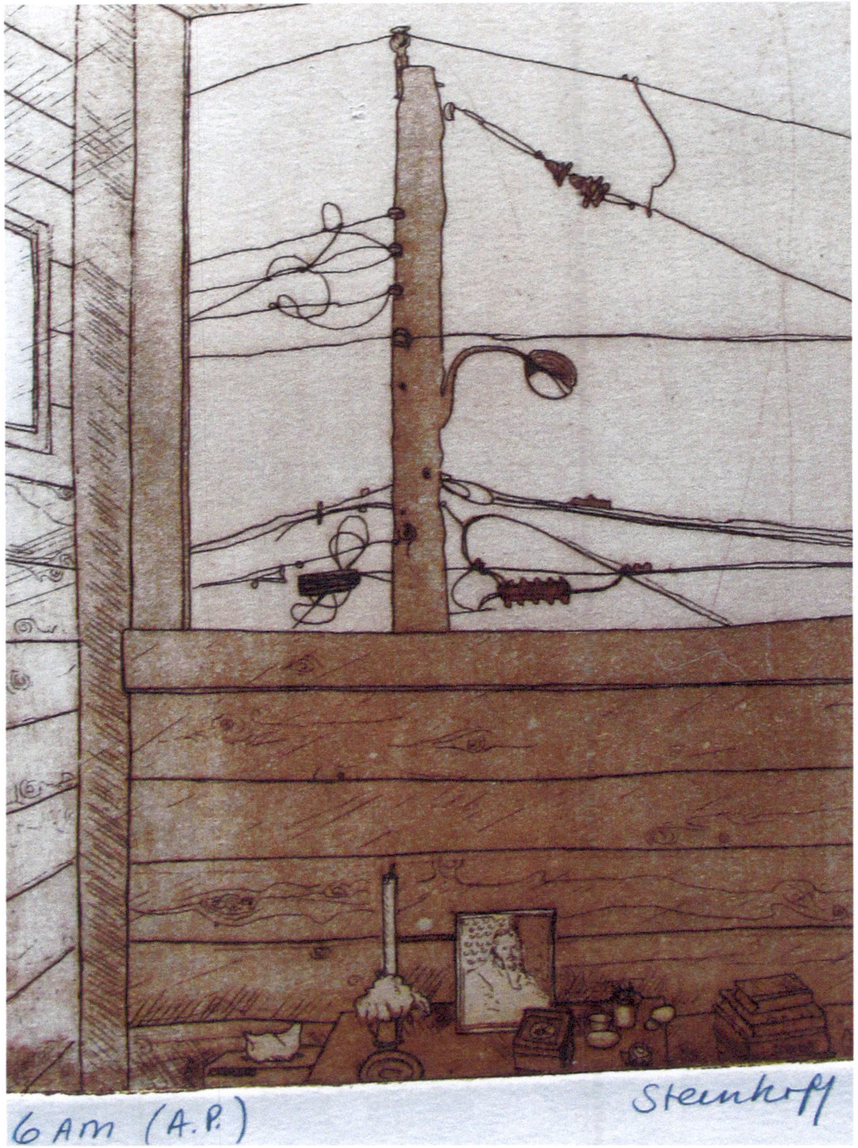

6 A.M.

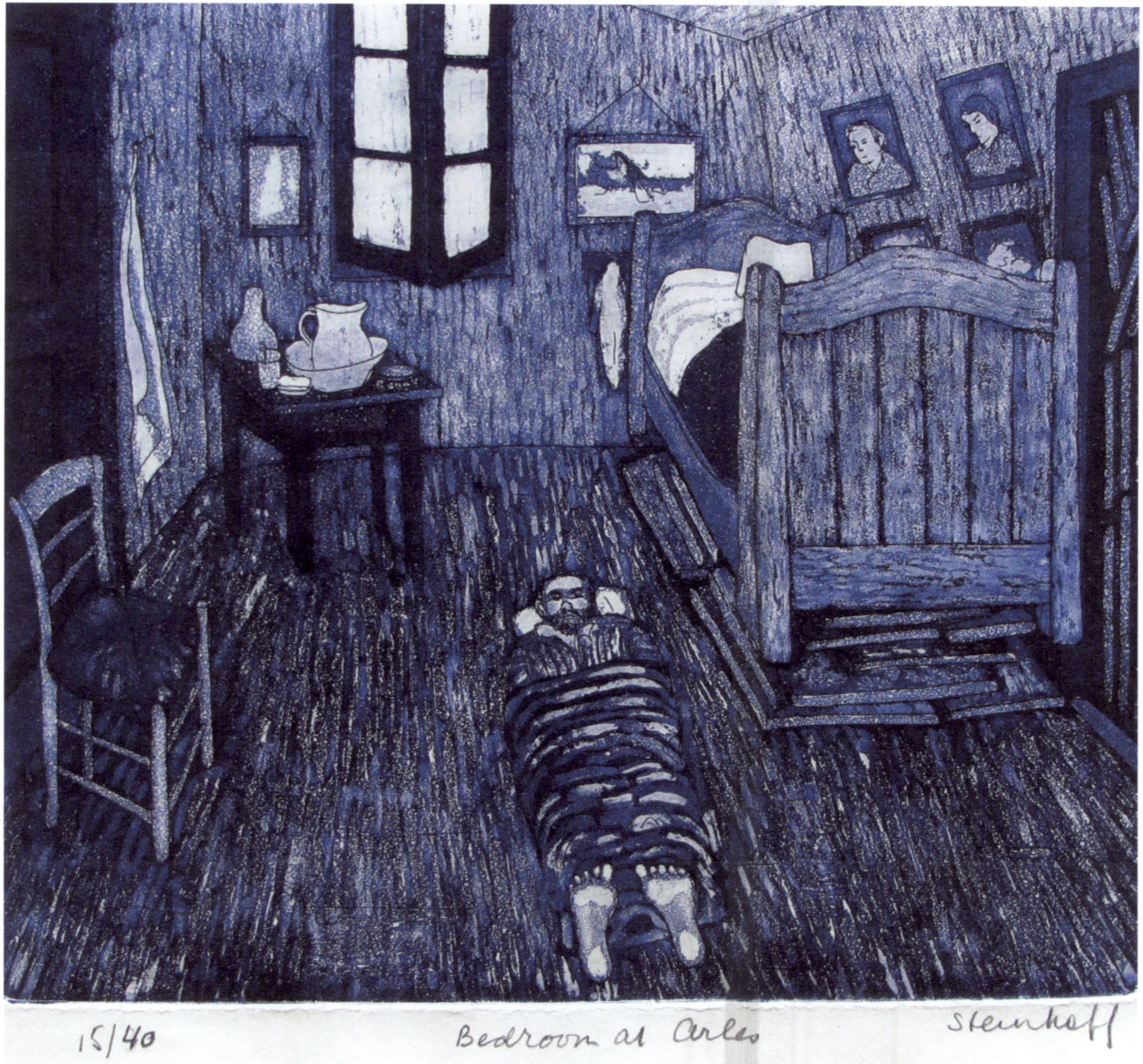

Van Gogh's Bedroom

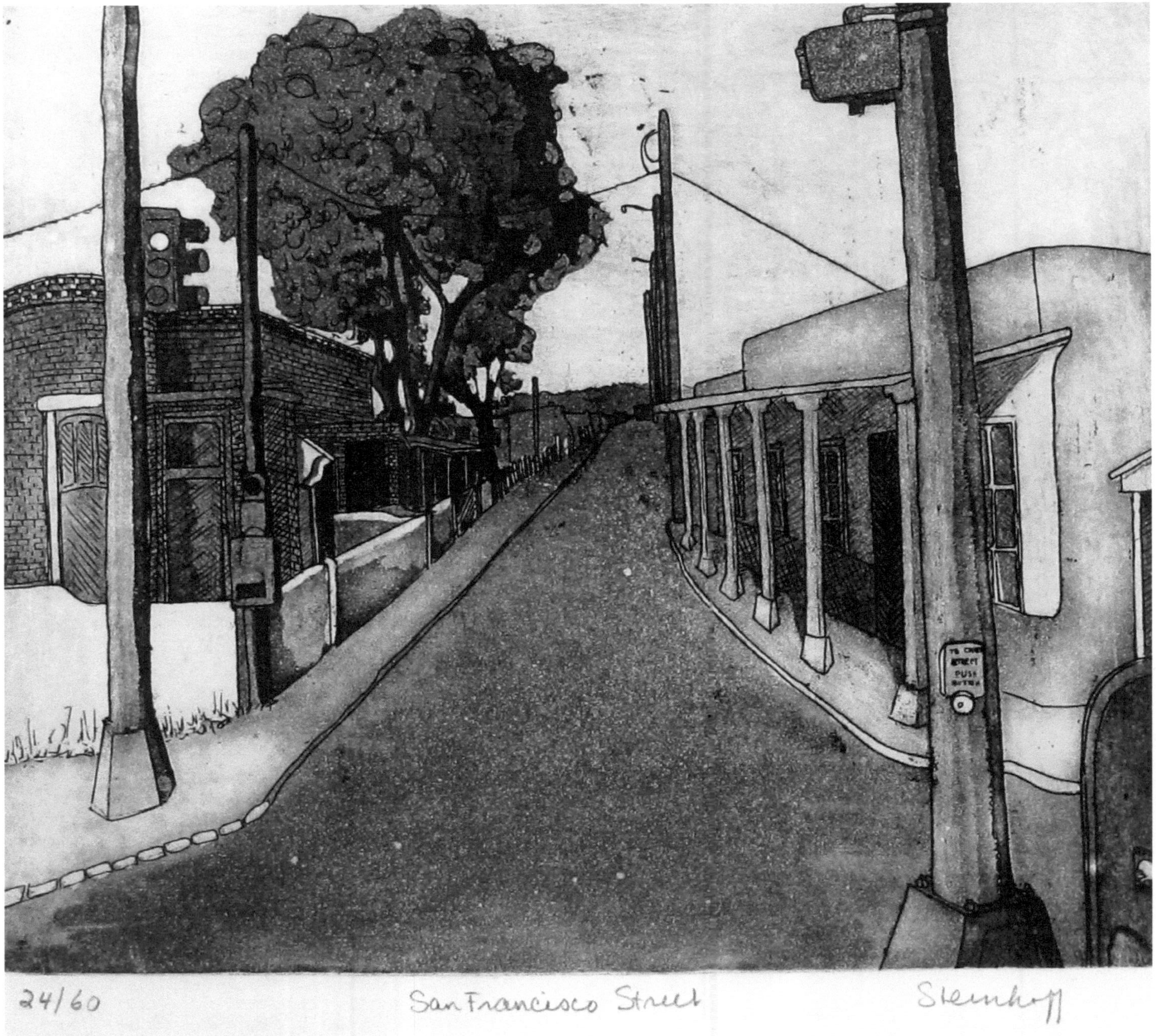

San Francisco Street

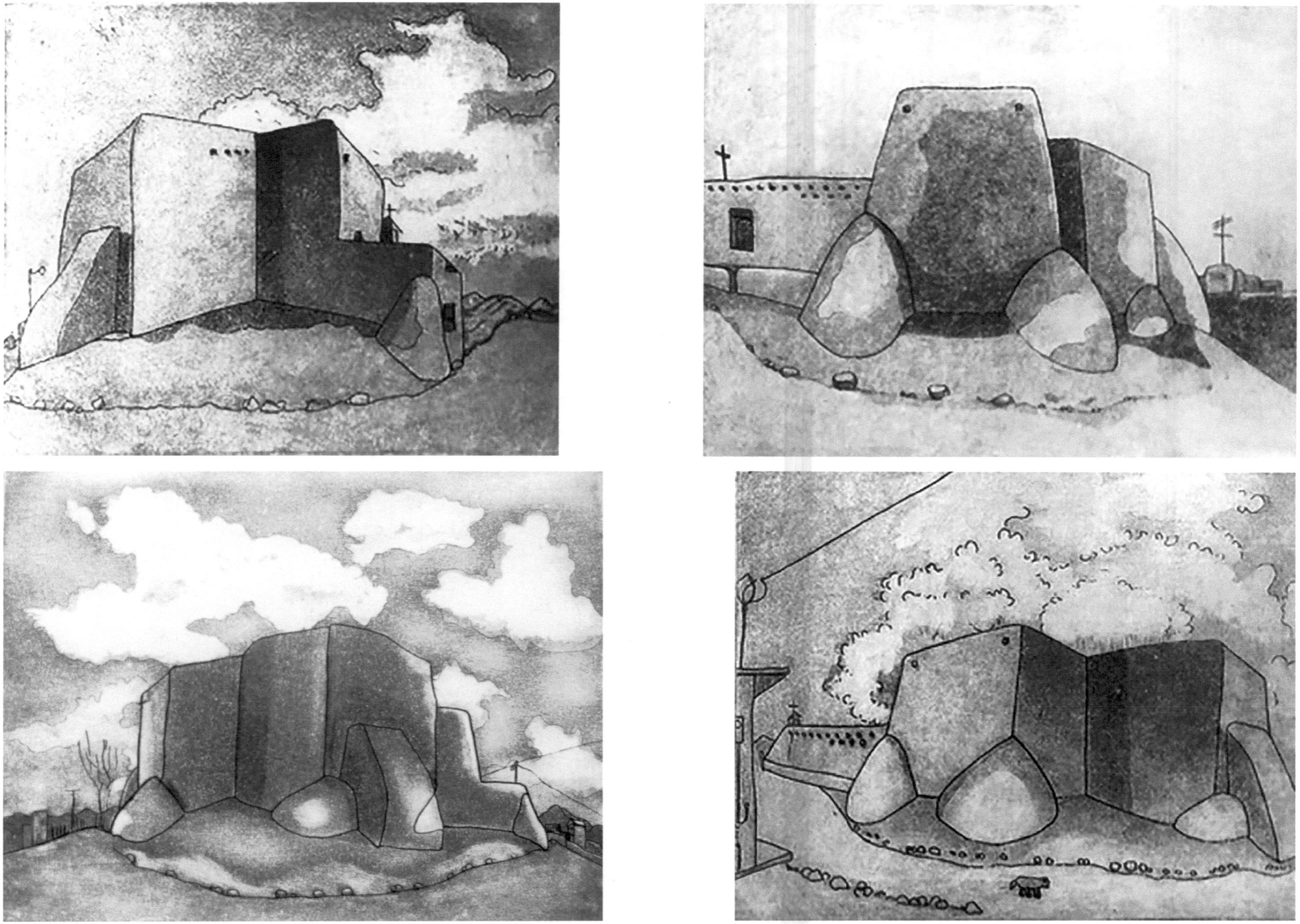

Rancho de Taos (set of 4)

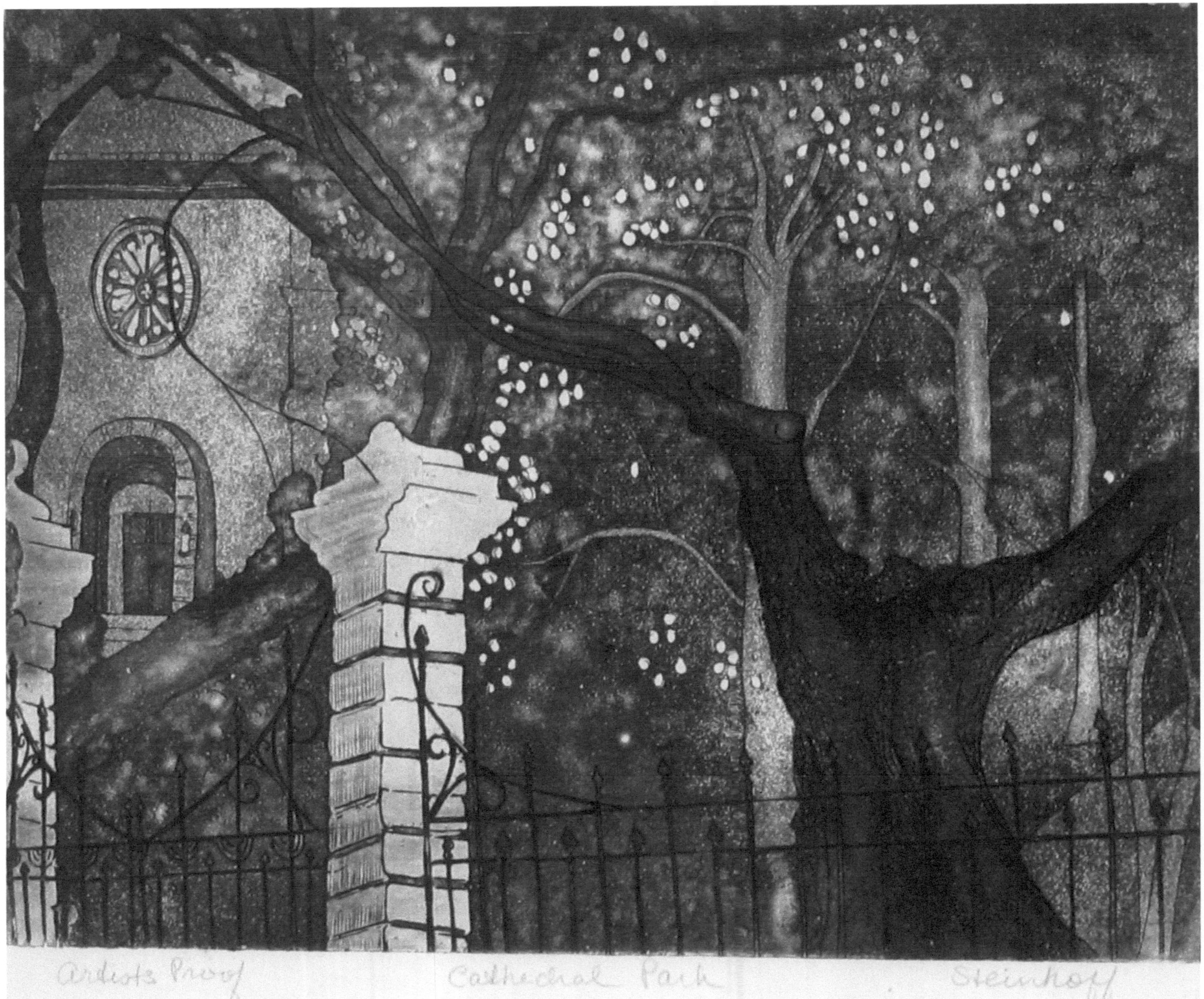

Cathedral Park

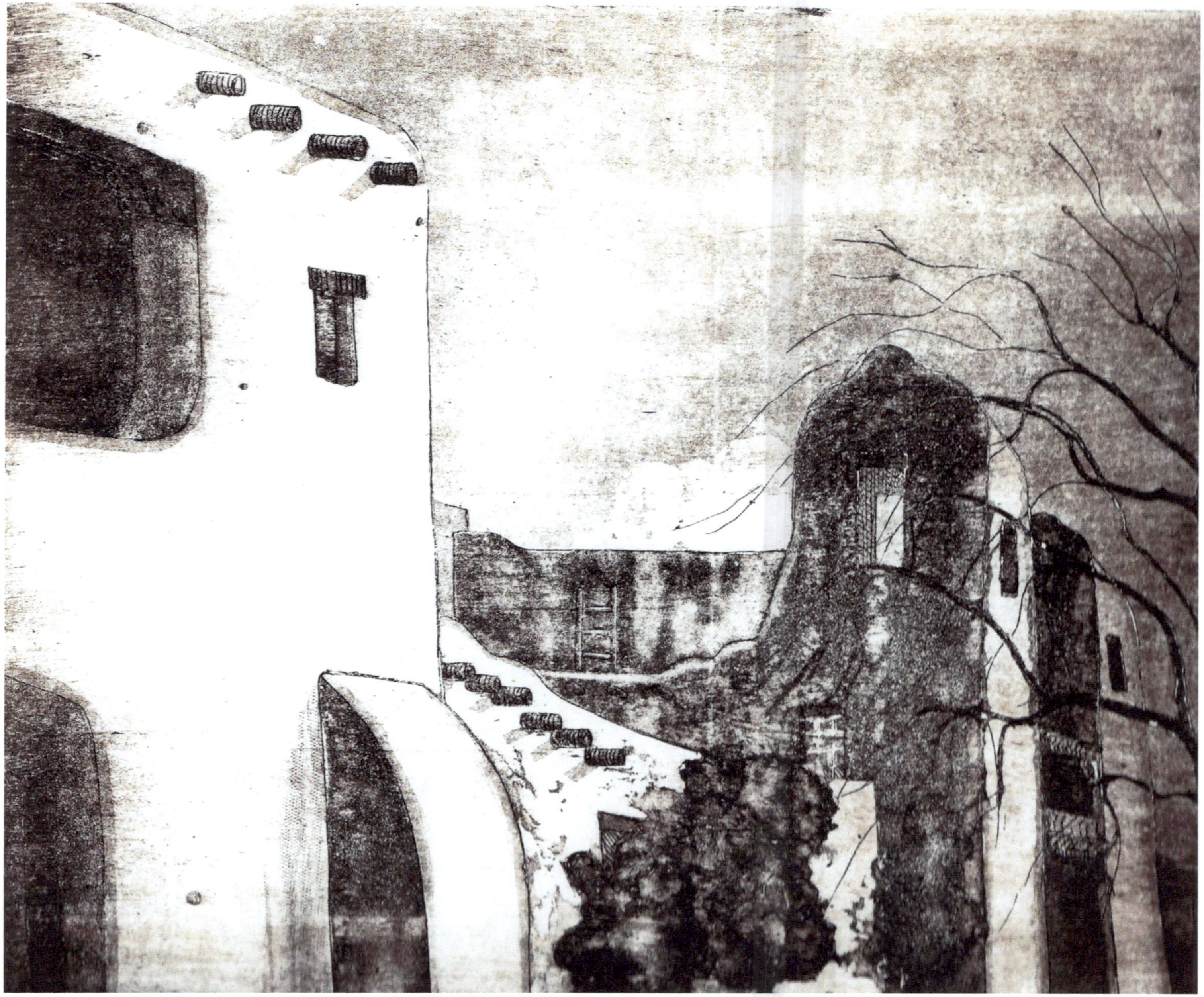

St. Francis Auditorium

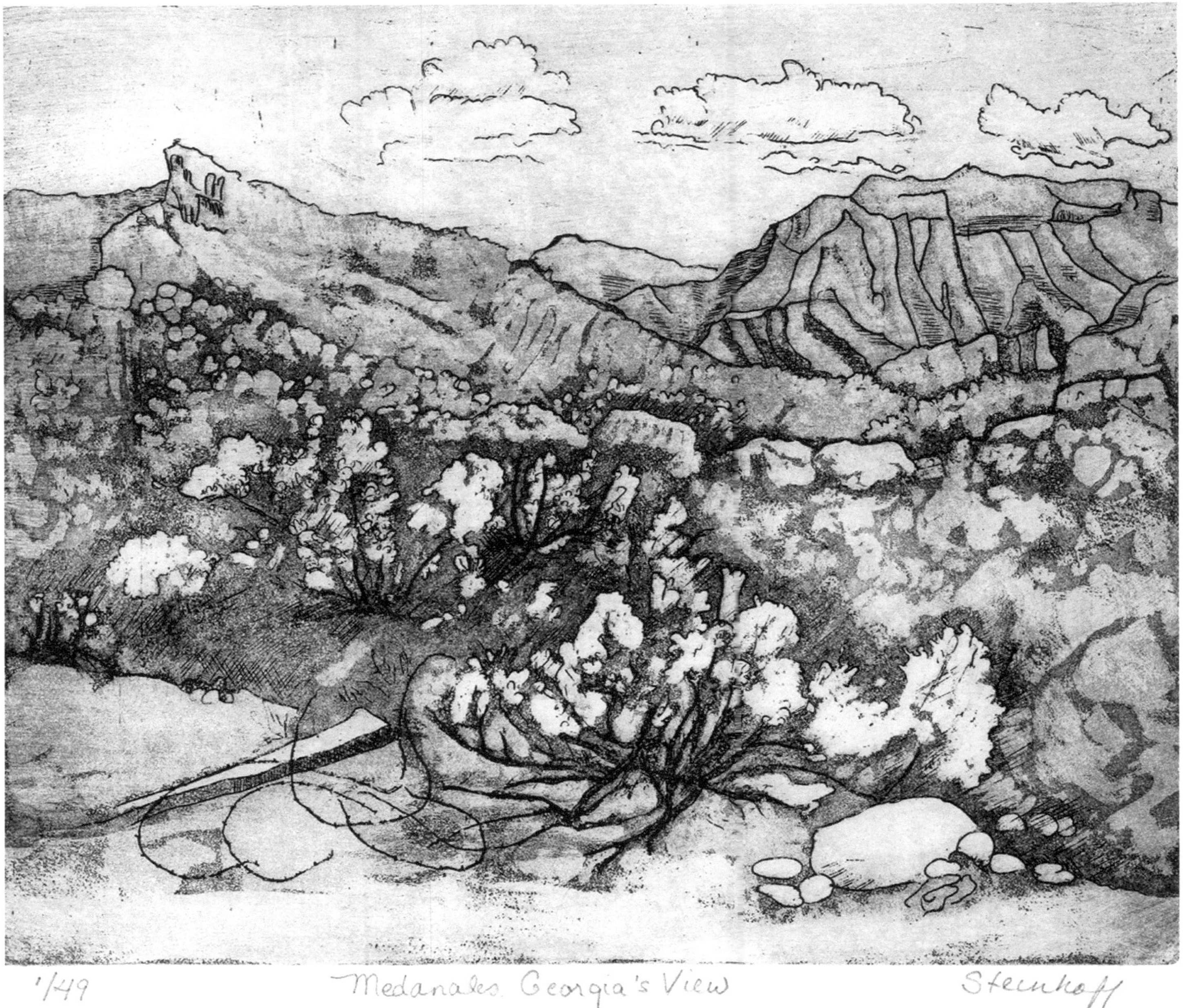

Medanales Georgia's View

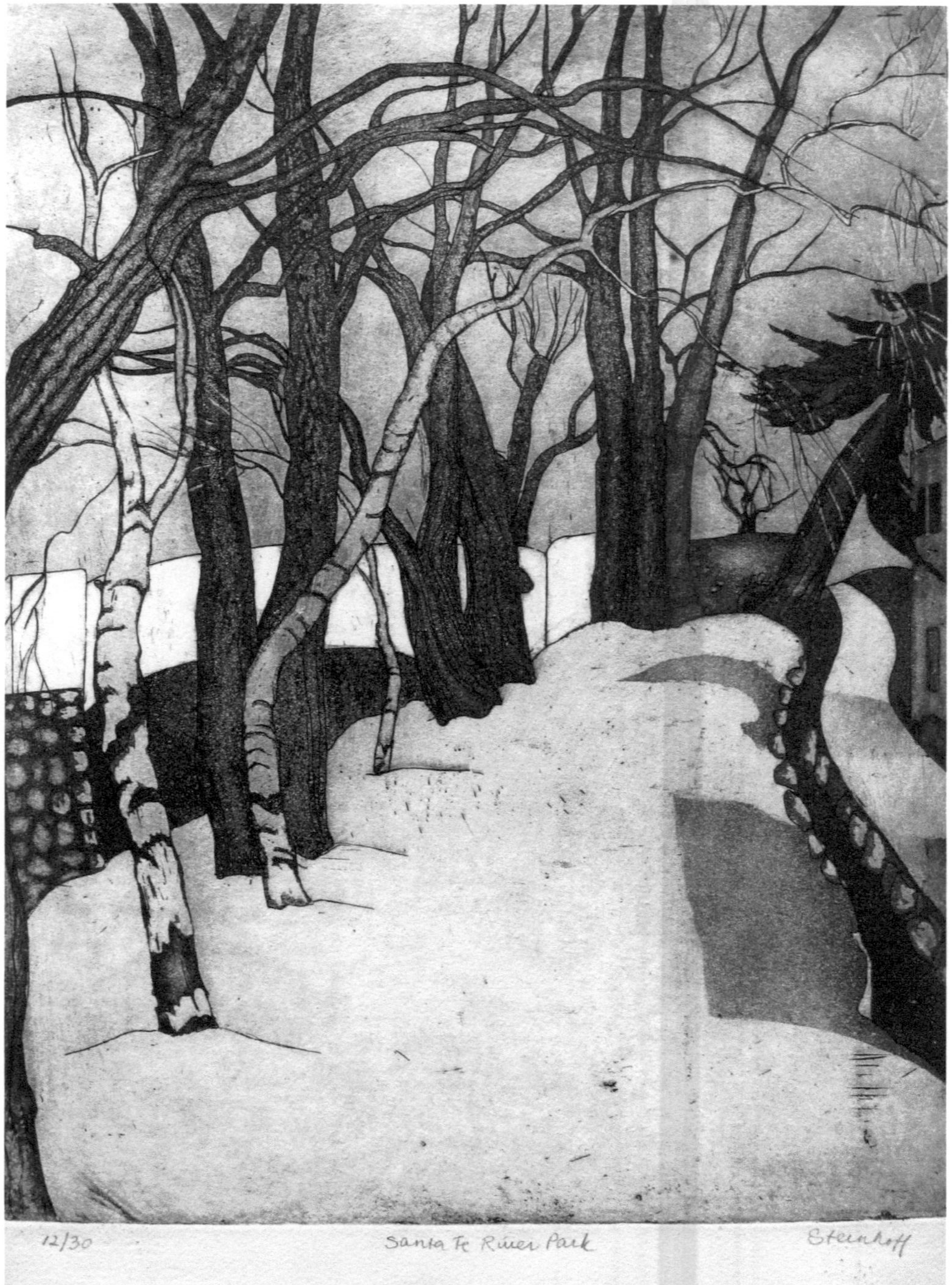

Santa Fe River III

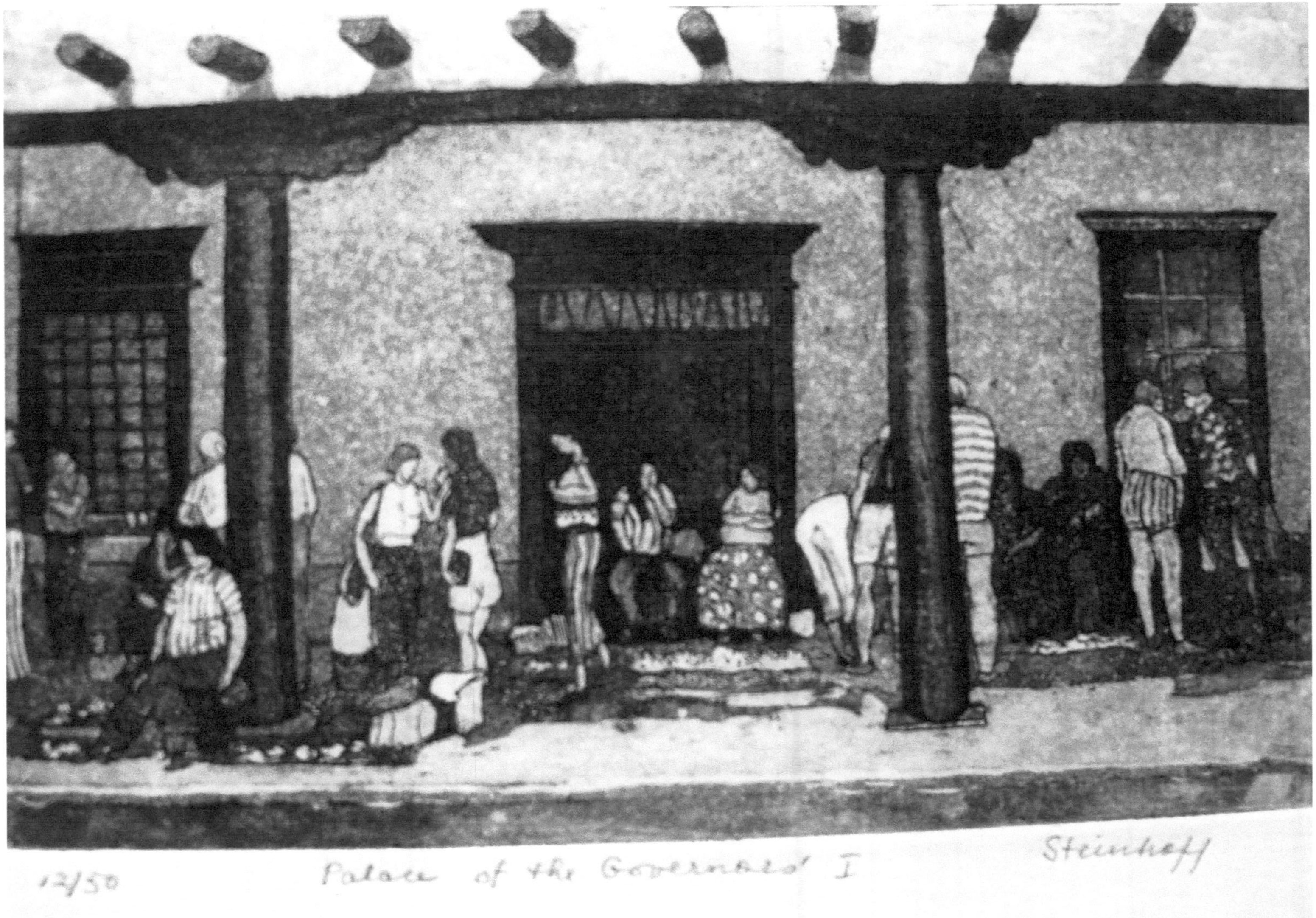

Palace of the Governors I

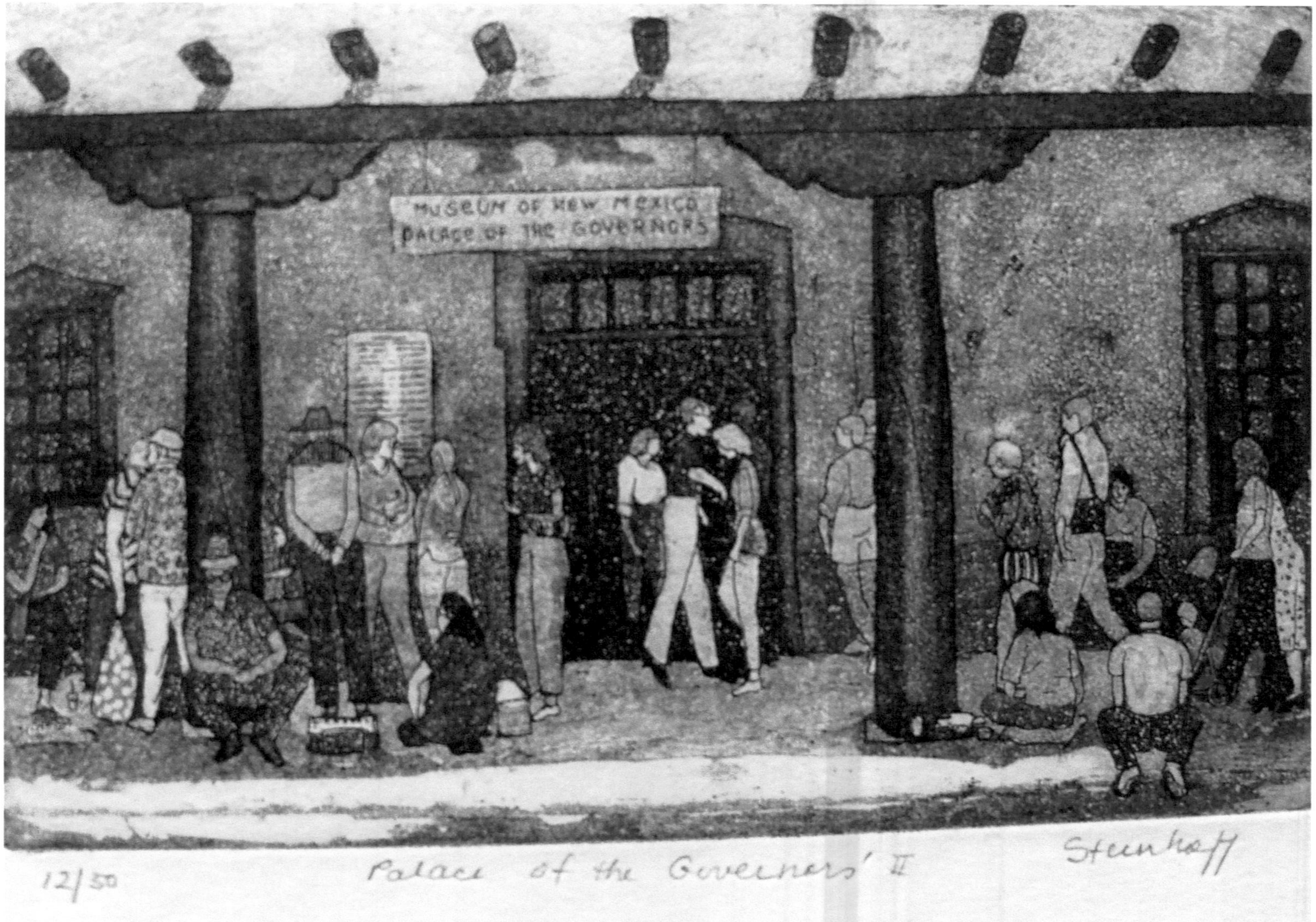

Palace of the Governors II

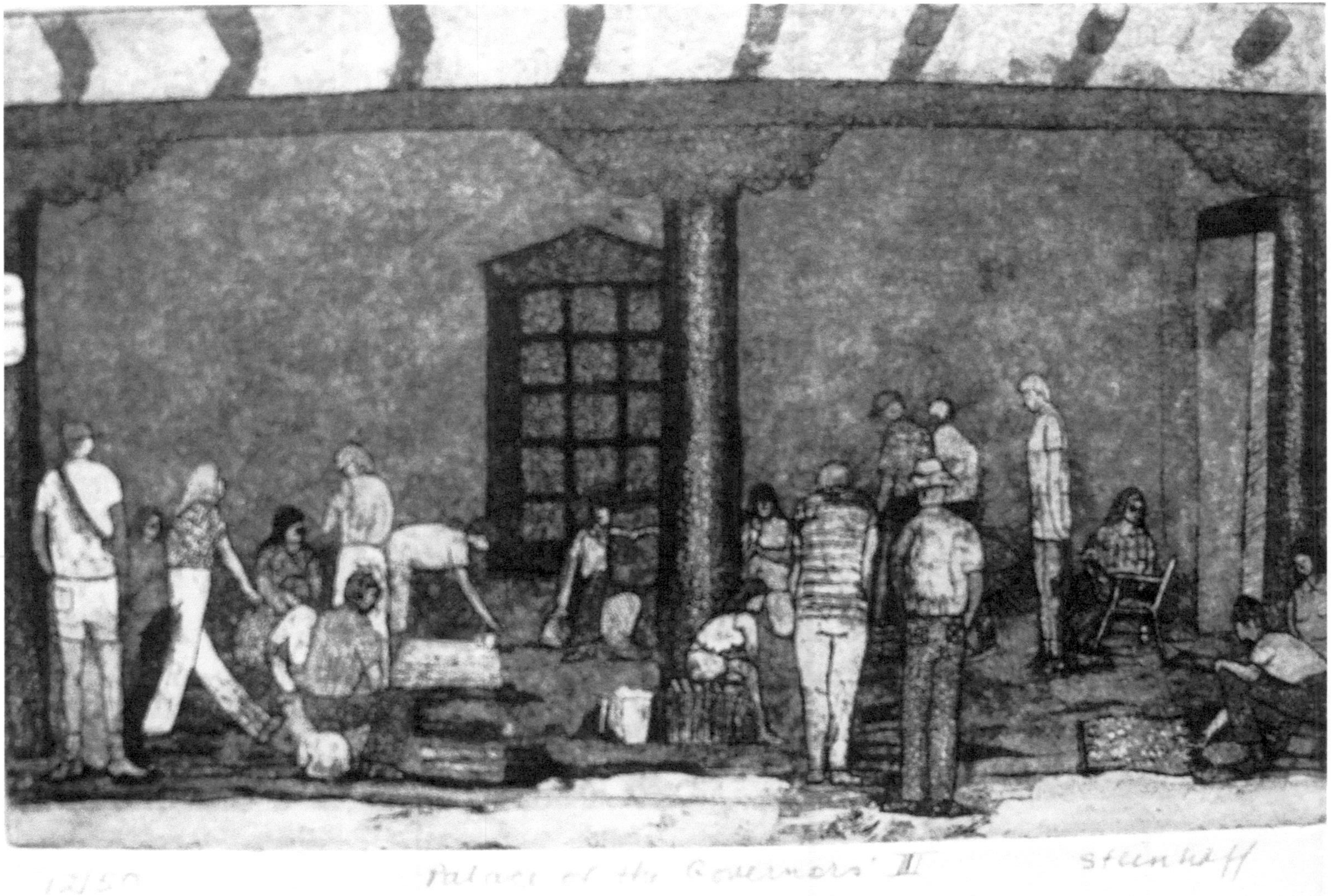

Palace of the Governors III

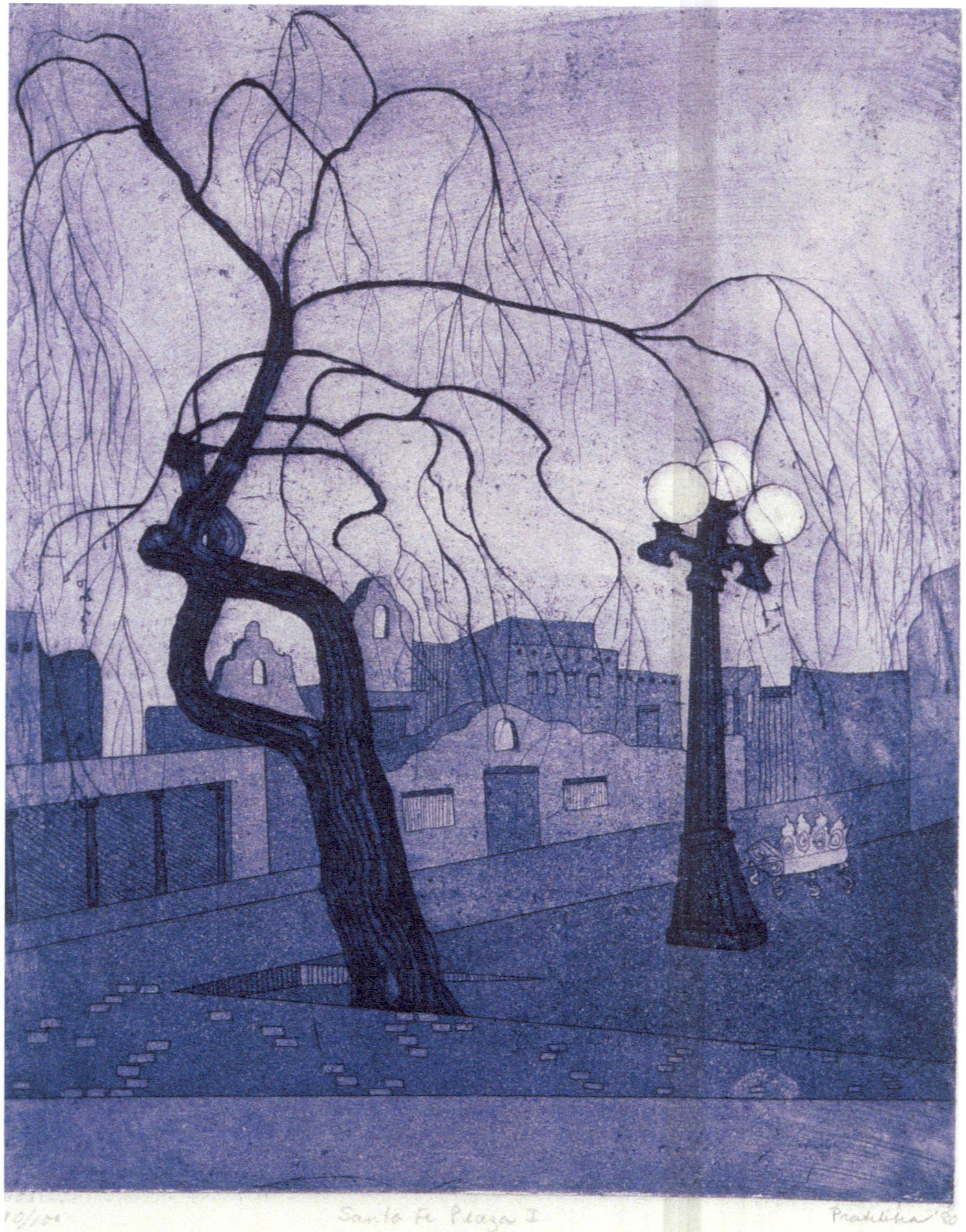

Santa Fe Plaza I

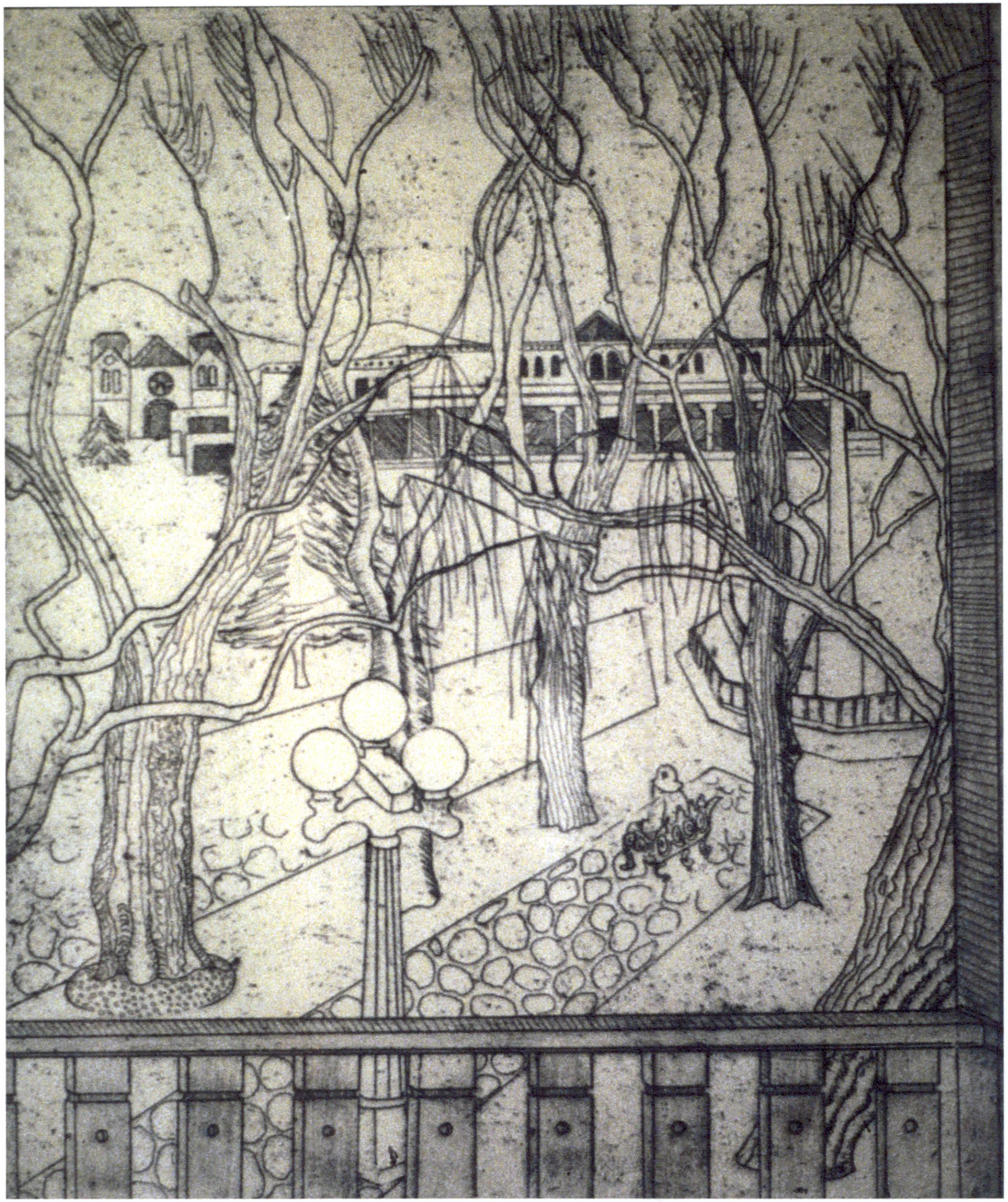

Santa Fe Plaza III

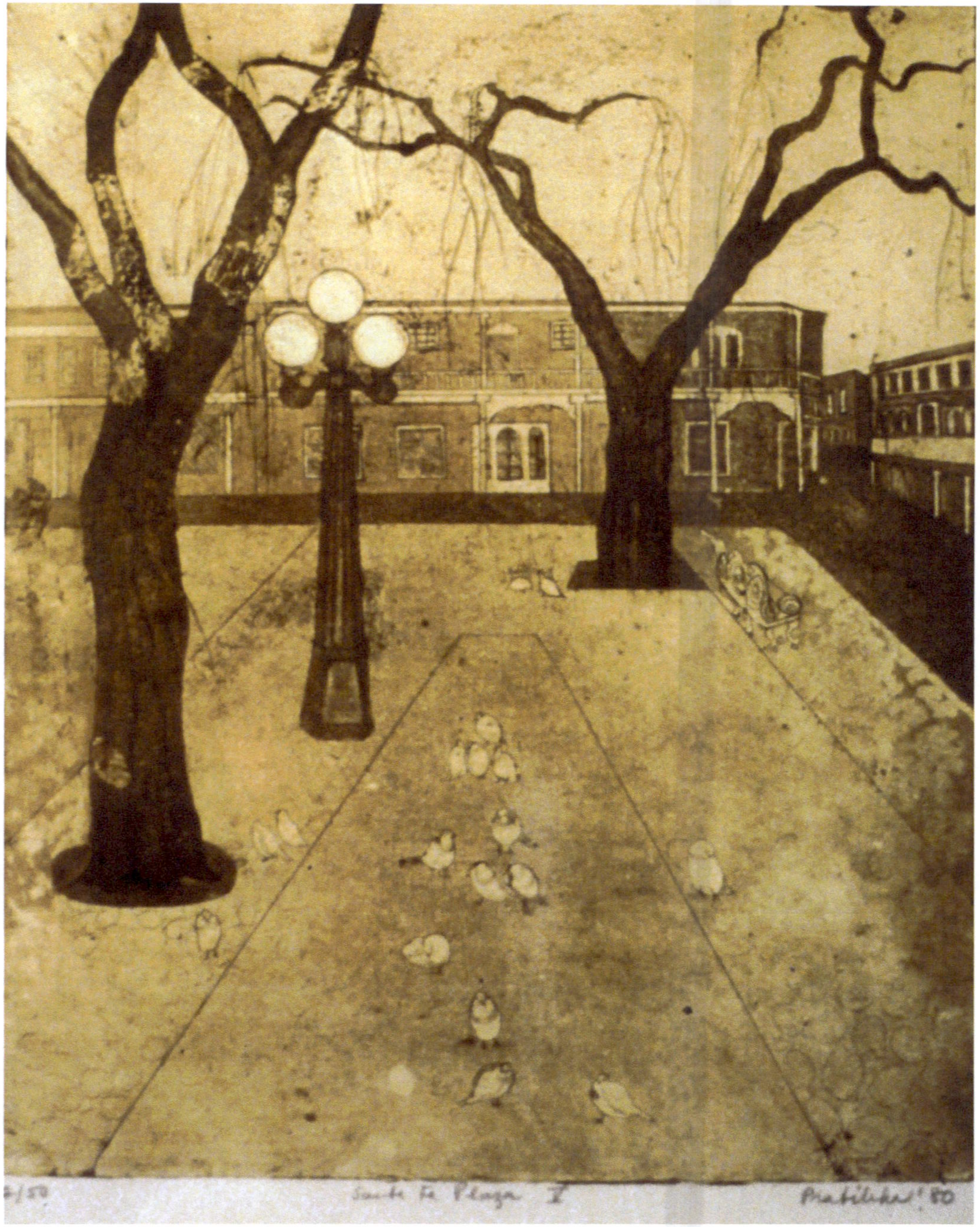

Santa Fe Plaza V

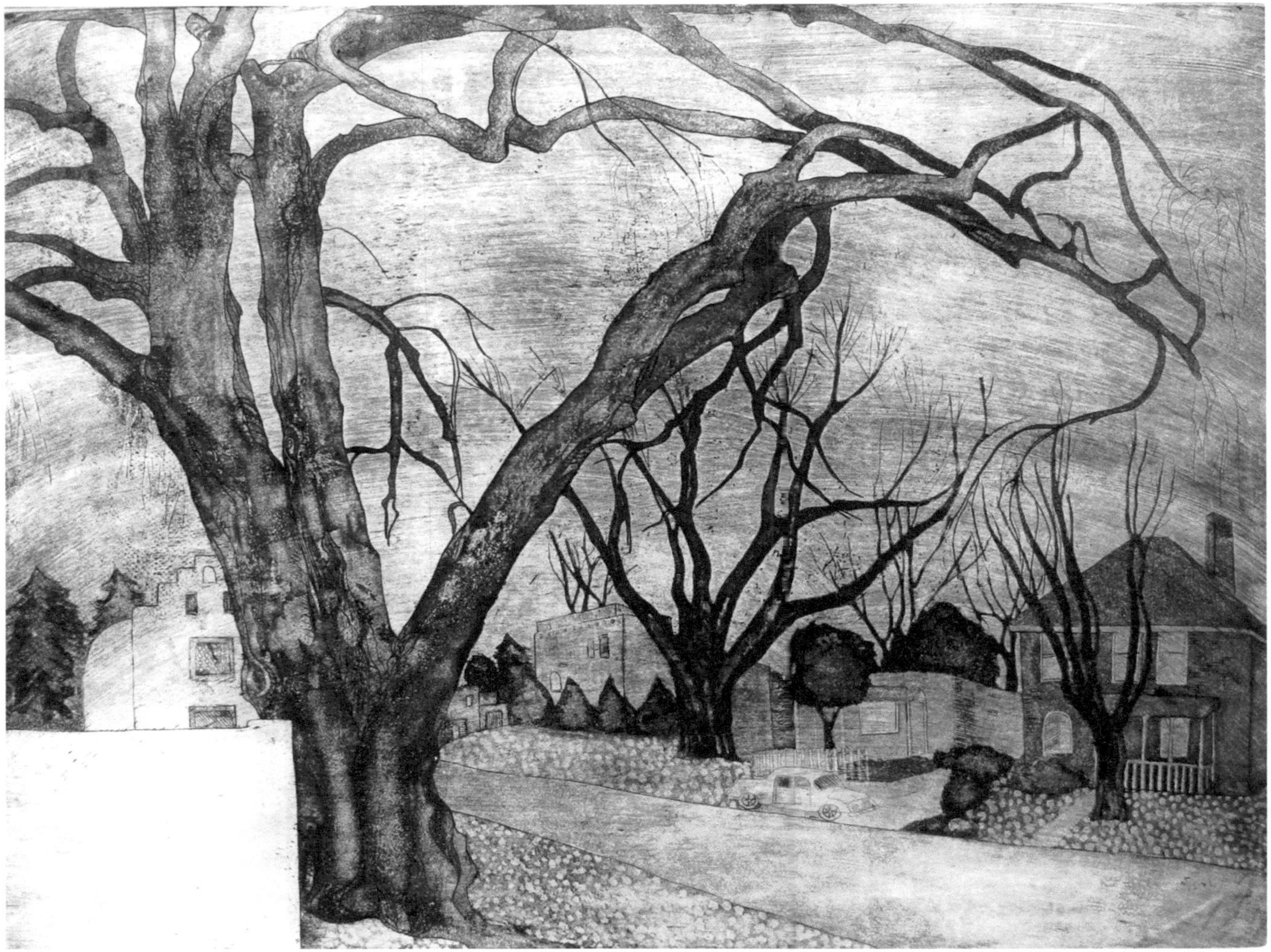

Santa Fe Winter

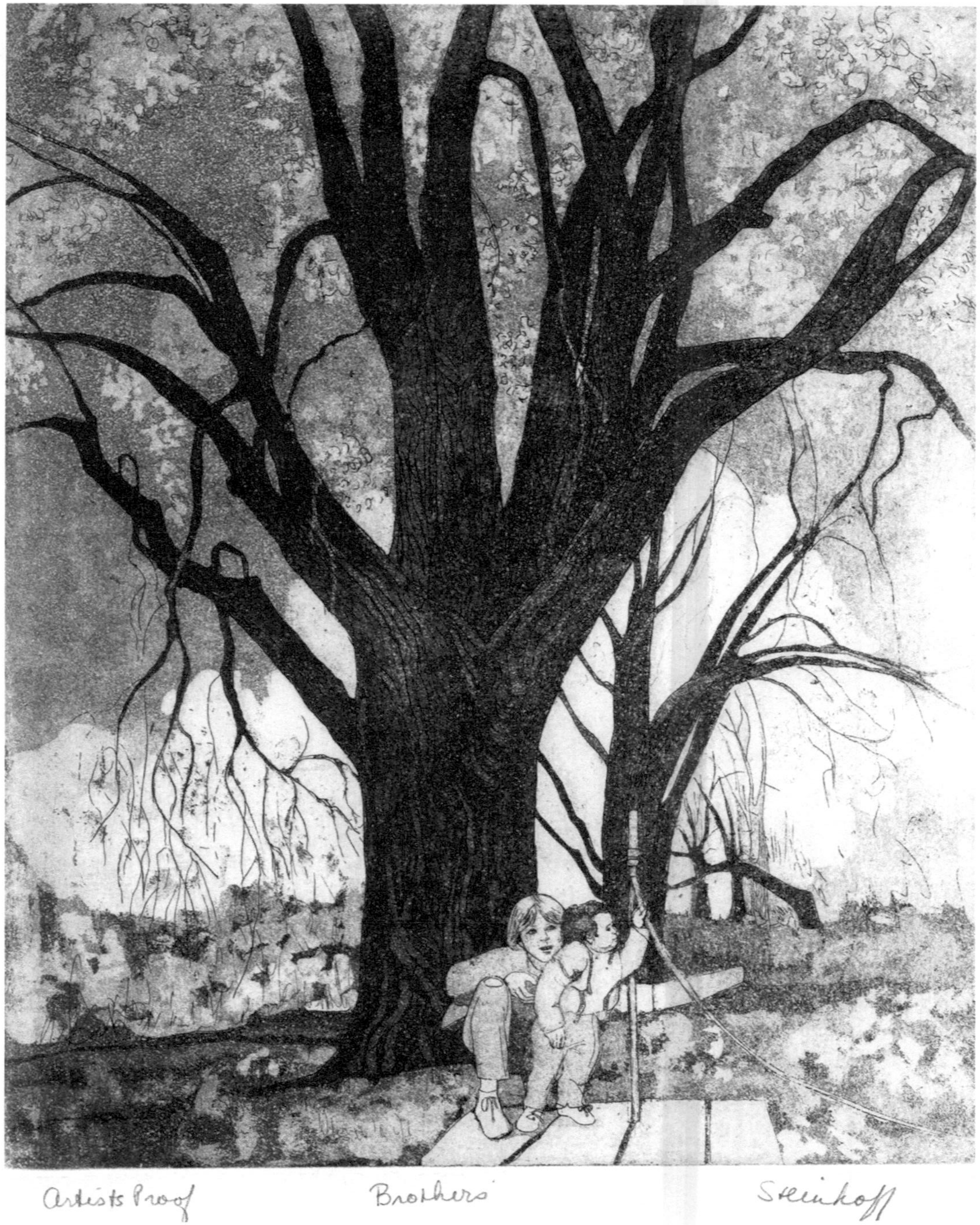

Brothers

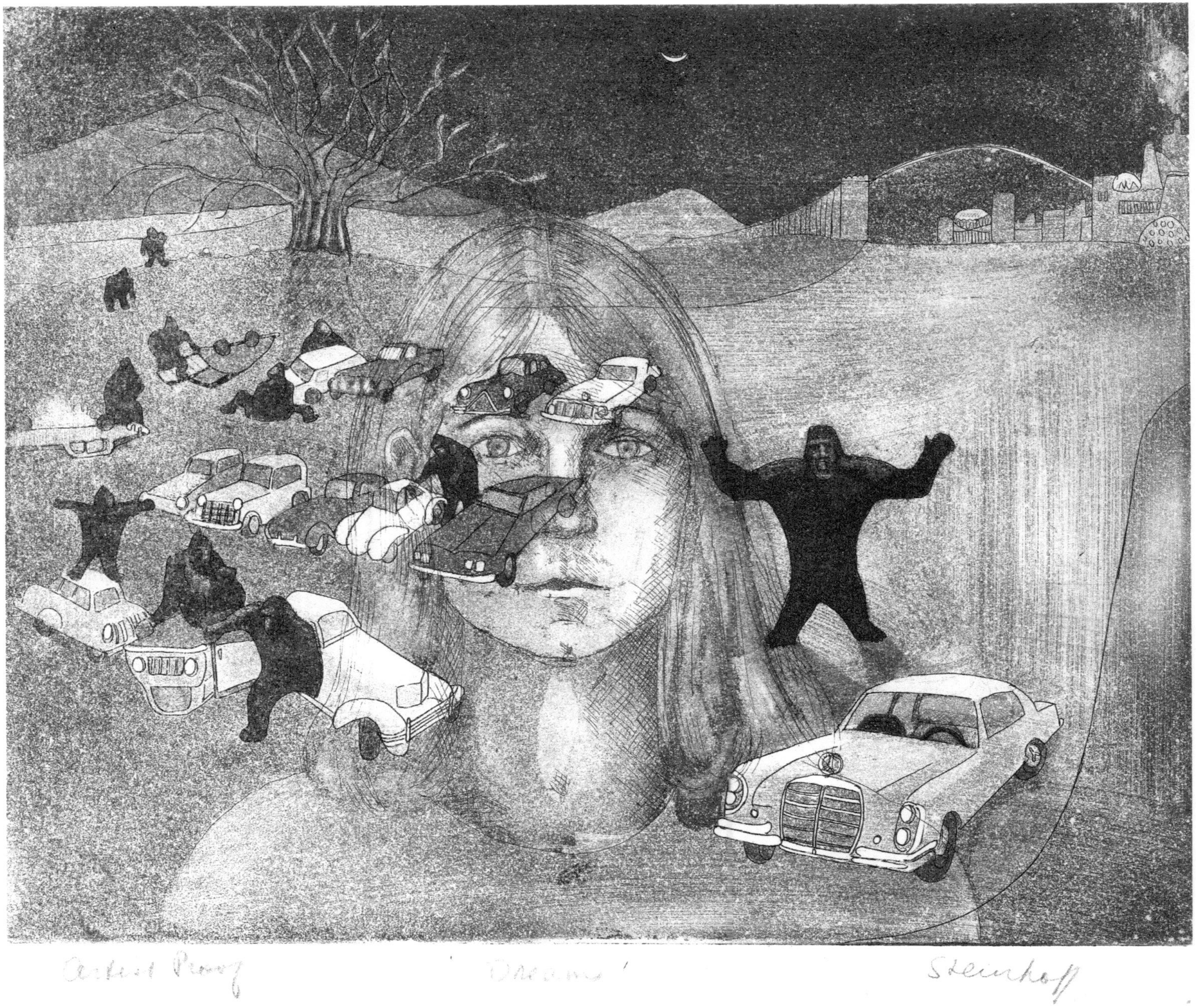

Gorilla Dream

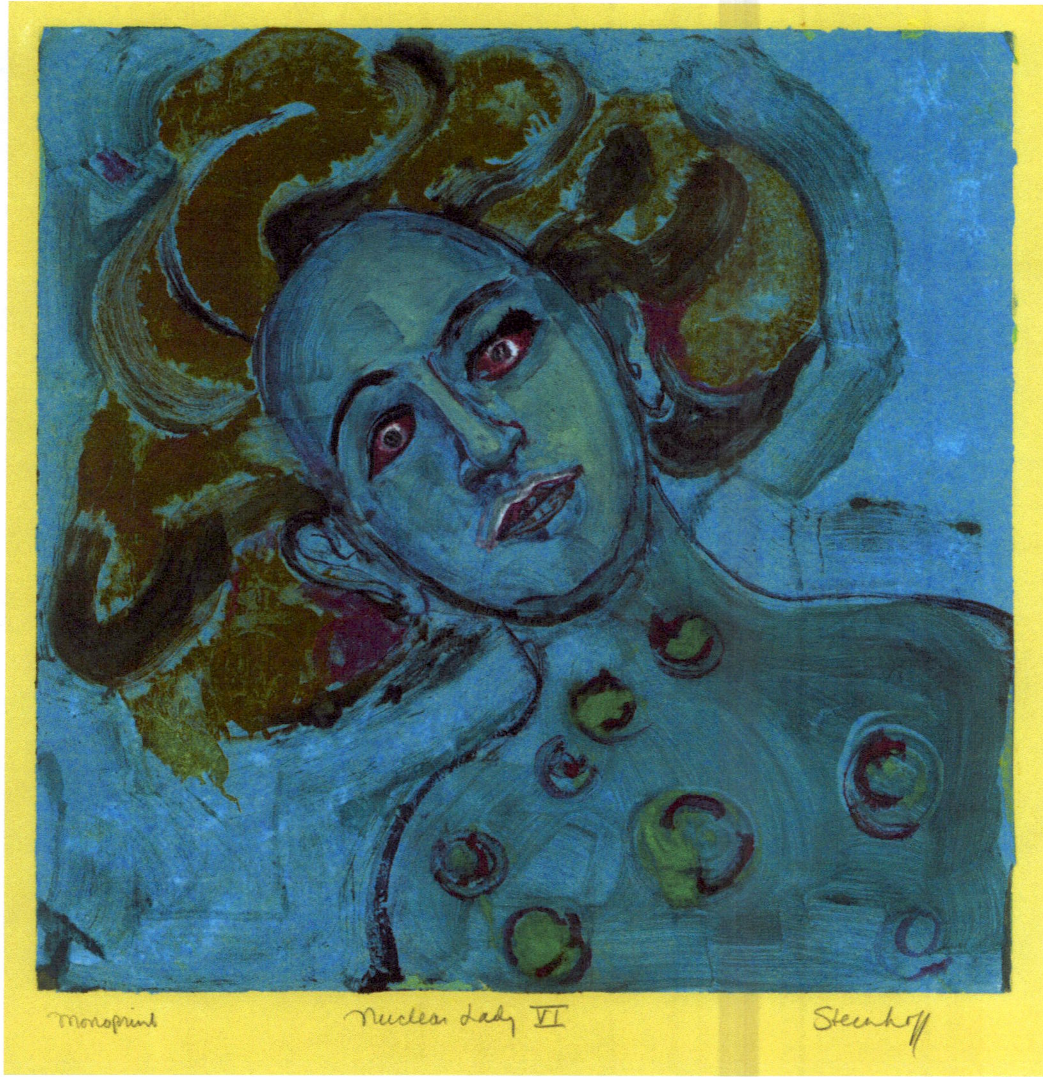

Nuclear Lady
Monoprint

NOTE ON THE DIMENSIONS OF MY ART

The size in inches and/or centimeters of art works are usually placed under the image of the work in a publication, but as that is a tedious project for an artist like myself and many of the works have been sold, I chose not to do this. Instead I have chosen to provide this note that will give the reader broad guide lines. The documentation for each work exists, but digging it up for over fifty years of work will wait for another publication.

While the Etchings are last in this book, they were the earliest, so I will start with them. The first few were on zinc plates, and were between 7 x 4 inches, to as large as my press could print, which was 14 x 11 inches. "Santa River III" and "Santa Fe Winter" and two of the "Santa Fe Plaza" series are 11 x 9 inches; all other etching plates are copper. The series of Santa Fe such as "Governor's Portal" I,II and III are approximately 4 x 6 ½ inches; "Rancho de Taos, I, II, III and IV" are approximately 6 x 4 ½ inches. The "Picasso for the Right" series are approximately 7 x 4 inches each. My average etching size is about 8 x 10-11 inches.

My early "interiors" in oil were mostly not standard sizes in that I "gesso-ed" my own panels or canvases with rabbit skin glue and all were individually framed by professionals; later, when I first began using egg tempera, I continued the same practice, but from the time I discovered and changed to using clay panels sizes became more uniform: from the smallest (not in this book) of my "Gallery of Heroes," which are 4 x 3 ½ inches and 5 x 4 inches up to 36 x 48 inches. For larger paintings I began to create Diptychs like "From Eden to Assange," two panels 48 x 36 inches each, "Waves/Migration," 36 x 28 inches each, and finally a six-part painting, "My Cosmology," 48 x 90 inches, each panel being 24 x 30 inches. The largest single is "Berkeley," which is 54 x 48 inches, which I had to gesso (and endlessly sand), as I could not get (or afford?) a panel that size. Prior to that, twenty years earlier, for one of my first egg tempera paintings, I gessoed and painted on three hollow core doors to create "Mural of my Life" (not in the book). Then in the same decade my infamous "...and God gave Dominion," 36 x 48 inches, became very heavy due to the "cradle" I built to support the panel (and then laboriously chiseled back down!). In my middle and latest period, the larger panels are usually 48 x 36 or 36 x 48 inches while the more frequent smaller paintings are 28 x 22 or 24 x 18 inches. The "Contemporary Icons" are usually 10 x 8, 11 x 9 or 12 x 10 inches. Which category an art work fits into can be fairly easily judged in the image by its size in the book and how much detail is revealed.

FINALE

And the people bowed and prayed, to a Neon God they made... And the Words of the prophet are written on the Subway wall..." For more than a decade the transformation of society to wireless communication and the Internet has occurred with, seemingly, little resistance. To me, by comparison, the "Pandemic" is less disturbing. If one could see the whole picture, it could be clearer that we are not being told the whole truth. I and many others, including scientists, believe the "Pandemic" is connected to the "wireless revolution". Wireless/Virus—even sounds alike. From the beginning of wireless, people who questioned it's being totally benign, were seriously vilified. Starting with the head of the World Health Organization. Remember Trump's vilification of it? When she noticed, and expressed that the cell phone made her body significantly uncomfortable, she was ridiculed by the people around her to such a degree that she resigned. I began reading all I could find on the subject (having been trained as a scholar in graduate school): *Zapped, Disconnected, The Force* among others, and the most comprehensive: *The Invisible Rainbow, a History of Electricity*—all cite the suppressed studies showing this to be a worldwide, social and technological experiment. Just look around you: do people look healthy? Cancer rates, obesity, heart disease, etc. are spiking (just like the virus). Are our forests (which are strongly impacted by wireless radiation) healthy? (No, they are burning, just like the fever in our bodies (see *Inflamed*, a recent book by Marya and Patel). *Die Droggen im Wohnzimmer* (*The Drugs in Our Livingroom*) and *Irresistible*, by a psychiatrist, are the latest books about the deliberate intent behind making this tool as addictive as possible, along with earlier (now almost invisible) books: Underneath the radar of constant focus on the virus, number of people infected, number of deaths, etc. is the silent roll out of 5G: thousands of satellites placed in the Ionosphere, beaming radiation toward Earth. How is this affecting our weather patterns? Does anyone know or care? I've wondered for some time about the spots (and proneness to rot more quickly) on our fruits and vegetables. Many farmers, struggling to survive, welcome the income from a cell tower on their land. (My friend Carlos R. did this and is now dead of cancer.) We are all more prone to disease, not because we are not all vaccinated (that treats the symptom not the cause). People feel they have to use their smart phone. But there is no discrimination, no awareness of how much energy it uses or that it's EMF are not in harmony with the body's magnetic fields or the Earth's. We don't need to be absolute; it's a matter of degree; for example, turning off one's wireless when it is not being used, such as at night and especially when one is sleeping, is already a positive step.

> "Du Nachbar Gott.
> Wenn ich Dich manchmal stoere,
> so its weil ich Dich atmen hoere,
> und weiss Du bist im naechsten Saal"
> —Rilke, *Stundenbuch*

I have heard this story in its many iterations because I sought out the truth/reasons for the troubles we face on Earth; I have despaired to the core of my being about what I see, know and feel is happening. And I also know this time has been predicted in many ancient and more contemporary traditions. Perhaps it is inevitable that humanity pushes the envelope to the extreme. One problem that humanity is experiencing which has occurred before, is that the advances of technology that most have quickly come to depend on, far outstrip societies comprehension of it as to cause and effect, blindly assuming it is inevitable and progress. Also a selfish element might prevail: "I want what I want when and how I want it." Humanity has not learned to consider how every decision affects the whole: acting on the basis of what is for the highest good of all. We are facing a precipice. At each step of this evolution, there was opposition, but it was not respected. Industrialization and technology are not in themselves negative. It is how they evolve and are utilized, whether in harmony with the earth, all species and our bodies, or not.

Health II

I learned from my parents' generation and those around me. My mother was given a complete hysterectomy after the birth of her seventh child. It was assumed in those days: "the equipment is no longer needed; you are better off without it; fewer things can go wrong." After that my mother began having severe migraine headaches. Years later it was discovered that she was prescribed too high a dose of estrogen; once it was reduced, her migraines decreased. Seeing my Mutti suffer and take so much medicine, which my Vati did also as he grew older, made me choose a different path, becoming drawn to books on alternative medicine and healing. At 22 when I entered UCLA which had a well known medical center which was free for students, I consulted with a medical doctor there. I had been on thyroid medicine since sixteen and also on a medication for stomach aches and digestive problems. In case of the latter, I had read the small print and realized I had many of the warning symptoms. After the move to Santa Barbara my period had stopped. Both my younger sister and I were tested; low thyroid was the diagnosis. So I had been on thyroid for seven years. The doctor told me in the interview that it's difficult to get off thyroid: few succeed, because it takes six weeks for thyroid to kick in. The depression, fatigue, weight gain from no thyroid in the body is difficult to go through. Being busy with school, studying and my new active social life, it didn't seem so bad. When I was tested after the six weeks, I tested on the high end of normal. Some years later I was told I had appendicitis and needed immediate surgery to have my appendix removed. Doctors were taught it is a vestigial organ, not needed by the body. The doctor told me that I could die and he would take no responsibility if I did not listen. I felt threatened and did not trust him in my gut. I decided to get another opinion. The second doctor asked me if I was on any medicine. I was on an antibiotic. He recommended I stop taking it and call him in a couple of days. It turned out I was allergic to the antibiotic the first doctor had prescribed.

To this point I have had only two surgeries; the first, knee surgery due to a ski accident at age twenty-two, so my knee could bend (cartilage torn out). That surgery was crude compared to today's, soon causing a varicose vein problem that would become more serious later in life. But as I lay in the UCLA Medical Center hospital, enjoying the high on Morphine, I learned an important lesson: I realized that in our large family, and with all the stuff going on around us, and in us, we rarely or only got individual attention when we were sick. Here I was basking in attention: flowers, visitors who cared about me. There were two paths in front of me: the way of weakness, sickness, need or the way of strength and health, both physically (via the body) and mentally via the spirit, and what I had to offer. I consciously chose the latter.

The second, was an emergency C-Section at thirty-seven after fifty hours of labor in an attempted home birth. Some months later I was diagnosed with an ovarian tumor by two separate doctors but refused surgery. I "cured" it over an eighteen month period with fasting, colonics, herbs and Bentonite, which I still use for many purposes. Afterwards doctors believed it could not have been a tumor. The other possibility was that a sponge had been left in my body during the surgery; both my dreams and intuition, plus the Ayurvedic doctor confirmed the second. And amazingly, dreams continued to give accurate progress of its dissolution. I continued to learn about the recuperative powers of the body, and the equally important lesson of trusting my body.

Diet and exercise are fundamental for me. Herbs, homeopathy and acupuncture made sense to me and became part of my health care. From the beginning of my Berkeley years to the present I have practiced yoga and meditation. In the last five years I have also added the Nine Palaces Qi Gong (which I found serendipitously when looking for a smaller book to take when traveling) and happens to be the perfect complement to my other practices.

Artists are exposed to many toxic materials and consequently sometimes die younger, but for someone with Virgo Rising (health conscious) and Neptune conjunct Moon conjunct the ascendant (very high degree of sensitivity), being accused of hypochondria is quite natural. In fact my mother used to say/call me: "Krauetchen ruehr mich nicht an," an idiom something like: little untouchable plant or the princess and the pea syndrome.

The owner of the etching studio which had insufficient ventilation thought I was. My nose would bleed from using the nitric acid to etch the copper. Later the ventilation was perfected as it became known that the acid otherwise etches the lungs. When I was pregnant and the doctor was concerned that my nausea was lasting too long, he came to my studio and asked, "What's in these dyes you use for batik?" and called up Los Alamos National Laboratory and discovered they contained PCBs. On my own I realized that the Clorox I was using to bleach black cloth progressively to white, creating stunning batiks, emitted chlorine gas, poisonous to one's lungs also. It was time to stop batiking anyway.

Growing up in Alamogordo's northwest side, downwind from where the bomb was dropped in 1945 contributed to or even caused the thyroid problem and some other sensitivities and the death of three siblings from cancer. The government now admits that people in Tularosa, living there at the time could have a higher rate of cancer deaths. But radiation does not disappear; it lasts thousands of years. We experienced intense sandstorms on the farm: sand running down the walls inside our house; the winds blowing the stirred up radiation fallout for miles.

The early exposure to radiation could contribute to my EMS, one reason of many why accessible health care is necessary. In the public discourse many people assert the belief and conviction that everyone should have affordable health care. Others believe that would be impossibly expensive. Both are right to a degree. Unless one knows one's own body and how to care for it, taking responsibility for one's health, the government provided health insurance won't keep us healthy either. Add to this the man made pollutants, pesticides, air pollution, heat exhaustion, and radiation from many sources, and we have a lot less control over our health than in previous decades.

Belief System

I heard the term, Belief System, over fifty years ago and have pondered it periodically ever since. It's illusive yet encompasses many things. Grasping it is important because of its relation to the pursuit of Truth and to making art. I could/would say: "I believe in Astrology." So the saying goes: "now the Sun is in Virgo" but, does the sun move? Or is it a "fixed" star? Can anything in the Universe be utterly "fixed" or does it move, a little or a lot, in relation to everything else?

But this is only part of one level, the conscious one, which is broad and covers many areas, and is vital to the subject matter I choose for my art. Of equal importance but more difficult to access, are the unconscious contents of one's "Belief System," that rule our lives and creeps into everything one does, and in this case, certainly into my art—a way of discovering them, possibly.

There are beliefs we don't even consciously know we hold. Hidden within conscious beliefs are also and often many unconscious ones. Religion, codified into a particular branch, say "Catholicism" is a "belief system" as is Judaism, Mohammedism and Buddhism, not all equally across the world, have led to wars. In the West many hold this prevalent belief: Christianity is the only "True" religion. Those who don't believe they are saved from their sins through Christ's sacrifice, will go to hell forever. Of course there are many branches of Christianity, mitigating this to different degrees. This is what I grew up with, struggled with and have not believed for a long time.

First of all, nothing is forever and second, I believe no one can die for another, to save that other. We each are responsible for our acts. "God" did not create this belief system. Humans, in order to have power over others (Dostoevsky, *The Brothers Karamazov*) codified in the Council of Nicaea. Jesus, Buddha, Mohamed, all showed us reality and how to live. Striving to become more like one, or all, of these is the goal. (See my painting: "My Cosmography.") I believe Jesus walked on water, changed water into wine and returned to Earth in his body of Light. Whether he was actually crucified, I do not know. I believe he showed us how to live, and what we are all capable of, if we become enlightened enough. I don't believe he promised to save us from our "sins" (though we do sin) nor that there is an eternal, unchanging "hell" nor that anyone is ever banished forever. "Ask, and it shall be given you; seek, and ye shall find; knock, and it shall be opened unto you" and "Seek ye the Truth and the Truth shall set you free." Unfortunately humans continue to create hell on Earth.

Because I have been a teacher in periods of my life and still embrace that role, I have sometimes been asked: Why I do not teach art? First, a practical and possibly silly sounding reason: it's messy and I have enough trouble cleaning up the messes I make. But more importantly, since I am self taught, my knowledge is personal and subjective. I can happily and successfully talk about art history. I've done that plenty in the years of owning a gallery. Somehow I love to teach subjects that involve consciousness, it's growth and development. Kierkegaard said: "Purity of heart is to will one thing." This has been my aspiration. Goethe said: "Zwei Seelen leben, Ach, in meiner Brust." This is my personal experience, meaning: I have many contradictions in my personality. For instance, I have written this book to draw attention to my work, attract more collectors again, including new and younger collectors and get more paintings into museums around the world. Too many of my collectors are retired from collecting. But will the world return to a healthier state again? If not and that is my fear, part of the hyper-vigilance in my "belief system," I do hope there is still lots of time. I also have nine beautiful grandchildren.

Some years ago we visited Pompeii and saw the lava from Vesuvius that covered the town, preserving it almost totally, perfectly, and so astonishingly excavated. The people left everything when the volcano erupted and instantly ended their lives. There were children, and even babies. I've grappled with this for decades and believe death is not an end but a transition. Consciousness does not end, and everything is alive.

Another duality: "Ascension of the Earth" or "Existenz Angst" (Existentialism) This idea has been around at least since the 1989 harmonic convergence. Presumably it hearkens back to the Ascension of Christ and his return to Earth in the light body.

The Darkest Place and the Light

I have occasionally visited a "psychic" or "medium" as another way of learning what dwells below the surface of consciousness, or above. My first such experience was while I lived in Berkeley, an appointment with Zonette for a chiropractic session in Mendocino. She told me breathlessly while she channeled: "Your Aura is so beautiful I can hardly stay in my body." Of course I was flattered. It turned out not to be the last time I heard this. When I left her and took a walk through the village to get grounded again, to my surprise and delight, I felt like the pied piper, every dog in the village was following behind me. Perhaps they sensed or even saw my aura. (Virgo Ascendant, with Neptune and Moon conjunct it.)

I had already discovered the "Seth Material," first by the books and soon after by meeting Jane Roberts in New York. And the last twenty years or so I have studied and practiced Tibetan Buddhism which has been complimented for the last eight by the Laarkmaa teachings channeled through Pia and Cullen whom I met with several times while they still lived in Santa Fe. About six years ago also I discovered the nine Palaces Qi Gong which complements all the above and has made it possible during Covid, not to learn through Zoom, which everyone around me seems to be doing, but simply from books, some of which I read over and over.

So like my writings in the "Yellow Pages" section, my thoughts here are partially from an altered state of consciousness and part, putting together what I understand may be occurring and attempting to summarize it. I really feel that there are beings more evolved than we in the Universe, communicating through humans in order to help us evolve. Sometimes we are/were told: "The human experiment is coming to an end. We have tried for thousands of years to help humans evolve. We have given you guidelines—you have ignored them. We have tried over and over to give you rules for how to live on Earth. We created this beautiful Earth with everything needed for happiness." "We have told you, you can use all fruits that grow on Earth's surface," and perhaps that we must not dig up the minerals and gems, they each have a purpose. Digging up gold, silver, and diamonds has not brought welfare to humans but greed, jealousy, hatred.

The oil is another example of what perhaps should have been left alone, as it is said that it is the life blood of the Earth. We are drying the core and ruining the atmosphere by burning it just to speed around on the surface. "You create terrible instruments of destruction, to maim and kill each other. Instead of living fully in the present knowing you are safe and blessed, you create stories of past harms and future fears. Earth must now evolve herself out of the Third Dimension because humans are destroying her."

I believe the way to salvation is not "A I" nor the "Smart Phone," though perhaps it can be used to help find solutions. It is said that this is a very auspicious time. Human evolution can occur better and faster than any time in human history. To regain, re-awaken abilities that humans have forgotten, those of intuition, unconditional love; of perception beyond the Third dimension, and of course Ascension: embracing the Light.

One important and obvious solution to "Global Climate Change" has been around for a long time but is ignored and not popular at this time, is to roll back energy use. The USA uses the most energy by far in the world, so we are the most responsible. One example close to home is our bomb making factory: LANL which has been given Billions to ramp up PIT production. I think that anyone with a grain of sense knows it is absurd to make these triggers for hundreds of bombs. It is well known it is also extremely polluting as well. The citizens of Rocky Flats in Colorado shut it down due to the obvious radiation pollution and LANL embraced it. Pitt making also uses enormous quantity of water, prohibited in our ever more drought plagued landscape. Our situation is Biblical: "sin no more!" [Ritual of the Unlimited] " Do unto Others as you would have them do unto you." "I am another yourself; you are another myself." Human labor shared and rewarded, creates community. Technology, while promising connected-ness has created loneliness, alienation and chaos. Embrace each other and power down.

My art is the expression of a witness, (Jester, fool, lover), of the Darkness and the Light. I said at the beginning: there were many mysteries and unanswered questions in my childhood. And also secrets, mine too. Well, some questions were answered, and there are always many new ones. And writing a book is like looking at a tree: the trunk leads to many branches and those lead to many more, and one has to eventually, just appreciate the whole tree in the living landscape. Like many artists in the past hundreds of years, I have been drawn to earlier paintings (Durer and Blake) based on the Garden of Eden, not because I believe in the myth as stated and interpreted, but as a focus for engaging the myth. The story of the creation of Eve, clearly makes her subordinate to Adam, thus supporting the Patriarchy; being driven out of Eden (lain at the foot of Eve), condemned to suffering during childbirth and survival on Earth, are all part of the belief system that enslaves humans. I believe the Earth is still Eden, but we are losing it more and more. Eden is still a numinous subject and for now culminates in my large diptych: "From Eden to Assange," which takes a humorous view of the role of the apple, including Christ and the Devil, each with a smart phone, making a hero of Julian Assange and all watch dogs for truth.

Those of us who are EMS (Electromagnetically Sensitive), 1-3% in 100, are the "Canaries in the mine," joined by such luminaries as Mozart, Leonardo da Vinci, Rembrandt, Nietzsche, and others. If all voices were heard, respected in a real dialogue, there would be hope for a real solution.

"Let this life be spent in a state of uninhibited, naked ease. Whatever one does, joyful, practitioner of the Great Perfection; in any company happy, linage child of the Lotus Born... Heart Essence of the Dakinis. Having dispelled the Heart's darkness, great ignorance, in its own place the undiminished sun of luminous clarity shines continuously....

—Dudjom Tersar Ngondro.

I remind myself of this frequently to give myself courage. I have left out the (central) reference to "remember the Lama" because I believe in this time one must be one's own teacher; rather than look for authority outside of oneself, as if this 'authority' has the only access to Truth.

As life cycles in spirals, I return here to my first reading of Van Gogh's letters to his brother Theodor (from a 1911 edition I picked up in a used bookstore while studying at the University in Munich) to coming across the anti Vietnam war painting of Irving Petlin in the late 1990s, and finally, discovering the amazing paintings of former East German artist, Bernard Heisig just before Brusberg Gallery (Berlin) finally closed. In the first instance, I was moved by Van Gogh's awareness of the sensitivity of his soul, and the love he felt for nature, and wanting to share that with the world...a kindred spirit. In the latter two, the ability to turn terrible violence, hate, ignorance and evil into unbelievably expressive and beautiful paintings—darkness becoming light, which my art shares with all three.

An Astrological Postscript:

"April is the cruellest month, breeding/Lilacs out of the dead land, mixing/Memory and desire, stirring/Dull roots with spring rain." (T.S. Eliot) I always experience inward disagreement because it is one of my favorite months, having Mars in Aries (inherited from my father) and being more optimistic (Jupiter in Gemini on the Midheaven, my optimistic mother being a Gemini). In my life a pattern has repeated itself over and over though my 5 Retrograde planets always manage to create a lot of obstacles to overcome. In this case I started this memoir in October (I'm a double Libra) and finished it in the month of April, just before the (Christian) Ascension. What could be more fitting?

Walking Home

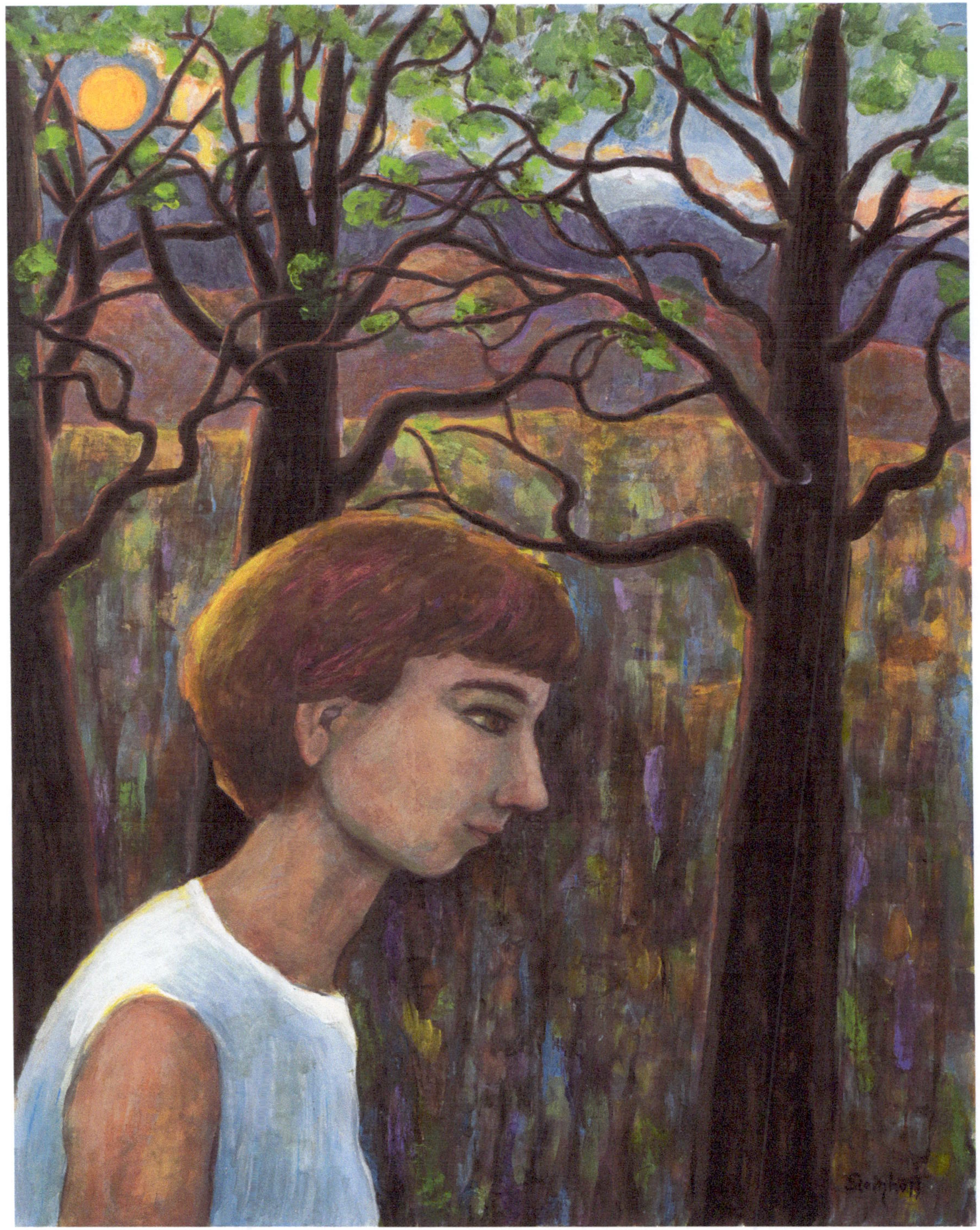

ALPHABETICAL INDEX OF PAINTINGS

Printed in the USA
CPSIA information can be obtained
at www.ICGtesting.com
JSHW041140291123
52539JS00004B/15